The Future of Public Administration around the World

Public Management and Change Series

Beryl A. Radin, Series Editor

SELECTED TITLES IN THE SERIES

Challenging the Performance Movement: Accountability, Complexity, and Democratic Values
Beryl A. Radin

The Collaborative Public Manager: New Ideas for the Twenty-First Century
Rosemary O'Leary and Lisa Blomgren Bingham, Editors

The Dynamics of Performance Management: Constructing Information and Reform
Donald P. Moynihan

The Greening of the U.S. Military: Environmental Policy, National Security, and Organizational Change
Robert F. Durant

How Management Matters: Street-Level Bureaucrats and Welfare Reform
Norma M. Riccucci

Implementing Innovation: Fostering Enduring Change in Environmental and Natural Resource Governance
Toddi A. Steelman

Managing within Networks: Adding Value to Public Organizations
Robert Agranoff

Public Administration: Traditions of Inquiry and Philosophies of Knowledge
Norma M. Riccucci

Organizational Learning at NASA: The *Challenger* and *Columbia* Accidents
Julianne G. Mahler with Maureen Hogan Casamayou

Public Values and Public Interest: Counterbalancing Economic Individualism
Barry Bozeman

The Responsible Contract Manager: Protecting the Public Interest in an Outsourced World
Steven Cohen and William Eimicke

Revisiting Waldo's Administrative State: Constancy and Change in Public Administration
David H. Rosenbloom and Howard E. McCurdy

The Future of Public Administration around the World

The Minnowbrook Perspective

Rosemary O'Leary
David M. Van Slyke
and
Soonhee Kim
Editors

Georgetown University Press
Washington, D.C.

Georgetown University Press, Washington, D.C. www.press.georgetown.edu

Library of Congress Cataloging-in-Publication Data

The future of public administration around the world : the Minnowbrook perspective / Rosemary O'Leary, David M. Van Slyke, and Soonhee Kim, editors.

p. cm.—(Public management and change series)

Consists of abridged and revised versions of the best papers from the third Minnowbrook Conference, which was hosted by Syracuse University in the fall of 2008.

Includes bibliographical references and index.

ISBN 978-1-58901-711-5 (hardcover / pbk. : alk. paper)

1. Public administration–Congresses. I. O'Leary, Rosemary, 1955– II. Van Slyke, David. III. Kim, Soonhee.

JF1351.F88 2010

351—dc22

2010007868

∞ This book is printed on acid-free paper meeting the requirements of the American National Standard for Permanence in Paper for Printed Library Materials.

15 14 13 12 11 10 9 8 7 6 5 4 3 2

First printing

Printed in the United States of America

We dedicate this book to those who are engaged in public service and who are trying to make the world a better place. In addition, we thank our families for their support and encouragement: Rosemary thanks Larry and Meghan; David thanks Wendy, Ryan, Ashley, and Anneke; and Soonhee thanks her mother, her late grandmother, and especially her late father, Oakchul Kim.

Contents

ILLUSTRATIONS

Tables

Figures

Boxes

Preface

The Minnowbrook Conference, held every twenty years, is one of the most significant academic conferences in public administration in the United States. Minnowbrook I, which took place in 1968, marked the beginning of the "New Public Administration." Minnowbrook II, which took place in 1988, reflected on the impact of the "New Public Administration." Both Minnowbrook I and Minnowbrook II resulted in significant, historic, publications.

Minnowbrook III was held in 2008 and was organized in two phases on the theme "The Future of Public Administration, Public Management, and Public Service around the World." Phase One, a preconference workshop that included fifty-five participants at the original Minnowbrook site on Blue Mountain Lake, New York, was for scholars who had completed their PhD programs within the previous eight years. Phase Two, which directly followed the new scholars' event, was held in Lake Placid, New York, for scholars and practitioners of all ages and degrees of experience. The Lake Placid group included at least thirty veterans of Minnowbrook I and/or Minnowbrook II.

The outcomes of both phases of Minnowbrook III involved analyses of the current state and future direction of the field. A total of 200 scholars and practitioners from thirteen countries participated in Minnowbrook III. The topics explored and debated included academic–practitioner relations; democratic performance management; financial management; globalization/comparative perspectives; information technology and management; law, politics, and public administration; leadership; methods; interdisciplinary research; networks; public administration values and theory; social equity and justice; and transparency and accountability.

This book brings together a group of distinguished scholars—seasoned, new, and in between—who critically explore public administration's big ideas and issues as presented at Minnowbrook III. A retrospective and prospective examination of the field of public administration is by definition multifaceted and complex, and an edited book such as this allows the reader to examine this complicated phenomenon from a variety of perspectives. The chapters in this book are a selection of the best papers presented at Minnowbrook III. An added plus is that authors critiqued and debated their chapters at the conference, edited them after the conference, and revised them again after anonymous peer reviews. Yet the best papers have not merely been republished here; they have been abridged to provide a concise and accessible overview of Minnowbrook III. Excerpts from the papers are seen as a means to an end—as catalysts for a rare critical examination of the field of public administration yesterday, today, and tomorrow.

The original Minnowbrook Conference ideas, which reflected the tumultuous 1960s, sparked a serious examination of public administration scholarship and practice and constitute the starting point for this book. We are joined in the first chapter by two scholars—George Frederickson and Harry Lambright—who participated in all three Minnowbrook conferences, in revisiting key Minnowbrook I and Minnowbrook

II concepts (e.g., "change" and "relevance") and in considering whether they have been successfully infused throughout, and implemented by, public administration. We also assess the applicability of these concepts today.

The book then moves beyond the original Minnowbrook concepts and focuses on public administration's challenges of the future. Public organizations of the future are examined, as well twenty-first-century collaborative governance, deliberative democracy, the role of information technology in governance, globalism, teaching tomorrow's leaders, and finally one of the enduring themes of all Minnowbrook conferences: the challenge of remaining relevant. The book closes by reflecting on the field of public administration, weaving in major themes of Minnowbrook III and the critiques of conference plenary speakers. We analyze the mix of enduring issues to which the field keeps returning, plus new emerging issues.

There is no other book like this. Simply stated, the ideas, concepts, and spirit of Minnowbrook are historic and one of a kind. Our goal was to create a book that captures the soul of public administration—past, present, and future—and that will be read by scholars and students of public administration for decades to come.

Many acknowledgments are due to those who made Minnowbrook III possible. First and foremost, Rosemary thanks Maxwell School alumnus Howard Phanstiel and his wife, Louise, for generously underwriting the conference, as well as Syracuse University Graduate School dean Ben Ware, and Maxwell School dean Mitchel Wallerstein. Rosemary also thanks her "sister" Esther Gray for commandeering the logistics of meeting rooms, hotel rooms, food, and transportation. Finally, she thanks Mary Pat Cornish and Dana Cook of the Maxwell School dean's office for support behind the scenes, as well as Lisa Mignacca and Carin McAbee of the Maxwell Program for the Advancement of Research on Conflict and Collaboration (PARCC). The Syracuse University Office of Conferences is thanked for registration assistance. We thank the staff of the Syracuse University Minnowbrook Conference Center for maintaining a beautiful setting that is conducive to thought and reflection.

We thank the 55 new scholars who participated in Phase One of Minnowbrook III at Blue Mountain Lake, whose enthusiasm for, criticisms of, and creative thinking about the field of public administration were both heartening and enlightening. And we thank the 200 participants in Phase Two at Lake Placid for the quality of their insights and the depth of their discussions. This book would not have been possible without the intellectual prodding and pushing of both groups of scholars.

Many acknowledgments also are due to the other people who made this book possible. We thank Beryl A. Radin, editor of the Georgetown University Press Public Management and Change series, for her vision and gentle nudging as we created this book. We also thank Don Jacobs and two anonymous reviewers for feedback that was 100 percent constructive, creative, and helpful. We thank Laurel Saiz and Debbie Toole (of PARCC) for their editorial and administrative skills. Finally, as coeditors, we all gratefully acknowledge our two recent department chairs, Jeff Straussman (now dean at the State University of New York at Albany) and Stu Bretschneider, for supporting the Minnowbrook III gatherings and for nurturing an intellectual environment at the Maxwell School that encourages these kinds of collaborative research and writing projects.

Introduction

The Legacy of Minnowbrook

Soonhee Kim, Rosemary O'Leary,
David M. Van Slyke, H. George Frederickson,
and W. Henry Lambright

The Minnowbrook conferences—held in 1968, 1988, and 2008 in the Adirondack Mountains in Upstate New York—are the cicadas of public administration: appearing every twenty years and having an impact on the landscape. These gatherings represent an extraordinary assembly of intellectual talent, past and present, new and seasoned. They are intended as an opportunity to take stock of where the field is, where the field is going, and where the field needs to go.

This book is an outcome of these gatherings, with a special focus on the 2008 Minnowbrook III Conference. The book's importance to the field of public administration is not simply as a record. Its contribution includes presenting a broad set of issues that new and seasoned scholars alike have sought to highlight with fresh perspectives, analytical research, and commentary shaped by years of scholarship and practical experience. The book is more than an artifact; it is a catalyst for discussion and debate. It is intended to be a vehicle that serves as both a reference for new scholars entering the field and an integrated architecture that connects disparate subfields and perspectives with a common purpose. It is a lens through which the learning and exchange of new knowledge may be evaluated. It is an avenue to new research directions and new ideas for public managers. The ideas presented are not exhaustive of the issues, opportunities, and challenges present in the field. They are intended, however, to be broad and representative of the many serious debates taking place, as well as a platform for relevant scholarship that tackles the complex problems facing government and governance today.

It could be regarded as a mark of their status in public administration that the Minnowbrook conferences can now be found on Google and on Wikipedia. The Minnowbrook I Conference is an objective subject, with a literature and a record (Marini 1971; Waldo 1971). More important, "Minnowbrook" is an enduring legend in public administration, a narrative with an attendant mystique and mythology. And so it is that every public administration generation now has its own Minnowbrook.

MINNOWBROOK I—1968: ENTER THE "NEW PUBLIC ADMINISTRATION"

The year 1968 was the most turbulent one in the most turbulent decade in the United States since World War II. It began with the Tet Offensive in Vietnam, which made it clear to the American people that we were not winning that war and that their government had not been telling the truth. This was followed by Lyndon Johnson's announcement that he was not running for reelection to the presidency. The assassinations of Martin Luther King Jr. and Robert F. Kennedy were both followed by a wave of urban riots. The Democratic National Convention in Chicago was marked by protesters chanting "The whole world is watching" and beatings by the police. Finally that year, the Soviet Union invaded Czechoslovakia.

The United States was tearing itself apart over the Vietnam War. The Great Society was collapsing. Universities were caught in the middle. Students, worried about the draft, were a source of continuous unrest. Authority of all kinds was being questioned.

With this momentous backdrop, Dwight Waldo, then holder of the Albert Schweitzer Chair of Public Administration at the Maxwell School of Syracuse University, organized the Minnowbrook I Conference. Waldo felt that public administration had to respond to the events and turmoil of the day. He especially felt that the new generation must have a voice. He asked three junior colleagues, all assistant professors—H. George Frederickson, Frank Marini, and William (Harry) Lambright—to organize a conference. He wanted the "best and brightest" of the New Public Administration generation. He contacted the leading scholars of the day and several practitioners and asked who they would recommend as their rising stars.

Thirty-four young public administration scholars came to Syracuse University in the fall of 1968 right after the annual conference of the American Political Science Association in Chicago. The university had had its own round of protests. The participants all boarded buses and traveled to the Syracuse University Minnowbrook Conference Center on Blue Mountain Lake, in New York's Adirondack Mountains. The conference center, named after the brook that runs through the property, is a quiet and remote place consisting of a lodge and several cabins.

Lambright recalled: "We all felt we were living at a pivotal point in time. There was passion in the air. The bus trip was helpful in our getting to know one another. All of us were young men—mostly in the late twenties and early thirties. Most of us came from universities all over the country."

Virtually all the academic participants at Minnowbrook were political scientists who tended to frame their perspectives on public administration along political science fault lines, particularly the so-called behavioral (logical positivism, rationality, science) versus antibehavioral (philosophical, historical, normative) debate. Although papers had been written for the conference, the conferees decided that these papers would not be given, although they were later published. (Waldo observed silently and did not participate in the group decision-making process on site.) The conference was raucous, characterized by "mau-mauing," a popular form of meeting disruption at the time.

Most conference participants were familiar with the debate between Waldo and Herbert Simon over the role of science in political science and public administration (Dahl 1947; Simon 1947, 1952; Waldo 1952a, 1952b; Drucker 1952). That debate tended to frame the Minnowbrook "conversation," dominated by the antibehavioral perspective associated with Waldo. Simon emphasized a more empirical investigation—some might argue technocratic—of organizational and behavioral approaches to understanding decision making, one that incorporated tools of management and social psychology. (Some now call the outcome of Simon's work the field of public management.) Waldo emphasized a more political, theoretical, and philosophical approach to thinking about the tensions between democracy and bureaucracy. His emphasis was more of a critique, less positivistic, and more directed at increasing the bureaucracy's involvement in developing processes for public participation and democratic expression. He feared that public administration as a field would become replaced by decision makers who were overly consumed with a set of values that focused on making government organizations efficient and effective at the expense of democratic values.

The group assembled at Minnowbrook I was interested in "action," not pure academic theory or quantitative techniques for their own sake. Lambright remembered: "I recall on the first day, Todd LaPorte was giving a paper—the first paper—and Peter Savage loudly said, 'Todd, that's a bunch of crap.' He may have used a harsher term. That was how it all began, and the meeting deteriorated immediately thereafter. We threw away the script and formed ad hoc groups around topics of interests, and the result was magical."

Frederickson reminisced: "Although the discussion was rather untidy, it was possible to discern, particularly after the fact, there were certain Minnowbrook themes. First, the relevance of public administration. Second, the democratic grounding of public administration. Third, public administration as a moral enterprise. Fourth, democratic (internal) administration, the so-called politics of love, which posited that if you 'change the institutions, . . . you will change the men' (Crenson 1971, quoted by Marini 1971, 86). Fifth, social equity. Not everyone agreed with every theme and, over time, particular 'Minnows'—the name for those who participated in a Minnowbrook Conference—came to be associated with particular themes."

Lambright recalled the themes a bit differently:

> There were two major themes that cut across the various panels. The first was change. Public administration academics had to "recover relevance." They had to go back to basics and deal with real problems. "Relevance" trumped "rigor," if rigor meant scientism for its own sake. The other was caring. Public administration in practice had to be more caring, more in touch with those served. Bureaucrats (like academics) were said [to be] more interested in themselves than their clients. The Minnows said that administrators had to think beyond accountability. There was lots of talk about equity, and socio-emotional needs as subjects of Public Administration.

The Minnowbrook I Conference was followed by several symposia, workshops, and other gatherings. The conference papers were published in a book, *Toward a New Public Administration: The Minnowbrook Perspective*, edited by Frank Marini (1971). This book is considered a classic, assigned in whole or in part in most courses on the history of public administration. The book is important to the intellectual development of the field, not only because it provides a historical perspective on the scholarly debates that took place at the time but also because it sets the stage for the themes to be explored after the conference. These themes were seen, in retrospect, as important markers for where the field was moving and what topics required more research.

It was clear that a disconnect existed between the passion and atmospherics of the conference and the more formal and cooler "scholarship" in the book (Marini 1971). Though the messages were essentially the same, the book could not possibly capture the Minnowbrook mood. Yet the mood continued to be influential. Versions of several of the original Minnowbrook themes later appeared as articles in the *Public Administration Review* and other journals in the field. Persons associated with Minnowbrook I, literally and figuratively, took over the next American Society for Public Administration conference in Philadelphia in 1969 and subsequently became society officers. Various streams of literature began to emerge that were particularly associated with the themes of social equity and the democratic administration. What is now the Public Administration Theory Network and the journal *Administrative Theory and Praxis* trace their origins to the Minnowbrook I gathering. Many persons associated with Minnowbrook I later became leaders in the field.

The Minnowbrook I perspective, and particularly what some regarded as youthful excess, stimulated a counterliterature. An example is Victor A. Thompson's book *Without Sympathy or Enthusiasm* (1975), a blistering critique of the New Public Administration's position that public administrators should promote social equity independently of a legal or other official mandate to do so. He called it "theft of the popular sovereignty," arguing against the idea that promoting social equity is either necessarily a good thing or something public administrators should try to force on the nation. He argued that procedural justice is crucial to public administration and democratic government and that like cases should be treated alike. He stressed that public administrators should not independently define their mission to include using their authority and governmental power to help poor people and minorities—the "powerless."

Perhaps the biggest omission in the original Minnowbrook Conference was the failure to include or even consider the then-new and relevant literature from economics—particularly that literature focusing on the public choice perspective exemplified by the works of Anthony Downs, as well as James Buchanan's and Gordon Tullock's perspectives. These scholars would soon become very influential in both public administration and political science. Thus, some scholars came to view the "New Public Administration" as too oriented toward political philosophy and insufficiently attentive to the need to operate government bureaucracies in more efficient and effective ways. Such tensions were evident even in long-standing and revered public affairs programs, such that of the Maxwell School of Syracuse University, where the influence and legitimacy of the "New Public Administration" faculty eventually gave way to the credibility of faculty trained in disciplines that were more aligned with the policy sciences and norms of empiricism.

The Minnowbrook "relevance" theme is also notable for another reason. At about the same time as Minnowbrook I, several leading public administration programs at prestigious universities were either closing or significantly changing. By the mid-1970s, the Ford Foundation was prepared to fund the establishment of several new public policy analysis schools, most of them at universities that previously had viable graduate programs in public administration. Examples include Harvard University, the University of California, Berkeley, the University of Chicago, and the University of Michigan. The argument made by the advocates of these changes was that academic public administration was no longer "relevant" to the real problems of the day, most of those problems being concerned with policy—and particularly policy analysis—rather than administration. Frederickson noted that Graham Allison, one of the leading voices in this movement, commented that it was important to get the study of public policy and the skills of public policy analysis out from under the "dead hand of social science."

The first Minnowbrook gathering was more than an extension of the Simon–Waldo debate. It involved new scholars wrestling with conflicting views of the field—past, present, and future. Indeed, the participants at this gathering identified the role they were to continue to play in the field's development primarily as one questioning the status quo. That development was not straightforward, easily reconciled, or aligned with common goals. The spirit of Minnowbrook I, however, was strong and enthusiastic.

MINNOWBROOK II—1988: CRITIQUING THE IMPACT OF THE "NEW PUBLIC ADMINISTRATION"

Minnowbrook II was much more prosaic than Minnowbrook I, notable mainly for the greater diversity of participants. It left a different mark on the field. Minnowbrook I reflected the stormy times. It made a difference, but—like the times—was guilty of overreaching. The 1960s were the high noon of big government. The United States tried to build a Great Society, fight an unpopular war in Southeast Asia, and go to the moon, all at once. The reaction was a sharp withdrawal from big government. The overreach of one decade led to an overwithdrawal the next.

Indeed, through the 1970s and early 1980s, the political and social context was steadily changing, and not generally in a direction favored by the "Minnows." The dominant political mood was increasingly antigovernmental and antibureaucratic. The "New Right" support for market solutions often included alarming examples of bureaucratic retreat, such as in the area of deregulation and new efforts aimed at devolution. The politics of bureaucrat bashing were increasingly effective as political leaders, the press, and civil society viewed government employees as detached from their work, unmotivated by results, and indolent in their work efforts. The public administration period that began with the Progressive Era reform movement and flourished as part of the "positive state" was coming to an end as new constraints were being implemented to limit bureaucratic discretion in program development, implementation, and evaluation.

This was the 1988 context in which Minnowbrook II occurred, organized by George Frederickson, distinguished professor and holder of the Stene Endowed Chair in Public Administration at the University of Kansas. It was held at the original Minnowbrook Conference Center, but it was organizationally somewhat different from Minnowbrook I. More people attended Minnowbrook II and almost half were female, whereas all the participants at Minnowbrook I had been male. About half the Minnowbrook II participants were younger public administrators, with the other half being original "Minnows," then mostly in their fifties.

Like Minnowbrook I, the papers commissioned for Minnowbrook II were not given at the conference. Instead one participant was assigned to respond to each paper on the assumption that participants had read the paper in advance, and a discussion ensued after each response. The responses were measured; they were sometimes critical, yet civil. So, too, were the ensuing discussions of the papers and the responses. The participants generally agreed that the mix of younger and more senior participants contributed to the comparatively placid mood, with the younger participants possibly being intimidated by the more senior participants. Though the debate between the normative and the behaviorist perspectives continued at Minnowbrook II, social equity and diversity were accepted as basic values among the participants (Guy 1989). Overall, Minnowbrook II was less controversial and probably less influential than Minnowbrook I.

Like the first one, Minnowbrook II produced a considerable literature (Frederickson and Mayer 1989; Bailey and Mayer 1992; Frederickson and Chandler 1997). There was less of a disconnect between the papers prepared for the conference and the actual themes that emerged. Frederickson summarized the themes from Minnowbrook II: "First, more technicist; second, more individualist; third, a social equity perspective that now included gender and age; fourth, an emerging importance on productivity and performance measurement; and fifth, a greater connection to mainstream social science and the positivist or Simon perspective."

Minnowbrook II mostly missed the coming importance of the reinventing government movement and the emergence of the so-called New Public Management. The scholars at the second gathering did identify some of the issues about which Waldo was concerned. They were less successful in setting forth an agenda whereby the field might strategically manage the challenges that it would soon confront, because of the more techno-bureaucratic systems and processes that were being championed, developed, and implemented.

In some ways, the themes that emerged from Minnowbrook II reflected changes in public administration as an academic field. The period between the two conferences was a time of considerable growth, in both the number of degree programs and number of students. In addition, many of the more established academic programs were no longer part of political science departments. Finally, the cautious mood of Minnowbrook II might have been a reflection of the emerging complexity of the process of achieving academic tenure.

Changes in the field, the maturation of the profession, and entry into the discipline by scholars and practitioners who were trained in a range of fields and with diverse specialties gave rise to a robust and fragmented professional landscape. Minnowbrook II grappled with issues that permeated the disjointed and growing study of public administration. These included contemporary challenges to the legitimacy and efficacy of government bureaucracies. The credibility of studying policies with "scientific" tools had to be compared with the more subjective analysis of practicing and influencing the art of administration. If these concerns seem less compelling now, it may well be a function of the power dynamics, the changing context of public administration, and the more risk-averse nature of the academics who participated and did not challenge conventional ideas. In addition, there was a lack of incentives to craft a future research agenda for the field.

MINNOWBROOK III—2008: THE FUTURE OF PUBLIC ADMINISTRATION, PUBLIC MANAGEMENT, AND PUBLIC SERVICE AROUND THE WORLD

Public administration as an academic field continued to grow through the 1990s and early 2000s. By 2008, more choices existed in professional associations, journals, public administration programs abroad, and conferences. Most degree programs were accredited, giving a kind of standardization and credentialing to curricula for master of public administration programs and to the field. Rankings of public affairs programs nationwide were fashionable and increasingly competitive in the development of subfield specialties, such as public management and/or administration, public finance and budgeting, nonprofit management, local government, and public policy analysis. The exigencies of achieving academic promotion and tenure were more rigorous than in 1968. In 1988, this led to a growth in the quantity of publications but also fewer "big picture" ideas, theories, and models. Although the field continued to be relatively diverse and "multitheoretical," it is a safe observation that mainstream public administration was embedded as a form of applied social science and that the field was growing increasingly scientific, rational, and positivist.

All these contextual factors appeared at Minnowbrook III in the themes that were written about, discussed, and pursued through individual and group work. The debate was significantly less strident than at Minnowbrook I, but it addressed more challenging core public administration themes, such as the scope and influence of government contractors and citizen participation, which were left largely unaddressed at Minnowbrook II. Frederickson described it as public administration settling "into a kind of middle age."

At Minnowbrook III, the conference organizer, Rosemary O'Leary, distinguished professor and holder of the Phanstiel Chair at the Maxwell School, responded to the possible problem of younger scholars being intimidated by their senior colleagues by organizing the conference in two parts. The first, a preconference workshop at the original Minnowbrook site on Blue Mountain Lake, was only for scholars who had been out of their PhD programs for eight years or less. (Frederickson and Lambright were invited to silently observe, as did O'Leary.) The second part directly followed the new scholars' event and was held in Lake Placid for scholars and practitioners of all ages and degrees of experience. This group included at least thirty veterans of either Minnowbrook I or Minnowbrook II.

The setting of Minnowbrook III was more like the first Minnowbrook than the second. The controversial presidency of George W. Bush, terrorism, the 9/11 attacks, wars in Iraq and Afghanistan, Hurricane Katrina, the impact of the internet, and a severe economic recession were forms of turbulence rather like 1968. The political landscape provided momentum to bureaucratic changes viewed as increasingly technocratic, performance oriented, and directed toward managing by results. Under President Bill Clinton, the Government

Performance and Results Act began to define operational changes to federal agency programs, states began to think more seriously about performance, and national philanthropic foundations compared state governments in terms of their performance, that is, the Government Performance Project. The federal government pushed the performance orientation of agencies further, requiring compliance with guidelines set forth by the Office of Management and Budget. The role that private contractors played in public service delivery (i.e., competitive sourcing) increased at every level of government.

Perhaps most dramatic of all was the fact that the Democratic Party was about to have its first African American nominee for president. Some viewed this as promising a significant departure in the roles and responsibilities of government and the marketplace should Barack Obama be elected. The social and political response to current events in 2008, however, was measured and more civil compared with 1968, though social issues dominated debates about the scope and influence of government and federalism in general. There appeared to be more citizen confidence in democratic and bureaucratic institutions, albeit coupled with a lack of trust of those institutional leaders. Some suggested that the absence of universal mandatory military service insulated most Americans from the specific sacrifices associated with the current wars and thereby reduced the prospects for open public protest. Still others suggested that because the younger generation of scholars had come of age in a governance environment where government was not the only or even the most important actor, this reduced the protests against the government. In the governance networks of 2008, nonprofit and private-sector actors complemented the work of governments in an increasingly fragmented intergovernmental and interjurisdictional environment at both national and global levels.

The first outcome of Minnowbrook III involved fifty-six critiques of the field written by the new scholar participants and presented by them at the preconference workshop. Box 1 lists examples of some of these new scholars' critiques. Numerous university public administration, public affairs, and public management programs used these critiques in their "intellectual history" courses and also as springboards for discussions concerning their own strategic planning.

Box 1 Examples of New Scholars' Critiques

"The Challenge of Remaining Relevant"
"Public Administration and the Black Public Administrator"
"The Challenge of Teaching Public Administration in Asia"
"Is There a Global Public Administration?"
"Has Public Administration Been Roofied (Drugged) and Rolled (Mugged) by Economics?"

After these presentations, a professional facilitator led the group in a "Future Search" exercise, where the new scholars were asked to envision public administration in 2018. The imagined future scholarly field of public administration was reminiscent of Minnowbrook I: relevant, practitioner friendly, and action oriented. It was interdisciplinary and included methodological diversity and acceptance of many ways of doing quality research. It included publications that were new, timely, open source, accessible, useful, and used. The imagined teaching in the future, as articulated by the new scholars, included opportunities for creativity, the presentation of applied and relevant ideas, the use of new technologies, learning through engagement, and producing students who would have the needed skills and competencies to address the world's most pressing public policy problems.

Also articulated in the "Future Search" exercise was a desire by the fifty-six new scholars to contribute to practice. They envisioned a stronger link between research and practice and themselves as being sought out for help by practitioners. They envisioned public administration scholars as valuable experts for real problem solving who would make a real difference. Tied in with this, they envisioned a culture in the field that was interdisciplinary, global,

Box 2 Statement of Commitment for New Public Administration Scholars

As we reflect on the state of Public Administration today, we feel that our strength is the diversity of disciplines, methods, theories and approaches that we bring to public problems. However, we believe that the future of public administration is limited by the institutional and personal barriers that researchers and scholars confront in their work. We recognize these barriers as:

- institutional incentives for promotion and tenure,
- curricular limitations (such as budgetary incentives to restrict interdisciplinary approaches),
- publication issues (including editor consistency, reviewer supply and reviewer timeliness),
- limited funding for PA research, and
- the challenge of conducting international and comparative public administration research.

We, the new scholars at Minnowbrook III, commit to serve as change agents to uphold and shape the culture of Public Administration, a culture that is open minded to and appreciates multiple theoretical and methodological perspectives, with an emphasis on "publicness." To achieve this goal we commit to do the following:

(*Continued*)

Box 2 (Continued)

In the research process we will . . .

- Expand our discipline's acceptance of various units of analysis (local, state, national and international actors; government, nonprofit and private organizations; individuals at various levels of organizational hierarchy; and stakeholders and citizens).
- Create a research environment that promotes the sharing of data and collaboration among our colleagues to advance the availability of quality data within our field.
- Acknowledge the limitations of our research methods and design in order to provide direction for future research and to avoid foreclosing questions that merit further attention.

In the classroom and community we will . . .

- Strive to create research-based tools that reinforce the utility of a good theory.
- Promote rigorous research methodological training and the use of mixed methods (qualitative and quantitative).
- Invest appropriate time in sharing knowledge with practitioners.
- Cultivate the ability among practitioners to reflect in the moment and adapt when faced with complexity.

In the publication process we will . . .

- Strive to publish relevant work (for practice and/or theory).
- Expand our field's use and appreciation of cross-disciplinary theory while emphasizing the role of "publicness."
- Seek to promote the inclusion of multiple methods and rigorous methods of all types.
- Review research within the paradigm in which they were conducted.

Drafted by Leisha DeHart-Davis, Mary Feeney, Beth Gazley, Yilin Hou, Stephanie Moulton, Rebecca Nesbit, Craig Smith, Jodi Sandfort, Scott Robinson, and David Van Slyke, with contributions from other Minnowbrook III participants.

and inclusive. Box 2 contains a "Statement of Commitment for New Public Administration Scholars," written by ten of the new scholars, which attempts to capture the sentiments of the group in this regard.

Other outputs from the preconference workshop included a special issue of the *Journal of Public Administration Research and Theory,* edited by two new scholars, Beth Gazley and David Van Slyke. This contains eleven multi-authored critiques of different aspects of the field, a wiki page, a wiki book, a Facebook site, conference panels, and joint research. The journal *Public Productivity and Management Review* published some of the new scholars' critiques that were not published in this book, and the journal *Administrative Theory and Praxis* published two special issues with essays on the Minnowbrook Conference.

Phase Two of Minnowbrook III involved formal paper presentations in a dozen focal areas and in a more traditional conference format, presented by two hundred scholars and practitioners from thirteen countries. The conference included a broad range of topics: academic–practitioner relations; democratic performance management; financial management; globalization and comparative perspectives; information technology and management; law, politics, and public administration; leadership; research methods and interdisciplinary research; networks; public administration values and theory; social equity and justice; and transparency and accountability. Box 3 contains examples of questions addressed at the Phase Two conference.

One theme that emerged was that scholars should rethink the role of government in view of the realities of 2008. The terrorist attacks of September 11, 2001, thrust homeland security to the top of the U.S. national agenda, although it had already been at the top of numerous other countries' agendas. Globalism linked the United States in a host of ways that added to its vulnerability and presented tremendous opportunities. The economies, financial systems, health concerns, energy systems, cybersecurity needs, and the climates of the world were, and still are, increasingly becoming integrated and interdependent with one another.

Box 3 Key Themes of the Minnowbrook III Lake Placid Conference

- How is the field of Public Administration different in 2008 from 1968 and 1988? What is Public Administration in 2008?
- Can we draw important theoretical and empirical conclusions about the market-oriented New Public Management that now has a 30-year history?
- Given the influx of scholars from many disciplines into Public Administration, is Public Administration closer or farther away from developing a core theoretical base?
- How are new ideas about networked governance and collaborative public management changing the way we look at Public Administration, Public Management, and Public Service? Are they changing the practice of Public Administration? Should they change what we teach in our programs?
- How has globalization affected our understanding of the key challenges that face the study and practice of Public Administration, Public Management, and Public Service in the United States, the developed world, and developing and transitional countries?

In addition, the participants recognized that since the 1970s, politicians around the world had campaigned against "big government." The result in 2008 was not only that big government was in disfavor but also a sense that "effective government" had been vanquished. At Minnowbrook III, scholars addressed issues of governmental capacity and the place of government in the twenty-first century. A perceived gap existed between public problems and government's capability and capacity to address them.

The two phases of the Minnowbrook III experience provide a useful analytical heuristic for understanding the evolution of the scholarly side of the field, as well as a set of benchmarks against which to measure the relevance of public administration scholarship in the future. Both Simonesque and Waldonian perspectives were alive in the analytical frames, methodological tools, foci of inquiry, and theoretically informed research that participants presented.

Those participants who might be classified as continuing a Simonesque tradition used theories whose roots are in economics, organizational theory, and management, although we suspect few of the presenters would classify themselves as disciples of either Simon or Waldo. Those more aligned with the perspectives offered by Waldo tended to use frameworks and models from political science, sociology, philosophy, and history.

Absent from the Minnowbrook III discussions was a poetic reminiscing about the gilded "Golden Age" of public administration. Rather, this group of participants was forward looking. They had access to a range of methodological, analytical, and technological tools, and were more likely to offer incremental contributions that are evidence based. This is not to suggest that they have a purely technocratic perspective on the field's future contributions, but rather a more sanguine assessment about the institutional realities of scholarship. They recognized a need to evaluate what works and what does not before offering up broad, untested theories and recommendations. What was missing were new idea-changing findings that altered the terms and debates of modern governance. It is fair to say, however, that the debates from the 1960s and 1970s remained rooted in twentieth-century notions of public administration.

The future, as represented by Minnowbrook III participants, clearly lies in a more global approach to thinking about institutions and the work of public administrators. Also present was a clear rejection of old ways of thinking about structure, form, and power within organizations. The complexity of the problems faced by public administrators and studied by scholars rivaled those during every other critical period of history. In addition, technology has lowered barriers to collaboration and engagement among scholars, practitioners, and regions of the world. Opportunities for broader engagement and learning among a diverse set of communities are reasons to be optimistic that the relevance of public administration can not only be restored but strengthened as well.

MOVING FORWARD

All three Minnowbrook conferences were celebrated in part as a legacy of Waldo. It is worth mentioning that after Minnowbrook I, Waldo edited a book titled *Public Administration in a Time of Turbulence* (1971). In the preface he indicated that the Minnows had gone too far in their critique of government. In tearing down government, there had to be a replacement model. One of the key discussions at Minnowbrook III was that we have yet to develop that replacement model—certainly not one apt for this new century.

During his career Waldo searched for a way to relate democracy and bureaucracy. As he articulated his case, democracy at its best provides legitimacy and demonstrates the government's responsiveness to the people. Bureaucratic administration involves the power to govern effectively. Finding the right balance of responsiveness and effectiveness was the challenge Waldo sought to address, and it is a challenge that emerged at Minnowbrook III. For the new generation of Minnows, the Minnowbrook III gathering represented an effort to discuss the components of this balance.

Although there was a greater acceptance of the role that markets and private organizations play in public service delivery, there was also a general consensus that the pendulum had swung too far in the direction of private enterprise. The fulcrum had moved to a position beyond the center in which government was now in a relationship not of interdependence but of dependence on private and nonprofit firms to deliver government services. From a perspective of democratic accountability, the 2008 Minnows were generally in agreement that government needed to reassert its place in the realm of governance.

As such, there was not a powerful shift back from Simon to Waldo, but a more nuanced recognition of and approach to the complexities of public problems and the work of government, including an articulated need for a greater distribution of power and responsibility. An outcome of Minnowbrook III may be greater involvement of scholars in the field with the challenges of balancing democracy and bureaucracy. They also recognize that the dynamic political environment of public administration shapes this desired balance in ways perhaps greater than the efforts of any one discipline or group of scholars. Despite these challenges, there was a sense that the field must and will work to achieve some semblance of balance.

THE CONTRIBUTION OF THIS BOOK

We now move beyond the legacy of Minnowbrook and focus on public administration challenges of the future. This book brings together a group of distinguished authors—both seasoned and new—who critically explore public administration's big ideas and issues as presented at Minnowbrook III. The best papers are not merely reprinted here; rather, the excerpts of the papers in this book are seen as a means to an end—as catalysts for a critical examination and discussion of the field of public administration.

This book is organized into six parts containing twenty-seven chapters written by seventeen seasoned scholars and twenty new scholars. The chapters in part I focus on the public organizations of the future. The possibility of a global paradigm is addressed in the chapters in part II. The chapters in part III concern twenty-first-century collaborative governance. The chapters in part IV analyze trends in deliberative democracy and public participation. The challenges of teaching the next generation of leaders are tackled in part V. And finally, the chapters in part VI return to an enduring Minnowbrook theme: the challenge of remaining relevant. In the conclusion we close with an essay reflecting on the field of public administration, weaving in the critiques of conference plenary speakers, and analyzing the mix of enduring issues to which the field keeps returning, coupled with new emerging issues and challenges.

Taken as a whole, the ideas in this book push us to think about the past, present, and future of public administration. The place, tradition, ideas, spirit, gatherings, and challenges of Minnowbrook are historic and one of a kind. By capturing the best of Minnowbrook III, we hope that we have created a book that will be read by scholars and students of public administration for decades to come.

REFERENCES

Bailey, Mary Timney, and Richard T. Mayer. 1992. *Public Management in an Interconnected World: Essays in the Minnowbrook Tradition.* Westport CT: Greenwood Press.

Crenson, Mathew A. 1971. Comment: Contract, Love, and Character Building. In *Toward a New Public Administration: The Minnowbrook Perspective,* ed. Frank Marini. Scranton, PA: Chandler.

Dahl, Robert. 1947. The Science of Public Administration: Three Problems. *Public Administration Review* 7:1–11.

Drucker, Peter. 1952. Reply to Dwight Waldo. *American Political Science Review* 46:496–500.

Frederickson, George F., and Ralph Clark Chandler. 1997. Democracy and Public Administration: The Minnowbrook Perspective. *International Journal of Public Administration* 20, nos. 4–5 (Special Issue): 817–1155.

Frederickson, George F., and Richard Mayer. 1998. Minnowbrook II. *Public Administration Review* 49 (Special Issue).

Guy, Mary Ellen. 1989. Minnowbrook II: Conclusions. *Public Administration Review* 49, no. 2:219–20.

Marini, Frank, ed. 1971. *Toward a New Public Administration: The Minnowbrook Perspective.* Scranton, PA: Chandler.

Simon, Herbert. 1947. A Comment on "The Science of Public Administration." *Public Administration Review* 7:200–203.

———. 1952. Reply to Dwight Waldo. *American Political Science Review* 46:494–96.

Thompson, Victor A. 1975. *Without Sympathy or Enthusiasm: The Problem of Administrative Compassion*. Tuscaloosa: University of Alabama Press.

Waldo, Dwight. 1952a. The Development of Theory of Democratic Administration. *American Political Science Review* 46:81–103.

———. 1952b. Reply to Simon and Drucker. *American Political Science Review* 46:500–503.

———. 1971. *Public Administration in a Time of Turbulence.* Scranton, PA: Chandler.

PART I

Studying and Managing Public Organizations of the Future

When we imagine public organizations of the future, many of us think of *The Jetsons,* the prime-time animated television show that was shown on Sunday nights in the early 1960s—with years of reruns and a cult-like following. The story of the Jetson family takes place in 2062. Aliens, flying people in special suits, flying cars that look like flying saucers with transparent bubble tops, and flying family pets that speak are the norm. Computers have human personalities and belong to the Society for Preventing Cruelty to Humans. Robots do most of the work, and a full-time job consists of three hours a day, three days a week. George Jetson's workday entails pushing one button on a computer, surrounded by an abundance of other labor-saving devices. Nonetheless, he often complains about his grueling schedule and the difficulty of his work.

Although we are certain that public organizations of the future will be more high technology than they were at the time of Minnowbrook III (see part III on the role of information technology in governance), the reality of the public organization of the future is much less glamorous than that portrayed in *The Jetsons.* The trend of tightening both human and financial resources is likely to continue as public organizations struggle to become more flexible, efficient, politically responsive, adaptable, and competitive. Contract management, network formation, and collaborative management will most likely continue to grow as public managers increasingly seek alternatives to better address society's most pressing public challenges.

In the midst of this turbulent environment, six of the seven chapters in part I focus on what is *missing* in the study and management of public organizations in 2009 and provide ideas for the future. These six chapters fall into three thematic groups: values, evidence, and race and ethnicity. A final chapter, on homeland security, chronicles a trend in public administration that has developed since Minnowbrook II.

Leading off in "From Performance Management to Democratic Performance Governance," Donald P. Moynihan writes that much has changed since the original Minnowbrook Conference in 1968. Many of the values that the Minnowbrook-inspired New Public Administration criticized—efficiency, effectiveness, and means/end rationality—are central to current approaches to governance. But traditional bureaucracies are still under attack. The start of the twenty-first century is characterized by limited faith in the expertise of managers and the capacity of governments. Instead, our current era places faith in quantitative indicators of performance, third-party government, and contracts as the new mechanisms of governance. Moynihan argues that a crucial task for public administration is to move beyond the study of performance management as a narrow technique, akin to personnel management, and instead conceptualize it as democratic performance governance.

Next comes "An Argument for Fully Incorporating Nonmission-Based Values into Public Administration," in which Suzanne J. Piotrowski maintains that a focus on nonmission-based values is conspicuously absent from the theory and practice of public administration. Nonmission-based values are those not associated with the central focus of an organization or program. For most public administrators, examples of these values include due process, equity, integrity, and transparency. Though some attention has been paid to these values and their associated laws, regulations, and policies, they are generally regarded in the public administration literature—either explicitly or implicitly—as subservient to the value of achieving results cost effectively. Piotrowski argues that there needs to be a coherent public administrative strategy to prioritize nonmission-based values in public-sector organizations. Public-sector employees need clear signals that these values and their associated laws, rules, regulations, and policies are an essential part of their jobs.

In "Are We There Yet? From Taylor's Triangle to Follett's Web; From Knowledge Work to Emotion Work," Mary E. Guy, Meredith A. Newman, and Sharon H. Mastracci focus on values of a different sort: those dealing with emotions. They question whether the field of public administration—in either theory or practice—has arrived at an appreciation for the worker as a whole person rather than as a cog in the machine where only cognitive skills are appreciated. Tracing the contributions of Frederick Taylor, Mary Parker Follett, and Peter Drucker to management theory, the authors argue that the field has stopped short of a full appreciation for public service work skills. Effective public service requires both emotional and cognitive work, they argue. The emotional part of public-sector work—dealing with trauma and death, working with citizens who may be unlikable, and interacting with needy, vulnerable members of society at the worst moments of their lives—is often not addressed in the official rhetoric of management efficiencies. The authors encourage public management scholars to amend public management theory to seek a more comprehensive understanding of the public service worker. Only then, they maintain, can we realistically comprehend public service work and all that it requires.

In "The Raised Fist and the Magic Negro: Public Administration and the Black Public Administrator," Domonic Bearfield writes about the second theme of this part—race and ethnicity. He argues that scholars in public administration have incompetently struggled with a changing racial and ethnic landscape, and that the field has consistently relied on old racial narratives to construct research questions and interpret data. What is needed is an examination of the images of race that are prevalent in the field and new robust analyses that catalyze our understanding of the role that race and ethnic background bring to public administration.

In a chapter on a similar subject but with a different twist, "Social Equity in Public Administration: The Need for Fire," Susan T. Gooden maintains that social equity in American public administration and policy is caught up in an unproductive cycle. She writes that there must first be solid data indicating whether social inequities exist. Second, there must be an acceptance of the research and a concrete plan to reverse identified inequities. Third, the reversal plan must be successfully implemented. These three steps can be expressed metaphorically as "ready, aim, fire." However, current practice suggests that a more appropriate metaphor is "ready, aim, study more," a cyclical process that results in very little fire, thus raising the question: How can research be more effectively used to reverse social inequities?

Next, shifting gears to the issue of evidence, is Kimberley R. Isett, in ". . . And the Pendulum Swings: A Call for Evidence-Based Public Organizations." Instead of "reactionary innovation," which is often based on what sells well to the public, Isett maintains that what the field needs is a body of knowledge that focuses on creating evidence concerning what works and under what conditions for a particular set of governmental, institutional, and environmental factors or characteristics. Such evidence-based organization and system design would entail an understanding of how particular organizational forms or permutations interact with the institutional, environmental, and normative contexts of government organizations. Evidence-based organizational analysis would take into account not only that the organization is in the public sector but also the substantive mission of the agency, as well as the set of constraints and opportunities facing the organization. Isett's goal is to retreat from faddish pseudosolutions that sound good but are often promoted without systematic analysis.

Finally, in "Public Administration: The Central Discipline in Homeland Security," Dale Jones and Austen Givens maintain that one of the most pronounced changes in U.S. government and public administration since Minnowbrook II has been the focus on homeland security as a major policy area, triggering immense changes in and challenges for U.S. public organizations. The national response to the September 11, 2001, terrorist attacks resulted in the most sweeping changes to federal government organization since the National Security Act of 1947. New legislation and executive branch actions after 9/11 brought significant changes for the first time in more than half a century, marking the beginning of a new era in American government and public administration. Jones and Givens explain the development of homeland security as a profession, argue that public administration is at the core of homeland security, and analyze what this means for the study and management of public organizations, as well as the education of current and future public affairs and public policy students.

Although these chapters do not address flying cars or people, robots, or talking dogs, taken as a whole they challenge us to think broadly and deeply about some of the most pressing issues facing public organizations now and in the future.

From Performance Management to Democratic Performance Governance

Donald P. Moynihan

Much has changed since the original Minnowbrook meeting in 1968. Many of the values that the Minnowbrook-inspired New Public Administration criticized—efficiency, effectiveness, and means/end rationality—remain central to current approaches to governance. But traditional bureaucracies are still under attack. The start of the twenty-first century is characterized by limited faith in the expertise of managers and the capacity of governments. Instead, our current era places faith in quantitative indicators of performance, third-party government, and contracts as the new mechanisms of governance.

This chapter argues that a crucial task for public administration is to move beyond the study of performance management as narrow technique, akin to personnel management, and instead conceptualize it as democratic performance governance. It is a task of profound importance because of how deeply embedded performance information is in the practices of governance.

The term "governance" reflects the reality that results-based reforms imply more than technical measurement processes, or even management. Performance routines are gradually altering the basic social and organizational processes whereby public services are considered and delivered. Within the traditional boundaries of government, agencies are required to state strategic goals and targets, and to report results. Governments continue to try, with little success, to connect pay systems to performance indicators. Within our growing state of agents, performance information is the primary basis on which contractual forms of accountability are established, and the means whereby webs of connected principals and agents allocate responsibility. To understand these mechanisms of governance, we need to understand the use and effects of performance information. The first three chapters of part I address these questions. But the Minnowbrook tradition calls us to do more than to consider matters of governance solely from an empirical point of view. Therefore, this final chapter of part I offers a normative argument that calls for the diffusion of democratic values into measurement processes.

HOW WE USE PERFORMANCE INFORMATION: PASSIVE, POLITICAL, PERVERSE, AND PURPOSEFUL

One of the difficulties of studying the use of performance information is that we think of it as a single construct, when in fact it has multiple categories and subcategories. Researchers usually focus on one or two of these categories and ignore others. There is a danger of conflating these different categories, and thus using the same name for different variables, with different causes and effects. If we are to emerge from this muddle, it would behoove us to conceptualize and measure these categories in the standardized way that we do for other multifaceted behavioral concepts, such as organizational commitment, public service motivation, and goal ambiguity. There are many possible ways to categorize the use of performance information, but for the sake of brevity, I will limit myself to the "four Ps"—passive, political, perverse, and purposeful—while collectively referring to bureaucratic and contract actors as "agents."

Passive

Results-based reforms may result in passive reactions, where agents do the minimum to comply with requirements to create and disseminate information but do not actually use this information (Radin 2006). This strategy is logical if (1) there is a high likelihood that the current approach to performance-based bureaucracy is temporary, (2) elected officials and stakeholders demonstrate little real interest in implementation, and (3) agency leaders see little additional benefit in implementing performance management tools. The struggles of previous versions of performance management, and growing bureaucratic disillusionment with current reforms, make such an outcome highly plausible. But where results-based reforms have a permanent statutory basis, it becomes more difficult for bureaucrats to assume that they can wait it out.

Political

Results-based reforms demand that agents provide evidence of performance. Agents may come to see data as a means to define their efforts and success as a means of advocacy in a political environment (Moynihan 2008a). Agents often have some discretion or input in selecting and measuring the performance goals and measures by which they are judged, and they are likely to select, disseminate, and interpret information that portrays them in a favorable light. External stakeholders may also seek to use performance data to support or criticize the agent, but the information asymmetry of the agents is likely to make them more effective as advocates.

Perverse

In some cases the pressures to maximize measured performance may be so great that agents will improve these measures in ways that are in conflict with the underlying or unmeasured goals of a program (Radin 2006, 207–8). Agents may game program indicators through a variety of tactics, including making up data, creaming easy-to-serve clients, changing performance goals to limit comparison across time, or manipulating measures.

Purposeful

The central hope of results-based reforms is that public employees will actually use the data to try to manage their program in ways that directly improve performance. Such improvements can come via goal-based learning that gives rise to efficiency improvements, better targeting of resources and more informed strategic decisions, or by tying indicators to rewards/sanctions in contract arrangements (Moynihan 2008a). As much of governance is devolved into ongoing contracts, a key question is whether principals can learn how to limit gaming on the part of agents, and actually encourage performance improvement rather than the exploitation of incomplete contracts (Courty and Marschke 2007).

WHY WE USE PERFORMANCE INFORMATION

Performance information use is contextual, influenced by incentives and the surrounding environment. As with many other initiatives, leadership and/or political support, organizational culture, and the supply of adequate resources are likely to be important factors to encourage the purposeful use of performance data. Where these factors are absent, passive use is more likely. Another important contextual factor is the nature of the task and how easy it is to measure. In an ideal situation, key goals are easily measured, measures capture the underlying goals of a program, outputs can be linked to outcomes, and individual effort can be clearly linked to outputs. In such a context, the purposeful use of indicators and effective contractual arrangements become more likely. But these desirable measurement characteristics are rare in the public sector. As a result, contracts are likely to be incomplete, making advocacy and gaming more feasible. Though measurement ambiguity should precede the decision to align performance indicators with incentives, it often does not, and the creation of market-type mechanisms forms another contextual factor that shapes use. The incentive for gaming and advocacy increases when measurement ambiguity and market-like arrangements interact.

The role and involvement of elected officials, central agencies, the public, and stakeholders is likely to affect the ways in which performance data are used. An external political environment that provides agencies with a great deal of autonomy may encourage passivity or the purposeful use of data, whereas a political environment that is adversarial might encourage political or perverse uses.

The use of performance information will also be shaped by individual traits, beliefs, and job characteristics. Organizational commitment, public service motivation, experience, task, role ambiguity, and other individual/job characteristics are likely to affect how performance data are viewed, and what forms of uses are appropriate and feasible.

HOW PERFORMANCE INFORMATION USES US: CHANGING THE NATURE OF GOVERNANCE

The previous section considered the use of performance information as a dependent variable. It is clear that we need to better understand how to build performance regimes, but we also need to understand their consequences. Performance regimes were intended to change the basic nature of governance, altering the culture, behavior, and actions of the public sector (Radin 2006). Performance information use is therefore also an independent variable. For example, Moynihan (2008a) has found that performance information was used to reshape organizational cultures and to build external political support for programs.

Depending on how it is used, performance data could negatively or positively affect intrinsic motivators, organizational commitment, client orientation, goal displacement, job satisfaction, and organizational morale (Moynihan 2008b). For example, studies have linked the use of performance targets among for-profit welfare services to employee disillusionment and frustration (Dias and Maynard-Moody 2007; Soss, Fording, and Schram 2008).

Many of the variables that shape performance information use can also be shaped by it. For example, the use of the performance data may become embedded as an appropriate norm in an organizational culture over time, reshaping the attitudes of individuals in that organization and making them more amenable to using performance data. This point recognizes that changes in governance are ultimately path dependent and incremental. A tendency to focus on key reforms or events simplifies these long-term historical trends. Though modeling why individuals and organizations use performance information is perhaps the more tractable question, examining how performance information use rewrites the causal processes that give rise to it is the more important long-term question, because it tells us how results-based reforms have ultimately affected governance.

THE DEMOCRATIC QUESTION (OR WHAT WOULD WALDO THINK?)

What would Dwight Waldo and the original scholars of the New Public Administration make of this era of governance by performance management? They might gently (or not so gently) remind us that causal modeling is important but that it cannot ultimately resolve normative questions of democratic accountability. They would surely worry that the New Public Management and performance management in many ways represent a continuity of values such as efficiency, effectiveness, and means/end rationality to the exclusion of other values such as social equity.

Some have explicitly made this argument, suggesting that though performance management has been portrayed as a neutral tool, it has legitimated certain values and excluded others, such as social equity, citizenship, transparency, due process, and individual rights (see also Piotrowski's chapter in this volume; Radin 2006; Rosenbloom 2007; and Wichowsky and Moynihan 2008). The Minnowbrook tradition of reconciling democracy and administration calls for a coherent strategy to make nonmission-based values a priority in performance management. Though this may be a difficult task, Wichowsky and Moynihan (2008, 917) argue that "there is no intrinsic attribute of performance measurement that prevents it from refocusing administrative attention to democratic concerns. Indeed, it could become a powerful means to do so."

The value-based critique addresses two important questions: What values does performance information represent? Can it represent other values? But it does not fully address many of the other key normative questions (and their logical empirical corollaries) that arise from performance regimes, such as these: Who sets the goals and measures? Who is empowered by performance regimes? What legitimate role should the public play? How should performance information interact with traditional forms of democratic involvement?

CONCLUSION

Performance management is sometimes treated as a narrow and technocratic topic. The opposite is, or should be, true. The study of performance management should be central to the study of governance. Some excellent research has begun this task, but there is much to do. This chapter has highlighted the need for better theories and evidence on the use of performance information and how this use affects governance over time. We also need to explicitly examine the normative implications of performance regimes and to tackle the question of how to reconcile the legitimate desire for performance with other administrative values.

All types of scholarship are needed. Argumentation can take on many of the normative questions of democratic accountability and judge whether the large-scale changes to governance are appropriate. The goal of testing some of the causal relationships suggested here implies large-*N* quantitative studies. Such work generally relies on survey data that bring both benefits and limitations. There is ample room for experimental analyses to examine how individuals perceive and use performance data. Given the variety of potential causal relationships suggested here, qualitative research can develop theory that maps out casual processes and identifies which of these processes are more likely and under what conditions. Regardless of the theory or research approach employed, we need analytical treatments of the key mechanisms of change if we are to understand and shape an era of democratic performance governance.

REFERENCES

Courty, Pascal, and Gerald Marschke. 2007. Making Government Accountable: Lessons from a Federal Job Training Program. *Public Administration Review* 67, no. 5:904–16.

Dias, Janice Johnson, and Steven Maynard-Moody. 2007. For-Profit Welfare: Contracts, Conflicts, and the Performance Paradox. *Journal of Public Administration Research and Theory* 17, no. 2:189–211.

Moynihan, Donald P. 2008a. *The Dynamics of Performance Management: Constructing Information and Reform*. Washington, DC: Georgetown University Press.

———. 2008b. The Normative Model in Decline? Public Service Motivation in the Age of Governance. In *Motivation in Management: The Call of Public Service*, ed. James L. Perry and Annie Hondeghem. Oxford: Oxford University Press.

Radin, Beryl. 2006. *Challenging the Performance Movement: Accountability, Complexity and Democratic Values*. Washington, DC: Georgetown University Press.

Rosenbloom, David H. 2007. Reinventing Administrative Prescriptions: The Case for Democratic-Constitutional Impact Statements and Scorecards. *Public Administration Review* 67, no. 1:28–39.

Soss, Joe, Richard Fording, and Sanford Schram. 2008. The Organization of Discipline: From Performance Management to Perversity and Punishment. Paper presented at annual meeting of Association for Public Policy Analysis and Management, Los Angeles, November 6–8.

Wichowsky, Amber, and Donald P. Moynihan. 2008. Measuring How Administration Shapes Citizenship: A Policy Feedback Perspective on Performance Management. *Public Administration Review* 68, no. 5:908–20.

AN ARGUMENT FOR FULLY INCORPORATING NONMISSION-BASED VALUES INTO PUBLIC ADMINISTRATION

SUZANNE J. PIOTROWSKI

Conspicuously absent from the theory and practice of public administration is a focus on nonmission-based values, which are those values not associated with the central focus of an organization or program (Piotrowski and Rosenbloom 2002). For most public administrators, examples of these values include due process, equity, integrity, and transparency. Though some attention has been paid to these values and their associated laws, regulations, and policies, they are generally regarded, either explicitly or implicitly, as subservient to the value of achieving results cost effectively in the public administration literature.

There needs to be a coherent public administrative strategy to prioritize nonmission-based values in public-sector organizations. Public-sector employees need clear signals that these values—and their associated laws, rules, regulations, and policies—are an essential part of their jobs. History has shown us that in times of crisis, war, and massive social and economic change, public administrators can ignore issues such as equity and ethical decision making (Adams and Balfour 2004). A commitment to the rule of law is essential (Rosenbloom 2003). Public administrators managing in the twenty-first century in times of global financial crisis, health care system overhauls, and ongoing wars must not forget to prioritize nonmission-based values.

To make the argument more concrete, I provide an example of how the value of transparency can be more fully incorporated into public-sector management. Gaining access to government information is a perpetual concern for citizens. This is due in large part to the relationship between transparency and the issues of ethics, corruption, administrative malfeasance, and accountability. Governmental transparency is an essential, though frequently overlooked, aspect of democratic accountability. Governmental transparency is the degree to which access to government information is available. Transparency is a prerequisite for full administrative accountability, and the more transparent a government is, the more readily the public can engage with this government and hold officials accountable for their actions. The argument has been made for increased global civic engagement to strengthen democracy (Barber 2004). Democracy, one of the key themes throughout the proceedings published by the first group of Minnowbrook scholars (Marini 1971), has still—forty years later—not been fully incorporated into the field of public administration.

It has been argued that transparency is the closest thing the field of public administration ethics has to a universally accepted value (Cooper 2004). Though the issue and study of governmental transparency has been gaining traction in recent years, it is not a new concept, and a wide range of theorists have written on it. Max Weber (1968) wrote about the tendency of bureaucracy toward secrecy. In a personal correspondence in 1822, James Madison wrote: "A popular Government, without popular information, or the means of acquiring it, is but a Prologue to a Farce or a Tragedy; or, perhaps, both. Knowledge will forever govern ignorance: And a people who mean to be their own Governors must arm themselves with the power which knowledge gives" (Madison 1999).

Before becoming a Supreme Court justice, Louis D. Brandeis wrote about access to the banking industry: "Sunlight is said to be the best of disinfectants; electric light the most efficient policeman" (Brandeis 1933). The imagery of sunlight has been frequently applied to governmental transparency.

The current literature on transparency focuses on a wide range of issues, including national security (Blanton 2003; Roberts 2004), targeted transparency policies (Fung, Graham, and Weil 2007), and international trends (Florini 2007). David Heald (2006) develops a particularly helpful framework for describing the different directions of transparency. His four-part framework includes "transparency inwards," the ability to see within an organization from the outside, which is the one direction most usually associated with governmental openness. Governmental transparency allows individuals to find out what is happening inside government through various mechanisms, including freedom of information–type requests, the proactive release of information by governments, open meetings, whistle blowing, and leaked information (Piotrowski 2007).

Although there is a growing consensus that transparency is a key part of good governance, there has been little discussion on how to tie transparency to the mission of an organization. I propose a simple solution for career bureaucrats, political appointees, and elected officials. Public-sector organizations of all types should not only work to fulfill their current stated mission and program goals but also expand these statements to include informing the public about the activities and processes associated with these functions. In the following paragraphs I provide three examples to illustrate this point. It is important to explicitly link the goal of transparency with organization and programmatic missions. If this is done, transparency indicators can be incorporated into strategic plans and performance measurement systems. This sends a clear signal to public employees that openness is valued to the same degree as other values already incorporated into the strategic planning process. It is common to hear local government officials say that they do not have the time to fill a freedom of information–type request because it "takes them away from doing their job." This argument is also used when minutes of open public meetings are not available for release and government records are not properly archived for future retrieval. In many governments, these functions are not given priority, even though there are laws, regulations, and organizational policies requiring their completion because there are few incentives to follow them and almost no real penalties for ignoring them.

First, take an environmental agency for example. Currently, "the mission of the Environmental Protection Agency is to protect human health and the environment" (Environmental Protection Agency 2008). I argue that the U.S. Environmental Protection Agency's mission should be expanded to include informing the public as to how it is working to protect human health and the environment. In practice, this could include prioritizing the release of key environmental statistics early and often, fully funding freedom of information offices to reduce a backlog of these requests, and widely publicizing proposed regulations changes. Of course, releasing only positive or favorable information equates to little more than propaganda. An organization that truly sees transparency as part of its mission, and as essential for the public good, will disseminate and facilitate access to all legally releasable information.

This suggestion does not only apply to federal government agencies. Local police forces could similarly expand their mission. For instance, "the Mission of the New York City Police Department is to enhance the quality of life in our City by working in partnership with the community and in accordance with constitutional rights to enforce the laws, preserve the peace, reduce fear, and provide for a safe environment" (New York Police Department 2008). Local police departments could prioritize providing access to accurate and timely information not only regarding crime statistics but also how they enforce laws, conduct internal investigations, and operate generally. Local police forces could—and many do—hold public forums to explain to residents what activities their organization is undertaking.

The focus on incorporating transparency into mission statements could also be applied to specific governmental functions. To illustrate this point consider the water supply of Syracuse: "The Syracuse Water Department is responsible for constructing, maintaining and operating all necessary and desirable facilities for the supply and distribution of a safe, potable water supply for the city of Syracuse" (City of Syracuse 2008). The Water Department should make it a priority not only to supply safe drinking water but also to inform the public about the character of the water and the water system as a whole. This includes not only releasing published reports but also facilitating requests for information.

These three examples could be exponentially expanded to include other organizations, such as nonprofits, and a wide array of functions, including the management of contracts. Archiving and maintaining documents gains importance for an organization when transparency rises in importance. The necessity of accessing contractor records can be explicitly written into government contracts. If the value of transparency is incorporated into the mission of an organization or program, then a wide array of tools open up. Nonmission-based values such as transparency also can and should be incorporated into organizations' strategic planning processes, performance measurement systems, and employee appraisal systems. Having these values more fully integrated in public management systems sends the message that they are valued equally with other organizational priorities.

To some extent this is already happening in a piecemeal fashion throughout public-sector organizations. In British Columbia, the Office of the Information and Privacy Commissioner has begun establishing and tracking performance measures for freedom of information requests in the provincial governments (Office of the Information and Privacy Commissioner for British Columbia 2009). At one time, the U.S. Department of Justice included facilitation of the Freedom of Information Act as part of its personnel appraisal system. Personnel evaluations could include components associated with processing freedom of information–type requests and other transparency-related functions. Within a larger discussion of the preeminent importance of the separation of powers with public administration, Anthony Bertelli and Laurence Lynn (2006, 147) write that "accountability is not an ideal for regimes or governments so much as it is an ideal for the individuals who serve in official capacities." Individuals can be held responsible for promoting transparency, and thus democratic accountability more generally. *In short, nonmission-based values, such as transparency, should be fully incorporated into the mission, strategic plan, and performance measurement system of public-sector organizations.*

Much of what I describe falls under the proactive release of information, one of the five avenues of access laid out above. Public organizations need to proactively, regularly, and routinely provide accurate and full information to the public. Though the focus is on the proactive release of information, this does not preclude organizations from improving their processes surrounding freedom of information–type requests or emphasizing the need to inform the public through open public meetings or hearings.

Most governments, including the ones I mentioned here, are already incorporating many of these transparency-related functions to some degree. The difference is that these tasks are not considered an integral part of the success of most organizations and a priority for their personnel. When resources are tight, these functions may make their way to the budgetary chopping block. This is unacceptable. Frequently, organizations are legally bound by freedom of information–type laws, open public meeting laws, and regulations requiring disclosure. They should embrace the spirit of these requirements and not seek loopholes or minimum standards. Including a focus on transparency in the mission, strategic plan, and performance measurement system of an organization or program sends a clear message to employees that openness and disseminating information are an integral, not ancillary, part of the job.

REFERENCES

Adams, G. B., and D. L. Balfour. 2004. *Unmasking Administrative Evil*, rev. ed. Armonk, NY: M. E. Sharpe.

Barber, B. R. 2004. *Strong Democracy: Participatory Politics for a New Age*, 3rd ed. Berkeley: University of California Press.

Bertelli, A. M., and L. E. Lynn. 2006. *Madison's Managers: Public Administration and the Constitution*. Baltimore: Johns Hopkins University Press.

Blanton, T. 2003. National Security and Open Government in the United States: Beyond the Balancing Test. In *National Security and Open Government: Striking the Right Balance*, ed. A. Roberts and H. Darbishire. Syracuse: Campbell Public Affairs Institute, Maxwell School of Syracuse University.

Brandeis, L. D. 1933. *Other People's Money, and How Bankers Use It*. Washington, DC: National Home Library Foundation.

City of Syracuse. 2008. Department of Water. www.syracuse.ny.us/deptWater.asp.

Cooper, T. 2004. Big Questions in Administrative Ethics: A Need for Focused, Collaborative Effort. *Public Administration Review* 64, no. 4:395–404.

Environmental Protection Agency. 2008. About EPA. www.epa.gov/epahome/aboutepa.htm.

Florini, A., ed. 2007. *The Right to Know: Transparency for an Open World*. New York Columbia University Press.

Fung, A., M. Graham, and D. Weil. 2007. *Full Disclosure: The Perils and Promise of Transparency*. New York: Cambridge University Press.

Heald, D. 2006. Varieties of Transparency. In *Transparency: The Key to Better Governance*, ed. C. Hood and D. Heald. New York: Oxford University Press.

Madison, J. 1999. Letter to William T. Barry, August 4, 1822. In *James Madison: Writings*. New York: Library Classics of the United States.

Marini, F., ed. 1971. *Toward a New Public Administration: The Minnowbrook Perspective*. Syracuse: Chandler.

New York Police Department. 2008. About the NYPD's Mission and Values. www.nyc.gov/html/nypd/html/home/mission.shtml.

Office of the Information and Privacy Commissioner for British Columbia. (2009). *Timeliness of Government's Access to Information Responses: Report for Calendar Year 2008*. Available at www.oipc.bc.ca.

Piotrowski, S. J. 2007. *Governmental Transparency in the Path of Administrative Reform*. Albany: State University of New York Press.

Piotrowski, S. J., and Rosenbloom, D. 2002. Nonmission-Based Values in Results Oriented Public Management: The Case of Freedom of Information. *Public Administration Review* 62, no. 6:643–57.

Roberts, A. S. 2004. National Security and Open Government. *Georgetown Public Policy Review* 9, no. 2:69–76.

Rosenbloom, D. H. 2003. *Administrative Law for Public Managers*. Cambridge, MA: Westview.

Weber, M. 1968. *Economy and Society: An Outline of Interpretive Sociology*. New York: Bedminster Press.

Are We There Yet?

From Taylor's Triangle to Follett's Web; From Knowledge Work to Emotion Work

Mary E. Guy, Meredith A. Newman,
and Sharon H. Mastracci

The theories of Frederick Taylor (and to a lesser extent those of Henry Gantt and Frank Gilbreth) and of Mary Parker Follett indelibly altered the management landscape. Taylor's hierarchical, top-down, command-and-control approach to management relies on a strong leader with autonomous authority. Follett's integrative approach values pluralistic decision making and a two-way flow of power and authority. In contrast to Taylor's focus on engineering to achieve performance, Follett's focus is on the webs that connect workers to one another and to management. The nature of the workplace framed their thoughts; for Taylor and his contemporary Henry Ford, it was industrial production, and for Follett it was interpersonal relations in the workplace.

Max Weber's (1922) prescription that a bureaucratic hierarchy ought to run like an efficient machine informs this discussion as well. Weber theorized that bureaucracies succeeded by depersonalizing, if not dehumanizing, the people within them (Clair et al. 2008, 129). "Its specific nature, which is welcomed by capitalism, develops the more perfectly the more the bureaucracy is 'dehumanized,' the more completely it succeeds in eliminating from official business love, hatred, and all purely personal, irrational, and emotional elements which escape calculation. This is the specific nature of bureaucracy and it is appraised as its special virtue" (Weber 1970, 215–16). Weber would assign specific tasks to each worker and arrange them along assembly lines, whether they produce car parts, financial reports, or customer services.

Although it may be appropriate to structure and evaluate work according to what is measurable in goods-producing industries, it is inappropriate to do so for service providers. Public administration scholarship has looked at this problem over time, but without sustained attention. The most problematic aspect of applying industrial thinking to public service is that it renders emotional labor invisible.[1] Peter Drucker nudged management thinking forward by forecasting the importance of knowledge work in a service economy, such that workers own the means of production—their knowledge. But even his paradigm-stretching work failed to acknowledge the importance of affect.

This brings us to the purpose of this chapter. We suggest that *emotional labor* and the values of caring and service represent powerful levers that advance public service. This perspective complicates the conventional founding narrative of our field, a narrative already made suspect by the work of Camilla Stivers, DeLysa Burnier, Cheryl King, O. C. McSwite, Ralph Hummel, Hindy Lauer Schachter, Robert Kramer, and a handful of others. Emotional labor exposes the missing links in our field—namely, an ethic of care and relationship tasks.

We begin by illuminating the path from the top-down management style of the industrial age to the participatory style of the postmodern era. Next, we fast-forward to the contemporary focus on knowledge work, exemplified by the work of Peter Drucker. We then transition to the service exchange, showing how cognition alone is not enough. The affective component of the exchange and the *caritas* function must also be appreciated. Rejecting Weberian orthodoxy and the "administrative science" paradigm (connoting impersonal detachment), we underscore the value of "service" (connectedness). In doing so, we demonstrate the value of emotional intelligence for public administrators, and emotional labor and affective leadership for public service.[2] If our colleagues will adopt this more comprehensive model of the worker as a whole person rather than as "the truncated remnant" that remains when only cognitive aspects are appreciated, the future of public administration theory will be much richer.

ADMINISTRATIVE *SCIENCE* OR PUBLIC *SERVICE*?

In reflecting on this chapter, we were reminded of a question that had been asked of one of our students at the completion of formal coursework: "If you had to choose between the value of efficiency and the value of responsiveness, which would you choose?" Without hesitation, the student responded "efficiency." Alas! To choose "efficiency" is to view public administration from a "how" perspective, from a (scientific) management approach. "Responsiveness" suggests a competing approach—that of "to what" government should be most attentive. Jane Addams said it this way: "[Municipal reform efforts led by business groups] fix their attention so exclusively on methods that they fail to consider the final aims of city government" (Addams 2002, as cited by Stivers 2008). The big issue for governments, Addams held, was not how they should be run but what they should do. The Bureau Movement's approach to running government agencies came increasingly to be seen as a matter of "management" and management expertise, legitimated by Taylorism and operationalized by Fordism.

The intellectual heritage of the field of public administration is replete with references to "how" to "do" government better. The reinvention movement is merely the latest in a long line of reforms focusing on methods and techniques. For example, Van Riper (1983, 487) characterizes the administrations of Grover Cleveland and Ronald Reagan as pursuing "how to do it" not "what to do" programs. Missing from much of the history of the field is any significant debate on "what" government should be engaged in.

It matters whether public administrators view themselves, and are perceived by citizens, as merely dispassionate cogs in the machine of government or whether they are viewed and treated as public servants engaged in "soul-work" where all public service is people service (Kramer 2003, 6). In reviewing the intellectual heritage of public administration, attention to the *science* of administration and the cult of efficiency trumps attention to the relational aspects of public *service*. Indeed, discourse on the field's development can be characterized as a testament to the values of rationality and efficiency, scientific principles, objectivity, and generic management processes. Excluded from much of this discourse is any reference to a service orientation and the value of caring.

In revisiting the field's canon, the prominence of science (detachment) over service (connectedness) is undeniable. From Woodrow Wilson to Osborne and Gaebler, the *business* of government and the marketization of public administration sanctify the values of (technical) efficiency and (objective) rationality. For example, in his 1887 essay, Wilson asserted the need for expertise and businesslike methods. In 1903, Frederick Taylor's *Shop Management* fueled the fledgling Progressive Era movement. In *The Principles of Scientific Management,* he states, "in the past the man has been first, in the future the system must be first" (Taylor 1911, 7). His conceptualization of the "mechanisms of management" was predicated upon a subdivision of labor, task allocation, and standardization.

Taylor's assertion that scientific research could improve work in public agencies became an article of faith of the Bureau Movement (Schachter 2002, 2004). In 1909 Frederick Cleveland, a leader of the New York Bureau of Municipal Research, wrote " 'science is a codification of exactly determined commonsense.' . . . Administration must therefore become a science in order to eliminate confusion . . . about the best method of accomplishing tasks" (as cited by Stivers 2002, 42). In 1912, the beginnings of management analysis came with the addition to the Civil Service Commission of a Division of Efficiency (Van Riper 1983, 482). In the 1920s "bureau men" were the standard-bearers for the ideals of economy and efficiency. In 1926 Leonard White asserted that the study of administration "assumes that administration is still primarily an art but attaches importance to the significant tendency to transform it into a science" (as cited by Green 2002, 558). In 1937 Luther Gulick argued that efficiency must be built into the structure of government just as it is built into a "piece of machinery" (as cited by Kramer 2003, 14). And Gulick and Urwick's *Papers on the Science of Administration* provided an anthology focusing on administration as a universal process (Van Riper 1983, 481). "Since the Progressive Era, public administration has moved in an increasingly instrumental, managerial direction, valuing the application of scientific methodology to the resolution of public issues and building an identity of neutral expertise" (King and Stivers 1998, 106).

Missing from the conventional narrative is the language of caring, responsiveness, and "publicness." Attention to an ethic of care and the relational tasks that are performed in emotion work are rendered moot in the process. The experiences of settlement women and their attention to healing social ills stand in stark contrast to the rational detachment of administrative science. An exception to this oversight is the work of Mary Parker Follett and Jane Addams. Follett's work emphasizes the human side of management, breathing life into the outline afforded by Taylor's work (see Newman and Guy 1998). "While those around her were focused on transforming people into efficient machines, Follett saw the importance and possibilities of treating people as individuals" (Clair et al. 2008, 152). As such, her ideas are a bridge between scientific management and the human relations movement. In contrast with Taylor, who atomized tasks and perceived workers as interchangeable parts, Follett's approach is based on mutualism and collective responsibility. She argued that "you may bring together all the parts of a machine, but you do not have the *machine* until they are properly related. The chief task of organization is how to relate the parts so that you have a working unit" (Follett 1940/1973, 177).

Follett believes that interpersonal relations are a critical dynamic in the work environment. Her management philosophy centers on the worker, not the work; on the person, not the task at hand. She is interested in workers' feelings and motivations, and her concern for the worker, the "doer," is explicit in her writings. Far from being a "mechanical" link in the chain of production, workers are multidimensional and not unidimensional. She views the workplace as an integrated whole, a synthesis between management and staff.

Another management theorist whose work informs the canon is Peter Drucker. About a decade after Follett's work, Drucker began to focus on what he felt were the central questions of organization: the distribution of power and responsibility, and the selection and training of leaders. His focus on human relationships led him to the conclusion that "an institution is like a tune; it is not constituted by individual sounds but by the relations between them" (Drucker 1946, 26). Drucker felt that organizations, like tunes, when in harmony could induce in their members an intellectual and moral growth beyond a man's original capacities (Drucker 1946, 28).

For decades afterward, Drucker focused on how to devolve control, autonomy, and discretion to workers. His goal was to substitute management by self-control for management by domination. This empowerment language echoes that encouraged by Follett, but Drucker did not like the notion of empowerment. "It is not a great step forward to take power out at the top and put it in at the bottom. It's still power. To build achieving organizations, you must replace power with responsibility" (Drucker 1995, 17). He saw organizations as concentric, overlapping, coordinated rings, rather than as pyramids, with knowledge workers being capitalists because they own their own means of production, that is, knowledge (Drucker 1980). In Drucker's words, it is now "the man who puts to work what he has between his ears rather than the brawn of his muscles or the skills of his hands" (Drucker 1967, 3) that controls our future. But it is difficult to monitor and measure knowledge work during the creation process; rather, it is not until completion that effectiveness can be known. The same can be said for emotion work.[3]

Thus comes the service economy, the next link in a chain of an educated workforce performing in a service economy. Follett's work as well as Drucker's, in contrast to scientific management precepts and command-and-control structures, presage the contemporary public service workplace and call into question the conventional wisdom about what *work* is. It is to this topic that we now turn.

THEORIES OF WORK

Our understanding of what it means to "work" derives from Wilsonian, Fordist, Taylorist, and Weberian assumptions. For the most part, theories of work and caring are treated as unrelated concepts. The ideology of *work* is buttressed by four institutional forces. First, the structural elements of organizing, articulated by scientific management and reinforced by top-down, command-and-control structures, taught us to treat workers as interchangeable parts whose contributions reside in the performance of clearly enumerated duties. The process of job construction—where tasks are lumped together to form clearly defined jobs—is designed to depersonalize work and separate it from the person who performs it. Workers are akin to cogs in a machine, one indistinguishable from the next, whose tasks are carried out in a neutral (dispassionate) manner.

The Weberian model of "man as machine" and the "dominance of a spirit of formalistic impersonality, '*sine ira et studio*,' without hatred or passion" (Weber 1922, 15–16, as cited by Kramer 2003, 13), requires that public administrators conduct relationships "without sympathy or enthusiasm." A Fordist–Taylorist system of division of labor, hierarchical control, performance standards, scientific selection, and advancement based on technical competence is ingrained in the way we think about job classification. Relational work is absent from the list of knowledge, skills, and abilities, except in the obligatory requirement "to establish and maintain good working relationships."

Second, civil service systems are built on a foundation of formal descriptions that specify the tangible elements of each job. Though reforms have been introduced over the years, the basic understanding of what does, and does not, constitute "skill" remains mired in tradition. The nature of bureaucracy itself shapes—if not predicts—the character of work. In his scathing critique of bureaucracy, Ralph Hummel (1987, 27) decries the Weberian orthodoxy, asking, "is not a public service bureaucracy, especially, set up to provide public service?" As the emerging body of work on emotional labor attests, the expression and management of emotions remain for the most part invisible and uncompensated. They get "disappeared," to use Joyce Fletcher's term, not fitting the prevailing pattern of "work."

Third, urbanization and industrialization meant that a dichotomy emerged between home and work, with each domain evoking different behaviors. Home became a refuge from the dehumanization of the workplace. The work of nurturing and sustaining while simultaneously performing manual labor, as had occurred on the family farm, disappeared from the definition of work. In its place came a paradigm of "formal" job duties; relational work was defined away. Work and accompanying job descriptions focused on the tangible production of marketable goods and services. Behavior that mediated the process and produced positive relationships, a sense of community, and the resolution of conflict did not fit into quantifiable elements, so it was treated as extraneous—despite the suasion of Mary Parker Follett. This "separate spheres" custom, and the separation of roles for men and women (with men designated as the breadwinners and women as the primary workers in the household), spills over into the valuation of skills in the labor market (Baines, Evans, and Neysmith 1998, 52).

The fourth institutional force is that of so-called market value. This is shorthand for cultural understandings of worth and is nothing more than a panoply of culturally based assumptions and biases. The economist Nancy Folbre (2001, 231) says: "I've worried aloud about economists' overconfidence in that abstraction called 'the market.'" The only tasks that matter are those that are quantifiable, *objective*.

These four institutional factors have cemented notions about what is, and what is not, *real work*. Emotional labor and relational tasks fall outside these parameters. Having become trapped in the canon of scientific management, notions of organizational effectiveness fail to account for the centrality of emotion work in public service, nor do they recognize that jobs "require workers to have emotions as well as muscle and brain" (Himmelweit 1999, 34). The emphasis on tangible, testable skills suppresses or "disappears" behavior that is inconsistent with industrial-era standards, even when that behavior is directly related to organizational goals.

In summary, this "objective" approach to tasks and to performance evaluation rests on a theory of work buttressed by norms suited to industrial but not service jobs. Missing is any mention of relational work that involves caring and nurturing, and the emotion work that is required to perform such tasks. Traditional administrative language is the language of scientific management—

span of control, hierarchy, authority, and division of labor. A conception of administrative practice that is relational rather than controlling would have a different vocabulary. The construct of emotional labor bridges the "how" and "what" of governance because it turns our attention to the *caritas* function that is at the heart of public *service*, and the *means* by which work is performed.

THE (HE)ART OF PUBLIC SERVICE

Emotional labor and caring are the silent partners of person-to-person transactions in the citizen–state encounter. Stivers (2002, 62) makes reference to leadership as having become public administration's "phlogiston—the mysterious substance that, prior to the discovery of oxygen, was believed to be the ingredient in substances that made them burn." The same term can be applied to the concept of emotional labor. Many, if not most, public service jobs require interpersonal contact, either face to face or voice to voice. This work is relational in nature and involves acts that "grease the wheels" so that people cooperate, stay on task, and work well together. They are essential for job completion but have only recently come under scrutiny as prerequisites for successful performance.

The term *emotional labor* shares similarities as well as differences with physical labor—both require skill and experience and are subject to external controls and divisions of labor. Emotional labor requires that workers suppress their private feelings in order to show the "desirable" work-related emotion. In short, the focus is on an emotional performance that is bought and sold as a commodity.

Emotional labor and caring are bound together by definition and practice. Not all emotional labor is caring labor, but caring labor is a type of emotional labor. Martin Heidegger, according to King and Stivers (1998, 38–39), states that "care is that attentiveness or concern that enables us to orient ourselves toward and connect with things and people in our world and to be aware of those connections."

The language of an alternative—and more complete—administrative theory has its own vocabulary. This language is relational; the care perspective emphasizes values such as attentiveness, responsiveness, and the importance of relationships and emotional connection. These "unscientific" words are not new at a personal level, but they are new to administrative theory.

This relational language was the mother tongue of the women of the settlement houses and city clubs. Stivers (2000) points out that, at its founding, the field of public administration faced a choice between two divergent paths: that advanced by the science of the bureau men, and that of the care orientation of the settlement women. "De facto rather than deliberately, American public administration chose one and rejected or forgot the other"

(Stivers 2005, 27). Gender dynamics at the time resulted in a bifurcation between what could have been complementary impulses of systematizing and caring.

More recently, Stivers (2005, 27) "explores the road less taken: public administration based on ideas of home. . . . Home offers a relational reality for public administration. This reality serves as an alternative to prevailing understandings based on efficiency, control, and competition." The ontology of home is associated with nurturing and caring. These values were reflected in the work of the settlement residents and club women (p. 35). In contrast to the bureau men's vision of the city as a business, settlement women viewed the city as a home, and the community as one great family; accordingly their reform efforts came to be known as "municipal housekeeping," and their work as "public motherhood" (Stivers 2000, 9). The Woman's City Club, for example, characterized its work in terms of " 'the Links that bind the Home to the City Hall.' The home and all life within the city were inextricably chained to City Hall—female concerns about food inspection, factory safety, and clean air" (Flanagan 1990, 1048).

Jane Addams, the founder of Hull House in Chicago, lived this reality. She articulated a pragmatic view of administration informed by ideas of home and community, and she rejected the notion that efficiency was the key to effective administration (Stivers 2008). She used "family" as a metaphor for the wider society in order to argue for a notion of governance rooted in the kind of caring and nurturing that is typical of home, where there is a commitment to treat people with the kind of respect and care due real human beings, as opposed to cases and statistics.

Although Burnier (2003, 538) has stated that "the voice of care is yet to be heard within public administration," the voices of Stivers, Addams, and others represent a rising undertone. Follett's organizational thinking anticipates the care perspective's emphasis on relationship (Burnier 2003, 536). Hummel and Stivers (1998, 29) are critical of government for becoming "a specialized enterprise increasingly devoted to the exercise of technical rules and procedures, whether or not these take care of real-life problems. Reason, especially instrumental reason, overwhelms care." Reminiscent of the feminist ethic of care as developed by Charlotte Perkins Gilman (Clair et al. 2008, 159), they advocate developing a "politics of care" that would be marked by attentiveness and connectedness (p. 38). Taken together, these and other like-minded scholars point public administration in a direction where care would become a guiding value (Burnier 2003, 531).

THE DISCONNECT BETWEEN THEORY AND PRACTICE

Dwight Waldo (1948) noted that the issues public administration practitioners and scholars wrestle with are issues of "human cooperation." Few if any questions in public administration are simply technical (Stivers 2000, 135). A social worker comforts a frightened child, a paralegal calms a teenage client, an investigator becomes a chameleon in order to secure information, a public attorney engages in crisis intervention, an administrator rallies her staff, while another acts as role model and surrogate mother figure to her charges. Theirs is not work of a "neutral expert" simply "doing the job" as a technician. Their work is relational in nature and involves considerable emotional labor demands. Yet much of their work, and that of others who engage in emotional labor and caregiving, is treated informally. It is not part of any formal job description, nor does it appear on performance evaluations. Nor is this work tangible or measurable. It is, instead, uncharted—even more uncharted than the knowledge work that Drucker had forecast.

The "rich and knotty texture" (Abel and Nelson 1990, 40) of emotion work—dealing with trauma and death, working with citizens who are unlikable, interacting with needy, vulnerable members of society at the worst moments of their lives—illuminates the chasm between the practice of public service and the official rhetoric of management efficiencies. Care as a value is tied to everyday judgments that citizens and administrators make about what it means to do a job well or what it means to be a good manager. Emotional labor is inherent in these practices. When what we observe in the world is inconsistent with the ways in which our theories require us to talk and think, it is time to amend our theories.

CONCLUSION

This chapter has charted the theoretical development of the field of public administration in order to illuminate its blind spot. Its lexicon remains dominated by the vocabulary of industrial-era production methods, hierarchy, and the market. Terms like "rigid controls," "reengineering," "restructuring," and "reinvention" all come to mind. This is the language of "how" government should work. Any dialogue is more likely to revolve around whether and how public administration can achieve scientific status, rather than question the appropriateness of its means and ends.

We argue for the insertion of caring and affect into the canon. Why not follow the lead of the Progressive Era social reformers, such that government would focus on improving the conditions of people's lives and "working to put science to the service of life"? (Stivers 2000, 136). It is clear that public service requires both affective and cognitive work. We live in a service economy. Service with a smile, long the mantra in the private sector, is equally important in the public realm. A service-to-citizens orientation is wrapped with care and emotion work. Relationship, rapport, interaction, compassion, service, connectedness, and stewardship—*soulwork*—constitute the vocabulary of this relational administrative perspective.

Looking forward, an accurate theory of public service would embrace the fact that knowledge work and emotion work are both integral to service delivery and citizen satisfaction. To focus only on the former is like wondering why a one-bladed scissor fails to cut.

To conclude, viewing public administration theory through the lens of emotional labor and the values of caring and service has pointed out the missing link in the field's founding narrative and has explicated what it means to "work." A focus on emotional labor in practice, including care work, underscores the (human) nature of public work. Indeed, it puts us in a "public service frame of mind" (King and Stivers 1998, 196). The most important challenge facing public administrators is not to make their work more efficient but to make it more humane and caring. This is the service imperative. The goodness of fit between the foundational values of rationality and efficiency and the actual demands of public service is, well, not very good. How long will it take to get there?

NOTES

1. The relationship between emotional intelligence, emotional labor, and emotion work is this: *Emotional intelligence* is the native ability one has to sense one's own affect and the affect of the other and to know when and how to act, based on that knowledge. It is a construct similar to cognitive intelligence. *Emotional labor* is the effort that is made to suppress or manage one's own feelings in order to elicit the desired affect of another person. *Emotion work* is a term that connotes the performance of emotional labor. These two latter terms are often used synonymously. For an elaboration of this, see Guy, Newman, and Mastracci (2008).
2. For an elaboration of the affective component of leadership, see Newman, Guy, and Mastracci (2009).
3. A results-oriented organizational culture can accommodate a recognition of both knowledge work and emotion work better than a process-oriented culture because the service delivery is manifest but the process is not.

REFERENCES

Abel, Emily K., and Margaret K. Nelson, eds. 1990. *Circles of Care. Work and Identity in Women's Lives.* Albany: State University of New York Press.

Addams, Jane. 2002. *Democracy and Social Ethics.* Champaign: University of Illinois Press.

Baines, Carol, Patricia Evans, and Sheila Neysmith, eds. 1998. *Women's Caring: Feminist Perspectives on Social Welfare,* 2nd ed. Toronto: Oxford University Press (orig. pub. 1902).

Burnier, DeLysa. 2003. Other Voices / Other Rooms: Towards a Care-Centered Public Administration. *Administrative Theory & Praxis* 25, no. 4:529–44.

Clair, Robin P., Megan McConnell, Stephanie Bell, Kyle Hackbarth, and Stephanie Mathes. 2008. *Why Work? The Perception of a "Real Job" and the Rhetoric of Work through the Ages.* West Lafayette, IN: Purdue University Press.

Drucker, Peter F. 1946. *Concept of the Corporation.* New York: John Day Co. (rev. ed., 1972).

———. 1967. *The Effective Executive.* New York: Harper & Row.

———. 1980. *Managing in Turbulent Times.* New York: Harper & Row.

———. 1995. *Managing in a Time of Great Change.* New York: Truman Talley Books / Dutton.

Flanagan, Maureen A. 1990. Gender and Urban Political Reform: The City Club and the Woman's City Club of Chicago in the Progressive Era. *American Historical Review* 95, no. 4:1032–50.

Folbre, Nancy.2001. *The Invisible Heart: Economics and Family Values.* New York: New Press.

Follett, Mary Parker. 1940 (1973). *Dynamic Administration: The Collected Papers of Mary Parker Follett*, ed. E. M. Fox and L. Urwick. London: Pitman Publishing.

Green, Richard T. 2002. Alexander Hamilton: Founder of American Public Administration. *Administration & Society* 34, no. 5:541–62.

Guy, Mary E., Meredith A. Newman, and Sharon H. Mastracci. 2008. *Emotional Labor: Putting the* Service *in Public Service.* Armonk, NY: M. E. Sharpe.

Himmelweit, Susan. 1999. Caring Labor. *Annals AAPSS* 561 (January): 27–38.

Hummel, Ralph P. 1987. *The Bureaucratic Experience*, 3rd ed. New York: St. Martin's Press.

Hummel, Ralph P., and Camilla Stivers. 1998. Government Isn't Us: The Possibility of Democratic Knowledge in Representative Government. In *Government Is Us: Public Administration in an Anti-Government Era*, ed. Cheryl King and Camilla Stivers. Thousand Oaks, CA: Sage.

King, Cheryl Simrell, and Camilla Stivers, eds. 1998. *Government Is Us: Public Administration in an Anti-Government Era.* Thousand Oaks, CA: Sage.

Kramer, Robert. 2003. Beyond Max Weber: Leading with Emotional Intelligence in Post-Communist Governments. In *Proceedings of 10th Annual Conference of Network of Institutes and Schools of Public Administration in Central and Eastern Europe.* Kraków: Network of Institutes and Schools of Public Administration in Central and Eastern Europe.

Newman, Meredith A., and Mary E. Guy. 1998. Taylor's Triangle, Follett's Web. *Administrative Theory & Praxis* 20, no. 3:287–97.

Newman, Meredith A., Mary E. Guy, and Sharon H. Mastracci. 2009. Beyond Cognition: Affective Leadership and Emotional Labor. *Public Administration Review* 69, no. 1:6–20.

Schachter, Hindy Lauer. 2002. Women, Progressive-Era Reform, and Scientific Management. *Administration & Society* 34, no. 5:563–77.

———. 2004. Public Productivity in the Classical Age of Public Administration. In *Public Productivity Handbook*, 2nd edition, ed. Marc Holzer and Seok-Hwan Lee. New York: Marcel Dekker.

Stivers, Camilla. 2000. *Bureau Men, Settlement Women. Constructing Public Administration in the Progressive Era.* Lawrence: University Press of Kansas.

———. 2002. *Gender Images in Public Administration. Legitimacy and the Administrative State*, 2nd ed. Thousand Oaks, CA: Sage.

———. 2005. A Place Like Home: Care and Action in Public Administration. *American Review of Public Administration* 35, no. 1:26–41.

———. 2008. A Civic Machinery for Democratic Expression: Jane Addams on Public Administration. In *Jane Addams and the Practice of Democracy: Multi-disciplinary Essays on Theory and Practice*, ed. Wendy Chmielski, Marilyn Fischer, and Carol Nackenoff. Champaign: University of Illinois Press.

Taylor, Frederick W. 1911. *The Principles of Scientific Management.* New York: Harper & Brothers.

Van Riper, Paul P. 1983. The American Administrative State: Wilson and the Founders—An Unorthodox View. *Public Administration Review* 43, no. 6:477–90.

Waldo, Dwight. 1948. *The Administrative State.* New York: Ronald Press.

Weber, Max. 1922. Legitimate Authority and Bureaucracy. In *The Great Writings in Management and Organizational Behavior*, ed. Louis E. Boone and Donald D. Bowen.

New York: Random House. (Reprinted from Max Weber, *The Theory of Social and Economic Organization*, trans. and ed. A. M. Henderson and Talcott Parsons. London: William Hodge & Co., Ltd., 1947.)

———. 1970. *Max Weber: Essays in Sociology*, trans. H. H. Gerth and C. Wright Mills. New York: Oxford University Press (orig. pub. 1946).

The Raised Fist and the Magic Negro

Public Administration and the Black Public Administrator

Domonic Bearfield

Before the 2008 Democratic Party's national convention, an article appeared in *The New York Times Magazine* under the headline "Is Obama the End of Black Politics?" The article called attention to the difference between a new wave of African American politicians represented by Barack Obama, Cory Booker, Michael Nutter, and Deval Patrick and traditional civil rights–style politicians like John Lewis (Bai 2008). Though there were several historic aspects to the campaign that eventually led to Obama's election as the forty-fourth president of the United States, making him the nation's first black president, one aspect was the way the campaign was run. Unlike previous black candidates such as Shirley Chisholm, Jesse Jackson, and Al Sharpton, whose careers were shaped by the civil rights struggles of the 1960s, Obama did not run a race-based campaign. Instead, when he spoke of issues affecting members of the black community, he would frequently frame them in the context of the struggles faced by all Americans. During the campaign there were several moments when many members of the media struggled in their attempt to cover him, appearing unsure that the rules normally governing race and minority political candidates were still applicable.

Watching this, I could not help but think of how scholars in the field of public administration have continued to struggle with the changing racial landscape. Unfortunately, far too often there has been no struggle at all. Instead the field has consistently relied on old racial narratives to construct research questions and interpret data. In this chapter I offer a critique of that approach. I argue that during the second half of the twentieth century, social and political events produced two narratives that have dominated descriptions of blacks in America—the Magic Negro and the Raised Fist. The hegemony of these narratives has resulted in a bias that influences the way scholars approach the study of race and black public employees.

WHAT DO YOU MEAN BY BLACK? RACIAL IMAGES SINCE 1950

Omi and Winant (1994, 100) define race as the result of social and historical conflicts, a process they describe as "race projects," which help to organize human beings into racial categories. These conflicts cause societies to experience periods of racial formation, where images and narratives emerge that shape the popular perception of different racial groups. According to the authors, the conflicts that arose from the civil rights movement of the 1950s and 1960s altered the image of blacks in America. The first change was the creation of a new, collective identity. There was an effort by civil rights leaders like Martin Luther King Jr. to recast blacks as "the moral, spiritual, and political leadership of American society. [Representing] not only their own centuries-long struggle for freedom, but the highest and noblest aspirations for white America as well." By the mid-1960s a second change occurred, reflecting the growing sense of despair felt by segments of the black population. Despite early victories, some blacks had become increasingly cynical about the promise of equal opportunity. This cynicism gave rise to the black power movement, a social movement closely associated with individuals like Malcolm X and Stokely Carmichael and political groups like the Black Panther Party. Being rooted in the tradition of black nationalism and separatism, the black power movement offered a counterforce to the mainstream civil rights establishment.

The narratives associated with these two changes had a particular resonance with the media, which often used them to shape perceptions of black life in America. An example was the "Black Mayor" narratives of the 1960s. According to Rich (2007), following the election of Carl Stokes in Cleveland, the first black mayor of a major U.S. city, the media applied one of two narratives to other black mayors as they won elections around the country. One narrative was the black mayor as a sign of racial progress. The other was the black mayor as a symbol of black takeover. With time, the two themes—integration versus black power—were applied not only to black mayors but also to other aspects of American life that reflected the changing relationship between blacks and the broader society. The pervasiveness of these narratives grew as the use of the images moved from the media into other areas of popular culture.

To describe the two narratives, I have adopted the terms "Magic Negro" and "Raised Fist."[1] The term "Magic Negro" has been used by journalists, film critics, and scholars in black studies to describe a type of black character often found in movies with interracial casts. According to the columnist Eugene Robinson (2005), Magic Negros "exist to provide moral, spiritual or even supernatural guidance to white characters." In what are sometimes described as "Touched by a Negro" movies (Graham 1999), the job of the Magic Negro is to help a white character resolve a deeply rooted problem or character flaw. However, instead of high intellect or cognitive ability, the Magic Negro typically relies on folk insight or magic to solve the dilemma (Glenn and Cunningham 2007). Sidney Poitier's portrayal of "Noah" in *The Defiant Ones* has been described as the classic example of the Magic Negro, which was originally coined in the late 1950s (Kempley 2003). Contemporary examples include Morgan Freeman in *Bruce Almighty,* Will Smith in *The Legend of Bagger Vance,* and Michael Clarke Duncan in *The Green Mile* (Glenn and Cunningham 2007).

The term "Raised Fist" refers to what has become both an iconic and frequently mocked symbol of the black power movement. Instead of integration, the movement argued for increased power, autonomy, and self-determination that reflect the uniqueness of the black experience in America. According to Chuck Stone, the author of *Black Political Power in America,* "at all times, in all organizations and in all strategies, the emphasis was on integration. Integration defined the goal, determined the method, and established the tradition. Two words ruptured that tradition: *Black Power*" (Stone 1968, 16; emphasis in the original).

Variations of this idea appeared in several popular texts during this time, including *The Crisis of the Negro Intellectual* by Harold Cruse (1967) and *The Report of the National Advisory Commission on Civil Disorders* (known as The Kerner Report; see National Advisory Commission on Civil Disorders 1968). For the sake of conceptual clarity, the two narratives are presented here as distinct and separate categories. However, in the popular consciousness, the lines between the two are not nearly as clear. For example, in a recent newspaper article describing the implementation of a mentoring program for at-risk black teens, the reporter seamlessly used aspects of both narratives to describe the goals of the program and the actors involved. The fact that these themes remain in use some forty years after their introduction reflects their widespread and enduring power.

RACE NARRATIVES MATTER

It is important to note that the influence of racial narratives does not stop conveniently at the front door of the social sciences. Instead, as Myrdal (2006) argued, despite the scientific ideal of "full objectivity," in practice social science research on race has often been infused, both explicitly and implicitly, with thoughts and opinions from the broader culture. Decisions about research questions, data collection, and interpretation of results are all biased by the researcher's reaction to the broader society's racial attitudes. For example, during the late nineteenth century popular tales of the natural inferiority of blacks were given the stamp of scientific legitimacy when married with Herbert Spencer's theory of Social Darwinism (Frederickson 1971; Zuberi 2001). During the same period, DuBois (1898) warned against researchers who "imbibe [deep, fierce convictions on the Negro question] from their environment." Because he was concerned with the "manifest and far-reaching bias of writers," he dismissed much of the research on blacks up to that point as "uncritical."

In public administration, themes associated with the Raised Fist narrative, such as minority autonomy and racial collective action, can be found in the contemporary literature. For instance, according to Robinson (1974, 553), the Conference of Minority Public Administrators was founded in 1970 "out of the frustrations of a small group of minority members of the American Society for Public Administration who perceived a reluctance on the part of the larger organization to direct its attention in any meaningful way to the special needs and concerns of minorities as administrators, future administrators and as consumers of public services." Other themes emphasizing the use of black economic and political strength appear in the research. In the chapter titled "Measuring Black Political Power," Stone (1968, 62) wrote, "The only way in which black people can develop political power in government is to be able to control the hiring process." This declaration has been reflected in several studies on the relationship between black executive or midlevel public managers, including mayors (Eisenger 1982), principals (Meier, Stewart, and England 1989), police chiefs (Lewis 1989), and other levels of black public-sector employment.

Examples from the Magic Negro narrative can also be found. Hunt's (1974) assertion that public administration from a "black perspective" might help the field resolve its lingering identity crisis is a demonstration of an early use of the Magic Negro narrative. Rice (2004) argued that traditional public administration departments in universities, many with nearly all-white faculties, often struggle in their ability to teach diversity and social equity. One way to resolve this problem, he suggested, was for the departments to add people of color to their faculties.

In perhaps the quintessential example of the Magic Negro narrative in public administration, Goode and Baldwin (2005) examined more than one hundred cities with populations of 50,000 or more with a black population of at least 10 percent in search of predictors for black local government employment. The study included several race-related and nonrace-related predictor variables, such as the percentage of black administrators, the existence of a black mayor, the municipal population, and the form of government. Through their analysis, the authors ultimately concluded that the size of the black population and the presence of a black personnel manager were the strongest predictors. After ruling out the manipulation of the city's black population "as neither an easy nor necessarily desirable task," the authors declared, "appointing an African American personnel director is a relatively simple and easy task that appears to hold much promise for enhancing racial diversity in American municipalities" (Goode and Baldwin 2005, 49). Or, put another way: Hire a Magic Negro.

Curiously, although clearly not intentionally, the authors drove home the point in the reference note attached to the previous statement: "This conclusion reflects the statistical associations found in this research and is not meant to imply that African American personnel directors unfairly advocate for African Americans or that non–African American personnel directors lack commitment to . . . their cities' affirmative action plans. Moreover, if African American personnel directors violate equal employment opportunity laws or the legal parameters of their cities' affirmative action plans, one can argue against the conclusion of this article" (Goode and Baldwin 2005, 51).

It is worth stating that the goal here is not to equate the contemporary literature on race in public administration with the blatantly racist research of the Social Darwinists. Nor is it meant as a strident DuBoisian criticism of our intellectual forbearers and contemporaries. Instead, the aim is to call attention to the influence that these racial narratives have on our research and to demonstrate how they shape the ways we consider and understand the issue of race. If there is an insidious aspect to the domination of these two narratives, it is that they promote outdated racial stereotypes.

MOVING BEYOND THE RAISED FIST / MAGIC NEGRO

In an examination of articles in *Public Administration Review*, Oldfield, Candler, and Johnson (2006, 160) noted a dramatic decline in scholarship on race since the 1970s, a record they describe as "woeful." When presented with such information, the first reaction is often a call for more race-focused scholarship. Yet I fear that an unfocused increase in scholarly output will only produce a slightly marginal benefit in terms of our understanding. Instead, to move forward, the approach must be twofold. For the first part, individual researchers who study race must do more to combat racial bias in their research. Though an overreliance on the two narratives reflects one form of bias, we must also guard against others. In addition to the concerns described in the previous section, both DuBois (1898) and Myrdal (2006) found that the researcher's positive or negative predisposition toward blacks represented a frequently overlooked form of bias.

For the second part, the field must return to the question that has already been asked by so many: "What do we mean by race?" (Yannow 2003; Alexander 1997). However, this question should not be posed in an overly philosophic or esoteric way. Instead, we must use it as an opportunity to review the literature of the field to see how we have constructed and examined the different racial and ethnic categories. One way to do this is through narrative analysis. Though narrative analysis has been used to understand how street-level bureaucrats make sense of their work environment (Maynard-Moody and Musheno 2003), recent scholarship has also revealed how the approach can be used to help scholars improve their understanding of research and the field (Miller and Jaha 2005). In a field so rooted in the tradition that theory should inform practice, it is essential that we examine the images of race that we are transferring to our students.

Although this chapter has presented evidence of two narratives, it is by no means comprehensive or exhaustive. Exploration must be done to detect the existence of new or competing narratives in the literature. During the last half century, the Raised Fist and the Magic Negro have held a hegemonic position in their ability to shape the way we talk about blacks in public administration. If we are to move past these narratives, we must first be able to assess the depth of their actual power.

NOTE

1. I acknowledge that the names used to describe these narratives are provocative and that there are readers who may consider the titles offensive. I would like to assure the reader that these names were not selected for shock value. They were selected in the tradition of Myrdal, who warned scholars engaged in race-based research not to avoid the use of value-loaded terms out of a fear that those terms might suggest a form of bias to the reader. Instead, the researcher should explicitly communicate the intended meaning conveyed by the terms.

REFERENCES

Alexander, J. 1997. Avoiding the Issue: Racism and Administrative Responsibility in Public Administration. *American Review of Public Administration* 27, no. 4:343–61.

Bai, M. 2008. Is Obama the End of Black Politics? *New York Times Magazine*, August 10.

Cruse, H. 1967. *The Crisis of the Negro Intellectual*. New York: Morrow.

DuBois, W. E. B. 1898. The Study of the Negro Problems. *Annals of the American Academy of Political and Social Science* 11:1–23.

Eisinger. P. 1982. Black Employment in Municipal Jobs: The Impact of Black Political Power. *American Political Science Review* 76, no. 2:380–92.

Frederickson, H. George. 1971. *The Black Image in the White Mind*. New York: Harper & Row.

Glenn, C., and L. Cunningham. 2007. The Power of Black Magic: The Magical Negro and White Salvation in Film. *Journal of Black Studies* 40, no. 2:135–52.

Goode, S., and J. Baldwin. 2005. Predictors of African American Representation in Municipal Government. *Review of Public Personnel Administration* 25, no. 1:29–55.

Graham, R. 1999. Life in the Pop Lane: The Myth of the Magic Negro. *Boston Globe*, December 7.

Hunt, D. 1974. The Black Perspective on Public Management. *Public Administration Review* 34, no. 6:520–25.

Kempley, R. 2003. Too Too Divine Movies: "Magic Negro" Saves the Day, but at the Cost of His Soul. *Washington Post*, June 7.

Lewis, W. 1989. Towards Representative Bureaucracy: Blacks in City Police Organizations 1975–1985. *Public Administration Review* 49, no. 3:257–68.

Maynard-Moody, S., and M. Musheno. 2003. *Cops, Teacher, Counselors: Stories from the Front Lines of Public Service*. Ann Arbor: University of Michigan Press.

Meier, K., J. Stewart, and R. England. 1989. *Race, Class and Education: The Politics of Second-Generation Discrimination*. Madison: University of Wisconsin Press.

Miller, H., and C. Jaha. 2005. Some Evidence of a Pluralistic Discipline: A Narrative Analysis of Public Administration Symposia. *Public Administration Review* 65, no. 6:728–38.

Myrdal, G. 2006. *An American Dilemma : The Negro Problem and Modern Democracy*. New York: HarperCollins.

National Advisory Commission on Civil Disorders. 1968. *The Report of the National Advisory Commission on Civil Disorders*. New York: Bantam Books.

Oldfield, K, G. Candler, and R. Johnson. 2006. Social Class, Sexual Orientation, and Toward Proactive Social Equity Scholarship. *American Review of Public Administration* 36, no. 2:156–72.

Omi, M., and H. Winant. 1994. *Racial Formation in the United States: From the 1960s to the 1990s*. New York: Routledge.

Rice, M. 2004. Organizational Culture, Social Equity, and Diversity: Teaching Public Administration in the Post-Modern Era. *Journal of Public Affairs Education* 10, no. 2:143–64.

Rich, W. 2007. *David Dinkins and New York City Politics: Race, Images, and the Media.* Albany: State University of New York Press.

Robinson, E. 2005. Oscar's "Ray" of Hope. *Washington Post*, March 1.

Robinson, R. 1974. Conference of Minority Public Administrators. *Public Administration Review* 34, no. 6:552–56.

Stone, C. 1968. *Black Political Power in America*. Indianapolis: Bobbs-Merrill.

Yannow, D. 2003. *Constructing "Race" and "Ethnicity" in America: Category-Making in Public Policy and Administration*. Armonk, NY: M. E. Sharpe.

Zuberi, T. 2001. *Thicker Than Blood: How Racial Statistics Lie.* Minneapolis: University of Minnesota Press.

Social Equity in Public Administration

The Need for Fire

Susan T. Gooden

This critique offers a normative argument that social equity in American public administration and policy is caught in an unproductive cycle. Instead of engaging in the process of "ready, aim, fire," we are operating in a continuous cycle of "ready, aim, study more." Examining social equity is an important part of public administration and policy research. First, there must be solid data indicating whether social inequities exist. Second, there must be an acceptance of the research and a concrete plan to reverse identified inequities. Third, the reversal plan must be successfully implemented. These three steps can be expressed metaphorically as "ready, aim, fire." But current practice suggests the more appropriate metaphor is "ready, aim, study more," a cyclical process that results in very little fire, thus raising the question: How can public policy research be more effectively used to reverse social inequities?

SOCIAL EQUITY IN U.S. PUBLIC ADMINISTRATION: A MISSION PARTIALLY ACCOMPLISHED

The concept of social equity in public administration is inextricably linked to John Rawls's *A Theory of Justice.* Rawls (1971, 250) developed a principle of justice as "fairness," whereby "each person is to have an equal right to the most extensive basic liberty compatible with a similar liberty for all." As Rawls argues, a modern theory of government equalizes the distribution of social and economic advantages. He challenges us to put ourselves behind a "veil of ignorance" and to use our innate sense of justice to derive principles of equity without the bias of knowing our own situation.

The participants in Minnowbrook I squarely identified social equity as an important concern for public administration. In the national 1960s context focused on civil rights, racial inequality, and injustice, the young Minnows noted that "a government built on a Constitution claiming the equal protection of the laws had failed in that promise. Public administrators, who daily operate the government, were not without responsibility" (Frederickson 1990, 228). Reflecting on this statement in 2005, Frederickson recalled that "it was during the 1960s that it became increasingly evident that the results of governmental policy and the work of public administrators implementing those policies were much better for some citizens than for others" (Frederickson 2005).

In February 2000, the National Academy of Public Administration's board of trustees authorized the establishment of a Standing Panel on Social Equity, which defined social equity as "the fair, just, and equitable management of all institutions serving the public directly or by contract, and the fair and equitable distribution of public services, and implementation of public policy, and the commitment to promote fairness, justice, and equity in the formation of public policy" (National Academy of Public Administration 2000). Additionally, the academy's board of directors recently adopted social equity as the fourth pillar of public administration, along with economy, efficiency, and effectiveness (National Academy of Public Administration 2005). Although the contributions of the academy's Standing Panel greatly elevated the acceptance of social equity into the "mainstream" of public administration, much work remains among twenty-first-century academics and practitioners in *realizing* social equity across public services, programs, and policies.

SOCIAL EQUITY AND RACE: A NERVOUS AREA OF GOVERNMENT

Social equity in public administration is largely focused on racial inequities. Race is a social construction with significant implications. As Lopez (1995, 196) contends, "Race is not a determinant or a residue of some other social phenomenon, but rather stands on its own as an amalgamation of competing social forces. . . . Races are constructed relationally, against one another, rather than in isolation." He continues: "The categories of race previously considered objective, such as Caucasoid, Negroid, and Mongoloid, are now widely regarded as empty relics, persistent shadows of the social belief in races that permeated early scientific thought." Social race, however, is not. "Race has its genesis and maintains its vigorous strength in the realm of social beliefs" (p. 200).

Race analysis is an important dimension in gauging social equity within public administration and policy: "Race analysis is the systematic application of the tools of historical and cultural analysis to understand the social and economic circumstances facing blacks and other racial minority group members" (Myers 2002, 170). All public policy analysis operates within a political context: "The reality that, outside the classroom policy analysis cannot be separated from politics has important practical and ethical implications" (Weimer and Vining 1992, 16). Writing in 1897, W. E. B. DuBois noted the importance of understanding the broad political context of race analysis in public policy: "It is necessary, therefore, in planning our movements, in guiding our future development, that at times we rise above the pressing, but smaller questions of separate schools and cars, wage-discrimination and lynch law, to survey the whole question of race in human philosophy and to lay, on a basis of broad knowledge and careful insight, those large lines of policy and higher ideals which may form our guiding lines and boundaries in the difficulties of everyday life."

As John Rohr (1989, 99) states in his classic work *Ethics for Bureaucrats*, "It is perhaps no exaggeration to say that questions of race, in one form or another, have been the most important issues in American politics." Put simply, examining racial disparities in public services, programs, and policies is a nervous area of government. An important and omnipresent emotional and historical context intervenes.

READY, AIM, FIRE: A SYNOPSIS

In an earlier article (Gooden 2008), I detail the "ready, aim, study more" problem and the need to replace this with "ready, aim, fire." I offer a summary of these concepts here. During the first phase, "ready," researchers devote considerable time and energy to identifying the existence of social inequities in various areas of public policy. Whether the focal topic is education, earnings, poverty, crime, or health, the common research story is characteristically predictable. The methods vary, the statistical models change, but the "takeaway" message is essentially the same: Minorities, especially African Americans and Latinos, fare worse than their white counterparts. A common response is to develop more sophisticated models, add additional control variables, and re-examine the extent of these inequities.

The second phase, "aim," analyzes specific policy interventions intended to combat social inequities. There are a number of public policy remedies that intend or *aim* to reduce disparities and promote social equity. For example, such policies include antidiscrimination legislation, fair housing laws, affirmative action policies, and minority business set-asides. It is important to evaluate how well or how poorly these remedies are implemented, and the extent to which that policy intent is achieved. "Aim" in social equity analysis fosters an empirical assessment of how well policy vehicles that are designed to foster the value of social equity actually do. Without such an analysis, policymakers may incorrectly conclude that a program or policy intervention designed to promote social equity resulted in those desired outcomes. The danger here is prematurely declaring victory.

"Fire" research is explicitly concerned with how organizations, policies, or programs significantly reduce or eliminate racial inequities. It develops criteria for social equity and analyzes how such equity was achieved. It becomes an effective learning tool for agencies and policymakers because it documents how equity was achieved, and it produces rigorous models for others to consider. Theoretically, "fire" research spreads because others—government agencies and policymakers—are eager to achieve social equity within their spheres of influence. An important precondition of "fire" research is that agencies, researchers, and policymakers seriously acknowledge that policies operate, and are affected by, a strongly embedded structural context. Most important, this embedded context of inequity exists within specific agencies and actions—not in a vague, general sense.

IMPLEMENTING THE FIRE

Why is there not more "fire"? Despite the utilization of sophisticated analytical techniques in "ready" and "aim" social equity analysis, the larger political research context is largely characterized by a schema that requests additional evidence to validate the findings. Researchers who analyze social equity find themselves in a disconcerting cycle. A fixed response to social equity analysis (by policymakers, agencies, and other academic researchers) is not to accept the research results because a higher standard of proof is needed. The burden of proof for "finding" social inequities becomes unattainable. It becomes a repetitive chase. The de facto "more evidence needed" response facilitates the avoidance of advancing public policy solutions. The bar for research acceptance is raised in ways not commonly seen when other relationships (particularly non-racial ones) are examined. Having an informal dual system of standards—one for social science research in general, and another when racial disparities are the subject matter—can function as a delaying tactic, both in discouraging further research on racial disparities and in causing additional delay in the successful implementation of policies specifically designed to correct these inequities.

Implementing the "fire" requires public administrators in the twenty-first century to overcome the nervous area of government that largely characterizes the area of social equity. This nervous context reduces social equity research and paralyzes organizations in their ability to openly examine their policies, practices, and managerial techniques. My colleagues on the medical campus of Virginia Commonwealth University informed me that nervousness in humans is typically overcome when we force ourselves to directly confront what makes us nervous. Similarly, an action that produces nervousness only increases when that action is avoided. In essence, social equity practice may not be perfect, but it may lead to significant improvements among the next generation of public administration scholars. Ultimately, the fulfillment of the social equity pillar in public administration requires us to dismount our current political-intellectual treadmill. We might then find ourselves brave enough to finally walk our social equity talk.

REFERENCES

DuBois, W. E. B. 1897. *The Conservation of Races*. American Negro Academy Occasional Paper 2. (Reprinted in *W.E.B. DuBois: A Reader*, ed. David Levering Lewis. New York: Henry Holt, 1995.)

Frederickson, H. George. 1990. Public Administration and Social Equity. *Public Administration Review,* March–April: 228–37.

———. 2005. The State of Social Equity in American Public Administration. *National Civic Review* 94, no. 4:31–38.

Gooden, Susan T. 2008. The Politics of Ready, Aim . . . Study More: Implementing the "Fire" in Racial Disparities Public Policy Research. *Journal of Race and Policy* 4, no. 1:7–21.

Lopez, Ian F. Haney. 1995. The Social Construction of Race. In *Critical Race Theory: The Cutting Edge,* ed. Richard Delgado. Philadelphia: Temple University Press.

Myers, Samuel L., Jr. 2002. Presidential Address: Analysis of Race as Policy Analysis. *Journal of Policy Analysis and Management* 21, no. 2:169–90.

National Academy of Public Administration. 2000. Standing Panel on Social Equity in Governance Issue Paper and Work Plan, November. www.napawash.org/aa_social_equity/papers_publications.html.

———. 2005. *Strategic Plan.* Washington, DC: National Academy of Public Administration.

Rawls, J. 1971. *A Theory of Justice.* Cambridge, MA: Harvard University Press.

Rohr, John. 1989. *Ethics for Bureaucrats: An Essay on Law and Values.* New York: Marcel Dekker.

Weimer, David L., and Aidan R. Vining. 1992. *Policy Analysis: Concepts and Practice,* 2nd ed. New York: Simon & Schuster.

. . . And the Pendulum Swings:

A Call for Evidence-Based Public Organizations

Kimberley R. Isett

As with all things in society, government is prone to pendulum swings of trends and fashions of the way things "ought" to be done (Abrahamson 1991; Tolbert and Zucker 1983). Though the field has moved away from the simple Taylorist notion of "the one best way" to organize (Taylor 1911), isomorphic tendencies to adopt or accept the newest best practice are still evident (DiMaggio 1986; DiMaggio and Powell 1983; Rogers 2003). In some cases, these new practices represent real innovations that are appropriate and beneficial for organizations. But sometimes they are not.

Perpetuating the movement toward finding the newest and best practice are the numerous awards presented by "good government" groups that reward invention and heap status upon those individuals or government entities that seem to get things done in a better way (e.g., Osborne and Gaebler 1992). "Seem" is the operative word here—too often, these awards are bestowed either before empirical investigation and validation of the innovation or only after initial success without regard to sustainability or long-term effects. The awards create a rash of early adopters reacting to the innovation news. Those governmental units that consider themselves "leaders" or "innovators" and do not want to be viewed as laggards or antiquated often adopt the new program or process, without a systematic analysis of its appropriateness for their particular set of circumstances.

Instead of reactionary innovation, what we need is a body of knowledge that focuses on creating an evidence base for what works under what conditions for a particular set of governmental, institutional, and environmental factors or characteristics. We need evidence-based organization and system design. What evidence-based organizational design would entail is understanding how particular organizational forms or permutations interact with the institutional, environmental, and normative context of governmental organizations. Evidence-based organizations would take into account not only that the organizations are in the public sector but also the interface with the substantive mission of the agency and the set of constraints and opportunities that the subcontext offers. Thus an organizational design solution for one agency may not be transferable to agencies in different operational domains. For example, organizational forms that work in engineering organizations (e.g., the Roads Department) that have strong technical components would not necessarily work for organizations with more indeterminate technologies (many social services, e.g., job placement).

To a student of organizations focused on public management studies, the need for evidence-based systems is nowhere clearer than in the pendulum swings of bureaucracy versus consolidation—centralization versus integration. This pendulum is always anchored on one side by bureaucracy, but on the other side are a variety of forms, ranging from umbrella and consolidated structures to the latest fashion in networks. This chapter focuses on the questions that these swings of the pendulum raise for students of public organizations—or at least for those focused on governance and structure.

TICK, TOCK

Just the word "bureaucracy" alone conjures up many different conceptualizations and gut reactions. But there is a reason why this form of government, as opposed to many others, is so enduring. Some authors argue (Wilson 1989; DiMaggio and Powell 1983) that bureaucracy is, despite some of its more egregious forms and foibles (cf. Mashaw 1983), the best form of organization—inside or outside government. When implemented effectively, bureaucracy offers many of the ideal aspects of organizations that early scholars of administration heralded as ideal, such as limited span of control, clear lines of authority, and delineated position descriptions and discretion (Weber 1946; Simon 1945; Gulick 1937; Knott and Miller 1987). Indeed, bureaucracy is the most ubiquitous form of organization in the world—likely due to these very factors.

Despite the benefits of bureaucracy, this form seems to be effective on a continuum—working well for some functions and services but less so than others. In cases where bureaucracy seems to work less well, alternate forms of organizations are often sought. The classes of services and programs that seem be better suited to nonbureaucratic organizations (or at least most often seek new forms of organization) are those that deal with intractable social problems like poverty and other social and family services. This is especially the case where the programs deal with vulnerable populations that seek, receive, and require services from a number of government programs.

When the confines of bureaucracy just do not seem to work, public entrepreneurs attempt to devise alternative forms of organization and governance that promise to address those multiple and overlapping needs of the clients they serve. These alternative forms have taken the shape of coordinating councils—see Mott (1968) for an early example of this, and Isett and Coleman-Beattie (2005) for a more recent example—umbrella structures (Agranoff 1991), and integrated service systems (Morrissey and Goldman 1984; Provan and Milward 1995). Though each of these alternatives is heralded as *the* solution when it comes on the scene, the problems of trust and coordination and contribution to the commons often overtake its benefits (Ostrom 1986; Ostrom and Walker 2003; Mott 1968). In consequence, these new alternatives that were recently thought to be solutions are abandoned as ineffective or cost-ineffective. When these forms are abandoned, the organization regresses back to the mean of bureaucracy (which, in various manifestations of these "new" forms, was never truly abandoned in the first place, just altered somewhat).

In the past ten years or so, the latest mode of organizing that has caught the attention of the public administration world is the interorganizational network. Networks are thought to increase organizational flexibility to respond to environmental dynamics while maintaining individual organizational independence and autonomy (Sabel 1989; Powell 1990). They have also been widely cited as one possible way to address "wicked problems" (Isett and Ellis 2007; Koppenjan and Klijn 2004; O'Toole 1997). The problem is, however, that we as a scholarly and practical community still do not know much about these forms or even how to measure network performance or effectiveness (Provan and Milward 2001; Isett et al. 2010). So as we continuously and increasingly use this form of organization, we are at a loss to objectively comment on whether or not these forms meet our purposes. To compound the uncertainty associated with these forms of organization, the network phenomenon has rapidly spread throughout government domains canvassing environmental issues, domestic and international security, and health and human services.

These pendulum swings back and forth from bureaucracy to alternative forms of organizing—at the moment, networks—represent what I call the Mae West problem. The Grande Dame of Vamps was attributed as saying: "When faced with a decision between two evils, I always pick the one I never tried before"—and this is certainly true of government organizational design. Because our public servants are clamoring to find something that works well to serve their stakeholders effectively, they try alternative forms without actually understanding how they work or their limits. And how could they? Scholarship often lags considerably behind innovation. When the research does appear, it may be too late in the adoption–sustain–de-adoption cycle to be of much use or is simply focused on understanding just how the innovation works rather than articulating its benefits and drawbacks or for what circumstances the innovation is particularly well suited.

The key dilemma is simple: As you peruse the body of public administration literature on forms of organizing, there are disparate streams of information on particular modes. However, there is a lack of scholarship on the comparative advantages of one form vis-à-vis others, or even the conditions of what works, when, how, and why. In short, there is a lack of an evidence base on forms of government organization.

So why would an enterprising reformer pick one form of organization over another? This decision is now relegated to some combination of the limitations of his or her personal experience, learned heuristics, guiding internal compass, professionalization/socialization, imperfect search routines, and idiosyncratic decision-making processes (Heikkila and Isett 2004). Whereas providing an evidence base is a tall task and requires immense efforts to investigate the nuances and antecedents of how organizing ought to be done (for a recent example of this type of effort in mental health services, see Drake and Goldman 2003), this is a logical and important next step to making our science of administration a more concrete and credible one. Though in recent years the notions of "evidence-based policy" (particularly in the health services and those articles appearing in journals like the *Journal of Policy Analysis and Management*) and "evidence-based management" (e.g., see Lynn, Heinrich, and Hill 2002; Meier and O'Toole 2002) have gained currency, the empirical work that drives the evidence bases is still emergent. Despite this emergent evidence base in policy and management, why do we not hear anything about evidence-based organization? The data exist; it is merely an empirical challenge.

THE FUTURE CHALLENGE

So what would a research agenda that builds an evidence base for public organizations look like? There is not ample space left in this chapter to fully flesh out a research program on evidence-based organizations, but I put forth some suggestions for where this line of inquiry might start.

Effectiveness and Efficiency

There is a theoretical trade-off between efficiency and effectiveness (e.g., Stone 2002), and there are well-established literatures on both these concepts. However, the potential effects of this trade-off for organizations have not been explored. Further research is warranted on the relevant dimensions of effectiveness and efficiency for the design of organizations. Additionally, understanding empirically the trade-off between efficiency and effectiveness would be an important step forward in our understanding of how organizations work.

Context

We also need to further understand how context affects organizations. Relevant variables here might include the continuum of organizational routines from technical to indeterminate processes, as well as the degree of standardization involved in organizational routines versus the number of exceptions involved in the work (Perrow 1967). These variables are related to the substantive focus of an organization and can affect how it might be designed, in terms of both its structure and its internal processes.

Performance

Although I consider performance to be a secondary issue related to evidence-based organizations (and a research program in its own right), it is an important aspect of it. What performance outcomes are important for particular types of organizations, and how are these outcomes related to organizational design? Building on the strategy-versus-structure debate in organization and management theory, does performance drive particular structures, or does structure affect performance? Though this is likely a recursive process, what does this process look like for public organizations?

SUMMING UP

One of the key dilemmas for public management scholars is how to be both theoretically compelling and practically relevant. Understanding the evidence for which organizations work well could be one way to do both. Though many of the important questions in this line of inquiry have yet to be addressed, scholars could contribute to theory by beginning to develop the evidence base on them. At the same time they could be aiding public organizations to understand how to avoid pitfalls or improve their organizations through the research they have conducted. This approach is a win for the intellectual field and a win for the applied field.

REFERENCES

Abrahamson, Eric. 1991. Managerial Fads and Fashions: The Diffusion and Rejection of Innovations. *Academy of Management Review* 16, no. 3:586–612.

Agranoff, Robert. 1991. Human Services Integration: Past and Present Challenges in Public Administration. *Public Administration Review* 51, no. 6:533–42.

DiMaggio, Paul. 1986. Structural Analysis of Organizational Fields: A Blockmodel Approach. In *Research in Organizational Behavior*, ed. B. M. Staw and L. L. Cummings. Greenwich, CT: JAI Press.

DiMaggio, Paul J., and Walter W. Powell. 1983. The Iron Cage Revisited: Institutional Isomorphism and Collective Rationality in Organizational Fields. *American Sociological Review* 48:147–60.

Drake, Robert E., and Howard H. Goldman, eds. 2003. *Evidence-Based Practices in Mental Health Care*. Washington, DC: American Psychiatric Association.

Gulick, Luther. 1937. Notes on the Theory of Organization. In *Papers on the Science of Administration*, ed. G. A. Urwick. New York: Columbia University Press.

Heikkila, Tanya A., and Kimberley R. Isett. 2004. Modeling Operational Decision Making in Public Organizations: An Integration of Two Institutional Theories. *American Review of Public Administration* 34, no. 1:3–19.

Isett, Kimberley R., and Brenda Coleman-Beattie. 2005. *Transformation of a Behavioral Healthcare System: The New Mexico Evaluation Project*. Chicago: John D. and Catherine T. MacArthur Foundation's Network on Mental Health Policy Research.

Isett, Kimberley R., and Alan R. Ellis. 2007. Explaining New Relationships: Sector, Network, and Organizational Impacts on the Growth of Linkages in Multi-Sector Service Delivery Networks. Paper presented at National Public Management Research Conference, Tucson.

Isett, Kimberley R., Ines Mergel, Kelly Leroux, Pamela Mischen, and Karl Rethmeyer. 2010. Networks in Public Administration Scholarship: Understanding Where We Are and Where We Need to Go. *Journal of Public Administration Research and Theory*, in press.

Knott, Jack H., and Gary J. Miller. 1987. *Reforming Bureaucracy: The Politics of Institutional Choice*. Englewood Cliffs, NJ: Prentice Hall.

Koppenjan, Joop, and Erik-Hans Klijn. 2004. *Managing Uncertainties in Networks*. London: Routledge.

Lynn, Laurence E., Jr., Carolyn J. Heinrich, and Carolyn J. Hill. 2002. *Improving Governance: A New Logic for Empirical Research*. Washington, DC: Georgetown University Press.

Mashaw, Jerry L. 1983. *Bureaucratic Justice: Managing Social Security Disability Claims*. New Haven, CT: Yale University Press.

Meier, Kenneth J., and Laurence J. O'Toole. 2002. Public Management and Organizational Performance: The Effect of Managerial Quality. *Journal of Policy Analysis and Management* 21, no. 4:629–43.

Morrissey, J., and H. Goldman. 1984. Cycles of Reform in the Care of the Chronically Mentally Ill. *Hospital and Community Psychiatry* 35:785–93.

Mott, Basil, J. F. 1968. *Anatomy of a Coordinating Council: Implications for Planning*. Pittsburgh: University of Pittsburgh Press.

O'Toole, Laurence J. 1997. Treating Networks Seriously: Practical and Research-Based Agendas in Public Administration. *Public Administration Review* 57, no. 1:45–52.

Osborne, David, and Ted Gaebler. 1992. *Reinventing Government: How the Entrepreneurial Spirit Is Transforming the Public Sector*. Reading, MA: Plume.

Ostrom, Elinor. 1986. Multiorganizational Arrangements and Coordination: An Application of Institutional Theory. In *Workshop in Political Theory and Policy Analysis*. Bloomington: Indiana University Press.

Ostrom, Elinor, and James Walker. 2003. *Trust and Reciprocity*. New York: Russell Sage Foundation.

Perrow, Charles. 1967. A Framework for the Comparative Analysis of Organizations. *American Sociological Review* 32, no. 2:194–208.

Powell, Walter W. 1990. Neither Markets nor Hierarchy: Network Forms of Organization. *Research in Organizational Behavior* 12:295–336.

Provan, Keith G., and H. Brinton Milward. 1995. A Preliminary Theory of Interorganizational Network Effectiveness: A Comparative Study of Four Community Mental Health Systems. *Administrative Science Quarterly* 40:1–33.

———. 2001. Do Networks Really Work? A Framework for Evaluating Public-Sector Organizational Networks. *Public Administration Review* 61, no. 4:414–23.

Rogers, Everett M. 2003. *Diffusion of Innovations*, 5th ed. New York: Free Press.

Sabel, Charles F. 1989. Flexible Specialisation and the Reemergence of Regional Economies. In *Reversing Industrial Decline*, ed H. A. Zeitlin. Oxford: Berg.

Simon, Herbert A. 1945. *Administrative Behavior*. New York: Free Press.

Stone, Deborah A. 2002. *Policy Paradox: The Art of Political Decision Making*. New York: Norton.

Taylor, Frederick W. 1911. *The Principles of Scientific Management*. New York: Harper & Brothers.

Tolbert, Pamela S., and Lynne G. Zucker. 1983. Institutional Sources of Change in the Formal Structure of Organizations: The Diffusion of Civil Service Reform, 1880–1935. *Administrative Science Quarterly* 28, no. 1:22–39.

Weber, Max. 1946. Bureaucracy. In *Essays in Sociology*, ed. H. H. Gerth and C. W. Mills. Oxford: Oxford University Press.

Wilson, James Q. 1989. *Bureaucracy: What Government Agencies Do and Why They Do It*. New York: Basic Books.

Public Administration

The Central Discipline in Homeland Security

Dale Jones and Austen Givens

A new period in American history began on September 11, 2001, when the United States was attacked within its own borders, thrusting homeland security to the top of the national agenda. America has faced a profound transformation in the years since the terrorist attacks. At the ten-year anniversary of the attacks, the United States is still in the initial stage of a long endeavor. America will be engaged with homeland security for many years to come.

Homeland security is an emerging discipline of study and practice. The early years are characterized as dynamic with constant change (Jenkins 2007). Public administration as a discipline is central in homeland security studies. This chapter provides an overview of the development of homeland security as a profession, makes the case for how public administration is at the core of homeland security, and suggests that more graduate-level public administration and public policy degree programs in homeland security will be offered and will expand in the future.

THE EMERGENCE OF HOMELAND SECURITY

According to the Department of Defense (DOD), the U.S. homeland is "the physical region that includes the continental United States, Alaska, Hawaii, United States territories and possessions, and surrounding territorial waters and airspace" (DOD 2005, GL-8). Fundamentally, homeland security is the protection of the nation and its citizens through public programs administered primarily by public employees with public funds.

The National Security Act of 1947 and its amendments had created the National Security Council, formed the Central Intelligence Agency (CIA), and combined the military services into the DOD. The policymaking structure and processes generated from that act served the nation well during the Cold War era, which lasted forty-five years. The dismantling of the Berlin Wall in 1989, the reunification of Germany in 1990, and dissolution of the Soviet Union in 1991 marked the end of the Cold War. The United States spent the majority of the 1990s examining threats to its homeland, trying to define the "new world order," and projecting its role in this order.

Throughout the 1990s, numerous studies, panels, task forces, and commissions warned of forthcoming dangers for the nation and the need for greater homeland defense as part of national security (Hart-Rudman Commission 1999; Tangredi 2001). In 1993, the bombing of the World Trade Center in lower Manhattan was a watershed moment in the development of homeland security. Ramzi Yousef, a terrorist from Pakistan, and a team of cohorts detonated a fertilizer-filled van in the underground parking garage of the complex (Naftali 2005). The attack shook U.S. policymakers concerned with terrorism. Indeed, then–national security adviser Anthony Lake in the Clinton administration noted that there was no "bureaucratic box" in which to place a terrorist attack on the homeland. At the time, the CIA, the Federal Bureau of Investigation (FBI), the Federal Emergency Management Agency, and various law enforcement agencies each had separate responsibilities in response to a domestic terrorist attack (Naftali 2005). Later efforts in the mid-1990s to reshuffle the federal government's approach to responding to domestic attacks were the seedlings of subsequent homeland security organizational changes after 9/11. The national response to the 9/11 attacks, including new legislation and executive branch actions, resulted in the most sweeping changes to federal government organization since the National Security Act of 1947.

LEGISLATION AND EXECUTIVE BRANCH ACTIONS

In 2001, President George W. Bush issued Executive Order 13228, which established the Office of Homeland Security and the Homeland Security Council within the Executive Office of the President. That same year, Congress passed the USA Patriot Act of 2001, officially the Uniting and Strengthening America by Providing Appropriate Tools Required to Intercept and Obstruct Terrorism Act, which created new crimes and new penalties, as well as new powers for searches, seizures, surveillance, and the detention of terrorist suspects. Then Congress passed the Homeland Security Act of 2002, which created the cabinet-level Department of Homeland Security (DHS).

In the largest federal government reorganization since the beginning of the Cold War, DHS was activated on March 1, 2003, with nearly 180,000 personnel from twenty-two federal organizations. The mission of DHS is to lead the unified national effort to secure America and ensure homeland security, defined as "a concerted national effort to prevent terrorist attacks within the United States, reduce America's vulnerability to terrorism, and minimize the damage and recover from attacks that do occur" (White House 2007, 3). Another significant action was the formation of the DOD's U.S. Northern Command, known as USNORTHCOM. With the responsibility for homeland defense and civil support, USNORTHCOM was established on October 1, 2002, and reached full operational capability on September 11, 2003. Another key law was the passage of the Intelligence Reform and Terrorism Prevention Act of 2004, which created the position of director of national intelligence and was designed to make the U.S. intelligence enterprise more unified.

The executive branch also developed a number of strategies and supporting plans to protect the nation from terrorism threats and natural disasters. These documents are continuously revised as circumstances change. For example, the 2002 National Strategy for Homeland Security was revised in 2007 (White House 2007), and the National Response Framework (DHS 2008) replaced the National Response Plan (DHS 2004).

Together, the magnitude of the actions after 9/11 establishes homeland security as a fixture in American government and society for the foreseeable future. Although DHS and DOD have the primary roles in homeland security and homeland defense, respectively, many other federal departments and agencies also play essential roles. Some of the more important agencies are in the departments of Agriculture, Energy, Health and Human Services, Justice, State, and Transportation. Others are independent federal agencies and offices. In addition, critical roles are performed by state, county, and city departments and offices of emergency management.

PUBLIC ADMINISTRATION AT THE CORE OF HOMELAND SECURITY

The embodiment of homeland security as a major policy area represents one of the most pronounced changes in U.S. government and public administration since Minnowbrook II in 1988. Moreover, homeland security is now integrated across a wide range of policy and program areas and within the highly decentralized and intergovernmental context. Public administration is at the core of homeland security, being essential for the success of the many professional practices involved. The 9/11 attacks reinforce the critical importance of effective public administration and public management (Goodsell 2002; Rosenthal 2003). This section discusses the centrality of public administration in addressing homeland security challenges and issues.

Homeland Security Challenges

A set of intractable challenges occupied policymakers during the first decade of the "homeland security era." Table I.1 identifies eleven broad homeland security challenges that are expected to persist. Public-sector leaders, administrators, and rank-and-file employees are serving in roles that deal with these concerns. A number of entities—nongovernmental organizations, the private sector, communities, individual citizens, and federal, state, local, and tribal governments—will have to remain engaged and work together to surmount these challenges in order to maintain a secure homeland. Hundreds of thousands of committed professionals and citizen volunteers are required. These

Table I.1 Current and Future Homeland Security Challenges

1. Understanding and communicating threats
2. Integrating security into society
3. Balancing trade-offs between security and liberties
4. Integrating collaborative processes into intergovernmental and interagency activities
5. Sharing information and intelligence
6. Strengthening border security
7. Achieving transportation security
8. Protecting critical infrastructure
9. Establishing maritime security
10. Advancing the national emergency management system
11. Researching, developing, and using technology

include civil rights and civil liberties attorneys, counterterrorism experts in the Department of State and FBI, intelligence analysts from intelligence community agencies like the CIA, border patrol agents with U.S. Customs and Border Protection, first responders and emergency managers from state and local governments, disaster relief workers with the American Red Cross, private-sector scientists and engineers involved in science and technology programs, citizen volunteers for community emergency response teams, and U.S. Coast Guard personnel protecting natural resources, the environment, and maritime regions.

Public Administration for Homeland Security

The nation's response to the terrorist attacks of September 11 has primarily involved government organizations and their activities. Federal, state, and local government organizations and their personnel are on the front lines performing critical actions daily to protect the American people. The roles of public-sector agencies and employees are essential to the welfare of citizens in the policy areas of education, health, the environment, the economy, and national defense. According to Hal Rainey, Distinguished Professor of Public Administration and Policy at the School of Public and International Affairs at the University of Georgia, "as Congress, the president, the media, experts, and interest groups deliberated over how to design the new Department of Homeland Security, they debated many questions long familiar to public administration scholars and practitioners. . . . The debate over these questions illustrated the issues and values that infuse the processes of organizing and managing in government" (Rainey 2003, 4). And Donald Kettl, director of the University of Pennsylvania's Fels Institute of Government, states that "homeland security, at its core, is about coordination" and "the skills that government needs to cope with these events [9/11 and Hurricane Katrina] are much the same as those that government needs to manage many programs effectively"

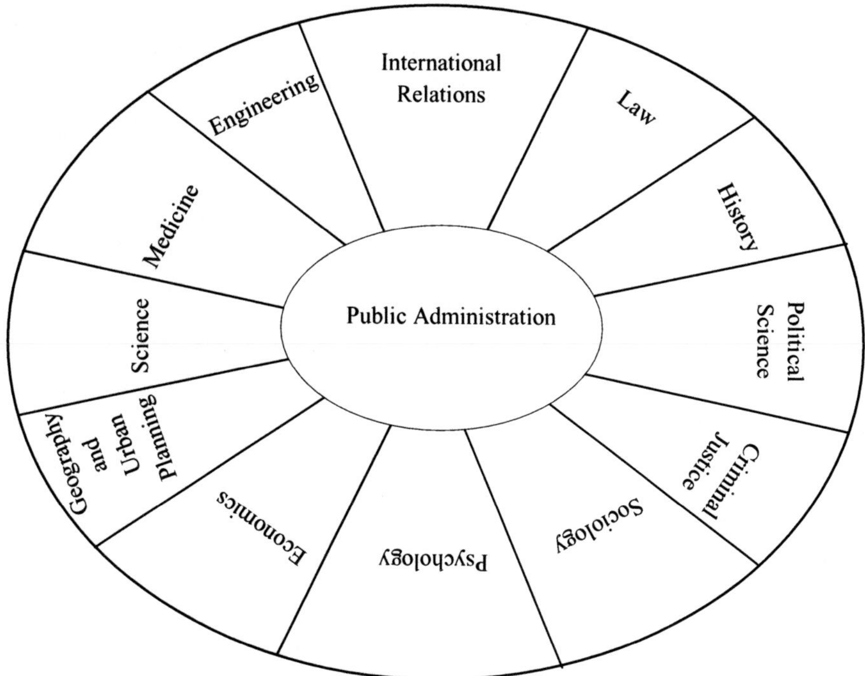

Figure I.1 Homeland Security: An Evolving Interdisciplinary Area of Study and Practice

(Kettl 2007, 32, 126). Thus, high-performing government organizations, administration, and management are all vital to homeland security.

Homeland security is an evolving interdisciplinary area of study and practice. Figure I.1 shows thirteen disciplines related to homeland security. The discipline of public administration is at the center of the figure to represent its standing at the core of homeland security.

Education Programs for Homeland Security

Since the 9/11 attacks, there has been a steady growth in the number of academic institutions across the United States that offer courses, concentrations, continuing education modules, certificates, associate degrees, bachelor's degrees, master's degrees, and professional master's degrees in homeland security. According to a report by the National Research Council (2005, 4), "The academic context of homeland security could be stretched to include almost every discipline and topic area imaginable, with 'homeland security' serving more as a target for the application of such studies, rather than as a descriptor of the studies themselves." The National Research Council report further finds that colleges and universities have important roles in support of homeland security. These roles are to prepare students for homeland security–related careers, provide knowledge concerning homeland security issues to the broad community, educate citizens about the nature of threats and about core democratic values to consider in responding to those threats, and serve as a forum for public debate on critical issues.

The propagation of programs and courses includes a wide range of content and variation in quality. Some programs existed in some fashion before 9/11 and then were simply revised to have a homeland security focus after 9/11. Other programs are newly established, based on deliberate efforts to design curricula and educate graduates for homeland security positions. Significant factors that influence program development are the continuing evolution of the homeland security profession and homeland security as an emerging academic discipline, as shown in figure I.1. Also significant are the absence of a consensus on a core curriculum and the nonexistence of a national governing or accrediting body to oversee homeland security education programs. Given these conditions, it is understandable that degree programs are diverse, based on multiple models, and rely on a multidisciplinary approach. Christopher Bellavita and Ellen Gordon, who teach in the homeland security master's degree program at the Naval Postgraduate School, express this view: "Homeland security is in a pre-paradigm phase. We understand this to mean that unlike medicine, law, engineering, and other professional disciplines, there is no general conceptual agreement about the range of topics that constitute homeland security as a field of study. Consequently there is not a dominant approach to teaching homeland security. We happen to think this is a good thing" (Bellavita and Gordon 2006, 1).

There is widespread agreement that homeland security as an academic discipline has not reached full maturity. Due to the extensive range of fields and topics within homeland security, no transcendent paradigm exists for a core curriculum. However, homeland security studies may follow the same evolutionary path that security studies did during the Cold War—as a field within the discipline of international relations. Eventually, security studies "became more rigorous, methodologically sophisticated, and theoretically inclined" and experienced "acceptance in the academic world" (Walt 1991, 211, 212). Today's students—who will be tomorrow's leaders—need to develop skill sets for performing pivotal functions in the complex environment of homeland security. The first wave of undergraduate and master's degree programs is paving the way. Doctoral programs are currently being planned. Much-needed scholarship will address key real-world research questions, develop and test theories to explain and predict phenomena, and apply new knowledge to critical concerns. Thus academic institutions will continue to determine their own orientations and curricula until a greater consensus emerges to guide them.

The remainder of this section argues why public administration and public policy graduate degree programs should offer homeland security courses, identifies pertinent topics for courses, and recommends research areas for public administration and public management scholars.

Public Administration and Public Policy Graduate Degree Programs

Since public administration is at the core of homeland security studies, it is imperative that graduate degree programs in public administration and public policy offer concentrations, focus areas, and certificates in homeland security. Schools of public administration and public policy have curricula that are ideal for teaching students with an interest in homeland security. At the American Society for Public Administration (ASPA) national conferences in 2007 and 2008, several public administration scholars with an interest in homeland security shared their common observation and dismay that few such programs existed.

To determine if any of the top public affairs master's programs have any degrees, certificates, or specializations in homeland security, a review was conducted of their program websites. The review of the top-ranked master of public administration (MPA) and master of public policy (MPP) programs, according to the March 2008 *U.S. News & World Report* rankings, confirms that very few of them offer homeland security courses. Of the top twenty-five programs, only three have homeland security offerings: Syracuse University's Maxwell School, Georgetown University's Public Policy Institute, and the State University of New York at Albany's Rockefeller College of Public Affairs and Policy. Furthermore, these offerings are certificates, tracks, or specializations. The descriptions of the homeland security offerings at those three institutions reflect some common foci: terrorism, national security, federalism, intergovernmental relations, leadership, public management, and emergency management.

Among all MPA and MPP programs, very few have started homeland security concentrations (Rollins and Rowan 2007), although they are gradually being established. For example, Texas A&M University's Bush School of Government and Public Service has a master of public service and administration degree with a concentration in security policy and management and an online certificate in homeland security. Virginia Commonwealth University's Wilder School of Government and Public Affairs offers an online master of arts degree in homeland security and emergency preparedness degree. Additionally, other doctoral research universities have homeland security degree and certificate programs, but operate them in schools other than schools of public affairs. For example, the University of Denver's Josef Korbel School of International Studies offers a master of arts in homeland security and a certificate in homeland security, the Michigan State University School of Criminal Justice has an online certificate in homeland security studies, and the Johns Hopkins University School of Education's Division of Public Safety Leadership is preparing a master of science program in management specializing in homeland security.

Topics for Homeland Security Courses

The diverse nature of homeland security programs throughout higher education institutions, along with the wide range of disciplines and fields involved, results in a plethora of courses and topics. According to a cursory review of homeland security courses and textbooks, fifty-one primary topics are commonly included as part of homeland security education (Bellavita and Gordon 2006). Twenty-three of the fifty-one topics, which equates to 45 percent, are related to public administration; they are listed here in the order they are most frequently mentioned:

- risk management and analysis
- homeland security policies and strategies
- an overview of homeland security mission areas
- the organization of homeland security
- the sociology of homeland security (politics, roles, behavior, power, conflict, and communication)
- systems integration and the administration of homeland security
- strategic planning and budgeting
- the federal role in homeland security
- preparedness
- public health and medical issues
- the role of state and local governments
- federalism
- strategic communications
- decision making
- ethical issues
- interagency coordination
- leadership
- the politics of homeland security
- recovery after an attack
- risk communications
- emergency management
- exercises and training
- human resource management

Although not many MPA and MPP programs currently have degrees, certificates, or specializations in homeland security, more public affairs programs are expected to offer them in the future. Five main factors should serve as drivers for this trend. The first is that the homeland security profession will continue to advance. Homeland security is now firmly a primary domestic public policy area, just like education, health care, the environment, and national defense (Dye 2005). The rapid emergence and growth of homeland security as an area of study and practice suggests a highly dynamic and progressive future field that will mature as an academic discipline.

Second, the number of students interested in studying homeland security as a way to prepare for careers in the public, nonprofit, and private sectors is expected to increase. Third, if other terrorism acts occur, the nation's commitment to homeland security will further solidify. Fourth, growth in government homeland security programs will require more leaders and managers with the education and competencies to administer those programs. And fifth, public administration and public policy programs will recognize, to a greater extent, the tremendous value of their curricula in preparing students for homeland security. The logical conclusion would appear to be that the expansion of public affairs programs is inevitable. When that happens, it will reinforce the reality that public administration is at the core of homeland security.

Homeland Security Research Areas

The homeland security challenges listed in table I.1 are momentous for the nation. University research is integral to finding solutions. All the homeland security disciplines shown in figure I.1 can be expected to contribute research toward overcoming these challenges. During the George W. Bush administration, DHS funded more than a dozen Centers of Excellence at major U.S. research universities to conduct multidisciplinary research in areas critical to homeland security, such as public administration and public management. Opportunities exist for scholars in these fields to conduct research with great

Table I.2 Areas in Need of Research for Homeland Security by Public Administration and Public Management Scholars

1. Public service
2. Leadership
3. Legal and managerial authorities
4. Organizational roles and missions
5. Organizational structure and alignment
6. Organizational culture
7. Strategic planning
8. Budgeting
9. Risk-management approach to decision making
10. Management, consolidation, and integration of information technology and administrative systems
11. Emergency management functions
12. Public health administration
13. Collaborative relationships through partnerships and networks
14. Interagency cooperation, communication, and coordination
15. Intergovernmental relations
16. Information and intelligence sharing
17. Human resource management
18. Performance measurement
19. Organizational learning, innovation, and change

relevancy to the challenges facing homeland security. Table I.2 lists nineteen recommended research areas with public administration and public management dimensions. Scholars who undertake research in these areas will help generate new knowledge and increased understanding that will prove valuable to homeland security. For example, homeland security and emergency management especially require interagency, intergovernmental, and multisector collaborative networks due to the requisite focus on security and safety, breadth of activities, and the wide range of organizations involved in each (Kelman 2007; Linden 2002; Milward and Provan 2006; O'Leary, Gerard, and Bingham 2006; Page 2003; GAO 2005; Waugh 2007; Waugh and Streib 2006). With the assistance of first-rate scholarship, organizations responsible for homeland security can, in the long term, be more effective and efficient in implementing programs, carrying out operations, and accomplishing statutory missions.

CONCLUSION

The unprecedented terrorist attacks of 9/11 marked the beginning of a new era in American government and public administration. This chapter has explained the development of homeland security as a profession, argued for how public administration is at the core of homeland security, and forecasted that public administration and public policy graduate degree programs that teach homeland security will continue to grow. One of the most important lessons learned from the 9/11 attacks was how vital public administration and public management are to homeland security. Given that the field of public administration is at the core of homeland security studies, graduate education in public administration and public policy will prepare tomorrow's leaders and policymakers to overcome the serious homeland security challenges confronting America. Furthermore, university research will help to address these challenges.

Homeland security continues on its evolutionary path and is multidisciplinary in nature. The field will continue to adapt as threats and priorities change. Since 9/11, intentional human-made disasters and natural disasters have captured the attention of scholars concerned with homeland security and emergency management. The variety of threats to homeland security, such as cyberattacks, critical infrastructure failures, agroterrorism, and bioterrorism compels new thinking from public administration and public management academics. Dwight Waldo reminded us that "public administration is a powerful, creative force" (Waldo 1980, 17). Regardless of the changing future foci of homeland security, public administration will continue to rest at the center of this critical area of study and practice.

REFERENCES

Bellavita, Christopher, and Ellen M. Gordon. 2006. Changing Homeland Security: Teaching the Core. *Homeland Security Affairs* 2, no. 1 (April): 1–19. www.hsaj.org/?article=2.1.1.

DHS (U.S. Department of Homeland Security). 2004. *National Response Plan.* Washington, DC: U.S. Government Printing Office.

———. 2008. *National Response Framework.* Washington, DC: U.S. Government Printing Office.

DOD (U.S. Department of Defense). 2005. *Homeland Security.* Joint Publication 3-26. Washington, DC: U.S. Government Printing Office.

Dye, Thomas R. 2005. *Understanding Public Policy,* 11th ed. Upper Saddle River, NJ: Pearson Prentice Hall.

GAO (U.S. Government Accountability Office). 2005. *Results-Oriented Government: Practices That Can Help Enhance and Sustain Collaboration among Federal Agencies.* Report GAO-06-15. Washington, DC: U.S. Government Printing Office.

Goodsell, Charles T. 2002. Insights for Public Administration from the Terrorist Attacks. *Administration & Society* 34, no. 3 (July): 255–60.

Hart-Rudman Commission. 1999. *New World Coming: American Security in the 21st Century, Major Themes and Implications.* Phase I Report on the Emerging Global Security Environment for the First Quarter of the 21st Century. September 15. Washington, DC: U.S. Commission on National Security / 21st Century.

Jenkins, Brian Michael. 2007. Basic Principles for Homeland Security. Testimony presented before the House Appropriations Committee, Subcommittee on Homeland Security, January 30. Santa Monica, CA: RAND Corporation.

Kelman, Steven. 2007. The Transformation of Government in the Decade Ahead. In *Reflections on 21st-Century Government Management.* 2008 Presidential Transition Series. Washington, DC: IBM Center for The Business of Government.

Kettl, Donald F. 2007. *System under Stress: Homeland Security and American Politics,* 2nd ed. Washington, DC: CQ Press.

Linden, Russell M. 2002. *Working across Boundaries: Making Collaboration Work in Government and Nonprofit Organizations.* San Francisco: Jossey-Bass.

Milward, H. Brinton, and Keith G. Provan. 2006. *A Manager's Guide to Choosing and Using Collaborative Networks.* Networks and Partnerships Series. Washington, DC: IBM Center for the Business of Government.

Naftali, Timothy. 2005. *Blind Spot: The Secret History of American Counterterrorism.* New York: Basic Books.

National Research Council, National Academy of Sciences, Committee on Educational Paradigms for Homeland Security. 2005. *Frameworks for Higher Education in Homeland Security.* Washington, DC: National Academies Press.

O'Leary, Rosemary, Catherine Gerard, and Lisa Blomgren Bingham. 2006. Introduction to the Symposium on Collaborative Public Management. *Public Administration Review* 66 (Supplement, December): 6–9.

Page, Stephen. 2003. Entrepreneurial Strategies for Managing Interagency Collaboration. *Journal of Public Administration Research and Theory* 13, no. 3:311–39.

Rainey, Hal G. 2003. Understanding and Managing Public *Organizations,* 3rd ed. San Francisco: Jossey-Bass.

Rollins, John, and Joseph Rowan. 2007. *The Homeland Security Academic Environment: A Review of Current Activities and Issues for Consideration.* Report prepared for Homeland Security and Defense Education Consortium. September.

Rosenthal, Uriel. 2003. September 11: Public Administration and the Study of Crises and Crisis Management. *Administration & Society* 35, no. 2 (May): 129–43.

Tangredi, Sam J. 2001. The Future Security Environment, 2001–2025: Toward a Consensus View. In *QDR 2001: Strategy-Driven Choices for America's Security,* ed. Michele A. Flournoy. Washington, DC: National Defense University Press.

Waldo, Dwight. 1980. *The Enterprise of Public Administration: A Summary View.* Novato, CA: Chandler & Sharp.

Walt, Stephen M. 1991. The Renaissance of Security Studies. *International Studies Quarterly* 35, no. 2 (June): 211–39.

Waugh, William L., Jr. 2007. Local Emergency Management in the Post-9/11 World. In *Emergency Management: Principles and Practice for Local Government,* 2nd edition, ed. William L. Waugh Jr. and Kathleen Tierney. Washington, DC: International City/County Management Association Press.

Waugh, William L., Jr., and Gregory Streib. 2006. Collaboration and Leadership for Effective Emergency Management. *Public Administration Review* 66 (Supplement, December): 131–40.

White House, Homeland Security Council. 2007. *National Strategy for Homeland Security.* Washington, DC: U.S. Government Printing Office.

PART II

GLOBALIZATION

The study and practice of public administration and international development management in the context of globalization, advanced information technology, and telecommunications have increasingly taken on new dimensions of connectedness, interdependency, and collaborative public management beyond state boundaries. Furthermore, a growing number of international organizations and regional networks of public organizations have begun to conduct more comparative studies on good governance, government effectiveness, the New Public Management, government reforms, transparency, and the level of decentralization at the international level. The scholars contributing to part II analyze how public administration research has responded to the challenges of globalization and explore how public administration scholars should prepare for future research with a global perspective.

An example of international interdependence in the context of globalization is an increase in international organizations handling regional and international issues, such as the European Union, the Asia-Pacific Economic Cooperation forum, and the countries party to the North American Free Trade Agreement. The EU, an economic and political partnership of twenty-seven democratic European countries with a combined population of roughly 500 million, takes an active role in international negotiations, including trade, the environment, food safety, international finance, foreign policy, and culture. Another example of international interdependence in a global context is regional collaboration for building public management capacity. For instance, in 2005, China, Japan, and South Korea approved and created the China-Japan-Korea Personnel Policy Network, which promotes collaboration and mutual exchanges between the three countries to improve personnel administration. Yet another example of the global economy's impact on public policy concerns and international collaboration is found in regulatory policy in the United States. In 2008, the U.S. Food and Drug Administration opened offices in Beijing, Guangzhou, and Shanghai to improve the speed and effectiveness of regulatory cooperation on food and drug safety overseas, and it also plans to open several offices in India, the Middle East, Latin America, and Europe.

The global economy and urban economic development together affect the decentralization of intergovernmental relations, the role of the state, and the demand for local-level autonomy in developing countries. The demand of social development and decentralization influences citizens' expectations about government responsiveness, transparency, and accountability. In an era of globalization, the decentralization of politics and administration in developing countries affects the evolution and strategy of international development management. The demand for broadening and contextualizing international development theory and practice has been increased because countries have different institutional frameworks, as well as different cultural and political understandings of democratic values and public administration development. In practice, international organizations—including the World Bank, the Asian Development Bank, the United Nations, Transparency International, and Global Integrity—seem to have taken the lead and have adopted various practices for development management regarding government effectiveness, democratic governance, and transparency. These organizations have also increased the attention given to comparative analyses of democratic governance values and performance at the national level.

These examples are only a few of many public administration concerns that cross international boundaries in the areas of environmental policy, financial crises, disaster management, crime, national security, terrorism, migration, trade policy, health policy, and food and drug safety. These cases suggest that public administration scholarship should focus on the emerging practice of international collaboration, which has an impact on knowledge transfer, policy transfer, strategic management, and diversity management in the context of the interdependent and globalized world of today. Thus public administration scholarship should include more discourses regarding the need for a global perspective in public administration research and practice in the twenty-first century.

Bidhya Bowornwathana leads off with "The Study of Comparative Public Administration: Future Trajectories and Prospects," in which he examines the evolution of comparative public administration (CPA) and discusses recent developments giving rise to the birth of the new CPA, for which the concepts and approaches of governance and public management are central. He suggests several trajectories in the emerging new CPA paradigm, including comparative studies of administrative reform among scholars from the same region and research on governance and public management reforms in all or many countries. By acknowledging the value of various research designs in CPA scholarship and increased professional networks of international public administration scholars, he suggests that CPA should be theory driven, under the common conceptual umbrella of governance and public management.

Yilin Hou shifts attention to the question of how to reinvent public administration in "Reinventing Public Administration for the Twenty-First Century: Toward a More Global and Generic Paradigm." He argues that CPA with a global perspective is not the field for a small group of scholars with foreign backgrounds or interest. Rather, it should be an inherent part of the discipline of public administration to seek higher explanatory power for the whole field, including its branch areas of research in the global community. He suggests that "internalizing" or "localizing" the global perspective in public administration scholarship will solidly transform the field, yielding a paradigm shift in the twenty-first century.

Ora-Orn Poocharoen shares "A Personal Memo from a Woman Teaching Public Administration in Asia," lamenting the lack of useful pedagogical materials as she teaches public administration to fellow Asians. She maintains that international public administration academics should become the core group that leads the field's development by taking a much broader global perspective in all areas of teaching, research, and service. Similar to Hou's suggestion, she notes that CPA in the global perspective is no longer a subfield but must now be considered mainstream public administration. She further suggests that more public administration scholars should conduct international and comparative studies and apply their accumulated knowledge from these studies in teaching the field's intellectual history.

The ideas discussed in these chapters provide important perspectives for understanding the challenges and future of public administration scholarship and pedagogy in the context of global concerns and interdependency.

The Study of Comparative Public Administration

Future Trajectories and Prospects

Bidhya Bowornwathana

Comparative public administration (CPA) is a field of study that seemed to die several times in the recent past but never did. This unusual ability to survive may indicate the usefulness of comparing public administration systems in differing countries. The beginning of the twenty-first century seems to signal the revival of CPA studies. The growing prominence of the governance paradigm and the increasing interest of scholars in studying administrative reform have brought scholars from many countries together to share their experiences and conduct comparative studies. Today, I would argue, CPA studies are centered on the subject of administrative reform. However, the term "administrative reform" is sharpened by new buzzwords like "governance," "public management," and the "New Public Management."

In this chapter I first discuss recent developments conducive to the birth of the new CPA. Then I argue that there is an emerging paradigm in CPA that centers on the concepts and approaches of governance and public management. Finally, I suggest possible development trajectories for the emerging new CPA.

DEVELOPMENTS CONDUCIVE TOWARD THE BIRTH OF THE NEW CPA

The observation that CPA is "a dying field that never dies" is well supported by recent developments. In 1971, the Ford Foundation discontinued its financial support for the Comparative Administration Group. The development administration approach of the 1960s and 1970s had difficulty distinguishing itself from the mother field of public administration. The study of public administration became inward looking (ethnocentric) rather than outward looking (global-centric). As a result, we know less about other countries' public administration systems. Since the 1970s, the popular master of public administration programs have not incorporated a core course on CPA. Though things seemed to go downhill for CPA in the 1970s, several developments during the

1980s, 1990s, and early 2000s slowly and quietly changed the nature of the old CPA.

Reforms and other innovations were introduced by some developed countries. Major administrative reforms were undertaken in the United Kingdom during the period when Margaret Thatcher was prime minister, from 1979 to 1990. Reforms such as the privatization of state-owned enterprises, the efficiency scrutiny program, the Next Steps Program, and executive agencies were implemented. At the same time, other countries—mostly Commonwealth member nations—were beginning to stage major administrative reform initiatives, with much borrowing and learning new ideas from each other. For example, New Zealand became the reform model that drew much attention from other countries.

It did not take long for reform among developed countries to spill over into developing countries, because the governments of developing countries tend to look to developed countries as models for these efforts. In short, everyone was learning from everyone else. In an effort to understand these new reform practices, scholars attempted to provide order to the ideas by subsuming them into larger concepts. These included the New Public Management (Hood 1991; Christensen and Laegreid 2002), the postbureaucratic paradigm (Barzelay 1992), reinventing government (Osborne and Gaebler 1992), governance (Rhodes 1996; Pierre and Peters 2000; Peters 1996; Bowornwathana 1997, 2000; Meier and O'Toole 2006), and public management (Pollitt and Bouckaert 2004; Kettl 2000; and Lynn 2006). With the creation of such new common concepts, it was possible to conduct comparative studies.

The borrowing of reform ideas among countries was further moved forward by the financial support from international agencies, such as the United Nations and the Organization for Economic Cooperation and Development (OECD). These international organizations released several documents in an effort to define new reform concepts (see OECD 1995; World Bank 2008; Levy 2007; United Nations Development Program 1997; UNDESA 2006). The international organizations also gathered basic data on reform in OECD member nations and other countries and made this information available on their websites. For example, the OECD website contains information about the background, history, and reform efforts of individual OECD countries. This makes it possible for students to conduct comparative administrative reform studies of the OECD countries. The World Bank, the United Nations (e.g., the United Nations Development Program), the Asian Development Bank, and the International Monetary Fund used the new reform principles of governance and public management to encourage and even coerce loan-receiving developing countries to reform their government administrations.

During the 1990s and early 2000s, some scholars began publishing new books showing their enduring commitment to the field of CPA. Some see CPA as the study of bureaucracies and show a strong political science influence. They are the followers of the old CPA, which focuses on the role of the bureaucracy in political development (Farazmand 2001; Tummala 2003; Jreisat 2002). Other books contain chapters that are foreign to the old CPA and do not recognize its "gurus." An example is Moshe Maor and Jan-Erik Lane's (1999) two-volume *Comparative Public Administration*, which collected new papers on CPA that went beyond the old classics of the 1960s. This book shows that CPA researchers were drastically changing their approaches and methodologies. The most recent book of readings on CPA is Eric Otenyo and Nancy Lind's (2006) *Comparative Public Administration: The Essential Readings*, which is interesting because it includes new papers on CPA written by both old and new CPA researchers. For example, part IV of the book clearly illustrates the importance of administrative reform in the literature of the new CPA. And the book's chapters use new key terms, including "globalization," the "New Public Management," and "governance."

A major comparative public administration study was done in the 1990s under the leadership of scholars from Indiana University in the United States and Leiden University and Erasmus University in the Netherlands. In October 1991, an international conference took place in Rotterdam and Leiden (Bekke, Perry, and Toonen 1996). In 1997, the second conference took place at the School for Public and Environmental Affairs at Indiana University. It was one of the largest gatherings of comparative administration scholars from all over the world, and they presented their empirical case studies within a common conceptual framework. Four edited volumes published by Edward Elgar came out of this second conference (Verheijen 1999; Bekke and Van der Meer 2000; Burns and Bowornwathana 2001; and Halligan 2003).

During late 1980s and throughout the 1990s, scholars from several countries formed new academic networks with the aim of becoming "international." They believed that something could be learned from other countries and that comparative work would be useful. They held conferences and launched academic journals that were comparatively oriented and not one-country journals. And in 1988 scholars formed the Structure and Organization of Government group, a research committee of the International Political Science Association, which publishes *Governance: An International Journal of Policy and Administration*. In 1991 American scholars in public administration under the leadership of George Frederickson, who wanted an academic journal that emphasizes theory and quantitative research, launched *The Journal of Public Administration Research and Theory* as an alternative to *Public Administration Review*, which was then more practitioner oriented. In 1998 the International Public Management Network began publishing the *International Public Management Journal* and the *International Public Management Review*. In March 1999 the first issue of the *Public Management Review* (originally *Public Management*) was published. *Public Management Review* publishes papers that are cross-disciplinary, based on cross-national or comparative research and focused on the management of intersectoral relations between government and the nonprofit/voluntary and private sectors. In Asia leading academicians in public administration have formed the Asian Forum, consisting of academicians from universities in such economies as Japan, South Korea, Hong Kong, Thailand, Singapore, Taiwan, China, Macao, Brunei, and Indonesia (Bowornwathana and Wescott 2008).

Besides the emergence of new journals that support comparative work, some existing journals also underwent major readjustments in favor of a comparative perspective. The national journal of British public administration, *Public Administration: An International Journal*, was "Europeanized" in 1999 with increased coverage of European public administration in a new European Forum. The editors aim to make the journal not only European in content and outlook but also international in its impact. In 2006 the American Society for Public Administration's *Public Administration Review* added a new international editor. *The International Review of Administrative Sciences: An International Journal of Comparative Public Administration* is the official journal of the International Institute of Administrative Sciences, the European Group for Public Administration, and the International Association of Schools and Institutes of Administration. It also became the official journal of the Commonwealth Association for Public Administration and Management in 2000.

Beginning in the 1990s, practitioners around the world seemed to become more interested in conducting administrative reform in line with governance and the New Public Management. When one attends conferences organized by practitioners in particular regions, one find that the conference themes, papers, and discussions center on the introduction of democratic governance institutions and public management methods into the public administration system. Reform ideas such as good governance, transparency, open government, combating corruption, and maintaining ethics and trust are common themes in conferences organized by the Latin American Center for Development Administration, the Network of Institutes and Schools of Public Administration in Central and Eastern Europe, and the Commonwealth Association for Public Administration and Management. Practitioners involved in administrative reform have also begun a tradition of holding Global Forums on Reinventing Government, with the first held in Washington in January 1999. Other international organizations—such as the World Bank, the United Nations Development Program, the OECD, and the Asian Development Bank—are also involved in encouraging research, publications, and implementation efforts related to governance reform. Developing countries that accept loans from these international organizations are obliged to reform their governments in line with the principles of governance and public management.

What do all these lively activities on governance and public management reforms carried out by practitioners and scholars mean to the field of comparative public administration? A new CPA seems to be slowly evolving, with practitioners and scholars striving to become "more comparative." The belief that one can learn from the administrative reform experiences of other countries is gradually gaining ground. What is now happening to the field of public administration is a reconfirmation of Woodrow Wilson's proposal in 1887 that the study of administration needs to be comparative in its method. Much can be gained by studying other countries' public administration systems (Wilson 1887).

THE EMERGING NEW COMPARATIVE PUBLIC ADMINISTRATION PARADIGM

It is clear that comparative public administration has been making a strong comeback as a field, but it is a new breed of CPA quite different from the old CPA. In the pages that follow, I argue that a new emerging CPA paradigm differs from the old in three major ways.

Although the old CPA compares bureaucracies, the new CPA compares administrative reforms. For the new CPA, "administrative reform" becomes the object of investigation. Proponents of the new CPA compare administrative reforms that are taking place in countries all around the world. The old CPA, conversely, focused on the development of bureaucracy, mainly in developing countries, and its role in the process of democratization and political development. As Heady (1966) asked, "Are bureaucracies usurpative or instrumental?" Though "administrative reform" was important for the old CPA, it was not the core for comparison. In the old CPA, there was a clear analytical and research distinction between developed and developing countries. The new CPA, however, advocates more studies that combine developing and developed countries.

The new CPA compares everything that is related to administrative reform policies and processes among countries. This comparison can look at particular phenomena, such as privatization, corruption, agencification (the process of creating "executive" agencies), downsizing, performance, accountability, transparency, trust and ethics, reform diffusion, and management tools. The comparison can look at the politics of administrative reform, politician–bureaucrat relationships, financial and budgeting reform, the reform of the human resources systems, and the reform of policy processes. It can also examine reform roles of such key actors as prime ministers and presidents, ministers and department heads, and legislative representatives. The "institutional where," or locus, of the new CPA is therefore broader than that of the old CPA. Though there are varieties of units and levels of analysis, the locus remains "administrative reform."

A group of scholars, mainly from Europe, has done extensive research on the subject of "agency" (Pollitt and Talbot 2004; Pollitt et al. 2004; Pollitt 2006; Bowornwathana 2005). Another group of scholars, more global in membership, does comparative work on politics and politician–bureaucrat relations with regard to administrative reform (Aberbach, Putnam, and Rockman 1981; Farazmand 1997; Peters and Pierre 2001; Bowornwathana and Poochareon 2006). Corruption is a unifying theme that draws comparative research (Rose-Ackerman 1999; Quah 1999). The relationship between culture and administrative reform is another topic that can foster comparison among countries (Schedler and Proeller 2007; Bowornwathana 2007). "Evaluation" of public-sector reforms can become another unifying concept for comparative work (Wollmann 2003; Pollitt and Bouckaert 2003). The governance concept of "transparency" is a central one for comparison (Hood and Heald 2006).

Thus, the pillars of the new CPA are different from those of the old CPA, which was closely connected to the field of comparative politics and had leaders who were mostly political scientists with a background in comparative politics. Public administration scholars play a much stronger role in the new CPA, which focuses more on public administration (Peters 1996). In this regard the new CPA fits well with the "Public Administration as Public Administration Paradigm," as put forth by Nicholas Henry (2004).

The old CPA was highly dominated by the ideas of American scholars, such as Fred W. Riggs (1964) and Ferrel Heady (1966). Theoretical frameworks and concepts were mainly coined by American professors. Conversely, several non-American scholars are leaders of the new CPA. Scholars from continental Europe and the United Kingdom build conceptual frameworks and conduct empirical research on the administrative reform experiences of European countries. The body of knowledge on administrative reform accumulates from both scholarly work and also the intense administrative reform efforts of European governments. Reform innovations are being tested by European governments, and much borrowing of reform ideas is going on among European countries. Non-European countries also borrow from the reform experiments of European countries by implementing European-style administrative reforms. For example, the British and New Zealand models of reform have been studied by scholars and practitioners around the world.

During the old CPA period, the objective behind the U.S. government's support of administrative reform in developing countries was to prevent communism from taking root. The assumption was that with a modern and efficient public administration, developing countries would be able to fight off communism and bring victory to democracy. The context of the new CPA is different. Today, communism has lost, globalization is in, and administrative reform all around the world seems to be heading toward one trend: the adoption of liberal democratic values, such as citizens as owners of government and the importance of accountability, transparency, fairness, and equity in the conduct of government.

The new CPA is replacing the structural-functionalism and systems theories that dominated the old CPA with new theories and concepts from governance and public management. Then the gurus were people like Gabriel Almond, Fred W. Riggs, and Ferrel Heady. Today the dominant theories and approaches of the new CPA are drawn from concepts of governance and public management, which, instead of a single theoretical framework, contain several interpretations. And the units and levels of analysis of the new CPA are much broader and more flexible than the grand theories of the old CPA.

Under the old CPA, studies on the bureaucracies of developing countries were mainly undertaken by scholars teaching in American universities. There were loose links among academicians, practitioners, and consultants. Under the new CPA, however, scholars, practitioners, and consultants collaborate closely and have a common focus on governance and public management reforms.

The old CPA saw developing countries as having characteristics that were obstacles to achieving higher levels of development. These included weak democratic institutions, military intervention in politics, the monopoly of power by the bureaucracy, the inability of the public to monitor the bureaucracy, and low levels of education. But the new CPA regards the development and reform of public administrative systems as an ongoing process for all countries—both developing and developed. The borrowing of reform ideas from abroad was a one-way, top-down process for the old CPA, but the borrowing process is a circle for the new CPA. Developed countries can learn from one another, and they can also learn from developing countries. Instead of blaming developing countries for being unable to develop at an expected pace, scholars of the new CPA focus on the process of reform diffusion. They ask questions like these: What happens when reform innovations from abroad enter a foreign country? Are reform hybrids produced? What are the intended and unintended consequences of reform?

FUTURE TRAJECTORIES

The emerging CPA paradigm consists of four future trajectories, or "tracks." First, the regional track refers to the practice of scholars from the same regions who form themselves into research groups that conduct comparative studies on administrative reform. For example, European scholars compare the governance reform experiences of European countries. The most active groups are those based in Western Europe, such as the European Group for Public Administration. Other groups include scholars from the Commonwealth nations, the Eastern Europe group through NISCAPee, the OECD group, and Spanish-speaking groups through such organizations as Crosscultural, Language, and Academic Development. The most important reason for the success of regional groups, besides funding, is a common language. Regions where member countries use different languages find it very difficult to conduct comparative research on administrative reform.

In the case of large countries like the United States and China, one may ask whether comparative studies of American states and Chinese regions can be included in the domain of comparative public administration. Recent examples of the regional track include a comparison of managerial reforms in Europe and the United States (Gualmini 2008), a comparison of the public-sector innovations in eight European countries (Vigoda-Gadot et al. 2008), and a discussion of developing countries in the Commonwealth in terms of their experiences in imitating the public-sector reforms of developed countries (Laking and Norman 2007). In another study, Verhoest, Bouckaert, and Peters (2007) identify the trajectory of specialization and coordination in four OECD countries—New Zealand, the United Kingdom, Sweden, and France.

Second, the "few-cases" track refers to the practice of scholars who compare several countries. Two, three, or four countries are usually drawn from the same region and compared within an administrative reform framework. The various dimensions of governance—such as accountability, transparency, the minimal role of the state, government trust and fairness—can serve as theoretical frameworks for the studies of the few-cases track. For example, George M. Guess (2005) compares the decentralization lessons of Pakistan, Indonesia, and the Philippines. Mark Turner (2006) also compares the decentralization experiences of the Philippines, Indonesia, and Cambodia. Another example is Marine Allix and Sandra Van Thiel's (2005) comparison of quasi-autonomous organizations in France and Italy. Linda McGuire (2001) compares the service charter initiatives in Australia, the United Kingdom, and the United States. Christopher Hood and Martin Lodge (2004) compare competency reform in the United States, the United Kingdom, and Germany. Myung-Jae Moon and Patricia Ingraham (1998) examine the shaping of administrative reform and governance in China, Japan, and South Korea. Another edited book compares public-sector reform in Britain and Germany (Wollmann and Schroter 2000). Samaratunge, Alam, and Teicher (2008) show how contextual factors influence the nature and outcome of New Public Administration initiatives in Singapore, Malaysia, Sri Lanka, and Malaysia. Lee and Haque (2006) compare the New Public Management reform and governance in Hong Kong and Singapore. Another recent study is a comparison of the politics of organizing reform work in six countries—Thailand, the United Kingdom, New Zealand, Malaysia, the United States, and Japan (Bowornwathana and Poochareon 2005).

Third, the "global" track refers to the tendency of some scholars to study the governance and public management reforms in all or many countries. In some cases, scholars provide macro conceptions of governance and public management. For example, Rhodes (1996) described the U.K. public sector as consisting of self-organizing networks. Hood (1991) summarized "the New Public Management" as consisting of seven characteristics: hands-on professional management, explicit standards and measures of performance, a greater emphasis on output controls, a shift to the disaggregation of units in the public sector, a shift to greater competition in the public sector, a stress on private styles of management practice, and a stress on greater discipline and parsimony in resource use. Peters (1996) envisions the state and governance as consisting of four models: the market model, the participatory state, the flexible government, and the deregulated government. The present author's democratic governance model outlines four principles: a smaller government that does less, flexible government and global vision, accountability, and government fairness (Bowornwathana 1997).

Other macroconceptualizations include network governance (Kickert, Klijn, and Koppenjan 1997; Sorensen and Torfing 2008; Goldsmith and Eggers 2004) and collaborative governance (Vigoda-Gadot 2003). Scholars use advanced quantitative statistical methods to compare the governance of many countries (Brewer, Choi, and Walker 2007). Scholars rank and rate the performance of an individual country in terms of governance reform by using complicated questionnaire items, scaling techniques, and quantitative methods (Arndt and Oman 2006; Arndt 2007; Hood 2007). In fact, several independent nongovernmental organizations such as Transparency International (using its Corruption Perception Index) and Global Integrity provide annual rankings of countries in terms of their governance performance, including levels of corruption and integrity. The World Bank also provides the Governance Indicators.

Fourth, the "one-country" track refers to studies of individual countries. This one-country approach to administrative reform is criticized by some scholars as being futile. They argue that one-country studies cannot be comparative. The concern here is the trade-off between quantity and quality. One is less able to do in-depth analysis when including a greater number of countries. But one-country cases can be useful if they are theory driven. One can then compare the country case studies done by other scholars who used the same theoretical frameworks and concepts. Governance concepts such as accountability, trust, integrity, and corruption can serve as comparative yardsticks for these individual country cases. In fact, if one surveys the papers published in public administration journals, one would be surprised to learn that despite all the calls for comparative cross-country studies, almost all are one-country cases.

Perhaps it is not necessary to choose from among the four trajectories of the new emerging CPA paradigm. All four tracks are useful, and they should all be developed simultaneously. An individual scholar can choose to concentrate on one track and learn to respect the work done by others in the remaining tracks. All levels of analysis are useful. However, all four tracks should be theory driven under the common conceptual umbrella of governance and public management. In each track, one must also decide which aspects of governance and public management one wants to study. These include accountability, corruption, integrity, and transparency. How many country cases one wants to use and how many scholars are, in fact, needed in a comparative research project to cover all the selected countries also need to be considered. I would also encourage studies of governance and public management reform that compare countries from different regions.

CONCLUSION

Comparative public administration—"the dying field that never dies"—seems to be making a strong comeback. Though the new CPA is quite different from the old CPA, both do share a common belief that comparative studies are useful for understanding and improving our administrative systems. In this chapter I have explained the developments leading to the revival of CPA, the distinction between the new and old CPAs, and the future trajectories of the new CPA. No matter which trajectory one chooses, most studies are likely to be driven by theories and concepts drawn from the growing literature on governance and public management.

REFERENCES

Aberbach, Joel D., Robert D. Putnam, and Bert A. Rockman. 1981. *Bureaucrats and Politicians in Western Democracies*. Cambridge, MA: Harvard University Press.

Allix, Marine, and Sandra Van Thiel. 2005. Mapping the Field of Quasi-Autonomous Organizations in France and Italy. *International Public Management Journal* 8, no. 1:39–56.

Arndt, Christiane. 2007. The Politics of Governance Ratings. Draft paper presented at Workshop Ranking and Rating Public Services of International Public Management Network, Oxford University, Oxford.

Arndt, Christiane, and Charles Oman. 2006. *Uses and Abuses of Governance Indicators*. Development Centre Studies. Paris: Organization for Economic Cooperation and Development.

Barzelay, Michael, with Babak J. Armajani. 1992. *Breaking through Bureaucracy*. Berkeley: University of California Press.

Bekke, Hans A. G. M., James Perry, and Theo A. J. Toonen, eds. 1996. *Civil Service Systems in Comparative Perspective*. Bloomington: Indiana University Press.

Bekke, Hans A. G. M., and Frits M. Van der Meer. 2000. *Civil Service Systems in Western Europe*. Cheltenham, U.K.: Edward Elgar.

Bowornwathana, Bidhya. 1997. Transforming Bureaucracies for the 21st Century: The New Democratic Governance Paradigm. *Public Administration Quarterly* 21, no. 3:294–308. (Also in *Comparative Public Administration: The Essential Readings*, ed. Eric E. Otenyo and Nancy S. Lind. Oxford: Elsevier, 2006.)

———. 2000. Governance Reform in Thailand: Questionable Assumptions, Uncertain Outcomes. *Governance: An International Journal of Policy, Administration and Institutions* 13, no. 3:393–408. (Also in *Governance and the Public Sector*, ed. Ron Hodges. Cheltenham, U.K.: Edward Elgar, 2005.)

———. 2005. Autonomisation of the Thai State: Some Observations. *Public Administration and Development* 26, no. 1:27–34.

———. 2007. Governance Reform Outcomes through Cultural Lens: Thailand. In *Cultural Aspects of Public Management Reform*, ed. Kuno Schedler and Isabella Proeller. Oxford: Elsevier.

Bowornwathana, Bidhyan, and Ora-Orn Poocharoen. 2005. Managing Reforms: The Politics of Organizing Reform Work. *Public Organization Review: A Global Journal* 5:233–47.

———. 2006. Bureaucratic Politics and Administrative Reform: Why Politics Matters. Paper presented at American Political Science Association Annual Meeting, Philadelphia, August 31–September 3.

Bowornwathana, Bidhya, and Clay Wescott. 2008. *Comparative Governance Reform in Asia: Democracy, Corruption, and Government Trust.* Bingley, U.K.: Emerald Group.

Brewer, Gene A., Yujin Choi, and Richard M. Walker. 2007. Accountability, Corruption and Government Effectiveness in Asia: An Exploration of World Bank Indicators. *International Public Management Review* 8, no. 2:200–219.

Burns, John P., and Bidhya Bowornwathana. 2001. *Civil Service Systems in Asia.* Cheltenham, U.K.: Edward Elgar.

Christensen, Tom, and Per Laegreid. 2002. *New Public Management: The Transformation of Ideas and Practice.* Aldershot, U.K.: Ashgate.

Farazmand, Ali. 1997. *Modern Systems of Government: Exploring the Role of Bureaucrats and Politicians.* Thousands Oak, CA: Sage.

———. 2001. *Handbook of Comparative and Development Public Administration.* New York: Marcel Dekker.

Goldsmith, Stephen, and William D. Eggers. 2004. *Governing by Network: The New Shape of the Public Sector.* Washington, DC: Brookings Institution Press.

Gualmini, Elisabetta. 2008. Restructuring Weberian Bureaucracy: Comparing Managerial Reforms in Europe and the United States. *Public Administration: An International Quarterly* 86, no. 1:75–94.

Guess, George M. 2005. Comparative Decentralization Lessons from Pakistan, Indonesia, and the Philippines. *Public Administration Review* 65, no. 2 (March–April): 217–30.

Halligan, John. 2003. *Civil Service Systems in Anglo-American Countries.* Cheltenham, U.K.: Edward Elgar.

Heady, Ferrel. 1966. *Public Administration: A Comparative Perspective.* Englewood Cliffs, NJ: Prentice Hall.

Henry, Nicholas. 2004. *Public Administration and Public Affairs,* 9th ed. Upper Saddle River, NJ: Prentice Hall.

Hood, Christopher. 1991. A Public Management for All Seasons? *Public Administration* 69, no. 1:3–19.

———. 2007. Public Service Management by Numbers: Why Does It Vary? Where Has It Come From? What Are the Gaps and the Puzzles? *Public Money and Management* 27, no. 2:95–102.

Hood, Christopher, and David Heald. 2006. *Transparency: The Key to Better Governance?* Oxford: Oxford University Press.

Hood, Christopher, and Martin Lodge. 2004. Competency, Bureaucracy, and Public Management Reform: A Comparative Analysis. *Governance* 17, no. 3:313–33.

Jreisat, Jamil E. 2002. *Comparative Public Administration and Policy.* Boulder, CO: Westview Press.

Kettl, Donald F. 2000. *The Global Public Management Revolution: A Report on the Transformation of Governance.* Washington, DC: Brookings Institution Press.

Kickert, Walter J. M., Erik-Hans Klijn, and Joop F. M. Koppenjan. 1997. *Managing Complex Networks: Strategies for the Public Sector.* Thousands Oaks, CA: Sage.

Laking, Rob, and Richard Norman. 2007. Imitation and Inspiration in Public Sector Reform: Lessons from Commonwealth Experiences. *International Review of Administrative Sciences* 73, no. 4:517–30.

Lee, Eliza W. Y., and M. Shamsul Haque. 2006. The New Public Management Reform and Governance in Asian NICs: A Comparison of Hong Kong and Singapore. *Governance* 19, no. 4:605–26.

Levy, Brian. 2007. *Governance Reform: Bridging Monitoring and Action.* Washington, DC: World Bank.

Lynn, Laurence E., Jr. 2006. *Public Management: Old and New.* New York: Routledge, Taylor & Francis Group.

Maor, Moshe, and Jan-Erik Lane. 1999. *Comparative Public Administration.* Dartmouth, U.K.: Ashgate.

McGuire, Linda. 2001. Service Charters-Global Convergence or National Divergence? A Comparison of Initiatives in Australia, the United Kingdom, and the United States. *Public Management Review* 3, no. 4:493–524.

Meier, Kenneth J., and Laurence J. O'Toole, Jr. 2006. *Bureaucracy and Democratic State: A Governance Perspective.* Baltimore: Johns Hopkins University Press.

Moon, Myung-Jae, and Patricia Ingraham. 1998. Shaping Administrative Reform and Governance: An Examination of the Political Nexus Triads in Three Asian Countries. *Governance* 11, no. 1:77–100.

OECD (Organization for Economic Cooperation and Development). 1995. *Governance in Transition: Public Management Reforms in OECD Countries.* Paris: OECD.

Osborne, David, and Ted Gaebler. 1992. *Reinventing Government.* Reading, MA: Addison-Wesley.

Otenyo, Eric E., and Nancy S. Lind. 2006. *Comparative Public Administration: The Essential Readings.* Oxford: Elsevier.

Peters, B. Guy. 1996. *The Future of Governing: Four Emerging Models.* Lawrence: University Press of Kansas.

Peters, B. Guy, and Jon Pierre. 2001. *Politicians, Bureaucrats and Administrative Reform.* London: Routledge, Taylor & Francis Group.

Pierre, Jon, and B. Guy Peters. 2000. *Governance, Politics and the State.* New York: St. Martin's Press.

Pollitt, Christopher. 2006. Performance Management in Practice: A Comparative Study of Executive Agencies. *Journal of Public Administration Research and Theory* 16, no. 1:25–45.

Pollitt, Christopher, and Geert Bouckaert. 2003. Evaluating Public Management Reforms: An International Perspective. In *Evaluation in Public Sector Reform: Concepts and Practice in International Perspective,* ed. Hellmut Wollmann. Cheltenham, U.K.: Edward Elgar.

———. 2004. *Public Management Reform: A Comparative Analysis,* 2nd ed. Oxford: Oxford University Press.

Pollitt, Christopher, and Colin Talbot. 2004. *Unbundled Government: A Critical Analysis of the Global Trend to Agencies, Quangos and Contractualisation.* New York: Routledge, Taylor & Francis Group.

Pollitt, Christopher, Colin Talbot, Janice Caufield, and Amanda Smullen. 2004. *Agencies: How Governments Do Things through Semi-Autonomous Organizations.* New York: Palgrave, Macmillan.

Quah, Jon S. T. 1999. Corruption in Asian Countries: Can It Be Minimized? *Public Administration Review* 59, no. 6:483–94.

Rhodes, R. A. W. 1996. The New Governance: Governing without Government. *Political Studies* 44, no. 4:652–67.

Riggs, Fred W. 1964. *Administration in Developing Countries: The Theory of Prismatic Society.* Boston: Houghton Mifflin.

Rose-Ackerman, Susan. 1999. *Corruption and Government: Causes, Consequences, and Reform.* Cambridge: Cambridge University Press.

Samaratunge, Ramanie, Quamrul Alam, and Julian Teicher. 2008. The New Public Management Reforms in Asia: A Comparison of South and Southeast Asian Countries. *International Review of Administrative Sciences* 74, no. 1:25–46.

Schedler, Kuno, and Isabella Proeller. 2007. *Cultural Aspects of Public Management Reform.* Oxford: Elsevier.

Sorensen, Eva, and Jacob Torfing. 2008. *Theories of Democratic Network Governance.* Basingstoke, U.K.: Palgrave Macmillan.

Tummala, Krishna K. 2003. *Comparative Bureaucratic Systems.* Lanham, MD: Lexington Books.

Turner, Mark. 2006. From Commitment to Consequences: Comparative Experiences of Decentralization in the Philippines, Indonesia and Cambodia. *Public Management Review* 8, no. 2:253–72.

UNDESA (United Nations Department of Economic and Social Affairs). 2006. *Innovations in Governance and Public Administration: Replicating What Works.* New York: United Nations.

United Nations Development Program. 1997. *Reconceptualising Governance.* Discussion Paper 2. Management Development and Governance Division, Bureau for Policy and Program Support. New York: United Nations Development Program.

Verheijen, Tony. 1999. *Civil Service Systems in Central and Eastern Europe.* Cheltenham, U.K.: Edward Elgar.

Verhoest, Koen, Geert Bouckaert, and B. Guy Peters. 2007. Janus-Faced Reorganization: Specialization and Coordination in Four OECD Countries in the Period 1980–2005. *International Review of Administrative Sciences* 73, no. 3:325–48.

Vigoda-Gadot, Eran. 2003. *Managing Collaboration in Public Administration: The Promise of Alliance among Governance, Citizens, and Businesses.* Westport, CT: Praeger.

Vigoda-Gadot, Eran, Aviv Shoham, Nitza Schwabsky, and Ayalla Ruvio. 2008. Public Sector Innovation for Europe: A Multinational Eight-Country Exploration of Citizens' Perspective. *Public Administration: An International Quarterly* 86, no. 2:307–30.

Wilson, Woodrow. 1887. The Study of Administration. *Political Science Quarterly* 56, no. 4:481–506.

Wollmann, Helmut. 2003. *Evaluation in Public Sector Reform: Concepts and Practice in International Perspective.* Cheltenham, U.K.: Edward Elgar.

Wollmann, Helmut, and Eckhard Schroter. 2000. *Comparing Public Sector Reform in Britain and Germany: Key Traditions and Trends of Modernisation.* Aldershot, U.K.: Ashgate.

World Bank. 2008. *Public Sector Reform: What Works and Why? An IEG Evaluation of World Bank Support.* Washington, DC: World Bank.

Reinventing Public Administration for the Twenty-First Century

Toward a More Global and Generic Paradigm

Yilin Hou

Since its inception, public administration has evolved through several substantive stages. At the turn of the twenty-first century, the field has encountered a serious challenge in that existing theories cannot well explain many of the recent happenings in a quickly changing world. This challenge, however, also presents a huge tract of new ground for theoretical explorations that could carry rich policy applications. We, the current generation of public administrationists, are fortunate to have met this historical occasion. If we face the challenge and seize the opportunity, we will make history.

These new challenges arise because current theories cannot offer adequate explanatory power; more exactly, some contemporary issues defy existing theories. Promise lies with these challenges because public administration, whether as practice or as discipline, maintains a great tradition of reinventing itself, which explains it has survived the vicissitudes of social change and flourished, though not as much as we would like, throughout all ideologies, political structures, and state/economic systems.

The globalization of trade, industries, capital flow, and human resources was a trend in the second half of the twentieth century; now it is a fact of life. Examples are easily identifiable at any level of government. The vice chairman of the U.S. Federal Reserve looks at foreign central banks for assistance in the fight against inflation (Blackstone 2008). After years of concerted efforts, the state of Georgia won an investment from the South Korean auto company Kia. In April 2008, the governor of Georgia led a delegation on a trip to China to celebrate the first flight on the new Delta–Shanghai route and to cut the opening ribbon for the state's business office in Beijing. Nationwide, 9/11 has permanently changed our way of life. In this changed environment, public administration as a discipline to study and support the operation of government should and must incorporate global views and perspectives.

Because the context of public administration operation has thoroughly changed, it is again time for the discipline to reinvent itself. Without fundamental updates, public administration would quickly lag behind the twenty-first century social dynamics. China is a typical love/hate case; consumers enjoy the low-priced, made-in-China products but loathe the loss of jobs presumably moved to that country. Big companies enjoy the huge profit margin obtained from their Chinese operations but have to suffer being accused of being unpatriotic. Above all, China's rapid economic growth occurred under resistance to Western political standards and lectures on "management experiences."

China has taken a unique route, as America did two centuries ago. It opened up a new path of development by "muddling through" reforms. As is widely acknowledged by expert consultants who have toured the country on numerous missions, China does not blindly accept or follow advice from the World Bank, the International Monetary Fund, or Western countries in general. The Chinese people's courtesy toward Westerners stops in most cases at the hotel door and dinner table. As a senior budgeting scholar said, smiling, "That is smart."

Decentralization was advocated to China almost as a panacea. It sounds good on paper; in practice it is a joke. It simply does not work in the Chinese context and tradition of hierarchy, where a highly centralized unitary, top-down system has been operating for more than two thousand years. The 1993–94 taxation reform was, above all, to centralize taxing power, increasing central control over resources. Among local governments, revenues were centralized to the province more than before the reform. In the absence of open local elections, decentralization does not work. It is not equal to effectiveness in service provision. Efficiency gains stem from the informational advantage of local governments' proximity to citizens; China harvests its benefit from increasing transfers, improving human capital via education, and gradually establishing institutions.

China's rapid economic progress toward prosperity amid relatively slow (in contrast to the economic side) political progress is an apparent paradox—that such a large, poor country largely rid itself of extreme poverty without fundamentally changing its old system defies existing theories. There are many explanations; none is convincing thus far. In this sense, the new challenge brings a window of opportunities, with as many puzzles, for us to further public administration explorations. After all, the intersection between practice and theory is the source of life for public administration research.

COMPARATIVE STUDIES: CONSTRAINTS AND PARADOXES

The nonnative factor has been the norm in America. The beginning of nation building in the United States was the fruit of cross-country comparisons, traces of which are abundant in the Federalist Papers, the Declaration of Independence, and the Constitution. After World War II, when public administration was still theoretically young, the expansion of international aid to newly independent countries triggered the need for comparative studies (Riggs 1976), for "a set of generalized principles independent of their peculiar national setting" (Dahl 1947, 8), because as a science, public administration would not be sufficient if its theory applied only to a particular country. Comparative public administration peaked in the late 1960s and early 1970s, and since has continued at a much lower level (Heady 1987).

The original intent of comparative public administration was to help Americans working in developing countries to better "transplant" U.S. administrative technologies; case studies of comparative budgeting appeared occasionally during this process. A surprise by-product was the finding that if the study includes not just foreign countries but also America, it will deepen and broaden our understanding of the U.S. system as well (Riggs 1998). Systematic comparative studies impose challenging demands on researchers in language, culture, and experience in the target countries. So far, comparative public administration has not established a widely accepted theoretical framework, thus falling short of the requirement for a science as set forth by Thomas Kuhn (1962) in his seminal book (Hou 2006).

The old view of comparative public administration was based on three false assumptions: (1) Researchers are mostly from other countries or those Americans who are interested in a specific foreign country because of their family background and personal experience; but (2) most American scholars do comparative work only after they become established, for pure curiosity or extension of their previous work; and therefore (3) the popular perception of comparative public administration is that it is less scholarly and nonmainstream.

These three false assumptions in turn contain three paradoxes about comparative public administration: (1) It is difficult to do because researchers need to have language proficiency, cultural background, and often personal ties for data and materials; thus (2) it is more difficult to do well; and (3) there may be a selection bias. Does the difficulty arise because lesser scholars, not well-qualified ones, study comparative public administration? Or it is not well done just because it is more difficult than general public administration?

TOWARD A NEW PARADIGM FOR PUBLIC ADMINISTRATION

Despite all the difficulties, globalization has made comparative public administration a promising enterprise. First, because most developing countries are open to the outside world, the necessary data are now increasingly becoming public information given that these countries are eager to join the world community and learn from the experiences of other countries. Second, the interwoven global markets and economies have converted everyone into an active part of the global community; Western scholars have enough interest and incentive to study the awakening partners. Finally, researchers for comparative United States–foreign projects are ideally those who can intuitively appreciate many subtleties between cultures. Foreigners who migrated to the West and received a systematic education there form one group; another group is formed by Westerners who have had the experience of living in a foreign country for extended periods and thus have acquired an appreciation of local affairs. Scholars of these two types are more likely to possess a third, comparative perspective from which to view seemingly familiar things.

Moving toward a new paradigm for public administration necessitates endorsing a new view of comparative public administration, which assumes: (1) Comparative public administration in the twenty-first century is equivalent to more general public administration; public administration is no longer U.S.- specific, because (2) the more general public administration seeks higher explanatory power for the whole field and its branch areas. The U.S.-specific public administration is but a special case of the more general theory. Thus, (3) comparative public administration is not the field for a small group with a foreign background or interest; it is an inherent part of the discipline. All public administration scholars need training in comparative studies and must conduct comparative work. Thereby, (4) comparative public administration merges into the mainstream as a global perspective, which will be one of the major sources of new blood for the discipline. Ultimately, (5) such endeavors are not foreign matters that fall under the responsibility of the State Department; instead, they are domestic affairs, part of the daily routine business of public administration. Internalizing or localizing the global perspective will solidly transform the field of public administration toward the new paradigm for the twenty-first century.

On the basis of this argument, it seems appropriate to declare that the time has come to reinvent public administration by moving toward a new paradigm with a newly defined comparative public administration under a global perspective. Endorsing this new paradigm will help generate generic theories with unprecedented explanatory power that will contribute toward making public administration a more solid science.

REFERENCES

Blackstone, Brian. 2008. Fed Looks to Developing Nations for Inflation Help. *Wall Street Journal*, June 27.

Dahl, Robert A. 1947. The Science of Public Administration: Three Problems. *Public Administration Review* 7, no. 1:1–11.

Heady, Ferrel. 1987. Comparative Public Administration in the United States. In *A Centennial History of the United States*, ed. Ralph Chandler. New York: Free Press.

Hou, Yilin. 2006. The Comparative Study of Budgeting and Chinese Budgeting in a Comparative Perspective. *Journal of Public Budgeting, Accounting and Financial Management* 18, no. 4:421–29.

Kuhn, Thomas. 1962. *The Structure of Scientific Revolutions.* Chicago: University of Chicago Press.

Riggs, Fred W. 1976. Comparative Administration: The U.S. Tradition. Unpublished paper, American Society for Public Administration, Washington, DC.

———. 1998. Public Administration in America: Why Our Uniqueness Is Exceptional and Important. *Public Administration Review* 58, no. 1:22–31.

A Personal Memo from a Woman Teaching Public Administration in Asia

Ora-Orn Poocharoen

I argue strongly that it is now time to once again critically rethink the field of public administration. This time it is not only about relevance to social issues—linking theory to practice, the focus of the Minnowbrook I Conference—but also about making the field truly relevant to public administration experiences around the world.[1] Public administration theories should be built from cases with different contexts. International academics should be the core group to lead the field. And the target audience should be practitioners from around the globe. I envision the field of public administration twenty years from now as a global field that is taught in every country and that offers much greater choice in international textbooks, journals, and conferences.

The field has been dominated by the U.S. experience for the past hundred years. Theories of public administration have been built on the U.S. experience, for a U.S. audience, by U.S.-based academics. This one-way influence of the United States' public administration establishment has led to domination by particular mindsets in the past thirty years, such as the New Public Management (NPM) paradigm.[2] We can only go in a new direction of global public administration by accepting that U.S.-based public administration is a subfield of public administration. The field needs to take a much broader global perspective in all areas of teaching, research, and service to the public.

WHERE WE ARE NOW

Upon graduation from university in the United States, I returned to Thailand to teach. In my course I had students read what I was taught, such as materials on politics and administration dichotomy, bureaucracy, accountability, governance, and ethics. But I soon realized the inadequacy of my knowledge about Asia's context in public administration. In one class, a midcareer student stood up to say, "Why are we learning all of these theories? These are all thoughts from the United States. They don't make sense in the Thai context."

The problem was that I was not presenting my students with theories from other parts of the world. I had not included topics relevant to Thailand, such as decentralization, corruption, and development. After this, I tried to develop cases in the Thai context. However, although the cases now focused on the local context, the theories were still from the U.S. experience.[3]

Currently, I am teaching in Singapore, where a cohort of about seventy students in the master of public administration (MPA) program represents at least twenty countries. Because there is no one dominant nationality, there is no one national context on which I am obliged to base the design of my course. Midcareer students, who come from different national settings, would not be able to relate to some debates common in the United States. For example, in China the separation between the Communist Party and the bureaucracy is not a topic of great concern, in Myanmar issues of collaboration and contracting-out make little sense under the military regime, and in Papua New Guinea the issue of total quality management might be of little use. And the list could go on.

Many academics rely on examples of course syllabi available on the internet and existing online textbooks to form course syllabi. This reliance, coupled with the long history of public administration as a field in the United States, has created an eschewed list of options available for scholars. The spread of the NPM in syllabi and courses around the world in the new millennium is a prime example. The NPM movement, which is grounded in economics, a rational approach, neoliberalism, capitalism, and market-based decision making, began with practitioners in the United States and Anglo-Saxon countries and is used in academic texts throughout the world. Most MPA courses in countries like China and Thailand would include the study of the NPM.[4] And now, moreover, although the NPM movement has faded in the original countries, alarmingly many countries around the world are just about to begin their great NPM experiment. This time lag in how U.S.-based theories are transferred to practice elsewhere usually runs ten to fifteen years.[5]

Most public administration and public policy schools have an economics orientation that focuses on the rational approach and quantitative methods, and is problem-solving oriented and aligned with the NPM movement. Not many focus on understanding problems, critical approaches, or discourse-based approaches. However, more recent debates in the field of public administration would include the perspectives of postmodernism, feminist theories of public administration, social discourses and public administration, interpretative approaches, critical theory, network theory, and so on. Managerial practices have shifted to collaborative governance, networking, and building a consensus through discourse. This will probably be the next phase in public administration. In this phase one must know the development of social sciences and be able to comprehend perspectives outside the rational, positivist, and scientific approaches of public administration.

New schools of public policy and public administration are rapidly being opened around the world. For example, more than a hundred new MPA programs have been started in China in the last ten years. Also, many prestigious public administration or public affairs master's programs, such as Syracuse University's Maxwell School and Harvard University's John F. Kennedy School of Government, have applicants with more diverse backgrounds from all around the world. Many programs outside the United States are also increasingly becoming much more international. They are more international in terms of the student body, faculty members, and direction of research. However, the textbooks and case studies that are non–U.S.-based are not being produced fast enough to meet these emerging demands. This stems from the historical developments of the field, as explained above, together with the character of academic journals and conferences, which are predominantly for U.S. audiences.[6]

WHERE WE SHOULD BE

I envision the textbooks and journals of public administration in the near future as becoming highly international. We should focus on non–U.S.-based cases and theories and print more textbooks, in English, that make sense in different regions of the world, whether in Africa, Latin America, the Middle East, or Asia. These textbooks should be theoretically focused, with ample empirical studies of cases from a diverse set of contexts.[7] Comparative work is no longer a subfield but must be considered mainstream public administration. For example, a student who would like to learn about public motivation theory should be able to find at least one book with studies that cut across many countries. And this same principle can be applied to any other midlevel theories.

It is important to emphasize that I do not mean to enhance comparative public administration as a subfield of public administration.[8] Instead, I propose making U.S. public administration a subfield and replacing it with global public administration. All along, comparative public administration was seen as a subfield, because it was conceived from a U.S.-dominated public administration perspective. This new view of the field of public administration in global perspective would have great ramifications. For example, no longer would Woodrow Wilson's paper be given so much importance, and the first textbooks on public administration would no longer be those produced in the United States in the early 1900s. The intellectual history of public administration would be taught in a global context. This would force academics to consider more historical perspectives, such as administration in different civilizations in the past and administrative practices in different political, cultural, social, and economic contexts in the present.

HOW WE GET THERE

To realize this new view of public administration as a global field, there would need to be major changes in the ways we teach and do research. In our teaching we would need to give importance to both local and nonlocal students. We have an obligation to provide diverse knowledge that does not only rely on one context. We must be able to provide examples and thoughtful insights into different contexts for different theories. We must avoid scenarios where international students come to study public administration in our institutions and then feel that they cannot apply the knowledge elsewhere. We must also train our doctoral students to be multilingual academics who are interested in different administrative systems and are comfortable doing international research.

As for our research, as a community we must foster international channels of information dissemination. Journals and conferences must be designed to answer to the international public administration community. Currently, some high-ranking journals are becoming more internationally oriented, but not most. Many universities use rankings of journals to judge the quality of publications of their faculty members. Because many of these journals are dominated by a preference for U.S.-based cases, currently it is much more difficult for cases from other countries to be accepted. For example, for a study of emergency management, the case of Hurricane Katrina is easily accepted, but the cases of Nargis in Myanmar or the tsunami in Aceh, Indonesia, will be seen as regional or comparative studies—even though, as a matter of fact, the emergency management of Nargis and the tsunami are probably more relevant to the rest of the world than Hurricane Katrina.

Hopefully, in the new global public administration, as international academic journals become ranked more highly, this would in turn force us to focus more on international research agendas, because these journals would only accept studies relevant to the global community that include cross-national cases. Similarly, international conferences would be the norm rather than the exception. Local or regional conferences would still exist but would be considered less prestigious than international ones, which would be much more vibrant.

These ideas are difficult to implement for scholars with a large domestic audience. For example, the United States has a large domestic market, which enables U.S.-based scholars to produce scholarly work only for the domestic market. Thus, if you were teaching human resources management to students who you know will work for the county or city where your university is based, then it would make no sense to teach the practice of other countries. You would also try to write articles that are directly linked to a practitioner audience in the area. Though this approach has value because it keeps the academician connected to the area-specific audience, it does not enhance the field as a whole. The same example can be given with scholars working in other large countries. For example, if you are a public administration specialist in Vietnam, Zambia, Hungary, Brazil, or any other country, if you only focus your research and ideas based on what is happening in this one country, you will miss the whole worldwide discourse on public administration. Your theories and cases, though of interest to your local group of practitioners, might not be contributing in any way to theories in the field, because what you have written might be unique to that particular country and others might have already written extensively on the same subject.

We need to better value international journals and conferences. The themes of journals and conferences should focus on theory rather than on a particular country. We can incorporate into our academic incentive systems new ways to rank publication in journals or conference attendances for tenure and promotion criteria. By doing so, more leading academics in the field would be able to function as international scholars continuously producing globally relevant knowledge. We would be agents of knowledge transfer responsible for what we teach and how it applies globally. We would be comfortable managing research projects that cross geopolitical boundaries. We would be creating knowledge that is relevant to local audiences and at the same time connected to discourses on a global scale. We would be able to produce more diverse textbooks that would be useful around the world. Only as it does these things will the field of public administration continue to be *relevant*.

CONCLUSION

I am waiting for that day to come when my midcareer MPA students are able to read and discuss cases from their own countries, are able to debate the development of the field in China versus the United States versus India, and are provided with a variety of ways to think about public administration other than U.S.-based approaches. This will be the day when I will never be asked again why we must study only certain histories and certain approaches, because I will then have many choices of texts to provide my students. This will be the day when the field of public administration will have become a coherent *global* field that has answers and can guide public administration students and practitioners in all political, social, economic, and cultural contexts. And this will be the day when we will have moved beyond the domination of specific country contexts and will have created a truly global public administration.

NOTES

1. For the literature from Minnowbrook I in 1968, see Marini 1971. For that from Minnowbrook II, see Bailey and Mayer 1992.
2. For the literature on New Public Management, see Christensen and Lægreid 2007; Lynn 2006; Dent, Chandler, and Barry 2004; McLaughlin, Osborne, and Ferlie 2002; and Barzelay 2001.
3. This experience is common in many countries—e.g., see Welch and Wong 1998, 40–49; Laohavichien 1984.
4. On China, see Wu and He 2008. As for on Thailand, this observation is based on the author's experience of teaching four years in an MPA program there.
5. This is based on the author's observation of the case on the transfer of Performance-Based Budgeting to Thailand and Malaysia from the United States. See Poocharoen 2005.

6. See Fritzen 2007.
7. A few good textbooks do exist; a recent one is Schiavo-Campo and McFerson 2008.
8. For leading literature on comparative public administration, see Riggs 1991; Heady 1995; Farazmand 1996; Jreisat 2005; and Otenyo and Lind 2006.

REFERENCES

Bailey, Mary Timney, and Richard T. Mayer. 1992. *Public Management in an Interconnected World: Essays in the Minnowbrook Tradition.* New York: Greenwood Press.

Barzelay, Michael. 2001. *The New Public Management: Improving Research and Policy Dialogue.* New York: Russel Sage Foundation.

Christensen, Tom, and Per Lægreid. 2007. *Transcending New Public Management: The Transformation of Public Sector Reforms.* Burlington, VT: Ashgate.

Dent, Mike, John Chandler, and Jim Barry. 2004. *Questioning the New Public Management.* Burlington, VT: Ashgate.

Farazmand, Ali. 1996. Development and Comparative Public Administration: Past, Present, and Future. *Public Administration Quarterly* 20, no. 3:343–64.

Fritzen, Scott. 2007. Public Policy Education Goes Global: A Multidimensional Challenge. *Journal of Policy Analysis and Management* 27, no. 1:205–14.

Heady, Ferrel. 1995. *Public Administration in Comparative Perspective.* New York: Marcel Dekker.

Jreisat, Jamil E. 2005. Comparative Public Administration Is Back In, Prudently. *Public Administration Review* 65, no. 2:231–42.

Laohavichien, Uthai. 1984. The Problems and Prospects of Public Administration in Thailand. *Asian Journal of Public Administration* 6, no. 1:46–60.

Lynn, Laurence E., Jr. 2006. *Public Management: Old and New.* New York: Routledge.

Marini, Frank, ed. 1971. *Toward a New Public Administration: The Minnowbrook Perspective.* Scranton, PA: Chandler.

McLaughlin, Kathleen, Stephen P. Osborne, and Ewan Ferlie. 2002. *New Public Management: Current Trends and Future Prospects.* London: Routledge.

Otenyo, Eric E., and Nancy S. Lind. 2006. *Comparative Public Administration : The Essential Readings.* Boston: Elsevier.

Poocharoen, Ora-Orn. 2005. Comparative Public Management Reform: Cases of Policy Transfer in Thailand and Malaysia. PhD diss., Syracuse University.

Riggs, Fred W. 1991. Guest Editorial: Public Administration: A Comparativist Framework. *Public Administration Review* 51, no. 6:473–77.

Schiavo-Campo, Salvatore, and Hazel M. McFerson. 2008. *Public Management in Global Perspective.* Armonk, NY: M. E. Sharpe.

Welch, Eric, and Wilson Wong. 1998. Public Administration in a Global Context: Bridging the Gaps of Theory and Practice between Western and Non-Western Nations. *Public Administration Review* 58, no. 1:40–49.

Wu, X., and J. He. 2008. Paradigm Shift in Public Administration: Implications for Teaching in MPA Programs. Paper presented at Interdisciplinary Approach in Policy Studies and Education Conference, Chungnam National University, Chungnam, South Korea.

PART III

COLLABORATION

The year Minnowbrook III was held, the term "collaboration" was widely used in all sectors—public, private, nonprofit—and was especially prevalent in the public administration and public management literature. Collaboration means to co-labor to achieve common goals, often working across boundaries and in multisector and multiactor relationships. Collaboration is based on the value of reciprocity. Collaboration is more than mere cooperation, as figure III.1 demonstrates.

Collaborative public management describes the process of facilitating and operating in multiorganizational arrangements to solve problems that cannot be solved easily by single organizations (O'Leary et al. 2008). There has been significant growth in both the theoretical and empirical literature describing the nature and breadth of collaboration and integration across the varieties of networks.

There are six main reasons for the increase in collaborative public management, both in the literature and in practice. First, most public challenges are larger than one organization, requiring new approaches to address public issues. Second, outsourcing has grown in volume and dollar amount. By its very nature, outsourcing is a collaborative endeavor between the public agencies awarding the contract and the organizations performing the contracted tasks. Third, changes in the regulatory environment have led to initiatives at the federal and state levels, which provide incentives for cooperation, collaboration, and information exchange. Fourth, improving the effectiveness of publicly funded programs is encouraging public officials to identify new ways of providing public services. Fifth, technology is helping government agencies and personnel share information in a way that is integrative and interoperable, with the outcome being a greater emphasis on collaborative governance. And sixth, citizens are seeking additional avenues for engaging in governance, which can result in new and different forms of collaborative problem solving and decision making.

In collaborative public management, solutions often transcend the position of any one participant. As Salamon (2005) put it, this "shifts the emphasis from management skills and the control of large bureaucratic organizations to enablement skills, the skills required to engage partners arrayed horizontally in networks, [and] to bring multiple stakeholders together for a common end in a situation of interdependence." The theme of collaboration played a prominent role at Minnowbrook III. The chapters in part III excerpt the papers presented there that best exemplify cutting-edge thinking about this important topic.

←---→

Cooperation.........Coordination.........Collaboration......... Service Integration

Figure III.1 Cooperation, Coordination, Collaboration, and Service Integration
Sources: Selden, Sowa, and Sandfort 2002; Keast, Brown, and Mandell 2007

The first chapter by Soonhee Kim explores "Collaborative Leadership and Local Governance." Kim argues that we need more theories and models that examine collaborative leadership in local governance in global communities. Her research agenda is informed by her experiences of living, learning, and working in Korea and receiving her graduate training and then teaching in the United States. She has been engaged in detailed case study research focusing on collaborative leadership capacity in several Asian countries and frames the local governance needs and challenges that are increasingly shaped by globalization. These challenges are prompted by different countries' experiences with decentralization, nested in a multitude of political, economic, historic, and social contexts. She provides insights into the competencies of collaborative leadership needed at the local government level.

In the next chapter, "The 'New Emergency Management': Applying the Lessons of Collaborative Governance to Twenty-First-Century Emergency Planning," Michael McGuire, Jeffrey L. Brudney, and Beth Gazley examine the modern challenges of collaborative emergency management. The chapter, primarily focused on the United States, provides a brief historical look at how the U.S. federal system has become increasingly involved in emergency management. The authors then turn to the complex emergency management environment that today includes a more diverse set of actors than ever before, stronger professional norms and training, greater attention to performance measurement, and tensions between command-and-control approaches to leadership relative to collaborative approaches to problem solving and service delivery. McGuire, Brudney, and Gazley present a research agenda for the future that includes greater attention to issues of predisaster planning, training, and partnering; capacity and preparation; and theory building. The new emergency manager, as both a generalist and specialist, leads a call for new approaches to training and research that addresses building innovative and responsive core competencies, evaluating performance, and modeling emergent and innovative frameworks and tools of emergency management.

In the next chapter, Theresa A. Pardo, J. Ramon Gil-Garcia, and Luis F. Luna-Reyes tackle the idea of "Collaborative Governance and Cross-Boundary Information Sharing: Envisioning a Networked and IT-Enabled Public Administration." They describe the intricate relationship between a networked, information technology (IT)–enabled public administration and the emerging complex global and regional problems in governance in both developed and developing countries. They note that a networked, IT-enabled public administration emerges not only as a possible vision for a prepared public administration of the future but also as a necessary one. They discuss transnational public problems and the need to share and integrate information from diverse sources, as well as to increase the level of informational interoperability among decision makers. Collaboratively governed networks for problem solving are needed to achieve these goals in multiorganizational settings. They conclude by discussing the new and complex challenges for public servants while framing the decision challenges of IT adoptions as being based not only on what public organizations do now but also on what they are likely to do in the future.

The final chapter in this part by Kirk Emerson and Peter Murchie concerns "Collaborative Governance and Climate Change: Opportunities for Public Administration." Former U.S. vice president Al Gore, a Nobel Peace Prize recipient for his campaign to curb global climate change, shared the prize with the United Nations Intergovernmental Panel on Climate Change, whose head, Rajendra Pachauri, told leaders at a climate conference in Indonesia that a well-documented rise in global temperatures has coincided with a significant increase in the concentration of carbon dioxide in the atmosphere. In this chapter, Emerson and Murchie explain the climate change challenges facing the public manager, including decision making under conditions of uncertainty and the need for multisectoral, organizational, and stakeholder collaboration to appropriately frame the question in order to engage in effective problem solving. They analyze what climate change challenges will demand in the public administration areas of budgeting and finance, service provision, planning, resource management, emergency management, contracting, personnel management, and other areas. And they call for a significant transformation of government and governance concerning climate change. Such change, they argue, can only take place through the collaborative efforts of multiple stakeholders with their own goals and motivations, but whose individual missions are aligned with the overall goal of combating the negative effects of climate change.

Taken as a whole, these four chapters provide a flavor of the collaboration agenda that emerged at Minnowbrook III. Public managers find themselves not solely as unitary leaders of unitary organizations but instead as collaborators across boundaries, often with a multitude of partners and stakeholders. The emphasis on local government as a key pivotal player in collaborating to meet our societies' most pressing public policy challenges now and in the future is a significant theme. Equally important is the skill set needed by the collaborative public manager. This issue of training was discussed by both scholars and practitioners. It includes skills in negotiation, facilitation, conflict management, consensus building and collaborative problem solving, big-picture thinking, strategic thinking, interpersonal communications and team building, boundary spanning, managing complexity and interdependency, and managing roles, accountabilities, and motivations. Taken as a whole, collaboration as a research, training, and practice agenda is a formidable challenge for the field of public administration. It will affect the future of public management, public administration, and public service around the world.

REFERENCES

Keast, Robyn, Kerry Brown, and Myrna Mandell. 2007. Getting the Right Mix: Unpacking Integration Meanings and Strategies. *International Public Management Journal* 10, no. 1:9–33.

O'Leary, Rosemary, Beth Gazley, Michael McGuire, and Lisa Blomgren Bingham. 2008. Public Managers in Collaboration. In *The Collaborative Public Manager: New Ideas for the Twenty-first Century*, ed. Rosemary O'Leary and Lisa Blomgren Bingham. Washington, DC: Georgetown University Press.

Salamon, Lester. 2005. Training Professional Citizens: Getting beyond the Right Answer to the Wrong Question in Public Affairs Education. *Journal of Public Affairs Education* 11, no. 1:7–9.

Selden, Sally Coleman, Jessica E. Sowa, and Jodi Sandfort. 2002. The Impact of Nonprofit Collaboration in Early Child Care and Education on Management and Program Outcomes. *Public Administration Review* 66, no. 3:412–25.

Collaborative Leadership and Local Governance

Soonhee Kim

The growing body of public administration literature on governance and governance networks suggests that there are new dimensions of connectedness, interdependency, complexity, uncertainty, and collaborative public management within government agencies, and even across international boundaries (Kettl 2000; Klijin 2008). Specifically, in the context of globalization, decentralization, and economic development, local government leaders depend on the support and understanding of citizens and businesses in order to conduct and effectively implement government policies.[1] Although the public administration literature mentions the importance of collaborative leadership in local governance (Hambleton and Gross 2007; Kim 2009; Morse and Buss 2008; Bingham and O'Leary 2008; U.S. Agency for International Development 2000), there are few quantitative or qualitative studies on the subject. Additional research is needed to better explain the nature of local government collaboration and effective leadership that builds democratic local governance with the values of citizen empowerment, transparency, and accountability.

This chapter explores the need for developing theories and models to better explain collaborative leadership in local governance in global communities, especially in the context of a new global economy, in which the different political, economic, historical, and social contexts of decentralization affect local governance networks, capacity, and collaboration strategies. In addition, the chapter proposes several competencies in fundamental collaborative leadership development for local governance.[2]

LOCAL GOVERNANCE AND COLLABORATION

Local governments face challenges related to economic development and community building in the new environment of decentralization, globalization, and urban economic development. This new environment also provides opportunities and challenges for urban government leaders to initiate new programs or adapt existing rules to their local context in order to build a management capacity that strengthens economic development, transparency, and accountability in local governance (Hambleton and Gross 2007; Kim 2009). Scholars have recognized these new forms of urban governance in the era of globalization that actively engage with local, national, international, and global economic concerns (Hambleton and Gross 2007; Kim 2009; Lo and Yeung 1996; Wei and Li 2002).

Furthermore, public–private partnerships, the roles of nongovernmental organizations (NGOs), and volunteer activities are expanded under the collaboration-based strategy for enhancing openness and citizen participation in local governance (Kim 2009). The demands of social development and decentralization also influence citizens' expectations of local government responsiveness, transparency, and accountability. For example, regarding urban development projects at the local level, citizens and community organizations have expressed their interest in transparency, accountability, and a more participatory approach to the decision-making process within local government (U.S. Agency for International Development 2000; Transparency International and United Nations Human Settlements Program 2004). Given the ongoing engagement of external actors in local governance, it is crucial to develop the elements of leadership competency in ways that enhance local governance capacity.

Collaboration is generally conceptualized as a strategy for increasing the value that a single organization is able to create on its own. Huxham (1996, 7), focusing on the advantages of collaboration, defines it as "a positive form of working in association with others for some form of mutual benefit." Other scholars have found that local government leaders in global communities identify and implement various interorganizational collaborations that contribute to successful economic development, social development, and democratic governance initiatives at the local level (Hambleton and Gross 2007; Kim 2009). Accordingly, effective public leadership is essential to the performance of ongoing projects that involve intergovernmental collaboration (e.g., national, subnational, and local), interagency collaboration within a government, intersectoral collaboration (e.g., public–private partnerships), and international collaboration (e.g., foreign direct investment, and international knowledge exchanges among local governments related to best practices for innovation).[3]

COMPETENCIES OF COLLABORATIVE LEADERSHIP IN LOCAL GOVERNANCE

On the basis of several case studies of local governments (Kim 2009), I propose eight fundamental competencies necessary for local governments to build collaborative leadership capacity. First, local government leaders must establish a clear vision and a set of goals for local governance that are shared with and articulated to stakeholders, both internal (e.g., senior management and employees) and external (e.g., citizens, community organizations, local, national and international NGOs, private corporations, and other governments). As a result, local government management capacity will be strengthened, which will generate political support from the citizenry and engender a sense of involvement and contribution among employees and local stakeholders.

Second, moreover, collaborative leadership demands innovation, creativity, and flexibility to adopt multiple frames for enhancing management capacity. Local government leaders need to encourage stakeholders to be creative and innovative as they develop new ideas and tools for enhancing local governance capacity. These could include partnerships among local businesses, universities, and local governments, as well as citizen coalitions for enhancing transparency and accountability in local governance.

Third, collaborative leadership must be strongly committed to creating conditions and consequences that support and sustain merit systems and strong performance for human resources management. Local government leaders must recognize that the management capacity necessary for collaboration to carry out an organization's mission and vision is dependent on the competency, professionalism, and innovativeness of its workforce. Furthermore, local government leaders can establish human resources management systems to recognize and reward the accomplishments of teams, divisions, and community members that help improve management practices for collaborative local government projects.[4] The performance of local civil servants who contribute to enhancing government effectiveness and accountability in local governance can, therefore, be evaluated and rewarded.

Fourth, collaborative leadership is important for enhancing transparency in local governance. Information and knowledge sharing across functional units and data sharing across heterogeneous information systems within the government are required by interagency collaboration in order to effectively manage the disclosure of government information to the public. Interagency collaboration is also important for supporting transparent government operations, integrating processes, facilitating management, streamlining workflow, and improving service quality, information technology adoption, and effectiveness.

Fifth, collaboration among central and local governments—both vertically and horizontally—is essential to ensure sufficient resources, avoid duplication, and deliver coherent action in a range of crucial areas, such as local tax systems, auditing systems, and human resources management. Furthermore, government leaders need to identify potential opportunities in the legislative and regulatory frameworks of central and local governments and make sure that the necessary management capacity is in place to facilitate and promote government performance and accountability.

Sixth, local government leaders must ensure that employees clearly understand the importance of interdivisional and intergovernmental collaboration and cooperation in building local government capacity. To establish proper management procedures, local government leaders must identify the organizational values prioritized by the majority of citizens and public agencies. It is also important to work with local news media to promote shared local governance values, including openness, citizen participation, accountability, and integrity. This can help generate support from local stakeholders and the citizenry.

Seventh, through partnerships and collaboration with local NGOs, volunteers, and citizens, local governments can overcome resource limitations. Collaborative processes for enhancing the value of transparency and accountability in local governance may help produce social capital and shape a community culture of inclusiveness and diversity, which can facilitate citizen participation and openness. Furthermore, local government leaders must collaborate and build networks with other local governments, both within the country and in other countries, to share best practices for local governance capacity building.

Eighth and finally, local leaders need to promote collaboration by assessing government performance and sharing this information with the public. Collaborative leadership can create a culture of organizational learning and managing for results by encouraging employees to analyze past successes and failures. It can suggest how the organization can apply those findings to further improve government performance and accountability in local governance.[5] The effective management of collaborative projects is not only driven by leaders' abilities to focus the government on its missions; it is also driven by mechanisms for tracking activities and performance relative to overall objectives (Ingraham, Joyce, and Donahue 2003). These three key components must be considered by local government leaders when adopting result management systems:

1. *Clear objectives for specific applications related to local government collaborative projects:* Clearly defined goals and objectives for a specific collaborative project may enhance the ownership of the project by all the participants (Newell, Reeher, and Ronayne 2007).
2. *Performance measurement (i.e., output and outcomes) of the applications:* To adopt performance management systems for collaborative projects, local government leaders need to develop various performance measurements by different collaboration types and models, such as networks, intergovernmental agreements, and public–private ventures.
3. *Continuous performance monitoring:* Local government leaders need to share performance evaluation reports with major stakeholders and citizens in the local community and solicit feedback.

CONCLUSION

In-depth empirical studies of collaborative leadership and local governance need to be conducted in the future. These studies can be based on the collaborative leadership competencies proposed in this chapter, which include diverse perspectives from local government leaders, local and international NGOs, community organizations, and the citizenry. Scholars in the field of local governance and public administration should take advantage of the multiple perspectives of organizational theories, including resource dependence theory, social networks, and ecological, institutional, organizational learning, strategic action, and transaction-cost approaches. These additional theoretical and comparative studies of collaborative leadership and local governance in a national or international context can improve our knowledge of the global–local connection, and can foster strategies to enhance local governance leadership capacity in global communities.

NOTES

1. Although there are various definitions of governance, local governance can be defined as the mechanisms, processes, and institutions through which citizens and groups articulate their interests, exercise their legal rights and obligations, and mediate their differences at the local level (United Nations Development Program 2001).
2. This chapter draws on the conclusions in the author's book *Management Strategy for Local Governments to Strengthen Transparency in Local Governance* (Kim 2009), which includes several case studies on urban local government in China and South Korea.
3. I am not proposing collaborative leadership as the only leadership style for local government leaders. To engage in various local governance challenges with high complexity and uncertainty, local government leaders should develop versatile leadership styles (Kaplan and Kaiser 2003) along with the collaborative leadership style.
4. Although it is difficult to measure employee performance related to effective collaboration processes and outcomes, job analysis and training programs for public managers facilitating collaborative projects should be carefully analyzed for developing performance appraisal systems that emphasize the skills, knowledge, and abilities of effective collaborators. In addition, collaboration participants may provide their feedback on public managers' performance regarding effective relationship building (Mandell and Keast 2008).
5. Managing for results is defined as "the dominant mechanism by which leaders identify, collect, and use the performance information necessary to evaluate the institution's success with respect to key objectives, to make decisions, and to direct institutional actions" (Ingraham, Joyce, and Donahue 2003, 22).

REFERENCES

Bingham, Lisa Blomgren, and Rosemary O'Leary, eds. 2008. *Big Ideas in Collaborative Public Management.* Armonk, NY: M. E. Sharpe.

Hambleton, Robin, and Jill Simone Gros, eds. 2007. *Governing Cities in a Global Era: Urban Innovation, Competition, and Democratic Reform.* New York: Palgrave Macmillan.

Huxham, Chris. 1996. Collaboration and Collaborative Advantage. In *Creating Collaborative Advantage,* ed. C. Huxham. Thousand Oaks, CA: Sage.

Ingraham, Patricia W., Philip G. Joyce, and Amy Kneedler Donahue. 2003. *Government Performance: Why Management Matters.* Baltimore: Johns Hopkins University Press.

Kaplan, Robert. E., and Robert. B. Kaiser. 2003. Developing Versatile Leadership. *MIT Sloan Management Review* 44, no. 4:19–26.

Kettl, D. F. 2000. *The Global Public Management Revolution: A Report on the Transformation of Governance.* Washington, DC: Brookings Institution Press.

Kim, Soonhee. 2009. *Management Strategy for Local Governments to Strengthen Transparency in Local Governance.* Seoul: United Nations Project Office on Governance.

Klijin, Erik-Hans. 2008. Governance and Governance Networks in Europe: An Assessment of Ten Years of Research on the Theme. *Public Management Review* 10, no. 4:505–26.

Lo, Fu-Chen, and Yue-Man Yeung. 1996. *Emerging World Cities in Pacific Asia.* Tokyo: United Nations University Press.

Mandell, Myrna P., and Robin Keast. 2008. Evaluating the Effectiveness of Interorganizational Relations through Networks: Developing a Framework for Revised Performance Measures. *Public Management Review* 10, no. 6:716–31.

Morse, Ricardo S., and Terry F. Buss, eds. 2008. *Innovations in Public Leadership Development.* Armonk, NY: M. E. Sharpe.

Newell, Terry, Grant Reeher, and Peter Ronayne. 2007. *The Trusted Leader: Building the Relationships That Make Government Work.* Washington, DC: CQ Press.

Transparency International and United Nations Human Settlements Program. 2004. *Tools for Support Transparency in Local Governance: Urban Governance Toolkit Series.* Berlin: Transparency International.

United Nations Development Program. 2001. *Country Assessment in Accountability and Transparency (CONTACT).* New York: United Nations. www.undp.org/governance/contactcdrom-contents/CONTACT_site/UNDP_manual/CONT01_Ch02.pdf.

U.S. Agency for International Development. 2000. *Decentralization and Democratic Local Governance Programming Handbook.* Technical Publication Series, Center for Democracy and Governance, Bureau for Global Programs, Field Support, and Research. Washington, DC: U.S. Agency for International Development.

Wei, Yehua Dennis, and Wangming Li. 2002. Reforms, Globalization, and Urban Growth in China: The Case of Hangzhou. *Eurasian Geography and Economics* 43, no. 6:459–75.

The "New Emergency Management"

Applying the Lessons of Collaborative Governance to Twenty-First-Century Emergency Planning

Michael McGuire, Jeffrey L. Brudney, and Beth Gazley

The organization and delivery of an effective public response in emergencies and disasters constitutes one of the most important public policy and management topics of the twenty-first century. As the scope of disasters grows, public officials find they must rely on a wider and more inclusive set of public and private partners, encompassing federal, state, and local levels of government, as well as businesses and voluntary organizations. Yet post hoc studies of disaster response suggest that the ability of emergency managers to marshal resources and cooperate across sectors and levels of government often lags behind public expectations of a coherent, organized disaster response (Comfort 2006; GAO 2008). In this chapter we describe the evolution of the field toward the "New Emergency Management." We introduce this term to characterize both the opportunities afforded by these new resources and the challenges that confront public managers as they integrate hierarchical emergency management systems, operating on principles of command and control, with a decentralized, privatized network of voluntary services found on the ground. We suggest that related research on collaborative governance and collaborative public management can thus offer the field of emergency public service many useful lessons. As well, we anticipate that studies of emergency management can inform the broader field of public management.

THE EVOLVING FIELD OF EMERGENCY MANAGEMENT

Over the last two centuries governments at all levels in the American federal system have become increasingly involved in emergency management. This involvement can be described in terms of eras through which the field has progressed, each era suggesting a distinctive role for the emergency manager.

Reactive Fragmentation, 1803–1950

Emergency "management" began as emergency "response" to natural disasters. This reactive approach called upon agencies in the vicinity of the affected area to respond to the disaster with assistance from a central government. The reactive approach ended in 1803 after a fire in Portsmouth, New Hampshire, destroyed more than 130 buildings. In that year Congress passed an act to assist the city in recovering from the fire. The act was the first piece of national disaster legislation in the United States and marked the first time that the federal government had made its resources available to subnational governments for disaster response activities (Drabek 1991). Some 128 pieces of legislation were passed between 1803 and 1950 (Canton 2007), resulting in a fragmented and reactive system of administration. A notable event in this period was the chartering by Congress of the American Red Cross in 1900 to play a major role in disaster relief.

This *emergency manager as reactor* phase was characterized by an emphasis on responding to and recovering from disasters with little attention given to planning. The manager was typically the lead first responder, for example, the fire chief, police chief, and/or a public works official. Although the role of government expanded during this period, responsibility for the management of disasters was not yet an explicit position held by a public official. But the creation and staffing of this position would change dramatically during the Cold War.

Command and Control, 1950–79

The advent of nuclear weapons and the threat of enemy attack on the civilian populace led to a shift in the emphasis in emergency management toward national security and civil emergency preparedness in the Cold War era (Drabek 1985). The passage of the Civil Defense Act and the Federal Disaster Act in 1950 defined a framework for federal, state, and local governments in disaster preparedness (Canton 2007). Throughout the 1950s and 1960s a number of federal, state, and local agencies were created or reorganized to address the threat of both conventional and nuclear attack. This paradigm shift toward a civil defense approach utilized what has come to be known as the traditional model of emergency management, also referred to as "the civil defense, command and control, bureaucratic, or emergency services perspective of disaster response and recovery operations" (McEntire 2007, 483).

This *emergency manager as controller* phase focused on a strict hierarchical response to disasters. Many emergency managers had military or law enforcement backgrounds and were therefore "comfortable with hierarchy, . . . centralized decision making, and a reliance on standard operating procedures" (McEntire 2007, 88). Despite its fit to the period, the hierarchical model had weaknesses that made this approach lose favor. For example, its focus on disasters resulting from war precluded the profession from adequately addressing the more common occurrence of natural disasters. This traditional approach also neglected the important roles that citizens and private entities played in emergency management activities.

Professionalization, 1979–2000

The professionalization era is tied very closely to the year 1979, when President Jimmy Carter consolidated the many fragmented programs addressing civil defense and disaster-related organizations into a single agency, the Federal Emergency Management Agency (FEMA). The formation of this federal agency provided the foundation for similar agencies in state and local governments. The name of the federal agency conveyed for the first time the recognition that a single field—emergency management—existed, with new responsibilities that could be formalized in this emerging profession. In 1978, a National Governors Association report described a new, comprehensive, systems-based approach to emergency management activities comprising four management phases: (1) mitigation activities that reduce or eliminate risks to persons or property or lessen the consequences of disaster; (2) preparedness, or efforts to identify threats, determine vulnerabilities, and specify required resources to mitigate risk; (3) response activities, which address the short-term effects of a disaster, including actions to save lives, protect property, and meet basic human needs; and (4) recovery, which develops and executes service and site restoration plans for affected communities and the reconstitution of government operations (McGuire and Silvia 2010).

We refer to the period from 1979 to the end of the twentieth century as the *emergency manager as professional era*. A profession emerges as occupational groupings mature, and there is an identifiable body of technical knowledge. Members begin to identify with colleagues in other jurisdictions, develop standards of conduct and professional practice, and establish minimum professional qualifications and experience (Stanley and Waugh 2001). Thomas Drabek has argued that the "single most significant societal change that has most altered community preparedness has been the increased professionalization of local emergency managers" (quoted by Canton 2007, 63). This era was characterized by several realizations:

- Emergency managers will be confronted by many different types of human and natural disasters.

- Hierarchical, command-and-control relationships are often impossible in response situations involving different levels of government, organizations, and the public.
- Standard operating procedures rarely hold up during times of crisis because no emergency plan can account for all contingencies.
- The public is a resource and will respond to disasters, whether it is invited or not (Neal and Phillips 1995).
- Planning and response cannot be undertaken by just one agency, or even one sector.

The move from "controller" to "professional" developed out of necessity during this period as several major human and natural disasters struck the United States, with effects that extended beyond a single jurisdiction. As a result, FEMA provided grants for subnational governments, created a system that focused on planning and response, and established a national training center that helped to standardize knowledge (Canton 2007). Thus, the role of the emergency manager was greatly expanded, formalized, and professionalized at the turn of the twentieth century.

THE NEW EMERGENCY MANAGEMENT FOR THE TWENTY-FIRST CENTURY

The New Emergency Management is developing to address the challenges of the twenty-first century. This *emergency manager as manager era* emphasizes these circumstances and performance expectations:

- an even more diverse set of actors spanning the business, nonprofit, and governmental sectors;
- a stronger professional understanding of how to manage public service delivery through horizontal, networked, or privatized means;
- increasing professionalization of the emergency management function;
- more attention to the proper administration of resources, human and otherwise, involved in planning for and responding to emergencies;
- greater attention to performance measurement;
- the need to establish a balance between the strengths of the command-and-control model with the strengths of the professional model; and
- the availability of emergency management training.

The new emergency manager is very much a generalist manager to the same extent as any other public-sector official who leads an agency, but is also a specialist in the field of emergencies and disasters, a boundary spanner, and a creator of networks. This broad and demanding job description calls for a new approach to training. Yet Waugh (2000, 3) remarks that although "emergency management is the quintessential government role, public administrationists have been slow to address the organizational and policy issues that define the role and the practice of emergency management." In this chapter we take a step toward filling this gap by describing the responsibilities of the new emergency manager and proposing a research agenda to guide further development of the field.

PROFILING THE NEW EMERGENCY MANAGEMENT

The New Emergency Management both expands and invigorates the role of the public manager. Fulfilling this role effectively will require greater professionalization on the part of the manager, including more training and education. In particular, the new emergency manager will need to develop and hone skills in undertaking collaborative activity and network management, involving emergent groups as well as the private sector, balancing command-and-control principles with collaboration, and planning and preparing for disasters.

Professionalization

More than two decades ago one emergency manager asserted that emergency managers should "get as much training as [they] can from whatever source" (Drabek 1987, 242). The New Emergency Management is grounded even more strongly in continuous training and education. In light of the relative failings of some emergency management procedures during the 2001 terrorist attacks and Hurricane Katrina in 2005, the need for training and education is evident. Avenues for training and education in emergency management and/or homeland security are widely available. They include certification training programs or stand-alone courses offered by state government, federal training through the Emergency Management Institute (the training and education arm of FEMA), professional training through the International Association of Emergency Managers, and formal education through more than two hundred college and university degree programs.

Collaborative Activity and Network Management

Intersectoral and intergovernmental collaboration is particularly important in emergency management, given the necessity of involving large groups of autonomous actors using limited public resources. Much has been written about the need for emergency management organizations to operate collaboratively (Moynihan 2005; Waugh and Streib 2006; Wise 2006). Emergency managers face extraordinary challenges, in both number and severity, which out of necessity require a more collaborative approach to service planning and delivery (Kapucu 2006b). The field of emergency management offers plentiful examples of both formal and informal joint efforts, ranging from formal purchase-of-service agreements and memoranda of understanding, to planning grants, joint exercises, and semicoordinated efforts (Gazley 2008). The new emergency manager, like many other public managers, acts as both a facilitator and broker of resources and a controller, operating in both a horizontal and vertical collaborative environment to implement all phases of emergency management.

Emergency management requires "professionals at various levels to work across boundaries, plan and negotiate future activities, and communicate during operations to resolve unanticipated problems" (Wise 2006, 315). The emergency manager thus works with an extensive range of organizations. FEMA, its equivalent state-level office, and other local governments command the most attention from a local emergency manager (McGuire and Silvia 2010). A second level of service provision occurs through voluntary organizations active in disaster (VOADs), including most prominently the American Red Cross, but also the Salvation Army, Citizens Corps, shelters, and hospitals (Brudney and Gazley 2009). Numerous case studies demonstrate a third tier of activity involving nonemergency voluntary organizations such as faith-based, social service, and civic organizations (Kapucu 2006a; Kendra and Wachtendorf 2003; Kiefer and Montjoy 2006; Drabek and McEntire 2003). In short, the emergency manager is also a network manager.

Emergent Groups

One myth that has been debunked in the emergency management literature is that individuals and groups will panic during disasters (Fischer 1998). To the contrary, research suggests that disaster victims are "more immune to the 'disaster syndrome,' more innovative in resolving their problems, and more resilient in the wake of severe challenges than they are given credit for" (Drabek and McEntire 2003, 99). A related assumption is that the volunteers who respond to disasters emerge spontaneously, in ways that cannot be anticipated. Such behavior would make it difficult or impossible to manage or coordinate these volunteers and to integrate their contributions with other organized emergency management efforts.

However, organizations have also found it possible—and useful—to organize and prepare volunteer resources well in advance of an untoward event (Brudney and Gazley 2009). With foresight, emergent groups and volunteers can support larger disaster management efforts by undertaking predisaster activities such as planning for a possible evacuation during a hurricane, preparing for expected eventual flooding, or training a neighborhood in how to respond to an earthquake. The organization of volunteers is rarely institutionalized, leaving groups to self-organize, sometimes without formal guidance. The new emergency manager must learn how to work successfully with the many paid and unpaid personnel who step forward to help, and to communicate needs effectively in order to manage the supply of human and material resources. Emergency managers are often involved in these coordination activities, despite a lack of formal training in volunteer management.

Private-Sector Involvement

The unprecedented scope of recent natural and human disasters in the United States demonstrates that the involvement of both businesses and voluntary organizations in response and recovery is sometimes a necessity. Some organizations (e.g., VOADS) are involved in routine planning and response, but most are involved on a temporary, ad hoc, or spontaneous basis (e.g., lay citizens or volunteers from churches, shelters, or social service organizations). The former are more likely to have relevant experience and/or formal training than the latter, and are also more likely to be involved in response as well as recovery efforts.

For-profit businesses are also involved as sources of supplies, funds, and personnel. One of the most active current areas of emergency planning on a national scale is a cross-sector effort led by the American Red Cross to involve corporate partners in coordinating their financial, human, and material resources in the event of a large-scale disaster. Like volunteers and voluntary organizations, the business community is part of disaster planning and response in the New Emergency Management.

Balancing Command and Control with Collaboration

The questions "How collaborative?" and "With whom?" address the dilemma faced by emergency managers as they operate in a partially networked, partially hierarchical environment that succeeds only through coordinated action but depends on diverse and autonomous resources that may be hard to control through directives. The laws and policy mandates emerging from Washington reflect the challenge of reconciling these two very different approaches to policy implementation. Although their language and scope have slowly expanded to recognize the greater breadth of emergency management, it remains an open question whether they provide the necessary direction and training to those responsible for coordinating emergency management.

A key directive guiding emergency planning and response is the National Response Framework. The framework is based on the idea that "communities, tribes, States, the federal government, . . . nongovernmental organizations, and the private sector should each understand their respective roles and responsibilities, and complement each other in achieving shared goals. . . . These responsibilities include developing plans, conducting assessments and exercises, providing and directing resources and capabilities, and gathering lessons learned" (U.S. Department of Homeland Security 2008, 4). The National Response Framework complements and builds upon the National Incident Management System, both of which are formal attempts to "sort out" intergovernmental and intersectoral collaboration in natural and human disasters. At the core of this process is the issue of when and how to coordinate multiple organizations toward a shared goal. A common but somewhat paradoxical structure for coordination is the Incident Command System, which "assumes that crises require a network of responders, but that these networks should be managed by a hierarchy" (Moynihan 2008, 205). The use of these "interorganizational hierarchies" reflects the practitioner sentiment that collaboration in emergency management is the result of a centralized authority in the form of an incident commander.

Emphasis on Planning and Preparedness

In addition to the growth in the number of potential institutional participants, the extent and scope of community-level planning have increased in the twenty-first century. The New Emergency Management is characterized not only by a focus on the four phases of emergency management but also by a heightened emphasis on the centrality of *preparedness* to effective response and recovery. Perry and Lindell (2003, 338) define emergency preparedness as "the readiness of a political jurisdiction to react constructively to threats from the environment in a way that minimizes the negative consequences." The primary mechanism for enhancing emergency preparedness is emergency planning. Jurisdictions often develop a written plan, but a plan is merely a snapshot in time, whereas engaging the community, including the government agencies and nongovernmental organizations involved in the response network, is a dynamic process. Plans are important; planning is indispensable.

The National Response Framework notes that planning (1) allows jurisdictions to influence the course of events in an emergency by determining in advance the actions, policies, and processes that will be followed; (2) guides other preparedness activities; and (3) contributes to unity of effort by providing a common blueprint for activity in the event of an emergency" (U.S. Department of Homeland Security 2008, 71). We suggest that planning has at least four additional potential benefits: the ability to resolve potential disagreements in advance of an emergency, strengthen mutual goals, build trust in partners, and identify and address gaps in resource needs. Mitigation plans, emergency operations/response plans, recovery plans, and continuity plans cannot possibly account for all contingencies, as was shown during the terrorist attacks of September 11, 2001. However, the emergency manager in the twenty-first century must learn appropriate planning principles and guidelines for developing and maintaining an effective planning process.

EVALUATING THE NEW EMERGENCY MANAGEMENT: A RESEARCH AGENDA

The New Emergency Management raises research questions with both practical and theoretical implications that warrant greater attention. First, much of the past emergency management research has focused on post-hoc studies of emergency response (Brudney and Gazley 2009). Despite this research emphasis on response, the need for a more proactive system of preparation for emergency is underscored in congressional reports, which acknowledge that "80 percent . . . of the problem lies with planning" (Chertoff 2005). Thus, more attention should be paid to understanding the efficacy of planning systems, training, and partnership-building efforts.

Next, from a practical perspective, the emergency management field needs to address issues of capacity and preparation. The broad collaborative framework within which the New Emergency Management operates involves more than the "usual suspects" (Brudney and Gazley 2009). The entry of new actors raises vital questions about the effectiveness of coordination strategies, systems, and also about managerial attitudes toward collaboration. Are emergency managers trained to work with these new actors? How committed are they to seeking new partners to assist in disaster planning and response, and what policy guidance do they need? How prepared are they to work within this broader network, and how familiar and comfortable are they with the different norms and cultures that they will encounter? Do their offices have the budget, background, and training to involve these groups on an ongoing basis?

With respect to theory building, we suggest several avenues of further exploration to address questions important not only to the field of emergency management but also to the broader study of collaborative public management. Emergency management provides an ideal test case for exploring multiple hypotheses about the initial conditions for collaboration derived from the management literature (McGuire and Silvia 2010). Emergency management has all the ingredients, complexities, and challenges of networked and collaborative public management—but also some distinct circumstances given the interest of government, the nonprofit sector, and private sector in making emergency management more effective. We pose three questions (though not an exhaustive set) to understand the management capacities, both human and institutional, that support effective emergency management.

First, what are the professional competencies of the new emergency manager? McGuire (2008) has found that public managers who possess higher levels of training and whose responsibilities are focused solely on emergency management engage in more collaborative activity than their counterparts. Research models should be expanded to understand the nature of this training, including not only the role of formal emergency management education but also the nature of experiential learning in developing emergency management expertise. Gazley and Brudney (2007) have found, generally, that public and nonprofit managers with cross-sectoral experience are more willing to engage in collaborative opportunities, a finding that could be tested in emergency management. Given the current focus of this field on response rather than planning, we also suggest that researchers examine not only the outcomes of community *responses* to natural and human disasters but also the outcomes of joint exercises, drills, and other planning activities that occur *to prepare for* disasters. In addition, panel or time series studies of vulnerable communities over time might reveal how joint planning may subsequently support a more effective response should emergencies or disasters occur.

Second, how do we evaluate the performance of the New Emergency Management? We suggest that both the scope and the depth of emergency management performance evaluation be expanded. With respect to scope, many multidimensional models exist to understand management capacity and performance as a function of human, financial, infrastructural, and technical resources (Christensen and Gazley 2008; Ingraham, Joyce, and Donahue 2003). Issues of accountability, human capital, governance, and culture are all relevant to emergency management, but there are also gaps in present scholarship. Further, emergency management research must be targeted to be useful. Accountability and governance, for example, must be understood in the context of the National Response Framework as a set of operational guidelines. Culture and values can be addressed by assessing the willingness of emergency responders to work with members of the voluntary sector who may not share their particular background, training, or mindset.

Third, how do we model the New Emergency Management? With regard to depth, little scholarship has been devoted to understanding the extent of joint planning with multiple partners. The lessons and theoretical frameworks (e.g., social network analysis) that have been applied to emergency response can also be tested on planning systems to understand the qualitative dimensions of these joint efforts. We suggest that many of the theories developed from the extensive scholarship on collaborative public management can and should be tested in the context of emergency management to understand their applicability and relevance. At the same time, findings from emergency management might enhance the broader collaboration field. In the present era of the *emergency manager as manager*, this official is equally a public manager. As we anticipate the considerable challenges that emergency management will face in the new century, we look forward to building our knowledge of effective planning and preparation to inform not only emergency management but also collaborative public management.

REFERENCES

Brudney, Jeffrey L., and Beth Gazley. 2009. Planning to Be Prepared: An Empirical Examination of the Role of Voluntary Organizations in County Government Emergency Planning. *Public Performance and Management Review* 32, no. 3:372–99.

Canton, Lucien G. 2007. *Emergency Management: Concepts and Strategies for Effective Programs*. Hoboken, NJ: John Wiley & Sons.

Chertoff, Michael. 2005. Testimony before the House Select Bipartisan Committee to Investigate the Preparation for and Response to Hurricane Katrina, Hearing on Hurricane Katrina: The Role of the Department of Homeland Security, October 19. Available at http://katrina.house.gov.

Christensen, Robert K., and Beth Gazley. 2008. Capacity and Public Administration: Analysis of Meaning and Measurement. *Public Administration and Development* 28:265–79.

Comfort, Louise. 2006. The Dynamics of Policy Learning: Catastrophic Events in Real Time. Paper presented at annual meeting of National Association of Schools of Public Affairs and Administration, Minneapolis, October 19–21.

Drabek, Thomas E. 1985. Managing the Emergency Response. *Public Administration Review* 45, no. s1:85–92.

———. 1987. *The Professional Emergency Manager: Structures and Strategies for Success.* Boulder: Institute of Behavioral Science, University of Colorado.

———. 1991. The Evolution of Emergency Management. In *Emergency Management: Principles and Practice for Local Government,* ed. Thomas E. Drabek and Gerard J. Hoetmer. Washington, DC: International City/County Management Association.

Drabek, Thomas E., and David A. McEntire. 2003. Emergent Phenomena and the Sociology of Disaster: Lessons, Trends, and Opportunities from the Research Literature. *Disaster Prevention and Management* 12, no. 2:97–112.

Fischer, Henry W., III. 1998. *Response to Disaster: Fact versus Fiction and Its Perpetuation,* 2nd ed. Lanham, MD: University Press of America.

GAO (U.S. Government Accountability Office). 2008. *FEMA Should Take Action to Improve Capacity and Coordination between Government and Voluntary Sectors.* Report GAO-08-369. Washington, DC: US Government Printing Office.

Gazley, Beth. 2008. Beyond the Contract: The Scope and Nature of Informal Government-Nonprofit Partnerships. *Public Administration Review,* 68, no. 1:141–54.

Gazley, Beth, and Jeffrey L. Brudney. 2007. The Purpose (and Perils) of Government-Nonprofit Partnership. *Nonprofit and Voluntary Sector Quarterly,* 36, no. 3:389–415.

Ingraham, Patricia W., Philip G. Joyce, and Amy Kneedler Donahue. 2003. *Government Performance: Why Management Matters.* Baltimore: Johns Hopkins University Press.

Kapucu, Naim. 2006a. Interagency Communication Networks during Emergencies: Boundary Spanners in Multiagency Coordination. *American Review of Public Administration* 36, no. 2:207–25.

———. 2006b. Public–Nonprofit Partnerships for Collective Action in Dynamic Contexts of Emergencies. *Public Administration* 84, no. 1:205–20.

Kendra, James M., and Tricia Wachtendorf. 2003. Elements of Resilience after the World Trade Center Disaster: Reconstituting New York City's Emergency Operations Center. *Disasters* 27, no. 1:37–53.

Kiefer, John J., and Robert S. Montjoy. 2006. Incrementalism before the Storm: Network Performance for the Evacuation of New Orleans. *Public Administration Review* 66, no. s1:122–30.

McEntire, David A. 2007. *Disaster Response and Recovery.* Hoboken, NJ: John Wiley & Sons.

McGuire, Michael. 2008. The New Professionalism and Collaborative Activity in Local Emergency Management. In *The Collaborative Public Manager: New Ideas for the Twenty-first Century,* ed. Rosemary O'Leary and Lisa Blomgren Bingham. Washington, DC: Georgetown University Press.

McGuire, Michael, and Chris Silvia. 2010. The Effect of Problem Severity, Managerial and Organizational Capacity, and Agency Structure on Intergovernmental Collaboration: Evidence from Local Emergency Management. *Public Administration Review* 70, no. 2:279–88.

Moynihan, Donald P. 2005. *Leveraging Collaborative Networks in Infrequent Emergency Situations.* Washington, DC: IBM Center for the Business of Government.

———. 2008. Combining Structural Forms in the Search for Policy Tools: Incident Command Systems in U. S. Crisis Management. *Governance* 21, no. 2:205–29.

Neal, David M., and Brenda D. Phillips. 1995. Effective Emergency Management: Reconsidering the Bureaucratic Approach. *Disasters* 19, no. 4:327–37.

Perry, Ronald W., and Michael K. Lindell. 2003. Preparedness for Emergency Response: Guidelines for the Emergency Planning Process. *Disasters* 27, no. 4:336–50.

Stanley, Ellis M., and William L. Waugh, Jr. 2001. Emergency Managers for the New Millennium. In *Handbook of Crisis and Emergency Management,* ed. Ali Farazmand. New York: Marcel Dekker.

U.S. Department of Homeland Security. 2008. *The National Response Framework.* Washington, DC: U.S. Department of Homeland Security.

Waugh, William L., Jr. 2000. *Living with Hazards, Dealing with Disasters: An Introduction to Emergency Management.* Armonk, NY: M. E. Sharpe.

Waugh, William L., Jr., and Gregory Streib. 2006. Collaboration and Leadership for Effective Emergency Management. *Public Administration Review* 66, no. s1:131–40.

Wise, Charles R. 2006. Organizing for Homeland Security after Katrina: Is Adaptive Management What's Missing? *Public Administrative Review* 66, no. 3:302–18.

Collaborative Governance and Cross-Boundary Information Sharing

Envisioning a Networked and IT-Enabled Public Administration

Theresa A. Pardo, J. Ramon Gil-Garcia,
and Luis F. Luna-Reyes

Within the context of emerging complex global and regional problems, a networked and information technology-enabled public administration emerges not only as a possible vision for a prepared public administration of the future but also as a necessary one. To be prepared for this future, we must understand how information is shared among government and nongovernmental organizations as they come together in collaboratively governed national and international networks to provide public services and solve complex public problems. The new generation of public servants must understand the changing landscape of society and the new and emerging complexity underlying the traditional role of the public administrator. They must understand the tensions between traditional bureaucratic organizations and emerging network forms of organizations as sometimes competing and sometimes complementary mechanisms for carrying out the role of government. They must become facile working within these tensions. They must understand the need for and power of collaborative approaches and the important role of information and technology in both creating conditions for collaboration and as the object of multiorganizational collaborative efforts. Overall, they must learn anew what capabilities must exist within networks of organizations to ensure that government programs serve citizens effectively within this evolving context.

This chapter contributes to the exchange of knowledge about the future of public administration by presenting a view that considers global trends in public management. In particular, we outline five topics for inclusion in the public administration classroom of the twenty-first century: postbureaucracy and organizational networks, information technologies and interorganizational information integration, collaborative governance and interoperability, the internationalization of public administration, and analytical tools to deal with complex problems. As a backdrop we first discuss some relevant global trends starting with the emergence of postbureaucratic organizations and interorganizational networks. E-government and cross-boundary information sharing are then introduced as part of the new context of public administration. Collaborative governance and interoperability as core capabilities of the public administration of the twenty-first century are then introduced. We then bring the focus back to the importance of collaboration and information sharing in transnational public problems and international cooperation and characterize the need for new capability in working across the boundaries of organizations, governments, regions, and nations. Finally, drawing on this discussion, we outline the five topics of critical importance for inclusion in today's public administration classroom to fully prepare students to work in the government of the twenty-first century.

POSTBUREAUCRATIC ORGANIZATIONS AND INTERORGANIZATIONAL NETWORKS

Traditional hierarchies, as described by Max Weber almost a century ago, are increasingly challenged by the new and complex public problems of the twenty-first century. Many of the services traditionally provided by single government agencies are now the responsibility of complex interorganizational networks, which sometimes include multiple government agencies, as well as nonprofit and private-sector entities. These interorganizational networks challenge the traditional hierarchical government organization, creating new pressure to innovate in the structure of institutions (Gascó 2004). They challenge government managers and researchers alike to understand the creation of networks of public and/or private organizations that need to share what they know about a specific problem domain and to work together in new ways to respond to those problems (Fountain 2001; Snyder and de Souza Briggs 2003; Zhang, Cresswell, and Thompson 2002).

Because the relational features of networks greatly enhance the ability to transmit and learn new knowledge, network organizations are particularly apt for circumstances that require efficient, reliable information and for the exchange of commodities with value that cannot be easily measured. These relational features are central to the sharing of both knowledge about a specific policy domain, such as public health, pollution control, and city management. For example, to effectively respond to the emergence of West Nile Virus, most U.S. states had to create new networks of organizations to work collaboratively and to share information both about the disease itself and about how each entity would work as part of the network response effort (Gil-Garcia, Pardo, and Burke 2009; Burke et al. 2010).

The traditional view of a manager's role is changing as well, and thus is focusing less on command and control and more on facilitation and coordination. In network forms of organizations, managers engage in team leadership, and thus they negotiate integrated efforts across boundaries, inspire and promote organizational learning, and conceive and facilitate change (Hales 2002, 55). Managerial roles as well as the authority for decision making are not necessarily possessed by individuals who hold formal managerial positions but can be assumed by different stakeholders belonging to the network. In this context, an individual needs to act as a "broker" whose role is to build and maintain a network, to negotiate agreement and commitment, and to present new ideas.

ICTs AND CROSS-BOUNDARY INFORMATION INTEGRATION

The central role of information and communication technologies (ICTs) in the formation and operation of government programs and services, and in network forms of government, requires public administrators to understand more fully the nature of this role. In particular, network coordination requires effective ways to share information and knowledge from different sources. Perhaps because of its usefulness for this particular purpose, the use of ICTs in government, or what some called "electronic government," has become a prominent strategy for government administrative reform (Fountain 2001; Gil-Garcia and Luna-Reyes 2006; Kraemer and King 2003).

Some of the most promising benefits from the use of ICTs in government are associated with the integration of information across organizational boundaries (Caffrey 1998; Cresswell et al. 2004; Dawes 1996; Gil-Garcia et al. 2005). In this way, interorganizational information integration has become a priority in many public programs and services, particularly those managed by a network of organizations. The capability to share information across boundaries has become "one of the basic goals of modern information management in government" (Rocheleau 2006, 308). The most common case of information sharing in the public sector is information transfer between two government agencies; however, holder and receiver entities can also be governmental units, for-profit organizations, nonprofit organizations, or individuals.

Information sharing and information integration have often been considered as closely related but distinct concepts (Gil-Garcia, Pardo, and Burke 2008). Though "information sharing" is the transference of information from one agency to another, "information integration" not only involves the transference of information but also a translation and transformation of information preparing it for new, joint uses (Carlile 2004). Both concepts converge when an integrated information system provides more comprehensive data sources shared among contributors in a Network (IACP 2000; U.S. Department of Justice 2003).

One way to think about integration is to focus on the social aspects, specifically on information sharing relationships among individuals and organizations

(Gil-Garcia, Pardo, and Burke 2008). Researchers who focus on social aspects pay attention to such issues as mutual trust, which alleviates conflict and reduces transaction costs and risks between information sharing entities (Dirks and Ferrin 2001; Lane and Bachmann 1998; Thompson 2003). In contrast, other researchers focus on the technical aspects of information integration. Jhingran, Mattos, and Pirahesh (2002, 555) propose that information integration is a process wherein "complementary data are either physically or logically brought together, making it possible for applications to be written to and make use of all the relevant data in the enterprise, even if the data are not directly under their control." A few scholars combine these two aspects and recognize the sociotechnical nature of information sharing (Gil-Garcia, Pardo, and Burke 2008).

COLLABORATIVE GOVERNANCE

Collaboration among networked organizations to provide services to citizens requires effective ways to share information, certainly, but new kinds of coordination principles and mechanisms are also necessary. The new kinds of capabilities and resources require changes in policy, management, and technology; however, recent research highlights that these changes necessary for cross-boundary information sharing are among the most complex, deeply functional, and institutional changes organizations face (Fountain 2001). To achieve these changes, collaboration must be institutionalized as a principle and facilitated as a management strategy within our traditional bureaucratic institutions as well as within our networks. Governance provides ways to institutionalize coordination and to establish decision-making processes that work in multiorganizational settings such as networks of government agencies.

Unfortunately, though leaders have the unique power to make these changes, experience shows that the policy environments they have created, or in many cases inherited, often limit the capability of governments to share authority, to collaborate, and to jointly and strategically manage enterprise-wide initiatives. To change this, government executives must understand the link between their policy decisions and the capability of governments to create the systems necessary to share information across boundaries and building effective networks. The government of the future must have the capability to engage in collaborative efforts including decision making.

INTEROPERABILITY

We define "interoperability" as the mix of policy, management, and technology capabilities (e.g., governance, decision making, resource management, standards setting, collaboration, and ICT software, systems, and networks) needed for a network of organizations to operate effectively. Government interoperability emphasizes the ability of network members to share knowledge and other resources *in addition to* creating interoperable technological infrastructures. Moreover, it also assumes that governments must take responsibility for improving their own capabilities in order to be effective partners with other nongovernmental network organizations (e.g., private corporations, nonprofit groups, and academic institutions).

Interoperability is a key enabler of the information and knowledge sharing necessary for ICTs to deliver on the promise of government transformation. Interoperability is not an end in itself; interoperable systems deliver value to the public through the opportunities they enable. Value is realized through the creation of connected systems that facilitate better decision making, better coordination of government programs, and enhanced services to citizens and businesses. The following list provides examples of how interoperable systems can contribute to the creation of public value:

- *Democracy and citizen participation:* (1) Access to information for engaging in political action activities such as advocating, debating, and voting. (2) Creation of new electronic forums for citizen engagement.
- *Transparency and trust:* Access to integrated, holistic views of government resources and operations create transparency and build citizen trust in and allegiance to government.
- *Citizen and business services:* (1) Information about benefits and services available to citizens that they would otherwise be unaware of or unable to acquire. (2) Easy-to-use, accessible, and geographically distributed citizen and business services (multichannel access to payment services and applications and forms).
- *Government management and economic development.* (1) Internal, modernized infrastructure for government operations to support the back-office processing of citizen and business services and provide information for financial transparency and accountability. (2) Improved government-wide coordination for responding to crisis such as natural disasters or public health problems. (3) Facilitating the creation of consumer–producer networks and alternative, more sustainable markets such as fair trade.
- *Government long-term strategy and policymaking:* (1) Consolidated databases and data warehouses provide information to support strategic planning and policymaking in government. (2) Stimulate local, regional, and national economies by attracting investments through an enhanced reputation for improved government operations and new and innovative services available to citizens and businesses.

Realizing the value of interoperability requires government managers to be prepared to face three distinct but related problems:

1. Creating interoperability requires potential network members to invest in changes to internal organizational arrangements, practices, and

technical resources in response to an externally agreed-upon set of priorities.

2. Creating interoperability requires potential network members to create new, and in some cases, renew cross-boundary relationships; recognize and manage the challenges to network formation including the creation or modification of a sufficient legal framework to enable new ways of sharing resources including money and data, as well as barriers to communication, collaboration, and issues such as divergent policies and practices.
3. Participants seeking to improve interoperability for coordination across government agencies do not know in advance all the tools or resources needed or how to acquire them, or precisely what configuration of old and new capabilities will be needed to achieve initiative goals (Cresswell et al. 2004).

Agency leaders are often well versed in creating the necessary environment to build interoperable systems within their organizations. However, creating cross-agency interoperability requires the kind of authority only available at the topmost levels of governments, particularly when the goal is to create interoperable systems across government levels or national boundaries. Though public officials at all levels play important roles in a wide range of interoperability efforts, government leaders alone have the power to alleviate the institutional constraints that impede these potentially transformative, but highly complex, enterprise-wide interoperability initiatives.

FIVE TOPICS OF CRITICAL IMPORTANCE FOR THE PUBLIC ADMINISTRATION STUDENT OF THE TWENTY-FIRST CENTURY

Working through collaborative mechanisms across networks of organizations to create policy, management, and technology infrastructures that enable governments to work together and with other organizations in the interests of citizens is the challenge that lays ahead for public administration professionals of the future. To be prepared to deal with these new challenges, we argue that students of public administration need to acquire a new set of skills and capabilities. Five topics of critical importance for inclusion in the public administration classroom are outlined here. These topics provide a frame of reference for evolving our collective efforts to fully prepare students to work in the networked and information technology (IT)–enabled government of the twenty-first century.

Postbureaucracy and Organizational Networks

Public administration students must learn how to operate within the new interorganizational environment of the public sector. To fuel this effort we must first develop more understanding about this emerging form, and in particular how networks and hierarchies work together in the governmental context. More research on how networks and hierarchies work together in carrying out traditional service delivery in new and innovative ways is needed. Case studies that explore the role of networks across a range of policy domains and levels of government are necessary. These case studies should highlight the challenges of network formation and operation, in particular as it relates to creating new governance capability. They could be used to discuss the role of public policy in enabling and constraining the ability of governance agencies to operate fully as network organizations.

For example, current resource allocation models tend to limit the ability of networks to share or blend resources toward a common interest. Further, case studies could be used to show the critical and shifting role of executive authority and leadership in network forms of organizations. Cases from across policy domains, such as public health and human services, would illustrate how some of the characteristics of network formation and operation may be universal, whereas others are more context specific. Students must understand these differences and be prepared to work within each form, as well as to bridge them.

Information Technologies and Interorganizational Information Integration

The complexity of creating interoperability to support information sharing across organizational boundaries increases with the number of boundaries crossed, the number and type of information resources to be shared, and the number of technical and organizational processes to be changed or integrated. To create an IT-enabled public administration, students of public administration must be exposed both to the complexities introduced when boundaries are crossed and also to the dynamic nature of the conditions that create these complexities. They must be provided with opportunities to understand capability for success in the use of technology and information integration as comprising the collective and sometimes complementary capabilities of the organizations involved.

How networks of organizations individually and collectively leverage their capabilities to manage their technology and information resources matters. Students must understand the complexity of cross-boundary information sharing, the opportunities to create public value, and the limitations of technology innovations, as well as the factors that determine the capability of government agencies to deploy a technology infrastructure that enables information sharing and integration across the boundaries of organizations. Finally, students must learn to ask questions about public value and to employ mechanisms for identifying and monitoring sources of value within the context of interorganizational information-sharing networks.

Collaborative Governance and Interoperability

The distinctions outlined above between capabilities are critical to understanding the complexity common to many collaborative governance and interoperability efforts. Students of public administration must be exposed to the concepts of collaborative governance if they are to be effective when operating within networks as well as creating the conditions in which networks succeed. Understanding the factors that influence governance within networks is necessary. Orienting students to the potential complementary roles that organizations can play in building information-sharing capability and learning to identify and leverage those strengths is also necessary. Organizations that are highly capable in collaborating and communicating may have limited information policy and technology capability. Research and case studies outlining the dynamic and complementary nature of capability within networks as a backdrop for creating collaborative governance can provide a foundation of knowledge here.

Collaborative governance and information sharing come at a high price; if value is not delivered through the investments being made in management, policy, and technology capabilities, then this same governance structure must be capable of halting or redirecting investment efforts. Students must be aware of the issues of IT investment decision making and planning, and of the mechanisms through which these decisions are made.

Transnational Problems and the Internationalization of Public Administration

Despite significant advances in knowledge about governmental collaboration within the context of a single country, we still know little about the factors influencing governmental collaboration across borders. Research in this domain is clearly scarce, and an analysis of the interactions of political, economic, and cultural contexts and the information needs of cross-border interoperable systems is largely missing. Creating an IT-enabled public administration requires us to consider how networks that bridge the borders of countries create collaborative governance and information-sharing capability. Case studies of international efforts, such as cross-border airshed management initiatives in the United States–Mexico and United States–Canada border regions, are necessary to support this process. Other cases related to border security, international trade, mobile workforces, and public health provide similar opportunities.

Reaching out beyond the traditional framework of the public administration curriculum to engage scholars from the fields of public health and education might provide additional case examples of how governments are collaborating across borders to connect systems and share information. Faculty and students need to engage in comparative and transnational studies of government information sharing and other efforts across borders to provide new knowledge about this phenomenon. Drawing on the experiences of the United States, the European Union, and other regional integration efforts will provide students with insights into how collaborative governance efforts have created sustainable capability for interoperability and information sharing.

Analytical Tools for Dealing with Complex Problems

Building understanding of complex problems requires the use of relevant analytical tools and the development of models of both problems and possible solutions. Moreover, it is always possible to find more than one technical solution when a network of organizations collaborates to face a complex problem. In this way, analytical tools are also required to compare and decide among alternative solutions. To create an IT-enabled public administration for the twenty-first century, students need to be exposed to such analytical tools and models that help them to understand complex problems, recognize the characteristics and dynamics of organizational networks, and devise alternatives and choose the most appropriate one. Students need to develop tool kits made up of a mix of qualitative and quantitative methods, as well as modeling methodologies.

The analytical tools applied at the Center for Technology in Government and the State University of New York at Albany's Rockefeller College of Public Affairs and Policy to facilitate interorganizational teams to develop solutions to public problems include process models, capability assessments, social network analysis, multiattribute decision tools, judgment analysis, simulations, and system prototypes. These tools have been found to support a focus on issue articulation, the identification of solution strategies, and the analysis of alternatives, including public value assessments. Case studies dealing with problem analysis and decision strategies are critical to facilitating an understanding of the tools and methods. Through these hands-on experiences, students will build the knowledge necessary to apply the tools in real situations. Further research on the use of these analytical tools and modeling methodologies in the context of interorganizational and international groups is needed.

CONCLUSION

A quotation from a U.S. local government public health official characterizes the public administration environment in this way: "While we can't predict future challenges, we know they will be there. We know they will be difficult, surprising in complexity, and growing in frequency and severity." The next generation of public servants must understand the changing landscape of society and the new and emerging complexity underlying the traditional role of the public administrator. Creating capability for collaborative governance and cross-boundary information sharing to enable governmental transformation and response efforts is part of this emerging role. Additional research on this new landscape and the underlying complexity surely will be necessary as we move forward, but new attention to these challenges, ideas, tools, and techniques in the classroom is needed now if we are to adequately prepare students to lead in the networked and IT-enabled public administration of the twenty-first century.

NOTE

A previous version of this chapter was presented at the Minnowbrook III Conference, Lake Placid, New York, September 5–7, 2008. The authors thank Anthony Cresswell, Sharon Dawes, Brian Burke, and Hyuckbin Kwon for their valuable contributions to the research on which this chapter is based, and Anna Raup-Kounovsky for her valuable help in copy-editing the last version of this chapter. This work was partially supported by the U.S. National Science Foundation under Grant 37656 and Grant ITR-0205152, and by Mexico's National Council of Science and Technology (Consejo Nacional de Ciencia y Tecnología, CONACYT) under Grant I0110/127/08 and Grant SEP-2004-C01-46507. Any opinions, findings, and conclusions or recommendations expressed in this material are those of the authors and do not necessarily reflect the views of the National Science Foundation or CONACYT.

REFERENCES

Burke, G. Brian, Chris M. Wirth, Theresa A. Pardo, Amy D. Sullivan, Hyuckbin Kwon, and J. Ramon Gil-Garcia. 2010. Moving beyond Hierarchies: Creating Effective Collaboration Networks for West Nile Virus Biosurveillance in Oregon. In *The Practice of Strategic Collaboration: From Silos to Action*, ed. Dorothy Norris-Tirrell and Joy A. Clay. Oxford: Taylor and Francis.

Caffrey, L. 1998. *Information Sharing between and within Governments*. London: Commonwealth Secretariat.

Carlile, P. R. 2004. Transferring, Translating, and Transforming: An Integrative Framework for Managing Knowledge across Boundaries. *Organization Science* 15:555–68.

Cresswell, A. M., D. S. Canestraro, J. R. Gil-García, T. A. Pardo, and C. Schneider. 2004. Inter-Organizational Information Integration: Lessons from the Field. Paper presented at 65th National Conference of American Society for Public Administration, Portland.

Dawes, S. S. 1996. Interagency Information Sharing: Expected Benefits, Manageable Risks. *Journal of Policy Analysis and Management* 15, no. 3:377–94.

Dirks, K. T., and D. L. Ferrin. 2001. The Role of Trust in Organizational Settings. *Organization Science* 12:450–67.

Fountain, J. E. 2001. *Building the Virtual State: Information Technology and Institutional Change*. Washington, DC: Brookings Institution Press.

Gascó, M. 2004. *¿Luces? Y sombras de la reforma del Estado en América Latina*. Documentos de Trabajo, Número 8. Barcelona: Institut Internacional de Governabilitat de Catalunya.

Gil-Garcia, J. R., and L. Luna-Reyes. 2006. Integrating Conceptual Approaches to E-Government. In *Encyclopedia of E-Commerce, E-Government and Mobile Commerce*, ed. M. Khosrow-Pour. Hershey, PA: Idea Group.

Gil-Garcia, J. R., T. A. Pardo, and G. B. Burke. 2008. Conceptualizing Inter-Organizational Information Integration in Government: A Comprehensive and Empirically Grounded Definition. Unpublished manuscript.

———. 2009. Executive Involvement and Formal Authority in Government Information-Sharing Networks: The West Nile Virus Outbreak. In *Public Sector Leadership:*

International Challenges and Perspectives, ed. Jeffrey Raffel, Peter Leisink, and Tony Middlebrooks. Cheltenham, U.K.: Edward Elgar.

Gil-Garcia, J. R., C. Schneider, T. A. Pardo, and A. M. Cresswell. 2005. Inter-Organizational Information Integration in the Criminal Justice Enterprise: Preliminary Lessons from State and County Initiatives. In *Proceedings of the 38th Hawaiian International Conference on System Sciences*. Los Alamitos, CA: IEEE Computer Society Press.

Hales, C. 2002. "Bureaucracy-Lite" and Continuities in Managerial Work. *British Journal of Management* 13:51–66.

IACP (International Association of Chiefs of Police). 2000. Toward Improved Criminal Justice Information Sharing: An Information Integration Planning Model. www.theiacp.org/documents/pdfs/Publications/ cjinfosharing.pdf.

Jhingran, A. D., N. Mattos, and H. Pirahesh. 2002. Information Integration: A Research Agenda. *IBM Systems Journal* 41, no. 4:555–62.

Kraemer, K. L., and J. L. King. 2003. Information Technology and Administrative Reform: Will the Time after e-Government Be Different? Paper presented at Heinrich Reinermann Festschrift, Post-Graduate School of Administration, Speyer, Germany.

Lane, C., and R. Bachmann. 1998. *Trust within and between Organizations: Conceptual Issues and Empirical Applications*. Oxford: Oxford University Press.

Rocheleau, B. A. 2006. *Public Management Information Systems*. Hershey, PA: Idea Group.

Scholl, H. J., and R. Klischewski. 2007. E-Government Integration and Interoperability: Framing the Research Agenda. *International Journal of Public Administration* 30: 889–920.

Snyder, W. M., and X. de Souza Briggs. 2003. *Communities of Practice: A New Tool for Government Managers*. Washington, DC: IBM Center for the Business of Government.

Thompson, G. F. 2003. *Between Hierarchies and Markets: The Logic and Limits of Network Forms of Organization*. New York: Oxford University Press.

U.S. Department of Justice. 2003. Alabama Justice Information Pilot Project Guidance. http://it.ojp.gov/manage/files/SW-Alabama-Justice.pdf.

Zhang, J., A. M. Cresswell, and F. Thompson. 2002. Participants' Expectations and the Success of Knowledge Networking in the Public Sector. Paper presented at annual conference of Americas Conference on Information Systems, Dallas.

Collaborative Governance and Climate Change

Opportunities for Public Administration

Kirk Emerson and Peter Murchie

Collaborative governance integrates structures for decision making, deliberative processes, leadership, and information to resolve and manage difficult public policy problems. Collaborative governance presents alternative and complementary approaches to engaging multiple interests from the public, private, and civic spheres to work toward more robust and durable solutions. Advocates of collaborative governance suggest that stakeholders will be able to share their diverse interests, become better informed, and become more invested in mutually beneficial joint solutions. Those solutions are understood to go beyond what any one entity or sphere could accomplish individually by generating synergy and leveraging resources.

The future challenges posed by climate change are global in scale and will be significant in the United States. There is emerging consensus that we need to limit warming to 2°C to 3°C; the 2007 Intergovernmental Panel on Climate Change report makes clear the severity of international climate change effects. In the United States, evidence is mounting: the decline of forest health and catastrophic fires; changes in planting zones and crop ranges; and the expansion of ranges of pest- and vector-borne disease species, drought, increased flooding, severe weather events, and the relocation of native Alaskan communities due to erosion and melting permafrost.

Climate change and clean energy are complex issues. Causes and effects are separated spatially (around the world) and may not be immediately evident. In addition, the issue and potential solutions remain controversial, and some groups continue to be skeptical or even combative. Solutions will likely require not only regional, state, tribal, and local action but also, and more important, household and individual engagement.

To achieve reduction goals and prepare for adaptation, diverse groups in the public and private sectors with varied interests, expertise, and resources will need to work together. Many states and local governments are already setting aggressive goals and outlining actions to reduce greenhouse gas emissions. Regional cooperation is producing, in the absence of federal policy, carbon trading or offset programs. Corporations are getting involved, and nongovernmental organizations and the international community continue to work, post–Kyoto Protocol, toward a consensus on global strategies.

COLLABORATIVE GOVERNANCE

Collaborative governance has become the new paradigm for democratic public administration (Frederickson 1991; Jun 2002; Kettle 2002). Writ large, collaborative governance characterizes processes and structures of public decision making and management that enable constructive engagement within or across public agencies, levels of government, private and public interest sectors, and the public at large. At its most ambitious, it includes "a variety of processes in which all sectors—public, private, and civic—are convened to work together to achieve solutions to public problems that go beyond what any sector could achieve on its own"(Carlson 2007, 6).

Collaborative governance is a big construct, and it embodies at least three converging strands of theory and practice in public management, negotiation, and participatory democracy developed during the past twenty years. Within public management, intergovernmental relations and public-sector network theory have given rise to concepts of horizontal network management and collaborative public management (Wright 1988; Agranoff and McGuire 2001; Kamensky and Burlin 2004). Collaborative management is defined by Agranoff and McGuire (2003, 4) as "the process of facilitating and operating in multiorganizational arrangements to solve problems that cannot be solved by single organizations."

From negotiation theory in interest-based and mutual gains bargaining (Raiffa 1982; Axelrod 1984; Fisher, Ury, and Patton 1991) have come alternative dispute resolution, conflict management, and consensus-building methods practiced in labor relations, personnel management, contracting, and environmental and public policy (Goldberg, Sanders, and Rogers 1992; Susskind, McKearnan, and Thomas-Larmer 1999; O'Leary and Bingham 2003).

Out of participatory democracy has emerged new forms of civic engagement—sometimes termed civic, shared, or participatory governance—all promoting new levels of public deliberation through different forums and at varying scales (Gastil 2000; Fung and Wright 2001; Torres 2003). This strand is often referred to as a movement that not only increases citizens' ability to exercise their voice but also aspires to improve the responsiveness of government, providing "an opportunity to embed governance systems and institutions with greater levels of transparency, accountability and legitimacy" (Henton and Melville 2005, 5).

The multifaceted provenance of collaborative governance can make it somewhat difficult to talk about and assess, because researchers and practitioners are coming at the concept from quite different theoretical, normative, and applied frames. Across these perspectives, however, a few key features or principles of practice have emerged that are designed to foster more effective engagement or deliberation, including

- providing balanced, equitable, and voluntary representation;
- creating conditions (transparency, coordination) and capacity for people to engage constructively (resources, skills, availability);
- building on, generating, and making accessible all requisite information; and
- securing committed leadership and direct links to formal decision making and implementation.[1]

This list can be expanded depending on the context of collaboration. For the purposes of this chapter, however, we are interested in effecting climate change mitigation and adaptation by marshalling all the contexts for effective governance.

CURRENT CLIMATE CHANGE CONDITIONS AND PROJECTED EFFECTS

The body of scientific research related to climate change has grown significantly in the past twenty years. Coordinated international and North American climate science funding, synthesis, and assessment have been driven by the Intergovernmental Panel on Climate Change (IPCC) and the U.S. Climate Change Science Program (CCSP). Climate change is not just a problem for the future; it is already affecting us globally and in North America. Recent studies and synthesis assessments show that human activities are the primary cause of global warming, and there is an urgency to take action now to help reduce future warming and adapt to the current level of warming (IPCC 2007).

In 2007 the IPCC found that global warming is "unequivocal" and primarily due to human emissions with significant negative global and regional effects (IPCC 2007). Global emissions of carbon dioxide are accelerating, increasing from 1.3 percent a year in the 1990s to 3.3 percent a year between 2000 and 2006 (Canadell et al. 2007). The level and magnitude of change in the future will depend on the choices we make now. We have had a 1.5°F warming and can expect to see another 1°F in the next twenty years, even if we produce no new emissions today (Trenberth et al. 2007).

In the United States, human-induced climate change is apparent. Researchers have observed temperature increases and heat waves, sea-level rise, changed precipitation patterns, regional droughts, and effects on habitat and wildlife including wildfires, retreating glaciers, early snowmelt, and altered timing and amount of river flows. These changes have effects on public health, energy, water quality and supply, transportation, agriculture, and ecosystems.

Sea-level rise, storm surges, and hurricane intensity have increased recently and are projected to continue increasing, putting coastal and island communities at greater risk (CCSP SAP 3.3 2008; CCSP SAP 4.7 2008). Clean water supply and quality will be harder to ensure in many parts of the United States due to declining snowpack and hotter, drier conditions in the Southwest. Overall, water availability and seasonal stress will lead to greater competition among agricultural, urban, industrial, and ecosystem water needs (CCSP SAP 3.3 2008).

Public health effects in the United States are also projected, with predicted increases in morbidity and mortality due to extreme heat; poor air quality; extreme weather events; the spread of infectious diseases through food, water, and pests; and rising allergy and asthma rates. All these health stressors will disproportionately affect vulnerable populations such as children, the elderly, and the poor (CCSP SAP 4.6 2008). Our energy and transportation systems will be affected with greater energy demand and energy and transportation infrastructure risk due to increased temperature variability and weather events. In the United States 27 percent of major roads, 9 percent of rail lines, and 72 percent of air and sea ports are built on land at or below an elevation of 4 feet (CCSP SAP 4.5 2008; CCSP SAP 4.7 2008).

In the United States, projected agriculture and forestry yields are mixed; in some regions the warming trends will improve crop production, while in others higher levels of warming and changed precipitation patterns will most likely have an adverse impact (CCSP SAP 4.3 2008). Our ecosystems are changing due to warming; these changes include shifts in species ranges, fire, pests, invasive plants, the timing of seasons, and animal migration. Coastal (wetlands and coral), mountain, and arctic ecosystems are particularly vulnerable to the effects of climate change (CCSP SAP 4.3 2008).

The current and projected climate effects—combined with other societal, environmental, and economic factors—present a complex challenge. Pollution, the overuse of resources, economic challenges, and other existing stressors when combined with climate change could amplify negative outcomes, especially for more vulnerable populations.

Activities that decrease our vulnerability to climate change and in some cases take advantage of them are known as "adaptation." A key goal of adaptation is to make communities and their economic systems more resilient to the kinds of stresses that are expected to occur due to climate change. Additionally, options for reducing greenhouse gas emissions are often referred to as "mitigation" and include measures such as energy efficiency, low-to-no-carbon energy (renewable, nuclear, etc.), and capturing and storing greenhouse gases (sequestration). Society must use our understanding of climate change to inform our planning and activities that will better manage climate risk. We will be required to make difficult choices concerning water allocation, economic development and urban planning, and energy investments.

Past climate patterns no longer provide an adequate guide as we plan for future water, energy, transportation, and health services.

As noted above, global average temperature has already risen 1.5°F above preindustrial levels. To avoid increasingly severe and irreversible effects will require arresting the temperature rise to no more than 3.5°F above preindustrial levels. Results from analyses suggest that stabilizing concentrations at today's level of 400 parts per million of CO_2 would give us an 80 percent chance of avoiding exceeding the 3.5°F threshold (Meinshausen 2006). It is the consensus of most climate change scientists and many policymakers that we need to stop increasing our global greenhouse gas emissions by 2015 and reduce them to 60 to 80 percent below 1990 levels by 2050 (IPCC 2007; Pew Center on Global Climate Change 2008). Achieving this stabilization will require immediate and significant reductions in emissions worldwide.

THE CHALLENGES OF CLIMATE CHANGE FOR PUBLIC ADMINISTRATION

As summarized above, the effects of global warming are upon us. Despite the absence of a national climate change policy, in the United States responses to changing climate and energy economics have permeated virtually all areas and levels of government, for example in

- budgeting (e.g., Congress quadrupled funding in 2001 for forest fire suppression in the first year of the National Fire Plan; Stephens and Ruth 2005);
- finance (e.g., the Federal Crop Insurance Corporation increased its exposure 26 times to $44 billion between 1980 and 2005 due to weather-related losses; U.S. Government Accountability Office 2007);
- service provision (e.g., twenty-two states have renewable portfolio standards for electric utilities; Rabe 2006);
- planning (e.g., the seven Colorado River Basin states signed an agreement on managing for future water scarcity on December 13, 2007);
- permitting (e.g., 150 wind energy permit applications were pending before the U.S. Bureau of Land Management as of January 2008; American Wind Energy Association 2008);
- resource management (e.g., interagency restoration efforts to save Louisiana's collapsing coastal ecosystem; U.S. Army Corps of Engineers 2008);
- emergency management (e.g., the Emergency Managers Mutual Aid Program in California supplemented disaster operations in affected locales; California Office of Emergency Services 1997);
- purchasing (e.g., the Commonwealth of Massachusetts increased its green product purchasing from $7.3 million in 1994 to more than $40 million in 2000; Resource Conservation Alliance & Government Purchasing Project 2008);

- contracting (e.g., seven states have legislated Leadership in Energy and Environmental Design certification for government buildings; U.S. Green Building Council 2008); and
- personnel management (e.g., San Francisco Bay Area counties offer multiple incentives for car and van pooling for their commuting public employees; Metropolitan Transportation Commission 2008).

Beyond such basic functional developments, eighteen states and four regional initiatives have adopted a variety of greenhouse gas (GHG) emissions reduction targets (Pew Center on Global Climate Change 2008).[2] The imperatives of climate change are inspiring (and demanding) governmental, corporate, and civic leaders to heed the call and begin to take action. Without such leadership at the international, national, state, regional, and local levels, it is unlikely that we will generate and sustain the political will needed to reduce the rate of global warming or ease the transition to altered climatic conditions. Leadership will also be needed to address the concomitant financial challenge; the costs of transforming the generation and consumption of energy will be daunting.

The challenges and understanding of *how* we govern in response to climate change are less discussed. We have identified four such challenges to public administration: (1) the need for multiple strategies and policy instruments; (2) handling increasing uncertainty; (3) integrating models of governance; and (4) addressing accountability. It is our position that the developing field of collaborative governance has much to offer and much to gain by addressing itself to climate change and to these particular challenges for public administration.

Investing in Multiple Strategies and Scales

Climate change is the ultimate global commons problem. Because of its "wicked" policy nature, there is no one solution or authority to solve it for us. There are multiple interconnected sources and effects, and multiple jurisdictions and sectors that need to be part of the solution. Climate change requires us to think *and* act globally, nationally, regionally, and locally.

There are certainly those who prefer that innovation be spurred by oil price signals, for example, instead of by fuel efficiency standards. And there are disagreements among those committed to natural gas or nuclear power or wind generation as priorities for future energy investment. There are also those who advocate more aggressive strategies driven by the worst-case GHG emissions models and those with more tempered responses. But stepping back from these science, policy, or ideological differences, there is a remarkable consensus among climate scientists and policy experts that we must work simultaneously on many fronts using a "portfolio approach" (IPCC 2007).

The challenge for public leaders and managers is to acquire a *policy versatility* to match the polyphony of policy strategies and instruments that need to be designed, analyzed, tested and refined, implemented, and monitored to maximize their collective contribution to mitigation and adaptation objectives. The intersections with other policy sectors—energy, economic development, transportation, housing, air quality, agriculture, emergency management, and resource protection—require a coordinated, multifaceted strategy.

Collaborative governance lends itself to these kinds of complex problems whereby multiple options must be sorted, prioritized, and adjusted to geographic location, socioeconomic conditions, and governing capacity. Cultivating policy versatility requires an acknowledgment of this complexity and the interconnectivity of means and ends. The interdependence of analysis and prescription points to a constructive negotiation of trade-offs and collaborative engagement across spheres of responsibility, expertise, resource control, and decision making. Particularly, as public investments must be made or forgone, more open deliberation will be demanded among public managers, experts, corporate and public interests, and private citizens.

Managing for More Uncertainty

The 2007 IPCC report from its Nobel Prize–winning team of international scientists was unequivocal about the accelerating rate of global warming and the appreciable contribution of anthropogenic GHG emissions to this trend (IPCC 2007). In a recent ABC–Planet Green–Stanford University poll, 80 percent of those surveyed reported that global warming "was probably happening," while six in ten respondents thought the causes were "mainly by things people or businesses do" (ABC–Planet Green–Stanford University 2008).

Just as we in the United States have come to accept (albeit belatedly) these all-important conclusions, we are faced with more uncertainty—uncertainty in the face of predictions for more extreme and more variable weather conditions, uncertainty about how to use the science at regional and local scales, and uncertainty concerning the extent to which policy interventions will slow the rate of global warming. Uncertainty, of course, is what public managers strive to reduce. We model problems and analyze effects to minimize risk and enable people and organizations to make choices in a more predictable environment. However, the uncertainties being created by climate change and all its reverberations through the geophysical environment and the global economy will demand more of what might be called *judicious flexibility* from public administration. Governmental decisions and actions will have to be made based on a much larger range of probabilistic outcomes. This will require cultivating a greater tolerance for risk by otherwise conventionally risk-adverse public servants, and a greater tolerance for failure. Looked at another way, we will need to view governance more as an experiment and less as a predictable machine.

Managing risk by acknowledged experimentation at high levels of investment and potential loss will not work without the trust and confidence of the public, along with corporate, nonprofit, and other organized interests. Dealing with higher levels of uncertainty requires more transparency in how and why public decisions are being made and a greater public understanding of the potential risks at hand.

Stephen Schneider (2008) of Stanford University, one of the IPCC's lead authors, argues that "the science is settled enough for policy" based on a consideration of various standards of proof in the scientific, judicial, and public arenas. What is not settled is the public's confidence in the judgment and efficacy of its political leaders and the institutions of government. To turn public administration into more open and experimental governance with respect to climate change interventions will require a reengagement with the public, private, and civic spheres.

Collaborative governance makes sense not only when there are complex problems to address but also in the context of uncertainty. When facing unknowns, we have to weigh the odds of something occurring or not, compare the risks of holding back or moving forward, make measured judgments or leaps of faith. Collaborative governance can help surface these uncertainties, generate a broader understanding of their implications, and determine the collective tolerance for risk. This requires access to and confidence in the most current and available science and a collective appreciation of its limits. Collaborative governance creates pathways for gathering, translating, and analyzing information so that it can be integrated into the deliberative process in a timely fashion.

The social, political, and informational capital built through collaborative governance allows for more experimentation to take place, and for more flexible, adaptive management to be practiced. Managing for more uncertainty through collaborative means may be a key to preparing for and activating the community resilience and adaptive capacity now being called for by advocates for climate change action.

Integrating Models of Governance

Not only will mitigating actions to reduce GHG emissions be essential, but adaptive actions to reduce transition effects on natural and social systems will be needed as well (IPCC 2007). The portfolio approach to climate change will then extend to include both the use of high-level executive authority and extensive intergovernmental and cross-sector cooperation. The challenge will be how to simultaneously advance progress through all governance structures and management approaches, both mandatory and voluntary.

As mentioned above, in the past couple of decades, public administration scholars have observed and advanced the conduct of government through horizontal networks. Coordinated network interactions help managers build social capital, leverage resources, and get work done (Agranoff and McGuire 2003). Network theory and practice incorporate a recognition of the limits of governmental action and resources, the need for cooperation beyond institutional and jurisdictional boundaries, and the potential for partnerships and collaboration. Network management requires learning how to interface with private-sector initiatives as a public partner, not just as an expert, funder, or decision maker. Communication, collaboration, and conflict resolution skills thus become increasingly essential management competencies.

Cooperation through networks of formal and informal interactions is often presented in contrast to the centralized, command-and-control approaches of earlier public administration orthodoxy, as if collaborative management were normatively the better way to govern in a democracy. This presents a false dichotomy for dealing with climate change, however. Here, we will need to better *integrate* a more assertive use of governmental authority with a more responsive model of public partnership to adequately address the climate change imperative. We will need to more effectively use the governmental power at hand to prepare, design, test, communicate, enact, and enforce mandatory climate change policies, in such a way that the initiatives of nongovernmental actors (whose compliance is needed to be successful) will be fully encouraged, not dampened.

The use of top-down, command-and-control authority is not in itself orthogonal to collaborative governance. That depends on whether the centralized authority permits and encourages flexibility and adaptation in managing implementation. Indeed, collaborative governance thrives when the authorities are clear and purposeful. Collaborative governance does not mean working somehow outside government priorities or structures in some extralegal, extraregulatory realm. Quite the contrary. In fact, the clearer the judicial, statutory, and administrative sideboards, and the more directive and firm the leadership guidance, the easier it is to focus collectively on the problem at hand and generate creative, workable options. It is when leadership flounders or is intentionally opaque that collaborative governance tends to be less productive. Collaborative governance can also enable strong leadership and policy direction by generating better-grounded and well-informed ideas upfront, broadly vetted feedback on proposed directions, and support to leverage resources and commitment to implementation.

Addressing Accountability

If, as we argue, governmental responses to climate change will need to be more assertive and more engaged, more agile and experimental, then public accountability will become an even more essential part of governing. The imperatives of climate change solutions require us to make, chart, and reward progress. Because time is of the essence, it will be important to invest in what works. Knowing when something works or does not, and why or why not, and then integrating this knowledge back into policy and program refinements or reinvestments, is essentially adaptive management. At a minimum, it requires a justifiable logic for taking specific actions, reliable and reportable information, and accountability mechanisms. Adaptive management has been most prominently practiced in the natural resource arena (Koontz et al. 2004; Scholtz and Stiftel 2005).

With so much to accomplish and so many strategies and sectors engaged, it will be a challenging task to track and adjust performance at such a scale in a timely manner. It will also be challenging to do this in a transparent way that generates and builds on broad agreement around chosen policies, necessary targets, and reporting protocols.

Accountability is an important theme and challenge for collaborative governance as well as climate change. It is often incorporated into statements of principle underscoring the need for shared responsibility as well as shared decision making in collaborative engagement (Carlson 2007; Office of Management and Budget and President's Council on Environmental Quality 2005). Shared responsibility incorporates a dual accountability to both the principles and practice of collaborative governance and to its performance in the effective delivery of, in this case, some impact on desired climate change conditions (Emerson 2008). When engaged in a shared organizational network, a community problem-solving group, or a dispute resolution process, the conveners, supporters, moderators, and participants all commit to ground rules and decision-making protocols that assure inclusion, transparency, informed consent, and so on. They commit to work toward practical recommendations, agreements, and settlements that solve collective problems. As part of that commitment, they should also be explicitly establishing agreed-upon performance targets and processes for determining their progress.

CONCLUSION

Moving from an oil economy to a sustainable economy, and from a consumer society to a conserving community, is not expected to be easy—and not likely to occur within one or two generations. But such shifts have occurred before—from whale oil to petroleum, from horse and buggy to automobile, from lamp light to rural electrification. Whether spurred by resource depletion or competitive innovation, profound changes in infrastructure, energy, transportation, agriculture, and urban development have occurred throughout the centuries.

The climate change imperative requires another such significant transformation. The costs of not reducing carbon emissions will indeed be borne around the globe and for many generations with broad-scale resource depletion, energy scarcity, environmental degradation, and economic dislocation. The greatest burdens, however, will fall disproportionately on the most vulnerable and least resilient communities (IPCC 2007). Collaborative governance may help broaden and redistribute the responsibility for responding to these challenges through shared engagement, decision making, and action.

NOTES

The authors express their appreciation for the support provided to them by the Morris K. Udall Foundation, the Policy Consensus Initiative, and the University of Arizona during the writing and presentation of this chapter.

1. For examples of sets of collaborative process principles, see Society for Professionals in Dispute Resolution 1997; Henton and Melville 2005; Office of Management and Budget and President's Council on Environmental Quality 2005; Carlson 2007.
2. Arizona, California, Connecticut, Florida, Hawaii, Illinois, Maine, Massachusetts, Minnesota, New Hampshire, New Jersey, New York, Oregon, Rhode Island, Utah, Vermont, Virginia, Washington, the Western Climate Initiative, the Regional Greenhouse Gas Initiative, the Midwest Regional Greenhouse Gas Reduction Accord, and the Climate Change Action Plan signed by New England Governors and Eastern Canadian Premiers (Pew Center on Global Climate Change 2008).

REFERENCES

ABC–Planet Green–Stanford University. 2008. Fuel Costs Boost Conservation Efforts; 7 in 10 Reducing Carbon Footprint. http://abcnews.com/pollingunit.

Agranoff, R., and M. McGuire. 2001. Big Questions in Public Network Management Research. *Journal of Public Administration Research and Theory* 11:295–326.

———. 2003. *Collaborative Public Management: New Strategies for Local Governments.* Washington, DC: Georgetown University Press.

American Wind Energy Association. 2008. *Ensuring Adequate Resources for BLM to Process Wind and Solar Energy Applications.* www.awea.org/policy/regulatory_policy/pdf/BLM_wind_permitting_initiative_backgrounder.pdf.

Axelrod, R. 1984. *The Evolution of Cooperation.* New York: Basic Books.

California Office of Emergency Services. 1997. Emergency Managers Mutual Aid Program. www.oes.ca.gov/Operational/OESHome.nsf/PDF/Emergency%20Managers%20Mutual%20Aid%20Plan/$file/Emma.pdf.

Canadell, J. G., C. Le Quéré, M. R. Raupach, C. B. Field, E. T. Buitenhuis, P. Ciais, T. J. Conway, N. P. Gillett, R. A. Houghton, and G. Marland, 2007. Contributions to Accelerating Atmospheric CO2 Growth from Economic Activity, Carbon Intensity, and the Efficiency of Natural Sinks. *Proceedings of the National Academy of Sciences* 104, no. 47:18866–8870.5.

Carlson, C. 2007. *A Practical Guide to Collaborative Governance.* Policy Consensus Initiative. Available at www.policyconsensus.org.

CCSP (U.S. Climate Change Science Program) SAP (Synthesis and Assessment) 3.3. 2008. *Weather and Climate Extremes in a Changing Climate, Regions of Focus: North America, Hawaii, Caribbean, and U.S. Pacific Islands. A Report by the U.S. Climate Change Science Program and the Subcommittee on Global Change Research,* ed. Thomas R. Karl, Gerald A. Meehl, Christopher D. Miller, Susan J. Hassol, Anne M. Waple, and William L. Murray. Washington, DC: NOAA National Climatic Data Center, U.S. Department of Commerce.

CCSP SAP 4.3. 2008. *The Effects of Climate Change on Agriculture, Land Resources, Water Resources, and Biodiversity in the United States: A Report by the U.S. Climate Change Science Program and the Subcommittee on Global Change Research,* ed. P. Backlund, A. Janetos, D. Schimel, J. Hatfield, K. Boote, P. Fay, L. Hahn, C. Izaurralde, B. A. Kimball, T. Mader, J. Morgan, D. Ort, W. Polley, A. Thomson, D. Wolfe, M. G. Ryan, S. R. Archer, R. Birdsey, C. Dahm, L. Heath, J. Hicke, D. Hollinger, T. Huxman, G. Okin, R. Oren, J. Randerson, W. Schlesinger, D. Lettenmaier, D. Major,

L. Poff, S. Running, L. Hansen, D. Inouye, B. P. Kelly, L. Meyerson, B. Peterson, and R. Shaw. Washington, DC: U.S. Department of Agriculture.

CCSP SAP 4.5. 2008. *Effects of Climate Change on Energy Production and Use in the United States*, ed. T. J. Wilbanks, V. Bhatt, D. E. Bilello, S. R. Bull, J. Ekmann, W. C. Horak, Y. J. Huang, M. D. Levine, M. J. Sale, D. K. Schmalzer, and M. J. Scott. Washington, DC: U.S. Climate Change Science Program.

CCSP SAP 4.6. 2008. *Analyses of the Effects of Global Climate Change on Human Health and Welfare and Human Systems: A Report by the U.S. Climate Change Science Program and the Subcommittee on Global Change Research*, ed. J. L. Gamble, K. L. Ebi, F. G. Sussman, and T. J. Wilbanks. Washington, DC: U.S. Environmental Protection Agency.

CCSP SAP 4.7. 2008. *Impacts of Climate Change and Variability on Transportation Systems and Infrastructure: Gulf Coast Study, Phase I—A Report by the U.S. Climate Change Science Program and the Subcommittee on Global Change Research*, ed., M. J. Savonis, V. R. Burkett, and J. R. Potter. Washington, DC: U.S. Department of Transportation.

Emerson, K. 2008. Synthesizing Practice and Performance in the Field of Environmental Conflict Resolution. In *The Collaborative Public Manager: New Ideas for the Twenty-first Century*, ed. Rosemary O'Leary and Lisa Blomgren Bingham. Washington, DC: Georgetown University Press.

Fisher, R., W. Ury, and B. Patton. 1991. *Getting to Yes*, 2nd ed. New York: Penguin Books.

Frederickson, H. G. 1991. Toward a Theory of the Public for Public Administration. *Administration and Society* 22, no. 4:395–417.

Fung, A., and Erik O. Wright. 2001. *Deepening Democracy: Institutional Innovations in Empowered Participatory Governance.* New York: Verso.

Gastil, J., 2000. *By Popular Demand: Revitalizing Representative Democracy through Deliberative Elections.* Berkeley: University of California Press.

Goldberg, S. B. , F. E. A. Sanders, and N. H. Rogers, eds. 1992. *Dispute Resolution, Negotiation, Mediation and Other Processes*, 3rd ed. New York: Aspen Law and Business.

Henton, D., and J. Melville, with T. Amsler and M. Kopell. 2005. *Collaborative Governance: A Guide for Grantmakers.* Menlo Park, CA: William and Flora Hewlett Foundation. Available at www.hewlett.org.

IPCC (Intergovernmental Panel on Climate Change). 2007. *Climate Change 2007: The Physical Science Basis. Contribution of Working Group I to the Fourth Assessment Report (AR4) of the Intergovernmental Panel on Climate Change*, ed. Solomon, S., D. Qin, M. Manning, Z. Chen, M. Marquis, K.B. Averyt, M. Tignor, and H. L. Miller. New York: Cambridge University Press. Available at www.ippc.ch.

Jun, J. S., ed. 2002. *Rethinking Administrative Theory: The Challenge of the New Century.* Westport, CT: Praeger.

Kamensky, J. M., and T. J. Burlin. 2004. *Collaboration: Using Networks and Partnerships.* Lanham, MD: Rowman & Littlefield.

Kettle, D. F. 2002. *The Transformation of Governance: Public Administration for Twenty-First Century America.* Baltimore: Johns Hopkins University Press.

Koontz, T. M., T. A. Steelman, J. Carmin, K. S. Korfmacher, C. Moseley, and C. W. Thomas. 2004. *Collaborative Environmental Management: What Roles for Government?* Washington, DC: Resources for the Future Press.

Meinshausen, M. 2006. What Does a 2°C Target Mean for Greenhouse Gas Concentrations? A Brief Analysis Based on Multi-Gas Emission Pathways and Several Climate Sensitivity Uncertainty Estimates. In *Avoiding Dangerous Climate Change*, ed. J. S. Schellnhuber, W. Cramer, N. Nakicenovic, T. M. L. Wigley, and G. Yohe. New York: Cambridge University Press.

Meinshausen, M., B. Hare, T. M. L. Wigley, D. van Vuuren, M. G. J. den Elzen, and R. Swart. 2006. Multi-Gas Emission Pathways to Meet Climate Targets. *Climatic Change* 75, no. 1:151–94.

Metropolitan Transportation Commission. 2008. 511 Rideshare. http://rideshare.511.org/rideshare_rewards/county.asp.

Office of Management and Budget and President's Council on Environmental Quality. 2005. Memorandum on Environmental Conflict Resolution, Attachment A: Basic Principles for Agency Engagement in Environmental Conflict Resolution and Collaborative Problem Solving. www.ecr.gov/Resources/FederalECRPolicy/FederalECRPolicy.aspx.

O'Leary, R., and L. B. Bingham. 2003. *The Promise and Performance of Environmental Conflict Resolution.* Washington, DC: Resources for the Future Press.

Pew Center on Global Climate Change. 2008. *A Look at Emissions Targets.* www.pewclimate.org/what_s_being_done/targets.

Rabe, B. 2006. Revisiting Regionalism: Multi-State Collaboration in Climate Change Policy. Paper prepared for annual meeting of American Political Science Association, August 30–September 3, Philadelphia. www.allacademic.com/one/apsa/apsa06/index.

Raiffa, H. 1982. *The Art and Science of Negotiation.* Cambridge, MA: Harvard University Press.

Resource Conservation Alliance & Government Purchasing Project. 2008. *Focus on Government Purchasing.* Available at www.gpp.org.

Schneider, S. 2008. Global Warming: Is the Science Settled Enough for Policy? Lecture sponsored by Institute for the Study of Planet Earth, presented at University of Arizona. Tucson.

Scholtz, J. T., and B. Stiftel, eds. 2005. *Adaptive Governance and Water Conflict New Institutions for Collaborative Planning.* Washington, DC: Resources for the Future Press.

Society for Professionals in Dispute Resolution (Environmental/Public Disputes Sector) and the Consortium on Negotiation and Conflict Resolution. 1997. *Best Practices for Government Agencies: Guidelines for Using Collaborative Agreement-Seeking Processes.* http://acrnet.org/acrlibrary/more.php?id=13_0_1_0_M.

Stephens, S. L., and L. W. Ruth. 2005. Federal Forest-Fire Policy in the United States. *Ecological Applications* 15, no. 2:532–42.

Susskind, L., S. McKearnan, and J. Thomas-Larmer. 1999. *The Consensus-Building Handbook: A Comprehensive Guide to Reaching Agreement.* Thousand Oaks, CA: Sage.

Torres, L. H. 2003. *Deliberative Democracy: A Survey of the Field—A Report Prepared for the William and Flora Hewlett Foundation.* Washington, DC: AmericaSpeaks.

Trenberth, K. E., P. D. Jones, P. Ambenje, R. Bojariu, D. Easterling, A. Klein Tank, D. Parker, F. Rahimzadeh, J. A. Renwick, M. Rusticucci, B. Soden, and P. Zhai. 2007. Observations: Surface and Atmospheric Climate Change. In *Climate Change 2007: The Physical Basis—Contribution of Working Group I to the Fourth Assessment Report of the Intergovernmental Panel on Climate Change,* ed. Solomon, S., D. Qin, M. Manning, Z. Chen, M. Marquis, K. B. Avery, M. Tignor, and H. L. Miller. New York: Cambridge University Press.

U.S. Army Corps of Engineers. 2008. Louisiana Coastal Area, Louisiana: Ecosystem Restoration—Comprehensive Coastwide Ecosystem Restoration. www.mvn.usace.army.mil/prj/lca/factsheet.asp.

U.S. Government Accountability Office. 2007. *Climate Change: Financial Risks to Federal and Private Insurers in Coming Decades Are Potentially Significant.* Report GAO-07-285. Washington, DC: U.S. Government Printing Office.

U.S. Green Building Council. 2008. Leadership in Energy and Environmental Design, Green Building Rating System. www.usgbc.org/DisplayPage.aspx?CMSPageID=1779.

Wright, D. S. S. 1988. *Understanding Intergovernmental Relations,* 3rd ed. Florence, KY: Wadsworth.

PART IV

Deliberative Democracy and Public Participation

With the backdrop of a historic presidential election in 2008, some have asserted that a new dawn in American democracy is about to begin. However, any optimism must be moderated by the low level of citizens' trust and confidence in government. The public is often critical of elected officials and public administrators who shape policy and implement programs. Citizens are concerned about whether their individual and collective voices will be heard by governmental decision makers.

Several trends are changing the way in which citizens interact with their government. The demographic and socioeconomic composition of the American populace is changing. With these changes comes a more diverse set of constituents, each seeking to have their interests heard and to be involved in the policymaking process. The government has been on a path toward greater decentralization, fragmented decision making, and an increasing reliance on nongovernmental organizations, including both nonprofits and for-profit organizations. These changes have challenged traditional notions of the government's accountability to citizens. A new presidential administration in the United States is seeking to centralize control over certain policy domains and to reduce its reliance on third-party contractors, which have been used by the government for substantial proxy implementation and governance capacity during the last two decades. Technology and globalization are changing the patterns of interaction between citizens and their government, with one another, and with the larger global community. Other changes are also altering traditional conceptions about citizen involvement and deliberative democracy, requiring a reconsideration of how the government engages the nation's citizens, how citizens interact and become involved with their government, and how public administrators can manage these changes and develop new processes for more deliberative connections with citizens.

These issues lead to a number of questions addressed by the authors of the chapters in this part of the book: Should the public be involved in the decisions traditionally made by public administrators? When should they be involved? Under what conditions should they be involved? What is the best way to involve them? How can a representative group of interests and citizen voices be engaged, not just those who feel strongly about an issue? How much influence should the public expect to have over a decision when they become involved? How should public managers manage the involvement process and the input they receive? What governance mechanisms lend themselves to harnessing and reporting on citizen involvement?

Tina Nabatchi makes the case for "Why Public Administration Should Take Deliberative Democracy Seriously." She defines deliberative democracy and discusses where it occurs and in what forms, reviews its intellectual history and the features it shares with other citizen engagement processes, and goes on to argue why it should be taken seriously—outlining the benefits of greater engagement for the government and the nation's citizens but also, more prescriptively, identifying what types of actions are necessary by the government to leverage these benefits. Perhaps the action most needed, she asserts, is to revive a democratic ethos. However, she argues, this will be a challenge because positivist norms and a bureaucratic ethos have kept public administration focused on technical and instrumental actions. This has led to generations of public administrators who are "ill equipped to manage wicked problems and public priorities in a political environment where citizens are taking (and want to take) more active roles." She concludes by outlining a research agenda for scholars focused on deliberative democracy and calls for practitioners and scholars to work on changes to public affairs education that will equip public administrators with the tools to engage the public.

In "When Should the Public Be Involved in Public Management? Design Principles with Case Applications," John Clayton Thomas raises the question of when the public should be involved in the decisions that public administrators make. He puts forth a framework to address collective action problems and incorporates design principles, while illustrating process elements for engaging citizens in the work of governance through case examples. In assessing the need for involvement, he is a realist. He identifies conditions under which the public should be involved and those where their involvement is likely to send signals about reciprocity and exchange that may not accommodate all parties' preferences. He points out conditions under which public involvement can be beneficial, but he stresses that public managers will need to actively manage to achieve win–win outcomes for government and those who participate. As such, his design principles are straightforward and can serve as decision heuristics for public managers seeking to decide whether or not and how much to involve the public. In addition, he outlines principles that address the issue of power sharing, expectations about involvement, and the need to be transparent—but not excessively deterministic—about the process. In conclusion, he draws on three examples to illustrate these principles while advancing several caveats. The principles articulated are those that can be taught and learned and can contribute to public managers thinking and acting more deliberatively about democratic engagement.

Ines Mergel presents a social media perspective for government and governance in "The Use of Social Media to Dissolve Knowledge Silos in Government." She draws the reader into a discussion of what is currently taking place with a range of knowledge-sharing and learning tools, reviews the implications of these new technologies for integrating knowledge across government and its networks and with citizens, and focuses on the various implications of adopting, modifying, developing, and using social media to exchange information, promote collaboration, transcend organizational boundaries, and engage stakeholders through a more efficient collection, diffusion, and transmission of information. The potential outcomes are greater levels of civic engagement, more transparency, and increased accountability. But as Mergel notes, technological transformations challenge bureaucratic structures and traditional modes of information exchange in ways both known and unknown. Thus any attempt by government to adopt a one-size-fits-all approach to incorporating social media into the mission and programs of agencies is likely to be met by institutional challenges and a culture of communication that is still very much established in twentieth-century systems and processes. This chapter complements the contributions by Nabatchi and

Thomas because it suggests new avenues for increasing access to information for many engaged in the process of governance, while presenting a clear set of management challenges that will need to be understood before appropriate actions can be implemented by government.

Each contributor to this part is passionate about citizen involvement and deliberative democracy. Their prescriptions, however, are fundamentally grounded in reality, because they recognize that there are many interests, preferences, and motivations among the different supporters and opponents of these initiatives. Each author offers a framework within which to consider information exchange and public involvement, while offering guidance that public administrators should consider when engaging citizens. The lessons from each chapter can inform research, teaching, and practice for those seeking to strengthen democratic governance.

Why Public Administration Should Take Deliberative Democracy Seriously

Tina Nabatchi

This chapter argues that public administration must take deliberative democracy seriously. The chapter first describes the concept of deliberative democracy. It then identifies and explains three reasons why public administration should take such work seriously. It concludes with a brief discussion of recommendations for future research and practice.

DELIBERATIVE DEMOCRACY

Broadly defined, "deliberative democracy" refers to infusing government decision making with the reasoned discussion and collective judgment of citizens. Although definitions of deliberative democracy vary, there is some agreement on its core elements: it requires giving reasons, must take place in public and be accessible to (some, if not all) citizens affected by decisions, seeks to produce a decision that is binding for some period of time, and is dynamic and keeps open the option for continuing dialogue (Gutmann and Thompson 2004, 3–7). Deliberative democracy builds on the theory of principled negotiation, which emphasizes the interests that underlie and form individual preferences and positions. By promoting political judgment through the consideration of different perspectives in unconstrained dialogue, deliberative democracy provides a basis for reciprocal questioning and criticism (Young 2000). It gives citizens a "voice" in public decisions, fosters cooperation and understanding (as opposed to winning and losing), and supports reasoned decision making before the act of voting and preference aggregation. Thus, most scholars generally think of deliberative democracy as an expansion of (not alternative to) aggregative or representative democracy.

In practice, deliberative democracy is an umbrella term for a wide variety of processes, such as study circles, National Issues Forums, deliberative polling, consensus conferences, citizen juries, the AmericaSpeaks 21st Century Town Meeting, and various e-democracy initiatives. Key features shared among deliberative processes include a focus on action, an appeal to values, the absence of preexisting commitments, mutuality of focus, the free exchange of knowledge and information, and activities occurring within small groups, although the overall process may involve several thousand participants (Torres 2003). Salient differences include, but are not limited to, who participates in deliberation, how participants exchange information and make decisions, the link between deliberation and public action, and the connection to the policy process (Bingham, Nabatchi, and O'Leary 2005; Fung 2006).

TAKING DELIBERATIVE DEMOCRACY SERIOUSLY IN PUBLIC ADMINISTRATION

There are at least three reasons why public administration should take deliberative democracy seriously. First, at a practical level, the deliberative democracy movement is gaining momentum. As the use of deliberative practices and processes grows, so too do the prospective effects of deliberative democracy on public administration. Second, deliberative democracy presents public administration with an opportunity to rediscover a democratic ethos and the role of the public in shaping societal affairs. Finally, the institutional designs of deliberative democracy provide mechanisms with which the field can address the citizenship and democratic deficits.

The Deliberative Democracy Movement

Since the mid-1990s, there has been a rapid proliferation of private and nonprofit organizations, university and research institutions, and scholarly and popular work devoted to the subject of deliberative democracy. There are also growing numbers of public officials, practitioners, and scholars seeking to implement and institutionalize deliberative democracy at all levels of government in the United States. Hundreds of deliberative projects and structures have emerged at the local level in the last ten years, in cities and towns of all sizes, initiated by many different kinds of local leaders. They have been used to address a wide range of public issues, such as crime, land use, education, housing, racism and race relations, poverty and economic development, criminal justice and corrections, youth development, and neighborhood planning (Leighninger 2006). Some of the most visible and well-documented examples include municipal budgeting and strategic planning efforts in Washington (e.g., Moynihan 2003), neighborhood governance councils addressing policing and public education in Chicago (Fung 2003a), and recovery planning efforts in New Orleans (Williamson 2007).

At the state level, California engaged nearly 3,500 residents in CaliforniaSpeaks, a statewide, day-long deliberative forum on health care reform held in 2007. Many of the recommendations that emerged from the process were reflected in the health care legislation before the state legislature (www.californiaspeaks.org). At the federal level, the Centers for Disease Control and Prevention convened the Public Engagement Pilot Project on Pandemic Influenza in

2005 and again in 2009 to enable public deliberation about priorities for the use of vaccines during a period of anticipated shortage, and to revise the National Vaccine Plan accordingly (www.pandemicflu.gov/plan/federal/pepppi maintext.pdf). Moreover, President Barack Obama recently signed the "Open Government Memorandum," calling for more transparency, public participation, and collaboration in government. This memo signals interest in and commitment to public engagement, and it heightens the possibility of future federal-level deliberative efforts.

Reviving the Democratic Ethos

Two distinct intellectual frameworks can be identified in the history of American public administration: a democratic ethos and a bureaucratic ethos (see Pugh 1991). Though there has always been (and may always be) an inherent tension in public administration between the democratic and bureaucratic ethoses, the field has tended to favor the latter. The bureaucratic ethos is guided by market logic and values such as efficiency, efficacy, expertise, loyalty, and hierarchy. These norms are found throughout the intellectual history of public administration; simply consider the politics/administration dichotomy, the Weberian model of bureaucracy, the theory of scientific management, and the application of rationalism to public administration.

The operational values of the bureaucratic ethos have also dominated the practice of public administration. For example, they are clearly evident in Wilson's (1887) argument for a neutral and "practical science of administration," Gulick's (1937) articulation of POSDCORB (an acronym for planning, organizing, staffing, directing, coordinating, reporting, and budgeting), and Simon's (1947) emphasis on bounded rationality and satisficing decision making. The most obvious examples in modern public administration are New Public Management and other recent reform movements, such as Reinventing Government and the National Performance Review, which actively promote bureaucratic and managerialist norms. Finally, the bureaucratic ethos and its attendant values are implicit in the "new governance" era, which is characterized by the "hollowing of the state" through systems of partnerships, privatization, contracts, and networks, and is focused on values such as efficiency, effectiveness, and results (Stivers 2008).

The favoring of the bureaucratic ethos has serious implications for public administration. To the extent that the field focuses on bureaucratic and managerialist issues, it fails to adequately confront and understand the issues of public administration in a democracy, such as the ability of the political system to make and act on collective choices, and opportunities for effective citizenship, political leadership, and nurturing the civic infrastructure (Kirlin 1996, 418). In addition, the overemphasis on the bureaucratic ethos has limited the ability of public administrators to address effectively the new pressures and dynamics evident in twenty-first-century democracy. Because administrators must now focus on selecting contractors and ensuring that contract deliverables and other provisions are met, they are increasingly ill equipped to manage wicked problems and public priorities in a political environment where citizens are taking (and wanting to take) more active roles (Stivers 2008).

In contrast, the democratic ethos prepares administrators for twenty-first-century conditions because it embodies a very different set of norms and principles, such as regime values, citizenship, the public interest, and social equity (Pugh 1991). Among other things, these values require the field to accept responsibilities for the promotion and maintenance of civic education and democratic operations. Implicit in the democratic ethos is the idea that government is obligated to facilitate intelligent and effective participation and create politically educative processes that develop a rich understanding of community and the common good. Several seminal scholars in public administration—such as John Gaus, Marshall Dimock, Paul Appleby, Norton Long, Frederick Mosher, and Dwight Waldo—emphasized the integration of administrative practices and democratic values. Many modern scholars are also guided by the democratic ethos.

Deliberative democracy provides a means for the rediscovery of the democratic ethos in public administration; the values implicit in each are the same—inclusion, equity, participation, and the public interest, to name a few. Deliberative democracy supports institutional designs for the involvement of citizens in discussions and decisions about public policy problems. Such designs are sensitive to the value plurality inherent in policy issues and function well within the networked environment of modern government. Deliberative processes also present a concrete way of bringing together views and insights in a manner that is more than the mere aggregation of individual interests. In this way, deliberative democracy can help rediscover the public in the discipline of shaping public affairs, and in doing so, provides a way to help balance the tensions between the bureaucratic and democratic ethoses in public administration.

Addressing the Citizenship and Democratic Deficits

By valuing the bureaucratic ethos over the democratic ethos, public administration may be nourishing the citizenship and democratic deficits in the United States. The term "citizenship deficit" broadly refers to the erosion of traditional civic skills and dispositions among the general public. Evidence of a citizenship deficit in the United States is seen in the numerous statistics that show a decline in the voting behaviors, political engagement, social capital, and civic attitudes, among other areas. For example, voter turnout rates in presidential and off-year elections steadily decreased from 1960 to 1996 (Rimmerman 2001), when they slowly began to rise. In addition, fewer Americans are engaging in other political activities and participating in associational groups (Putnam 2000). Similarly, data from the American National Elections Survey show declining levels of political efficacy and trust in government among citizens since the 1960s. In the context of the United States, the term "democratic deficit" generally refers to the disconnect between citizen opinions and preferences, political decisions, and policy outcomes. It is useful to note, however, that although citizens have withdrawn from traditional civic and political activities, the advent of the internet and other digital technologies has stimulated new citizen attitudes and engagement capacities.

Nevertheless, for both practical and ethical reasons, public administration has a responsibility to address the deficit problems, not only because it has contributed to them with its embrace of the bureaucratic ethos but also because it is obligated to do so by the democratic ethos. Deliberative democracy has the potential to help public administration meet this obligation. Advocates assert that such processes have "educative effects" that produce "better citizens" by fostering and increasing political efficacy, sophistication, interest, trust, respect, empathy, and public-spiritedness (e.g., Fung 2003b). Moreover, advocates claim that deliberative democracy has benefits for government and governance in that it can produce "better" decisions and improve the quality of public policies (e.g., Fung 2003b; Gutmann and Thompson 2004). To the extent that deliberative democracy produces these effects, it may help reduce both the citizenship and democratic deficits.

DIRECTIONS FOR THE FUTURE AND CONCLUSION

Several scholars have identified research agendas relevant to deliberative democracy (e.g., Bingham, Nabatchi, and O'Leary 2005; Bingham and O'Leary 2006; Collaborative Democracy Network 2006; Levine and Torres 2008; Roberts 2008); therefore, this chapter presents only a brief list of recommendations for future research and practice. Scholars need to give critical and sustained attention to the role of public administration in a democracy, and refocus attention on the tensions between bureaucracy and democracy, particularly as they play out within the framework of the new governance. We also need research that better examines the trade-offs between the bureaucratic and democratic ethoses and how those might be managed vis-à-vis deliberative democracy processes. Academics and practitioners need to join forces and work in concert to address several other pressing areas of research and practice. For example, further research is needed on whether and how deliberative processes benefit citizens and governance, as well as how they affect the citizenship and democratic deficits. The connections between deliberative democracy and public administration, particularly with regard to decision-making and policymaking processes, need to be articulated. Research is also needed to identify the factors that enable or hinder the use of deliberative processes by public managers. Finally, scholars and practitioners need to address public affairs education, specifically focusing on the knowledge, skills, and abilities that are required of public managers to effectively engage in such work. Work in these areas will develop understanding about the role of deliberative democracy in public administration.

There is no doubt that as efforts to increase public participation in policymaking spread, public administration will need to understand deliberative democracy. But the importance of deliberative democracy to public administration reaches much further. Deliberative democracy builds on the democratic ethos of the field and seeks to actively involve decision makers, government officials, and citizens in inclusive discussions of public policy problems. Its institutional designs work well within networked environments, are sensitive to value plurality, and allow for a union of views and insights on important public matters. As such, deliberative democracy can help rediscover the role of the public in the discipline of shaping public affairs. In doing so, it provides a way to address the tensions between the bureaucratic and democratic ethoses and improve the citizenship and democratic deficits. These returns require those engaged in both the professional practice and academic study of public administration to take deliberative democracy seriously.

REFERENCES

Bingham, Lisa Blomgren, Tina Nabatchi, and Rosemary, O'Leary. 2005. The New Governance: Practices and Processes for Stakeholder and Citizen Participation in the Work of Government. *Public Administration Review* 65, no. 5:528–39.

Bingham, Lisa Blomgren, and Rosemary O'Leary. 2006. Conclusion: Parallel Play, Not Collaboration: Missing Questions, Missing Connections. *Public Administration Review* 66, no. s1:161–67.

Collaborative Democracy Network. 2006. A Call to Scholars and Teachers of Public Administration, Public Policy, Planning, Political Science, and Related Fields. *Public Administration Review* 66, no. s1:168–70.

Fung, Archon. 2003a. Deliberative Democracy, Chicago-Style: Grass-Roots Governance in Policing and Public Education. In *Deepening Democracy: Institutional Innovations in Empowered Participatory Governance*, ed. A. Fung and O. Wright. New York: Verso Press.

———. 2003b. Recipes for Public Spheres: Eight Institutional Design Choices and Their Consequences. *Journal of Political Philosophy* 11, no. 3:338–67.

———. 2006. Varieties of Participation in Democratic Governance. *Public Administration Review* 66, no. s1:66–75.

Gulick, Luther. 1937. Notes on the Theory of Organization: With Special Reference to Government in the United States. In *Papers on the Science of Administration*, ed. L. Gulick and L. Urwick. New York: Institute of Public Administration.

Gutmann, Amy, and Dennis Thompson. 2004. *Why Deliberative Democracy?* Princeton, NJ: Princeton University Press.

Kirlin, John J. 1996. The Big Questions of Public Administration in a Democracy. *Public Administration Review* 56, no. 5:416–23.

Leighninger, Matt. 2006. *The Next Form of Democracy: How Expert Rule Is Giving Way to Shared Governance—and Why Politics Will Never Be the Same*. Nashville: Vanderbilt University Press.

Levine, Peter, and Lars H. Torres. 2008. *Where Is Democracy Headed? Research and Practice on Public Deliberation*. Washington, DC: Deliberative Democracy Consortium.

Moynihan, Donald P. 2003. Normative and Instrumental Perspectives on Public Participation: Citizen Summits in Washington, D.C. *American Review of Public Administration* 33, no. 2:164–88.

Pugh, Darrell L. 1991. The Origins of Ethical Frameworks in Public Administration. In *Ethical Frontiers in Public Management: Seeking New Strategies for Resolving Ethical Dilemmas,* ed. S. Bowman. San Francisco: Jossey-Bass.

Putnam, Robert D. 2000. *Bowling Alone: The Collapse and Revival of American Community.* New York: Simon & Schuster.

Rimmerman, Craig A. 2001. *The New Citizenship: Unconventional Politics, Activism, and Service,* 2nd ed. Boulder, CO: Westview Press.

Roberts, Nancy C. 2008. Direct Citizen Participation: Coming of Age. in *The Age of Direct Citizen Participation,* ed. N. C. Roberts. Armonk, NY: M. E. Sharpe.

Simon, Herbert. 1947. *Administrative Behavior: A Study of Decision-Making Processes in Administrative Organizations.* New York: Free Press.

Stivers, Camilla. 2008. *Governance in Dark Times: Practical Philosophy for Public Service.* Washington, DC: Georgetown University Press.

Torres, Lars H. 2003. *Deliberative Democracy: A Survey of the Field.* Report prepared for William and Flora Hewlett Foundation.

Young, Iris Marion. 2000. *Inclusion and Democracy.* Oxford: Oxford University Press.

Williamson, Abigail. 2007. *Citizen Participation in the Unified New Orleans Plan.* Washington, DC: AmericaSpeaks. www.americaspeaks.org/_data/n_0001/resources/live/citizenpartstudy1.pdf.

Wilson, Woodrow. 1887. The Study of Administration. Reprinted in *Classics of Public Administration,* ed. J. M. Shafritz and A. C. Hyde. Fort Worth: Harcourt Brace, 1997.

When Should the Public Be Involved in Public Management?

Design Principles with Case Applications

John Clayton Thomas

A half century ago, a citizens' revolution came to public administration. Coming both bottom-up from citizens and top-down from government, this revolution pushed for greater involvement by citizens in the administration of government programs and in the shaping of other community decisions about public values. Gradually, too, the revolution spread from citizens and citizen groups to encompass a broad range of stakeholders.

As a result of this revolution, public administrators today work more closely with citizens and other stakeholders than did their predecessors of only decades ago. With networks and partnerships apparently growing in importance (Considine and Lewis 2003; Agranoff and McGuire 2001), public engagement also seems likely to be an important component in the future of public administration.

Yet administrators still frequently struggle with when and to what extent to invite public involvement in their decision making, and scholars of public administration have not offered much helpful counsel. Scholars frequently encourage public managers to engage citizens and other stakeholders more actively, but they have formulated few theories or guidelines for when and how to do so. As Nancy Roberts (2004, 335) has observed, "Theory building is an art but, on the topic of direct citizen participation, not a particularly well developed one."

The purposes of this chapter are to propose and illustrate guidelines for answering the all-important first questions public administrators ask about public involvement: Should I involve the public and other stakeholders in making this decision? And if so, to what extent? These guidelines are designed to assist public managers in answering these questions to promote decision making that is both democratic and effective. The guidelines draw from my prior work on public involvement (Thomas 1990, 1993, 1995), which in turn drew on the small-group decision-making research of Victor Vroom and others (Vroom and Jago 1988; Vroom and Yetton 1973).

These guidelines are detailed below as "design principles," using Ostrom's (1990, 90) term for "essential elements or conditions for success," for when and to what extent the public should be involved in making specific decisions. Design principles are defined more narrowly here than in Ostrom's work as limited to essential elements for success that *are or might be under the control* of those who lead decision-making processes, thereby excluding factors that could affect a decision's success but that lie outside leadership control (e.g., geography, population). Once explained, the principles will be illustrated relative to three previously reported cases of public involvement.

ASSESSING THE NEED FOR INVOLVEMENT

The decisions of interest here are those made—or in some cases considered, but not resolved—on the administrative side of government, where the public and other external stakeholders were or might have been involved, such as:

- What environmental regulations, if any, should be imposed on developers of specific sites?
- Where should a hazardous waste disposal facility be located?
- How should a city's discretionary community development funding be allocated?

The relevant decisions share three characteristics: (1) placement in public administration, (2) some administrative discretion in decision making, and (3) the possible involvement of actors, ranging from citizens and citizen groups to traditional interest groups, in addition to the legally responsible public administrators. As such, these decisions probably reflect the principal locus for involvement and influence by external actors on public administration. Our specific concern with these decisions relates to how more or less involvement of external actors contributes to, or detracts from, their effectiveness, where effectiveness refers to both the outcomes of the decision itself and the process that led to the decision (Beierle and Cayford 2002, 14–15).

To determine when and to what extent to involve the public in these decisions, public administrators should focus first on two factors: (1) the need for information to make a better decision, and (2) the need for acceptance of the decision in order to achieve its implementation where acceptance cannot be assumed with involvement in decision making. Prior research suggests the centrality of these factors to the desirability of public involvement (Thomas 1990, 1993, 1995).

The need for information could pertain to technical questions, citizen preferences, or both. For example, administrators who are charged with launching a program in a community may lack information on what citizens would like to see the program offer. Or citizens may see a need for technical information from other external stakeholders, such as contractors, or again from citizens and citizen groups, which can sometimes be excellent sources of technical information (Manring 1993). Obtaining either kind of information will likely require engaging external actors.

A need for the acceptance of a decision provides grounds to involve external actors if implementation hinges on this acceptance, which cannot be assumed without involvement. Many administrative actions do not require citizen acceptance to be implemented; the "consent of the governed" often can be assumed when those actions flow directly from the decisions of elected policymaking bodies. As well, some decisions that require external acceptance promise so many benefits that key external actors can be expected to support the decisions without being involved. For the most part, however, administrative decisions that substantially affect the public or other external stakeholders require that they be extensively involved in order to gain the acceptance necessary for implementation. U.S. highway engineers learned this principle the hard way by attempting to run highways through neighborhoods without consulting residents. Residents frequently resisted, sending many a planner back to the drawing board.

Application of the information and acceptance principles, as detailed elsewhere (Thomas 1990, 1993, 1995), will often result in a clear recommendation *not* to involve others, as expressed in this first design principle (DP):

> DP 1: The public and other external stakeholders should not be engaged where decision makers need neither more information nor public acceptance in order to implement the decision.

Absent those needs, involving external actors unnecessarily adds complexity to decision making. The manager is better advised to use the "autonomous agency decision" decision-making approach (see table IV.1), deciding alone or at least without involving external actors.

This recommendation may be welcomed by many public administrators, who recognize intuitively that external involvement is frequently undesirable. As for citizens and other stakeholders, they have limited time and energy to work with government, and so may appreciate it if public officials respect those limits and ask for outside assistance only sparingly.

On some issues, managers will perceive a need for information but not for acceptance, or they will perceive an *initial* need for information with uncertainty about whether acceptance will eventually be needed. In either case, the manager should seek the information and then plan to decide the issue without sharing influence, using a "modified autonomous agency decision" approach, as detailed in the second design principle:

Table IV.1 Options for Decision-Making Approaches with Public and other External Stakeholder Involvement

- AI = Autonomous agency decision: The agency solves the problem or makes the decision alone without public involvement.
- AII = Modified autonomous agency decision: The agency seeks information from segments of the public but decides alone in a manner that may or may not reflect group influence.
- CI = Segmented public consultation: The agency shares the problem separately with segments of the public, getting ideas and suggestions, then makes a decision that reflects group influence.
- CII = Unitary public consultation: The agency shares the problem with the public as a single assembled group, getting ideas and suggestions, then makes a decision that reflects group influence.
- GII = Public decision: The agency shares the problem with the assembled public, and together agency representatives and the group attempt to reach agreement on a solution.

> DP 2: On issues where only information is needed from the public and other external stakeholders, the manager should seek that information from segments of those external actors, but may alone decide in a manner that may or may not reflect those actors' influence.

Ordinarily, this information should *not* be pursued by convening external stakeholders as a whole, as in a public meeting. Public meetings demand significant time and energy, in exchange for which participants may expect influence. Where information is needed with no desire to share influence, external actors are better involved individually or in segments, as through citizen surveys, telephone calls to key contacts, and the like.

On many issues, finally, managers will perceive acceptance of a decision as a precondition for implementation where that acceptance cannot be assumed without involving external actors. Here managers should consider a third factor: the extent to which those external stakeholders share the agency's goals on the issue (Thomas 1990; Vroom and Yetton 1973), which may include legislative requirements, scientific and technical standards, and budgetary limitations.

If managers believe external actors share those goals, they should pursue extensive involvement. After all, the goals appear unlikely to be threatened by the input of external actors, and extensive involvement offers a greater likelihood of gaining decision acceptance. This logic leads to the third design principle:

> DP 3: On issues where external acceptance is needed and requires external involvement and the public is expected to agree with agency goals, the

> agency should share the problem with the assembled public, and agency representatives together with the public should attempt to reach agreement on a solution.

This is termed the "public decision" approach, meaning that a decision is pursued jointly by the agency and its public (and other external stakeholders).

Finding the best approach to decision making becomes more challenging when the principles conflict, especially when external acceptance is necessary for implementation and will require involvement, but external actors are expected to disagree with agency goals. These situations call for external involvement, but with protections for agency goals, as embodied in the fourth design principle:

> DP 4: On issues where external acceptance is needed and requires external involvement but external actors are expected to disagree with agency goals, the agency should share the problem with the public, assert essential agency standards, obtain ideas and suggestions, and then make a decision that reflects group influence.

This is a consultative approach. The agency consults with external actors, promising influence over the decision—the quid pro quo for their input—but retains ultimate decision-making authority. Typically here, an agency should pursue what is termed a "unitary public consultation," consulting with the relevant external actors as a single assembled group, as through public meetings or an advisory committee. To protect their goals, administrators should assert at the outset any essential standards to ensure that a decision is respected.

On especially difficult issues where external actors are united in disagreement with agency goals, administrators may prefer a "segmented public consultation," consulting separately with segments of the relevant stakeholders rather than with all of them (or their representatives) at once. This approach avoids the risk of assembling in one place external actors who are united in opposing agency goals.

Obviously, public administrators cannot always determine in advance whether (1) external actors can provide useful information, (2) involvement is necessary to obtain external acceptance, and/or (3) the public and other external actors are sympathetic with agency goals. This reality demonstrates that public officials move cautiously in *either* involving *or* excluding external actors, leaving latitude to increase or decrease the public's involvement as circumstances may warrant.

APPLYING THE DESIGN PRINCIPLES

A review of several recently profiled administrative decisions illustrates how the design principles can help in understanding and informing planning for public involvement.

Addressing a Gang Problem in Chicago

An effort to combat youth gangs in Chicago illustrates when little or no external involvement may be necessary (Spergel and Grossman 1997, 457–58). The Little Village Project brought together "a team of community youth workers, probation officers, tactical police officers, and a community organization" pursuing a variety of strategies to reduce the role of gangs and gang violence. The project focused especially on "hard-core gang youths (those who possess guns, are repeat offenders, and are influentials in gang crime)," seeking to reduce their criminal involvement through job opportunities, counseling, and, when necessary, surveillance and arrest.

Judging from the case description (Spergel and Grossman 1997), the project included limited involvement of the broader Little Village community. Several neighborhood meetings were held, but they were mostly informational with "limited follow-up" on issues raised by residents. Despite the minimal involvement, the evidence strongly suggested that the project substantially reduced violent crime in the area.

Reviewing the project relative to the design principles, especially DP 1, implies a four-part explanation for how the project succeeded despite limited involvement:

1. Community support was either unnecessary for implementation, or, if necessary, did not require public involvement. Residents may have readily accepted—even embraced—a program offering the prospect of less gang violence.
2. By including professionals on the project team, the project may have achieved the necessary involvement of external stakeholders other than the public.
3. With those professionals as information sources, additional information may not have been needed from community residents.
4. The several open community meetings may have provided a safety valve in case community members did have information to provide or concerns to voice.

Watershed Planning in the Omaha Area

The principles also help to explain a seemingly failed process of public involvement in watershed planning in the Omaha area (Irvin and Stansbury 2004). In contrast to the Little Village case, project planners here anticipated and encouraged broad public participation in the planning, then saw only *one* person come.

This planning targeted the Papillion Creek system, which originates northwest of Omaha, joins the Missouri River south of the city, and, at the time of the case, had become seriously polluted. The project's intent was to recommend choices between such creek-management options as environmental upgrades, real estate development, recreational development, and flood protection (Irvin and Stansbury 2004, 60).

The planners attempted to attract recreational creek users, developers, residents of surrounding areas, and other stakeholders to a public meeting to discuss the options, using newspaper articles, a broad distribution of brochures, direct contacts with landowners, and an offer of free pizza at the meeting. With all those efforts, fifteen people said they would come, but only one did, prompting an assessment of the involvement process as "ineffective and wasteful" (Irvin and Stansbury 2004, 62).

A review of the case relative to the design principles suggests a different conclusion, with three aspects. First, the issues in the case embodied a potential competition of values—the environment versus recreation versus development—that frequently mobilizes citizens and other stakeholders. These competing values usually mean that external actors must be involved in decision making in order to obtain the acceptance necessary for implementing any decision (DP 3).

Second, the mistake may have been to assume that the competing values *definitely* required involvement. In retrospect, the planners appear to have lacked enough information on the attitudes of external actors to know to what extent involvement would be needed. Consequently, the better approach might have been to seek more information—as through phone calls to key contacts, focus groups, surveys, and the like—before holding a public meeting (DP 2). That information search might have revealed, as the case study authors eventually concluded, that the "project failed to spark widespread public interest" and that "the environment was not an issue many people felt strongly about" (Irvin and Stansbury 2004, 61). It might have shown, in short, that successful implementation would not require public involvement in decision making.

Third, at the same time, a one-shot failure at public involvement does not mean that an issue will never arouse the public's interest. The literature on public involvement includes many cases where the public initially showed no interest, only to mobilize, usually in opposition, once a specific proposal took shape (for two cases, see Iglitzen 1995 and Talbot 1983). Seen in that light, the public's failure to appear at the initial meeting in this case should not have dissuaded decision makers from retaining options for later public involvement.

Oil and Gas Leasing in Pennsylvania

At the other end of the continuum, the risks of *not* inviting external involvement in decision making are illustrated by the efforts in 2002 of Pennsylvania's Department of Conservation and Natural Resources (DCNR) to auction tracts of public land for oil and gas drilling (Welsh 2004). In planning the auctions, DCNR officials met only with the oil and gas industry representatives who were interested in drilling on the land. After the meetings, DCNR sanctioned an auction of the desired land.

Only then did word of the possible auction reach the department's two citizens' advisory committees. Committee members immediately notified environmental groups, which objected and asked for a process of public involvement and input. DCNR responded that it was "not required to solicit public comment or prepare an environmental impact analysis" (Welsh 2004, 190) and that, in any event, it planned to closely monitor the work of the leasing companies once the lands were leased. That strategy mollified no one, as DCNR's opponents, now including many newspaper editorial pages, continued to object.

DCNR eventually agreed to hold "public information sessions" around the state to explain its plans and to solicit public comment (Welsh 2004, 192). The meetings drew 165 participants, and almost 5,000 comments were received at the meetings, via regular mail and the internet, most in opposition to the plan. DCNR still went ahead with an auction, making "moderate changes" in the bidding process and lease parameters and leasing only a fraction of the land originally targeted. At the same time, prompted by DCNR's lack of public involvement, the state legislature enacted requirements for environmental impact assessments and public involvement in any similar future efforts.

Seen through the prism of the earlier principles, there are two lessons from this case. First, DCNR officials ignored the reality that public acceptance—from environmental groups, in particular—was an essential precondition for successful implementation of the auction and that this acceptance could not be assumed without involvement (DPs 3 and 4). DCNR should have anticipated resistance from these groups if they were shut out of its planning.

Second, the lack of opportunity for input is sometimes more important than actual influence. In this case, "Opponents in effect [were] mobilized more by outrage at their own exclusion and mistrust of an agency claiming expertise than by specific concerns about the proposal itself" (Welsh 2004, 191). In short, although DCNR still held the auction, it might have done so earlier and with fewer constraints had it consulted external stakeholders at the outset.

The DCNR case also illustrates how disdaining necessary external involvement can bring unanticipated negative consequences, here in the form of the additional strictures on DCNR imposed by the Pennsylvania state legislature.

CONCLUSION

Most evidence points to continuing pressures for more public and other external stakeholder involvement in the administration of public programs. Education levels continue to rise, and as people become more educated, they become more resistant to governmental edicts and more insistent on having opportunities to speak to the nature of programs that will affect them. The result is more pressure to involve the public in public administration.

Public managers should recognize this reality and be mindful of needs to increase external involvement in the programs they administer. The design principles and the case illustrations detailed here can provide guidance for these managers as they consider how to respond to these needs.

These principles imply first that there is no universal, across-the-board need for more public involvement in public programs. It is not always true that, as sometimes argued, "to be successful, state and local government bodies should involve the public in decision making" (Welsh 2004, 186). The desirability of public involvement hinges on needs for (1) information the public can provide that could improve program quality and/or (2) public acceptance, which is unlikely without involvement, as an essential prerequisite to successful program implementation. Absent either need, inviting public involvement may be unnecessary, as illustrated by the effort to combat gangs in Chicago.

However, when there are needs for information and, especially, acceptance, the involvement of external actors becomes desirable, and a choice not to involve them—or to involve them insufficiently—invites failure. Failure ensued in the Pennsylvania oil and gas leasing case when officials underestimated the need to involve the public.

To be sure, planning for effective public involvement is more complicated than an explanation based on only two factors might imply. Managers will often have difficulty defining the needs for information and/or acceptance on particular issues; and, even if they can confidently define those needs at one point in time, the needs could then change. Finally, the successful definition of these needs determines only when and to what extent the public should be involved; managers must still determine exactly how to engage the public, a task not addressed here.

But an understanding of these two principal factors and the related design principles represents a foundational step toward understanding and planning for public involvement. This can help managers realize the enormous promise that appropriate involvement of the public offers for improving the future of public administration, government, and society.

REFERENCES

Agranoff, Robert, and Michael McGuire. 2001. Big Questions in Public Network Research. *Journal of Public Administration Research and Theory* 11:295–326.

Beierle, Thomas C., and Jerry Cayford. 2002. *Democracy in Practice: Public Participation in Environmental Decisions.* Washington, DC: Resources for the Future Press.

Considine, Mark, and Jenny M. Lewis. 2003. Bureaucracy, Network, or Enterprise? Comparing the Models of Governance in Australia, Britain, the Netherlands, and New Zealand. *Public Administration Review* 63:131–40.

Iglitzen, Lynne B. 1995. The Seattle Commons: A Case Study in the Politics and Planning of an Urban Village. *Policy Studies Journal* 23:620–35.

Irvin, Renee A., and John Stansbury. 2004. Citizen Participation in Decision Making: Is It Worth the Effort? *Public Administration Review* 64, no. 1:55–65.

Manring, Nancy J. 1993. Reconciling Science and Politics in Forest Service Decision Making: New Tools for Public Administrators. *American Review of Public Administration* 23:343–49.

Ostrom, Elinor. 1990. *Governing the Commons: The Evolution of Institutions for Collective Action.* New York: Cambridge University Press.

Roberts, Nancy. 2004. Public Deliberation in an Era of Direct Citizen Participation. *American Review of Public Administration* 34:315–53.

Spergel, Irving A., and Susan F. Grossman. 1997. The Little Village Project: A Community Approach to the Gang Problem. *Social Work* 42:456–70.

Talbot, A. R. 1983. The Port Townsend terminal. In *Settling Things: Six Case Studies in Environmental Mediation,* ed. A. R. Talbot. Washington, DC: Conservation Foundation and Ford Foundation.

Thomas, John Clayton. 1990. Public Involvement in Public Management: Adapting and Testing a Borrowed Theory. *Public Administration Review* 50:435–45.

———. 1993. Public Involvement and Governmental Effectiveness: A Decision-Making Model for Public Managers. *Administration & Society* 24:444–69.

———. 1995. *Public Participation in Public Decisions: New Skills and Strategies for Public Managers.* San Francisco: Jossey-Bass.

Vroom, Victor H., and Arthur G. Jago. 1988. *The New Leadership: Managing Participation in Organizations.* Englewood Cliffs, NJ: Prentice Hall.

Vroom, Victor H., and Philip W. Yetton. 1973. *Leadership and Decision-Making.* Pittsburgh: University of Pittsburgh Press.

Welsh, Michael. 2004. Fast-Forward to a Participatory Norm: Agency Response to Public Mobilization over Oil and Gas Leasing in Pennsylvania. *State and Local Government Review* 36:186–97.

THE USE OF SOCIAL MEDIA TO DISSOLVE KNOWLEDGE SILOS IN GOVERNMENT

INES MERGEL

Knowledge sharing in the public sector is mostly regulated through rules, a clear sense of hierarchy with fixed reporting structures, standard operating procedures, and laws that tend to restrict the free flow of information across organizational boundaries. The result is that information produced in one agency might not be available to entities in other corners of the overall system. This can and often does lead to reinventing the wheel and innovative knowledge being detained within knowledge silos (Noveck 2009). Consequently, ideas that might meet the knowledge needs of several similar stakeholders in government are prevented from spreading through the whole system.

Social media tools are challenging this traditional "need to know" information-sharing paradigm (Dawes, Cresswell, and Pardo 2009) and are increasing the degree of participation of all stakeholders in the process of creating, maintaining, sourcing, and sharing knowledge. The resulting—partially informal—emerging interactions between the public and government itself are creating opportunities for increased transparency, accountability, participation, and collaboration (Orszag 2009). Moreover, social media tools are potentially disruptive and might have transformative effects on knowledge sharing that have not been fully covered in the public administration literature (Mergel, Schweik, and Fountain 2009).

UNDERSTANDING INFORMATION SEEKING AND SHARING IN THE PUBLIC SECTOR

In the public sector, we are usually operating within traditional bureaucratic interactions bound to predefined federal, state, and local levels, and to departmental or even team boundaries, with very clearly divided tasks and reporting structures. The nature of the tasks to be accomplished is usually so complex that they need to be divided into fine-grained and independent components that can be treated separately while still contributing to the overall objective of the task: service delivery to the public (Simon 1982). As Blau and Scott (1962, 7) point out, "The larger the group and the more complex the task it seeks to accomplish, the greater are the pressures to become explicitly organized." This bureaucratization has led to very elaborate rules and regulations that every member of the organization must follow. The free sharing of information is restricted, and legal and policy constraints highly regulate distribution, storage, and usage.

Hierarchies have proven to be inefficient in many ways when it comes to searching for information: Hierarchical organizational structures restrict vertical information sharing to predefined categories within single entities of the traditional service delivery model (Blau and Scott 1962; Eggers 2005). Everything beyond structured information that is not systematically covered disrupts regulated information flows and needs to be absorbed by other information-sharing mechanisms, such as informal networks or market mechanisms (Powell 1990), and even ad hoc bazaars without any rules at all (Demil and Lecocq 2006). From the management literature we know that not all the knowledge needed to perform certain tasks and to solve problems confronted by government actors is readily available within a single organization. On the contrary: Knowledge is only codifiable to a certain extent—and not everything that an organization knows is searchable in databases, handbooks, manuals, and standard operating procedures, or by experts within the focal agency (Anand, Glick, and Manz 2002; Grant 1996). Especially when it comes to knowledge—that is, information that is relevant, actionable, and in part based on experience—its transfer is difficult and flows mostly through informal processes such as socialization and internalization (Morrison 2002; Nonaka and Takeuchi 1995, 1996).

Prior research on knowledge sharing and advice seeking has shown that seeking knowledge from others has clear informational benefits, such as access to solutions, metaknowledge, problem reformulation, validation, and legitimation (Cross, Borgatti, and Parker 2001). This is in part the reason why members of an organization often rely on knowledge from external third parties and must reach out to their informal network contacts (Anand, Glick, and Manz 2002).

Both informal and formal networks of professionals help to access knowledge to conduct the tasks within a professional environment that is not accessible in codified form due to its highly intangible and tacit nature (Cross, Rice, and Parker 2001; Kram and Isabella 1985; Morrison 2002). To break up the resulting knowledge silos, social media tools can help to support horizontal and vertical information-sharing needs.

TOWARD THE SOCIAL WEB: A NEW INFORMATION-SHARING PARADIGM IN THE PUBLIC SECTOR

In the public sector we see more and more new types of information production and sharing tools that are emerging in the form of grassroots developments:

so-called social media, Web 2.0 tools, or the "Social Web." These are tools that are used in digital environments in which contributions and interactions among all stakeholders are enabling a high degree of collaborative knowledge creation and sharing (for more detailed overviews, see, e.g., Chang and Kannan 2008; O'Reilly 2005; Sternstein 2006). These are Web applications that emerged in private settings outside any business or government context. They are rapidly making their way into the public sector (O'Reilly 2007). Among those tools are, for example, the photo sharing website Flickr; video publication sites like YouTube; social networking sites, such as Facebook or LinkedIn; microblogging tools, such as Twitter; and forecasting and prediction markets such as Intrade.com.

Especially during Barack Obama's presidential campaign, these (usually free) applications showed that a traditional top-down approach was no longer needed—volunteers self-organized with the support of a knowledgeable campaign team and the use of collaborative social media tools (Eggers and Dovely 2008). Their success is attributed to bottom-up mobilization and the willingness to provide knowledge and insights with a minimum of regulatory and bureaucratic control mechanism (Surowiecki 2004). Supporters and new voters were reached "where there are"—on social networking services, instead of traditional town hall meetings.

A prominent example in the public sector is Intellipedia, often called the Central Intelligence Agency's Wikipedia (Lawlor 2008b; Andrus 2004), which was started by the Office of the Director of National Intelligence and is designed to collaboratively capture all knowledge available by content area across all sixteen intelligence agencies in the United States. Users have access on three different security levels, and knowledge areas are connected to knowledge specialists using a design component called "bread crumbs" in order to identify experts, access a wider knowledge pool more efficiently, and ultimately reach a more informed level of decision accuracy. The goal is to integrate knowledge created on the vertical as well as the horizontal levels across different agencies within government to break up knowledge silos and build a basis for improved decision making using a wiki application. The information-sharing environment is supported by a host of Web 2.0 applications, such as iVideo, blogs, shared documents, collaboration spaces, and photo galleries.

Similarly prominent wikis include Diplopedia in the State Department (Cohen 2008), and Techpedia in the Department of Defense. U.S. Army soldiers in the battlefield have implemented wiki technology to speed up peer-to-peer information about battlefield conditions and the initial concerns by higher-level officers about the break in chain-of-command information flow or the loss of control over the message. Other social media tools include online social networking sites, modeled on Facebook or LinkedIn. NASA launched a social networking site for employees called Spacebook (Mosquera 2009), and the intelligence community is using A-Spaces to connect their employees (Shaughnessy 2008). These examples of increased collaboration in unlikely environments such as the highly regulated and compartmentalized command-and-control culture of the intelligence community can serve as a model for other cross-organizational collaboration and might move government from a need-to-know to a need-to-share information paradigm.

The Obama administration is promoting a new Open Government Initiative that allows the public to use data sets produced by the federal government (www.whitehouse.gov/open), and it has produced a few remarkable initiatives (e.g., data.gov and the IT Dashboard to monitor information technology expenses, it.usaspending.gov). Data provided there can be used with Google Maps to be matched up with public transit schedules (McGray 2009), or flu search terms on Google can be used to predict virus epidemics and help to inform the public (Ginsberg et al. 2008; see also www.google.org/flutrends). Recently, social media tools have proven to be helpful in aggregating political information during the Iran election protests (Morozov 2009a), or the so-called Twitter Moldova Revolution (Morozov 2009b). In addition, more and more government agencies are using the multiplayer tool Second Life for online meetings in order to reduce travel and coordination costs. Second Life is also used as an informal collaboration space for municipal chief information officers (e.g., see MuniGov2.0 on CitizenServices.gov 2009).

These examples show that social media tools in the public sector create opportunities to enhance transparency, communication, and collaboration in government, and might promote deeper levels of civic engagement (Hinchcliffe 2006). This technological transformation is challenging the existing bureaucratic information paradigm. Social media tools can help to serve as organizational anchors for a higher degree of integration and inclusion of alternative knowledge sources and information acquiring techniques. So far new knowledge has mainly been created by a small number of early activists, and the trend can therefore still be labeled as a grassroots movement, following the Rogers (1995) diffusion curve to create public value. These new forms of information sharing open up possibilities for further research to understand the behavioral aspects of why public-sector employees on all levels, but also citizens, are willing to share their knowledge.

CRITICISM OF THE CURRENT STATE OF PUBLIC ADMINISTRATION

The current trend of social media applications and the rising expectations of citizens are pressuring government into understanding the implications for the existing ways knowledge is created and shared in the public sector. As with all new trends and initiatives, there is the potential for unknown outcomes, including the creation and diffusion of unexpected practices and underestimated relationships between evolving practices and policy requirements. So far, the public administration literature has mainly focused on (large scale) e-government projects and their contribution to increase the reach and performance of electronic service delivery. Research on e-government itself is still at an early stage and has so far not supported many of the expected outcomes (cost savings, downsizing, etc.) that the claims of the e-government literature have promised (Moon 2002). The public administration literature has not yet picked up on the new wave of social media tools in the public sector. The examples mentioned above clearly show advantages for collaborative participation to improve efficiency and service for citizens and for the potential for a higher degree of transparency and collaboration (Lawlor 2008a). Ethical issues have to be considered when social media tools are used in unanticipated contexts. Public participation in knowledge creation through blogs, wikis, and the use of publicly available data creates additional problems of data handling complexity, privacy issues, and responsibility of data provision and usage and records management that might be underestimated and need to be addressed in appropriate ways.

RECOMMENDATIONS FOR THE FUTURE OF THE FIELD

So far, relatively little research has been conducted in public administration to understand how intra-, inter-, and extraorganizational informal knowledge-sharing tools are applied and effectively used for information-sharing purposes in the public sector. New research needs to focus on the emerging interactions and the content of interactions in order to understand what technological structure might support what kind of knowledge-sharing needs (Morris and Moon 2005). The traditional bureaucratic context is currently extended with a parallel technological structure in which public-sector employees as well as citizens are voluntarily engaging to create and share public knowledge—and the managerial implications and challenges are slowly emerging.

The social media phenomenon has created a need for innovative research approaches in public administration to understand the underutilized resources of these emergent interactions and voluntary contributions in which citizens and public-sector employees are engaging (Surowiecki 2004; Watts 2007; Mergel, Lazer, and Binz-Scharf 2008). Social science itself is lagging behind in collecting and analyzing large-scale behavioral data, such as information created on political blogs or the content and contacts created on social networking sites (e.g., government Facebook groups). New forms of research, such as social network analysis, can help us to explain these informal dynamic structures and their content (Borgatti et al. 2009; Lazer et al. 2009). This will help scholars in public administration understand the empirical phenomena, become more expedient in interacting with students and practitioners, and stay relevant as researchers.

REFERENCES

Anand, V., W. H. Glick, and C. C. Manz. 2002. Thriving on the Knowledge of Outsiders: Tapping Organizational Social Capital. *Academy of Management Executive* 16, no. 1:87–101.

Andrus, D. Calvin. 2004. *The Wiki and the Blog: Toward a Complex Adaptive Intelligence Community.* SSRN–Social Science Research Network. http://ssrn.com/abstract=755904.

Blau, P., and W. R. Scott. 1962. *Formal Organizations.* San Francisco: Chandler.

Borgatti, S. P., A. Mehra, D. Brass, and G. Labianca. 2009. Network Analysis in the Social Sciences. *Science* 323, no. 5916:892–95.

Chang, Ai-Mei, and P. K. Kannan. 2008. *Leveraging Web 2.0 in Government.* www.businessofgovernment.org/report/leveraging-web-20-government.

CitizenServices.gov. 2009. *MuniGov 2.0.* www.usaservices.gov/bestpractices/MuniGov.php.

Cohen, Noam. 2008. On Web, U.S. Diplomats Learn to Share Information. www.iht.com/articles/2008/08/03/technology/link04.php.

Cross, Rob, Stephen P. Borgatti, and Andrew Parker. 2001. Beyond Answers: Dimensions of the Advice Network. *Social Networks* 23, no. 3:215–35.

Cross, R., R. E. Rice, and A. Parker. 2001. Information Seeking in Social Context: Structural Influences and Receipt of Information Benefits. *Ieee Transactions on Systems Man and Cybernetics Part C-Applications and Reviews* 31, no. 4:438–48.

Dawes, Sharon S., Anthony M. Cresswell, and Theresa A. Pardo. 2009. From "Need to Know" to "Need to Share": Tangled Problems, Information Boundaries, and the Building of Public Sector Knowledge Networks. *Public Administration Review* 69, no. 3:392–402.

Demil, B., and X. Lecocq. 2006. Neither Market nor Hierarchy nor Network: The Emergence of Bazaar Governance. *Organization Studies* 27, no. 10:1447–66.

Eggers, William D. 2005. *Government 2.0: Using Technology to Improve Education, Cut Red.* Lanham, MD: Rowman & Littlefield.

Eggers, William D., and Tiffany Dovely. 2008. Government 2.0's Inauguration. *Governing*, www.governing.com/mgmt_insight.aspx?id=6062.

Ginsberg, Jeremy, Matthew H. Mohebbi, Rajan S. Patel, Lynnette Brammer, Mark S. Smolinski, and Larry Brilliant. 2008. Detecting Influenza Epidemics Using Search Engine Query Data. *Nature* 457:1012–14.

Grant, R. M. 1996. Toward a Knowledge-Based Theory of the Firm. *Strategic Management Journal* 17:109–22.

Hinchcliffe, Dion. 2006. *Architectures of Participation: The Next Big Thing.* http://web2.socialcomputingmagazine.com/architectures_of_participation_the_next_big_thing.htm.

Kram, K. E., and L. A. Isabella. 1985. Mentoring Alternatives: The Role of Peer Relationships in Career Development. *Academy of Management Journal* 28, no. 1:110–32.

Lawlor, Maryann. 2008a. Governing in a Web 2.0 World. *Signal* 62, no. 8:59–63.

———. 2008b. Web 2.0 Intelligence. *Signal* 62, no. 8:63.

Lazer, David, Alex Pentland, Lada Adamic, Sinan Aral, Albert-László Barabási, Devon Brewer, Nicholas Christakis, Noshir Contractor, James Fowler, Myron Gutmann, Tony Jebara, Gary King, Michael Macy, Deb Roy, and Marshall Van Alstyne. 2009. Computational Social Science. *Science* 323:721–23.

McGray, Douglas. 2009. iGov: How Geeks Are Opening Up Government on the Web. *The Atlantic,* January–February. www.theatlantic.com/doc/200901/technology-government.

Mergel, Ines, David Lazer, and Maria Christina Binz-Scharf. 2008. Lending a Helping Hand: Voluntary Engagement in Knowledge Sharing. *International Journal of Learning and Change* 3, no. 1:5–22.

Mergel, I., C. M. Schweik, and J. Fountain. 2009. *The Transformational Effect of Web 2.0 Technologies on Government.* SSRN–Social Science Research Network. http://ssrn.com/abstract=1412796.

Moon, M. Jae. 2002. The Evolution of E-Government among Municipalities: Rhetoric or Reality? *Public Administration Review* 62, no. 4:424–33.

Morozov, Evgeny. 2009a. Iran Elections: A Twitter Revolution? *Washington Post*, June 17. www.washingtonpost.com/wp-dyn/content/discussion/2009/06/17/DI2009061702232.html.

———. 2009b. Moldova's Twitter Revolution. *Foreign Policy*, April. http://neteffect.foreignpolicy.com/posts/2009/04/07/moldovas_twitter_revolution.

Morris, Donald F., and M. Jae Moon. 2005. Advancing E-Government at the Grassroots: Tortoise or Hare? *Public Administration Review* 65, no. 1:64–75.

Morrison, E. W. 2002. Newcomers' Relationships: The Role of Social Network Ties during Socialization. *Academy of Management Journal* 45, no. 6:1149–60.

Mosquera, Mary. 2009. Social Media Tools Slow to Take Root. *Federal Computer Week*, February 6. http://fcw.com/Articles/2009/02/09/Web-2.0-adoption-taking-a-while.aspx?p=1.

Nonaka, I., and H. Takeuchi. 1995. *The Knowledge-Creating Company*. New York: Oxford University Press.

———. 1996. The Knowledge-Creating Company: How Japanese Companies Create the Dynamics of Innovation. *Long Range Planning* 29, no. 4:592.

Noveck, Beth. 2009. Open Government Laboratories of Democracy. In *Open Government Initiative: Transparency, Participation, Collaboration*. Washington, DC: White House.

O'Reilly, T. 2005. What Is Web 2.0? Design Patterns and Business Models for the Next Generation of Software. www.oreillynet.com/pub/a/oreilly/tim/news/2005/09/30/what-is-web-20.html.

———. 2007. What Is Web 2.0? Design Patterns and Business Models for the Next Generation of Software. *Communications & Strategies* 1.

Orszag, Peter R. 2009. Open Government Directive: Memorandum for the Heads of Executive Departments and Agencies. www.whitehouse.gov/sites/default/files/microsites/ogi-directive.pdf.

Powell, W. W. 1990. Neither Market nor Hierarchy: Network Forms of Organization. *Research in Organizational Behavior* 12:295–336.

Rogers, E. M. 1995. *Diffusion of Innovations*, 4th ed. New York: Free Press.

Shaughnessy, Larry. 2008. CIA, FBI Push "Facebook for Spies." *CNN/Technology*. www.cnn.com/2008/TECH/ptech/09/05/facebook.spies/index.html.

Simon, H. 1982. From Substantive to Procedural Rationality. In *Method and Appraisal in Econimics*, ed. S. J. Latsis. Cambridge: Cambridge University Press (orig. pub. 1976).

Sternstein, A. 2006. Web 2.0 for Feds. www.fcw.com/print/12_43/news/96857-1.html.

Surowiecki, J. 2004. *The Wisdom of Crowds: Why the Many Are Smarter Than the Few and How Collective Wisdom Shapes Business, Economies, Societies and Nations*. New York: Random House.

Watts, Duncan J. 2007. A Twenty-first Century Science. *Nature*, February 1, 489.

PART V

Teaching the Next Generation of Leaders

What should public managers know about managing into the future when faced with a multitude of changes? These include changes to the size and role of government, a significantly expanded involvement in markets and the regulation of those markets, a blurring of traditional sector boundaries in providing public services, greater levels of interdependence among the different sectors of the economy and among organizations, and the increasing globalization of economic activity and governance.

What should graduates of public administration programs know—theoretically, conceptually, empirically, experientially—to think critically and more effectively perform their jobs in public service, regardless of sector or policy area? Should they receive more academic training in constitutional law, administrative law, ethics, and financial management? Or should the additional training focus on how to collaborate with others?

What will differentiate graduates of public administration programs in the job market from graduates in business administration, social work, educational administration, or emergency management? Is it knowledge of government and the policy process generally? Or are certain tools, skill sets, and analytical frames needed to make public administration graduates attractive as managers and leaders to a range of public, nonprofit, and private organizations? Are there areas within public administration where organizational and program performance can be improved as a result of new knowledge, skills, and abilities about collaboration?

A number of challenges and opportunities exist in teaching the next generation of leaders. In this part, the authors focus on what the next generation of public managers should know. The authors teach in graduate public administration programs, and their contributions address this issue from different perspectives.

Scott E. Robinson leads off with "Rebranding Public Administration for a Post-sector Age," in which he tackles an important and difficult issue about the comparative value of a master of public administration degree relative to other specialized graduate degrees, such as those offered in business administration, educational administration, nonprofit administration, social work, and emergency management. His perspective is interesting because he raises the question of how competitive public administration graduate programs are relative to other graduate programs. What differentiates the programs and their graduates from one another? How do prospective employers view master of public administration programs relative to other programs' graduates? Robinson then offers a framework for articulating and branding the programmatic differences across graduate degrees and the analytical skills and tools that differentiate public administration graduates from those of other degree programs.

Finally, he advances a set of cross-sectoral and boundary-spanning skills and tools that he believes will further strengthen the reputation and value of hiring graduates of public administration degree programs.

Guy B. Adams and Danny L. Balfour ask "Can the Study and Practice of Public Service Ethics Be Recovered in a New Governance Era?" They argue that ethics continues to receive insufficient attention within public administration graduate programs, yet the need is ever greater because many of the ethical challenges that public administrators face are not the discrete black-and-white choices that past generations dealt with. Rather, many of the decisions that public administrators confront today are more nuanced, gray, and complex, but have farther-reaching implications. In a continued period of low citizen satisfaction and trust in government, the decisions that public administrators make have important implications for how a broader range of stakeholders view the work of government. The authors document the background and importance of "ethical decision making" in government and suggest that the changing context of governance requires changes in public administration curricula and a renewed emphasis within organizations and across government on public service ethics. They conclude with thoughts on what is necessary to create an ethical organization.

Next, in "The Status of the Law in Contemporary Public Administration Literature, Education, and Practice," David H. Rosenbloom and Katherine C. Naff maintain that public administration students are receiving insufficient exposure to the law and specifically to understanding the legal framework that undergirds public administration. They point out the importance of understanding the interdependent implications that the law and public administration decision making have on one another. They suggest that greater exposure and understanding about administrative law would strengthen decision making by public administrators and give them a more robust understanding for their regulatory and oversight roles regarding accountability. They consider some of the historical context for the interdependent relationship between the law and public administration and more recent and controversial issues regarding the separation of powers and the role of public administrators. They go further to suggest not only that the law's lack of prominence in public administration curricula has diminished the skill sets, training, and actions of public administrators but also that a renewed emphasis on lawfulness as a public-sector value is necessary to improve government performance, rulemaking, and enforcement.

In the next chapter, "Adding Value in a World of Diffuse Power: Reintroducing Public Management and Public Financial Management," Justin Marlowe and Daniel L. Smith present an interesting and important argument that public management and public financial management as subfields of public administration have much to learn from one another. They assert that the control and allocation of resources are essential for managers. However, while public budgeting, financial management, and public management share roots in public administration, their respective branches have grown apart. The authors trace the detachment of budgeting and finance from management within public administration and set forth to create a path toward integration and engagement. They argue that scholarship and practice can benefit from bringing the two branches together toward win–win outcomes. Those outcomes are in better understanding interorganizational networks and performance, strengthening discipline and accountability in markets, and improving governance and public-sector risk management strategies. In each of these areas, Marlowe and Smith articulate how these outcomes can be achieved through greater integration of public financial management with public management. They conclude with recommendations for curricula and teaching in order to achieve these goals.

Finally, in "Teaching Democracy in Public Administration: Trends and Future Prospects," Matt Leighninger surveys scholars and practitioners to identify what the leading experts in the field think is missing from public administration programs in terms of knowledge about democracy and what changes could and should be made in the curricula of these programs to strengthen governance. He synthesizes areas of agreement; discusses what concepts require more attention in the classroom, in practice, and through research; and advances an agenda designed to augment each of these areas. He then recasts the challenges and opportunities public administrators face today using a democratic governance frame and suggests that integrating a democratic ethos with a bureaucratic ethos is necessary and important, but not one that is easily achieved. To that end, he proposes incentivizing schools and programs of public administration to actively engage them in this type of learning and teaching.

In each chapter of this part the authors highlight the challenges and opportunities for current and future public administrators and address what academic programs can do to assist those currently engaged in practice and those preparing to enter public service. In addition, as scholars, they each put forth a research agenda for further study designed to strengthen scholarship, teaching, and practice.

REBRANDING PUBLIC ADMINISTRATION FOR A POSTSECTOR AGE

SCOTT E. ROBINSON

The evidence on the careers of our students makes it clear that some of the assumptions of our classic images, particularly the career bureaucrat serving in one office or even one policy domain, are becoming inaccurate. It is increasingly common for our students to spend time in various sectors—government, nonprofit, and private—throughout their career (Light 1999). In this chapter, I focus on a related development in public service. Even students who find themselves in government-sector jobs are likely to be surrounded by coworkers with different professional backgrounds (including training targeting other sectors). A student trained in public administration may soon find himself or herself working side by side with students trained in business administration or training specific to one policy domain (e.g., public health management, environmental management, and transportation administration). The major concern of this chapter is how our field can prepare students to work in this world.[1] How should we design public administration curricula to respond to these changes in the nature of the work our students are likely to do?

The chapter begins by discussing the competition public administration programs face as they seek to place the students they train. Much of this discussion is based on a series of interviews with homeland security / emergency management and educational administration professionals. The chapter concludes with a discussion of public administration programs' competitive advantages in training students and what these advantages suggest for the development of a brand identity for public administration students.

WHAT DOES THE COMPETITION LOOK LIKE?

The future of master of public administration (MPA) programs depends on our ability to continue to recruit and place highly qualified and well-trained students. Our survival depends on our ability to remain relevant to these students and their employers. This chapter addresses the transformation of the traditional public sector, with particular attention to issues related to student recruitment.

In discussions about the reform of public administration curricula, one seldom sees an active discussion of what programs actually serve as our competition. With whom do we compete when seeking to recruit highly qualified students? When there is a discussion of the competition for MPA programs, the discussion tends to focus on the competition between public administration and master of public policy (MPP) programs.[2] This competition is real but of a peculiar character, because the National Association of Schools of Public Affairs and Administration (NASPAA) accredits both types of programs using similar standards, and many public affairs programs offer degrees or concentrations in both tracks. The supposed competition presumes that potential employers tend to select a group of candidates from policy analysis and public administration and then select among them. As I describe below, this is not the hiring process I have heard about when I have asked various public managers about their human resource strategies.

Interviews with public servants in two fields (education and emergency management) suggest that the real competition lies elsewhere. Though I will not argue that the interviews informing my argument represent a scientific sample on the subject, I have found conversations with workers in these areas to be eye opening. As such, I recommend taking this evidence as suggestive rather than as a basis for inference. My hope is to use these experiences to start a dialogue. I will leave inferentially valid tests of some of what I argue to future papers.

On their face, emergency management and education management offices could be interesting opportunities for many of our students. These are largely (with the limited exception being some private school programs) public offices that perform many of the tasks we would expect students with an MPA degree to be qualified to do. The day-to-day business of these organizations involves the management of personnel, budgets, and program analyses within a specific policy domain. In this regard, the offices are much like city offices or welfare agencies, where we think our students can move easily into positions upon graduation. Indeed, local, state, and federal organizations are increasingly investing in specialized positions related to continuity of operations and emergency preparedness. On the basis of these similarities, one would think these are the sorts of organizations that would potentially hire many of our students trained in MPA programs. You may even expect these organizations to have many MPAs already.

However, you are not likely to currently find many MPA degree holders in these programs. Instead, you will find a number of people trained in management within a specific policy context. In education management offices, you will likely see many people trained in education administration from specialized education programs. This almost universal preference for personnel trained within specialized education programs indicates an important belief about the training needs of these professionals. It is clear that there is a widespread belief that training in the specifics of education and the context of education is seen as vitally important—even more so than generalized management training. Interestingly, many of the people in management positions in these organizations have little or no management training—often specializing in such topics as curriculum design or instructional technology. Though it is common to find individuals with education but no management training, it is rare to find people in these organizations with general management training from outside education programs.

The case in emergency management is somewhat more complex. There are degree programs that specialize in emergency management (though still small in number), and many offices include a majority of people with degrees from these emergency management programs. Some offices include people with backgrounds in criminal justice or fire prevention (a classic tension in emergency response). I even see a fair number of people—often in the analysis departments in these offices—with backgrounds in urban planning and geospatial sciences. What I seldom see are people in these offices with backgrounds in public administration. Here, again, there is an implicit preference for training in the specific policy area of emergency management over general management training.[3]

This suggests that we are failing to see an important source of competition for our public administration programs. Though I have not studied environmental agencies, welfare agencies, or public health agencies, I suspect that I may find similar patterns in these organizations. I do not see organizations populated by a mixture of students from general public administration and public policy programs. Instead, both administration and policy students are competing with specialized policy programs in a variety of areas. A student considering a career in management who visited one of the offices in which I conducted interviews may quickly come to the conclusion that they should enroll in a specialized policy domain program. They have to choose not between an MPA and an MPP program but between a general degree (in either administration or policy) and specialized training in a program such as a master of emergency administration and planning (MEM) or of educational administration (MEd) (or, I suspect, a master of social work, MSW, or a master of environmental management or public health administration, MPH).

The natural solution would be to use recent data on the frequency of career switching to promote our programs as training in management that crosses policy domains. We could say "train in our program for any policy area rather than limiting yourself to one area." This is very close to the case I have made to students in the past. But this argument runs into a problem. Specialist policy area programs are not our only competition. For those interested in general administration and management training, we also face competition from business administration programs.

If our core competency is teaching generalized management, how do we differentiate our programs from these general business administration programs? The same studies that suggest that our students need skills to move from office to office and policy domain to policy domain also suggest that they may move from sector to sector (including into and out of the private sector) (Light 1999). Our argument for the importance of generalized management/administration education may prove much more than we would like.

There is reason to believe that business administration will become an even more important source of competition for public administration programs in providing general management education—even for those interested in public service. As has been documented in many locations, public service agencies across all levels of government (and in the public sector—though to varying degrees) are facing potentially massive waves of retirements (Spence and Reester 2008). The demand for employees ready to serve in these organizations may soon outstrip our capacity to graduate students. This would seem to be a great problem to have. Increased demand is generally a great situation for training programs. This assumes, however, that there are no substitutable goods. If the demand for employees (on the part of public agencies) forces agencies to seek new sources for employees, we may never get these agencies back. It may prove easier for public agencies to hire master of business administration (MBA) students from the higher-throughput business administration programs than to continue to recruit from smaller MPA programs. As hiring public managers from MBA programs becomes common, the need for a distinguishing identity for public administration programs will become all the more acute.

Public administration programs should realize that they are fighting a war on two fronts. On the one hand, programs are competing against specific policy programs targeting particular policy domains—like environmental policy, social work, education management, and public health. On the other hand, they are competing against business administration programs (many of which dwarf the public administration programs in their markets in terms of enrollment, faculty size, and advertising) for general management training. In this situation, public administration needs to carefully rebrand itself to offer unique competitive advantages to recruit (and later place) students. MPA programs must understand that they are not simply competing with MPP programs but also with MSW, MEM, MPH, MBA, and other programs.

WHAT DO WE HAVE TO OFFER?

The core question we must face is "What do we have to offer students?" We need to have something to offer that competes with both the specific training of the policy domain programs and with the generalized management training available in business administration programs. Historically, public administration has relied on the distinctiveness of training for the public sector and public service motivation to carve a niche between these competing possibilities. We have told students that those interested in public service, and who recognize the possibility of switching from policy area to policy area, will need the general public service training offered in public administration curricula. We have told students that we can prepare them for government service—wherever that service may take them.

The first cracks in this strategy began to appear as students began to ask for preparation for moving into the nonprofit sector. We had defined our field in relation to a specific sector—what we then called the public sector, but which generally meant government employment. For years, the field struggled with how to handle these new demands (Cleary 1990; Mirabella and Wish 2000). Some argued that we needed to create a bevy of new courses specializing in nonprofit organizations (Young 1999). This argument led to the creation of courses on nonprofit leadership and nonprofit management, and other courses based in part on the motivation behind coexisting courses on public management and public leadership. Others argued that nonprofit organizations were sufficiently similar government organizations that much of our curriculum still applied and that students of nonprofit administration need to be trained directly alongside students of government administration (Salamon 1995).

These arguments led to the incorporation of examples and applications from nonprofit organizations into traditional courses like organization theory and human resource management. The compromise often led to the strategy of having a token week or two of material titled "[course topic] in nonprofits" or something of that kind. This solution seemed to make no one happy. Students of nonprofit organizations felt that it was a token gesture proving that the rest of the course was not really targeted for them. Students pursuing careers in government service thought that they could just ignore those weeks (the evidence of sector switching notwithstanding).

The unease over the incorporation of nonprofit management into traditional public management curricula stems from tensions in the disciplinary identity of the field. For decades the field has branded itself as the place to train for government service. The intrusion of students with interests outside government service clashed with this disciplinary identity. At this point it seems clear that nonprofit management will continue to be a component of the field (Wish and Mirabella 1998) and a growing component of many programs, but this requires a shift in the identity of the field itself.

The foundations for this shift in identity are present in the recent literature on governance structures (Lynn, Heinrich, and Hill 2002). Students of public management and policy implementation have come to accept that these processes no longer operate solely within the scope of government agencies. These processes operate across the government, nonprofit, and private sectors. The boundaries of these sectors themselves are becoming increasingly blurry.

The foundations of public governance as a process that calls for crossing sector boundaries may serve as the basis for a new brand for public administration. By defining the term "public" to cross sectors and include all elements of the governance system, the field can specialize in training boundary crossers. We can train students to cross boundaries related to sector with skills needed to manage collaborations between government and nonprofit organizations, for example. We can train students to cross professional and policy domain boundaries as traditional silos continue to erode. The result could be a brand that differentiates us from both the specialized policy programs and MBA programs. Our programs can specialize in training practitioners in governance concepts—whether the jobs happen to reside in government, nonprofit, or private organizations.

When talking with managers in education and emergency management, I got the sense that executives are looking for such boundary crossers—but that they did not know where to look. In one emergency management office, the leader of the office noted that most of what his employees do is work with other, dissimilar organizations. He needs employees who can work with public health specialists in preparing for pandemics, with education specialists to use schools to distribute information to parents about general disaster preparedness, with private-sector organizations to disseminate information and cultivate resources for response and recovery activities, and many more. To address these needs, he deliberately hired from a variety of specialized policy schools—including not only emergency management but also public health and urban planning. His experience had been that specialists in one area tended not to communicate well with people from these other fields.

This strategy contrasts sharply with a different emergency management office where the leader of the office hired exclusively within one professional community (law enforcement) to ease communication within the office. This leader noted that there was very little work with external organizations outside the law enforcement policy domain (from which his office almost exclusively hired new personnel). Though the end result of this strategy was to create an office that differed remarkably from the previously described collaborative office, both offices hired people based on the assumption that connections to external organizations required a shared specialized professional background. Neither office seemed to seriously consider hiring a public administration student.

We could train students to help in both these situations. We could brand ur field to train people to manage around and across these professional and icy silo boundaries. We could define our field as being at the nexus of asingly complex, interdisciplinary policy solutions. For the emergency ement offices, we can explain that our students may not have the mashe Incident Command System of someone with a master's degree in management—but that the office needs other skills as well. We vide them with students who specialize in the skills of connecting with the local public health agencies, local education agencies, local governments, and the like. We can train connectors.

A FUTURE FOR PUBLIC ADMINISTRATION

Training connectors could involve some shifts in the way that we train students. There have been subtle shifts in the content of curricula over the past decade and a half as it is—many of which were in the direction of training connectors. One example of these shifts is the increasingly common course on conflict resolution and negotiation. In many programs, this seems to have become central to their curriculum, and many stakeholders in the programs in which I have worked have pointed to it as an attractive element of the curriculum. This seems to be a rather obvious example of what a connector-trained curriculum would include.

There are less obvious examples of how a connector-training curriculum could evolve from the current standard curriculum. In budgeting, the most popular textbooks are strongly focused on government budgeting and federal budgeting almost exclusively—but that is just another type of sector specialization (e.g., Lee, Johnson, and Joyce 2008). There is little support for discussion of nonprofit or private-sector budgeting—though there are limited discussions of the peculiarities of budgeting at the state and local levels. Deemphasizing the specifics of the federal process (with its specific timetables, sources of revenues, financial regulations, etc.) and emphasizing the common elements of budgeting across organizations could free up the room to discuss the skills needed by a connector. A connector would need to understand the difference between budgetary processes to effectively bridge organizations with different budgetary processes. One example of how a connector could leverage different budgetary skills is the need to manage a project budget where the project consists of personnel and resources from different organizations in different sectors.

One could imagine other such modifications. Policy processes courses would need to incorporate attention to cross-sector policy network and processes at the state and local levels. Human resource management courses would need to address the complications of operating within multiple personnel systems from different organizations in different sectors. Administrative law courses would need to engage the issues related to the legal authorities and regulations related to hybrid entities like cross-sector working groups. These are becoming common practices, and we are poised to train students to serve in these capacities.

The training of boundary spanners may require a change in teaching methodology as well. Training in specific content areas like conflict resolution and organizational communication may help—as may the incorporation of cross-sector content in traditional courses like budgeting and policy process. However, many of the basic skills of boundary spanners lie in the development of specific interpersonal skills. In my interviews with the boundary-spanning emergency management office, the director emphasized that he needed to ensure that any hire is a "people person." This is not particularly specific, but he looks for people with demonstrated skills in interpersonal communication and a desire to build new relationships. These are skills that are difficult to teach with a traditional lecture format. Instead of merely introducing new courses taught in traditional ways (like lectures on media relations), we may need to consider adding new teaching techniques, assignments, and extracurricular activities to develop boundary spanner skill sets. In an individual class, this may include the extension of group-based projects with orally communicated deliverables. One may add more small-group/breakout sessions for classes. Instructors will likely have to experiment with different approaches that best fit their style and course content.

At the George Bush School of Government and Public Service at Texas A&M University, we have sought to supplement in-class assignments with extracurricular resources for skills building. We have previously developed supplemental resources for writing skills, mathematical foundations, and some general professional development skills (e.g., résumé development, etiquette, and similar topics). It seemed that oral presentation skills were not given the same support from these external activities as written communications. To help build the oral communication skills that are so important to boundary-spanner training, we have developed a speaking and presentation workshop to complement our support for written communication.

Changing our curriculum and support activities will not be enough, however. A perfect modification of our curricula will mean very little if we fail to get the word out about what we have to offer. I suspect that this may be the hardest aspect of our challenges. We must rebrand ourselves. We must decouple our discipline's brand from the government sector exclusively. This will require changing the image of the field in the eyes of the potential employers of our students. We need to convince stakeholders that we can and do train a cadre of boundary-spanning managers in a world where no organization can operate within the confines of traditional sector boundaries.

We need to advertise the versatility of our programs to employers and to our future students. This will be difficult, in part because the effort faces a significant collective problem. First, the effort will require significant investment. The activities of rebranding the discipline will take a lot of work. We will have to be in the field talking about what we do and what our students have to offer. This arduous work will likely take years—maybe decades. To make the investment more difficult, there are few rewards for the individual faculty members who undertake this challenge. At many institutions, faculty are rewarded for efforts in research and teaching—but our systems reward activities that reach out to new communities and redefine the field one person at a time. Second, free riding is tempting. Many programs have long relied on the leading programs to brand the field. With the need to reach new audience in local nonprofit networks and local governments, this will not be adequate. Regional associations (like state and local chapters of the American Society for Public Administration, ASPA) will need to take an active role in branding their programs in their home region. This will call for appeals to local agencies and organizations to which we may be relevant but that do not know us. Though a handful of recruiting and placement programs can operate on a national scale, programs of all sizes and in all regions will need to pitch in to change their local brand. In the end, the change in the perception of the field will have to emerge from local efforts up. The combination of investment costs and the temptation to let someone else do the work (free riding) suggest that the rebranding effort will be difficult to manage.

I do not think the public administration community is quite ready for this. The first step will be to learn more about two beliefs on the part of potential employers for our students. First, we need to better understand what potential employers think they would get from a student trained in our programs. Here we must press beyond the comfortable responses we are likely to get from the employers of our recent students. We need to hear from people who have never hired one of our students but could potentially do so in the future. We may not like what we hear.

Second, we need to listen to these employers about what they need. To some extent, we may need to educate them (likely indirectly) about the needs of their organizations. We can only persuade them that we can offer students who fit their organizations if we understand their needs. These processes are preconditions for any active branding effort. I strongly recommend that national organizations devote more attention to this (potentially with working groups in NASPAA, ASPA, and maybe the National Academy of Public Administration), but each degree program needs to commit to this investigation and share the results of its studies. Many programs have such information based on the recommendation of NASPAA to have external stakeholder groups—but that information is not widely shared (and is considered by some to be proprietary). If we work together, we may be able to create an effective new brand. Regardless of the potentially upsetting results of such research, our field needs to conduct such research to better understand the target employers for our students (as broadly defined as possible) if we can hope to effectively rebrand our field to these employers.

In conclusion, we face a new world of competition. Our students compete with a wide variety of specialized policy and general management MBA programs. I recommend that we strongly consider an active effort to rebrand MPA programs to reflect changes seen in our research about the emergence of cross-sector collaboration and public management networks. A new professional identity may be the only way to survive in a postsector age.

NOTES

The author thanks the National Science Foundation for its support of this research through CMS 0555993. The opinions expressed in this chapter are solely the responsibility of the author.

1. The eroding boundaries between historically differentiated sectors (like between the government and private sectors) have a variety of implications for a wide range of issues, including legal accountability, policy design, and civic engagement. This chapter focuses almost entirely on the issues this erosion raises for public affairs education—leaving discussion of the other related issues to other times.
2. Here I discuss competitors to the MPA degree itself—not simply competition among MPA programs.
3. I do have an important qualifier to these statements. Though I have not seen many people with general management backgrounds in the emergency management offices, I have seen many of our management students taking internships with emergency management organizations. Some of this is due to the association of our program with a certificate in homeland security. Our program has a concentration that combines science and technology policy with homeland security—but no concentration specially in emergency management. We are also in a state with an established, top master of emergency management program. Possibly for these reasons, I have yet to see much hiring of people for permanent positions in emergency management from our program. Given the growth in personnel with homeland security responsibilities in emergency management organizations—or in other types of organizations—it is likely that more opportunities will emerge in the near future. The demand we have found for internship students in emergency management is a good indicator for this development.

REFERENCES

Cleary, Robert E. 1990. What Do Public Administration Masters Programs Look Like? Do They Do What Is Needed? *Public Administration Review* 50, no. 6:663–73.

Lee, Robert D., Ronald Johnson, and Philip G. Joyce. 2008. *Public Budgeting Systems*, 8th ed. New York: Jones and Bartlett.

Light, Paul. 1999. *The New Public Service*. Washington, DC: Brookings Institution Press.

Lynn, Laurence E., Jr., Carolyn J. Heinrich, and Carolyn J. Hill. 2002. *Improving Governance: A New Logic for Empirical Research*. Washington, DC: Georgetown University Press.

Mirabella, Roseanne M., and Naomi Bailin Wish. 2000. The "Best Place" Debate: A Comparison of Graduate Education Programs for Nonprofit Managers. *Public Administration Review* 60, no. 3:219–29.

Salamon, Lester M. 1995. *Partners in Public Service: Government–Nonprofit Relations in the Modern Welfare State*. Baltimore: Johns Hopkins University Press.

Spence, Joseph, and Keith Reester. 2008. Dynamics Factors Driving Workforce Change. *PA Times*, October, 4.

Wish, Naomi B., and Roseanne M. Mirabella. 1998. Curricular Variations in Nonprofit Management Graduate Programs. *Nonprofit Management & Leadership*. 9 no. 1:99–109.

Young, Dennis R. 1999. Nonprofit Management Studies in the United States: Current Developments and Future Prospects. *Journal of Public Affairs Education* 5, no. 1:13–24.

Can the Study and Practice of Public Service Ethics Be Recovered in a New Governance Era?

Guy B. Adams and Danny L. Balfour

In the United States, the last decade has brought a succession of high-profile ethical debacles in both the private and public sectors—from Enron to Hurricane Katrina to Abu Ghraib, Blackwater, and the collapse of the financial sector—events that have eroded the public's trust in both private- and public-sector organizations (Adams, Balfour, and Reed 2006; Adams and Balfour 2008; Moulton and Bozeman 2008). With sustained attention within the academy to both public service and professional ethics for at least the past thirty-five years, and the concomitant growth of ethics programs—albeit in fits and starts—within both the public and private sectors, there appears to be a major disconnection between theory on the one hand and human actions in both public and private organizations on the other. Surely, one would have hoped not just for more progress but perhaps for *any* sign of progress. Instead, ethical transgressions appear just as bad, if not far worse in at least some cases, than ever, and the phrase, "culture of corruption," is widely used to describe not only the public and private sectors but even American society as a whole (Callahan 2004).

We argue here that the most fundamental problem with the theory of public service ethics is a radical disconnection between theory and action, which we believe arises in considerable part from the difficulty of adequately considering the cultural and organizational contexts within which those in public service produce ethical or unethical actions. In some respects, this theoretical disconnection is predictable, because it is the culture at large—and the way it conditions our assumptions and understandings of organizational life in particular—that appears to set the "range of the possible" for the actions of people in the public and private sectors (Hofstede and Hofstede 2005). One is tempted to describe the situation of public service ethics as a structural conundrum. That is, there are powerful, long-standing, but largely unseen assumptions and values at work both in organizations and in the culture at large that simultaneously enable some ethical and unethical actions, and constrain others.

In comparison with other topics (e.g., financial or human resource management, or more recently, network management), ethics continues to receive considerably less attention in the academic literature of public policy and administration in the United States and has never achieved a place of centrality in that literature. Moreover, its presence in the master of public administration (MPA) and master of public policy (MPP) curricula is often as an optional course, and the trend line for ethics education for public service is a negative one. This too reflects the disconnection between theory and action. The publication of articles on ethics topics in the field's leading academic journals—especially those most aligned with new governance or public management—is clearly in decline. Further, and more troubling, fewer and fewer of the newer U.S. scholars in the field research ethical issues. An ethical framework captured by the twentieth-century gestalt of technical rationality and the dominance of bureaucratic organizations appears unable to adequately address the disconnection introduced above. This disconnection is now exacerbated by the ethical challenges of a new governance era characterized by a market-based system of public service and the myriad new opportunities presented therein for serving or betraying the public interest.

This chapter provides an overview of the theory and practice of public service ethics, and raises some of the issues that might be addressed in future research by public affairs scholars. We begin by placing the study of public service ethics in the context of technical rationality—the cultural milieu of the modern era. Professionalism and technical expertise were the hallmarks of organizational life during the twentieth century and are still in the early twenty-first, and they represent the organizational and cultural context within which public service ethics has been conceived and acted out. We then turn to a brief discussion of the decline of the nation-state, and the concomitant devaluation of public service. We trace the evolution of "new governance," an emerging set of arrangements whereby governments engage in a variety of partnership activities with both private and nonprofit collaborators through contracting and many other configurations. We discuss the changes that new governance and the market state have brought to organizational life more generally, and note the impact on the "psychological contract" that individuals and organizations have always tacitly employed. These developments have further undermined an already poor cultural and organizational climate for ethical behavior.

We trace a parallel demise of ethics scholarship within the academic community of public affairs. Never achieving centrality in the literature, ethics now appears to be a disappearing topic within the field's top journals—especially those most associated with new governance and public management. Scholars who teach and write in the area of public service ethics are also in decline. We close by assessing in as cold a light as possible the future prospects of public service ethics, and by raising some potential directions for further research.

PUBLIC SERVICE ETHICS IN AN ERA OF TECHNICAL RATIONALITY

The organizational context of public service ethics follows largely from the cultural context of the modern age. The cultural context in the United States (among other nation-states) in the modern age can be characterized as one of technical rationality—that is, a way of thinking and a way of living that exalts the scientific-analytical mindset and a belief in technological progress (Vanderburg 2005). Donald Schon (1983, 21) and others have argued that technical rationality has been the most powerful influence on both thinking about the professions and the institutional relations of research, government, and business. Technical rationality emerged in full form in the twentieth century, and continues in the twenty-first century's new governance era as perhaps the central pillar on the mental map of globalization. We suggest that technical rationality underpins globalization and economic rationalism, which in turn energize and sustain the New Public Management and market-based government. One author has described technical rationality as the first universal human culture (Vanderburg 1985; see also Barrett 1979; Bauman 1989; Ellul 1954; Ritzer 2004).

How does technical rationality's combination of the scientific-analytic mindset and the concomitant belief in technological progress shape our culture? The scientific-analytic mindset has come to characterize—and ultimately define—how knowledge is thought to be developed, resulting in a narrowing of the concept of human reason, and the devaluing of other sources and processes previously thought to develop knowledge. The closely connected belief in technological progress is essentially both a fascination and a faith in each successive technological advance—and the typically unquestioned assumption that each new technology is in fact an advance. Both individual and social problems are thought to be fixable by a (new) technique or technology. These twin assumptions are reinforced within a self-sealing way of thinking and way of living that simultaneously produces the outcomes that are made inevitable by the prior assumptions.

PROFESSIONALISM, RATIONALITY, AND ORGANIZATIONAL ETHICS

The modern organization is largely a creature of the culture of technical rationality. Within organizations, technical rationality has led to task and knowledge specialization, the successive application of the "latest, most up-to-date" technique (including machines, information systems and/or management schemes), and an inhospitable context for ethics and morality. As both MacIntyre (1984) and Poole (1991) have argued, modernity has produced a way of thinking—an epistemology—that renders moral reasoning necessary but superfluous. Organizational practice is based largely on technical expertise and pragmatic action, and organizations continue to be staffed primarily by professionals, that is, by people who self-identify as a professional. Even those obviously not in a recognized profession still strive to be seen as "professional" in their actions.

Indeed, many have seen professionalism as a source of ethical standards for organizational practice. Professional ethics, however, has also been captured by technical rationality (Adams 2001), emphasizing as it does the technical expertise of the individual practitioner. Public service (and other) professionals do not see the technical rational model of professionalism as eschewing ethics; quite the contrary: They see the role model of "professional" as satisfying the need for a system of ethical standards. Many scholars in the field have assumed that ethical behavior can be treated as an afterthought that will follow from the accepted professional management practices of the day (Maesschalck 2004). The net result is an organizational context that defaults to leaving ethics as an afterthought. Here again, we see the disconnection between thought and aspiration on the one hand, and action on the other.

PUBLIC SERVICE ETHICS

Both public service and business ethics—as well as professional ethics more generally—in the technical-rational tradition draw upon both consequentialist and deontological ethics (Frankena 1973), and focus on the individual's decision-making process in the modern, bureaucratic organization and as a member of a profession. In the public sphere, deontological ethics is meant to safeguard the integrity of the organization by helping individuals conform to professional norms, avoid mistakes and misdeeds that violate the public trust (corruption, nepotism, etc.), and assure that public officials in a constitutional republic are accountable through their elected representatives to the people. At the same time, public servants are encouraged to pursue the greater good by using discretion in the application of rules and regulations and creativity in the face of changing conditions—consequentialist ethics. The "good" public servant should avoid both the extremes of rule-bound behavior and undermining the rule of law with individual judgments and interests. Like most people, public servants operate within a partly tacit mix of different ethical orientations, with the mix often shifting from one situation to the next. Virtue ethics (MacIntyre 1984), with its focus on moral character, does not align well with either the organizational or cultural context of technical rationality, especially if it is understood to be a social, and not just an individual, construct.

Attention to public service ethics in the U.S. literature appears to have waned considerably since the turn of the century. Its growth trajectory was, however, strong in the later decades of the twentieth century (Adams 2001). Ethics scholarship in the 1980s and 1990s in the United States built on the literature from a previous wave of ethics concern, prompted by the Watergate scandal of the early 1970s. However, attention to ethics in the field's literature in the United States appears to have diminished since 2000. In the last three decades of the twentieth century, each successive wave of ethics scandals in the public realm (e.g., Watergate, Iran-Contra, savings and loans) seemed to prompt renewed energy and attention both in the literature and among practitioners in both the public and private sectors. The first decade of the twenty-first century has had perhaps more than its representative share of ethics scandals (e.g., Enron/Worldcom, Hurricane Katrina, Iraq, the subprime mortgage meltdown), but the response in the literature has, at a minimum, yet to appear.

Internationally, a similar decline in attention to public service ethics is not evident. There appears to be strong, continuing interest in public service ethics in Europe and in Asia. There have been three "transatlantic dialogues" on public service ethics, involving primarily scholars from Europe and the United States, and there are active centers of public service ethics scholarship at the Free University in Amsterdam and the Catholic University in Leuven, Belgium. Further, there has been a great deal of activity worldwide throughout the past decade as many countries have begun or enhanced governmental ethics programs, in many cases, aided by consultations with the U.S. Office of Government Ethics. The United Nations and the Organization for Economic Cooperation and Development have both been very active players in promoting the development of public service ethics programs, with a strong focus on both anticorruption and transparency.

FROM NATION-STATE TO NEW GOVERNANCE: A CHANGING CONTEXT FOR PUBLIC SERVICE ETHICS

Despite many accomplishments, public service ethics in the nation-state offers a mixed picture at best, contributing perhaps to both the rise and fall of the nation-state. On the one hand, there have been many successes. The insulation of administration from (corrupt) politics and the proliferation of bureaucratic and professional norms and procedures have helped to reduce corruption and establish reliable and responsive organizations at all levels of government and industry. Professions and their standards for performance and conduct became the norm for ethical behavior and for translating scientific discoveries into practical means for solving societal problems and producing wealth (Schon 1983). On the other hand, these same organizations and professions were often blind to the limitations and destructive consequences of their actions, even as they pursued lofty goals and ambitious programs in the name of the public interest and economic prosperity (Adams 2001).

We have written elsewhere (Adams and Balfour 2009) about the moral and ethical failings of the technical-rational cultural and organizational context, especially the tendency toward moral inversions and administrative evil. There has been little recognition of the most fundamental ethical challenge to the professional within a technical-rational culture: that one can be a "good" or responsible administrator or professional and at the same time commit or contribute to acts of administrative evil. As Harmon (1995) has argued, technical-rational ethics has difficulty dealing with what Milgram (1974) termed the "agentic shift," whereby the professional or administrator acts responsibly toward the hierarchy of authority, public policy, and the requirements of the job or profession, while abdicating any personal, much less social, responsibility for the content or effects of decisions or actions. From a virtue ethics perspective, this seems to risk a kind of "moral schizophrenia" in the worst cases.

By the closing decade of the twentieth century, the world was changing in ways that began to transcend the limitations of the nation-state. The waves of change and reform in the public service—new governance—during this same time frame were a direct response to the undermined credibility of the state as a means for assuring continuous improvement in the welfare of its people. The end of the Cold War and of the era of nation-states was hastened by innovations in rapid computation, international travel and communication, and their integration and application to markets and organizations (Friedman 2007). The expansion of markets across national boundaries in a global system increasingly limited governments' ability to effectively promote the welfare of citizens or to effectively limit the purview of international corporations. At the organizational level, these developments have made it very difficult for even the most capable managers to create the "lean" and "nimble" organizations demanded by the global marketplace while basing their legitimacy on promoting the welfare of their communities (Bobbitt 2002). Cutbacks in the labor force and in the benefits offered by employers have been accepted as normal—and necessary—operating procedures in the global economy of the twenty-first century.

Organizations themselves are changing in many instances under the pressures of globalization. Some of these changes can have a great impact on individual workers (Sennett 1998). Workers, and even successful entrepreneurs, who achieve success in this new market environment may also suffer from deep anxieties about the future and the quality of their lives—anxieties that have become all too real for many thousands of people like them in the successive waves of market "rationalization." One result of this dramatic alteration of the "psychological contract" between workers and organizations is declining levels of trust and commitment (Rousseau 1995). Individuals are often whipsawed between valuing the independence of the new economy but also feeling adrift, with no strong bonds of commitment or trust. For managers and policymakers, individual employees are increasingly considered expendable. The notion that organizations should care for their employees, or make long-term commitments to them, is seen as an anachronism. Translated to the individual level, the short-term orientation of the new market state tends to undermine further character, especially those qualities that bind people to each other and furnish the individual with a stable sense of self. Callahan (2004, 107) notes three shifts over the last decade in particular that, taken together, undermine the possibilities for ethical action: Individualism has shifted to a hard-edged selfishness, money has become more important (well-being is understood as financial), and harsher norms of competition have emerged. All three are consistent with globalization and the rise of the market state.

Under these conditions, the requirements for success in organizations make the grounds for ethical behavior even more uncertain. Though bureaucracy and stable lines of authority and routine were valued in a nation-state environment, market state organizations emphasize flexibility and autonomous action. Corporations and governments want employees who can think on their feet and adroitly adjust to rapid change, but also want to retain the right (in the name of adaptability to market imperatives) to let these employees go at any time for the good of the organization. More flexibility does not necessarily mean more freedom for employees. The threat of expendability and fear of social breakdown make people all the more prone to protect their self-interest rather than consider the implications of their actions for the well-being of others. The context these developments provide for ethics in public life is significantly more difficult than in the past.

THE DEMISE OF PUBLIC SERVICE ETHICS

In recent years, the literature on public service ethics has not yet effectively addressed these dramatic changes in how public service is conceived and carried out. Government organizations and programs have been compared in a negative light with their private-sector counterparts. It has been widely assumed that private organizations are more effective than government if given the opportunity to perform (Frederickson 2005). Contracting, outsourcing, competitive sourcing, privatization, and public–private partnerships became the methods of choice for delivering public services, and public agencies must compete (competitive sourcing) and demonstrate cost savings and effectiveness before directly providing a service. A considerable literature has emerged on market-based service delivery and the principles for the successful management of contracts and outsourcing. Simply scanning recent issues of the *International Public Management Journal* or *Governance* provides ample evidence. Scant attention in the literature is given, however, to the ethical dimensions and consequences of market-based government.

Scholarly articles on ethics topics at their zenith hovered around 5 percent of all articles published in the field's top journals (e.g., the *Public Administration Review* or the *Journal of Public Administration Research and Theory*). However, in those journals most closely aligned with the New Public Management, ethics scholarship is disappearing. The *Journal of Public Administration Research and Theory* had 5 percent of its published articles devoted to ethics topics in the 1990s, but in the current decade only 2 percent. *Governance* over the past decade has had only 1 percent of its published articles on ethics topics. The *International Public Management Journal* has published almost nothing on ethics. This decline in public service ethics scholarship is mirrored in a decline in both required and optional ethics courses in both MPA and MPP programs. In MPP programs, ethics never has achieved a real foothold, with some programs offering some treatment of research ethics at least. In sum, the field is ill prepared to address ethics in the education and training of future leaders in public service, which calls for a more nuanced and beefed-up curriculum inasmuch as it now has to deal with all the ethical issues associated with the new governance and globalization—network ethics is just one small example. Arguably, the United States is ceding the field of public service ethics, including ethics education, to the rest of the world, where interest in these questions seems to be growing.

ACHIEVING ETHICAL ORGANIZATIONS

The road from compliance-based ethics programs to comprehensive ethics programs that are high on both compliance and social responsibility is a steep climb, with multiple switchbacks and precipitous drop-offs. The Sarbanes-Oxley Act of 2002, itself a response to the Enron-Worldcom cluster of widespread corporate misbehavior, sets a rather minimal compliance floor (Ethics Resource Center 2007, 20): written standards for ethical conduct, a mechanism for reporting misconduct anonymously, and disciplining employees who violate the standards of the organization or the law. According to the Ethics Resource Center (2007, 20), a comprehensive ethics program should also include training on company standards of ethical workplace conduct, a mechanism for seeking ethics-related advice or information, and assessment of ethical conduct as a part of employee performance evaluations. It is important to note here that there has been a strong private-sector reaction and opposition to the Sarbanes-Oxley provisions as overly onerous and damaging to the ability to compete in the global marketplace.

The Ethics Resource Center (2007, 37) suggests that developing strong ethics cultures in public organizations will be quite difficult:

> Traditional approaches will not be enough. Prevailing methods for addressing problems—the implementation of formal government programs, creation of policies, and, in some cases legislative action to improve internal controls—do make some difference. But at present, only half of government employees are aware that these programs exist, and only eighteen percent of government ethics and compliance programs are well-implemented. Even if all government agencies had well-implemented

programs, the most significant change will come only when effective government programs are coupled with a strong ethical culture. Reaching this point will require an "out of the box" approach for many government leaders.

Both strong ethics cultures in organizations and organizational (including corporate) social responsibility (McBarnett 2004) go against the grain of individualism (the classical liberal values inherent to American culture) and against the grain of technical rationality (professionalism, scientific-analytic mindset, and belief in technique). Arguably, the market state, globalization, and economic rationality have considerably exacerbated the difficulty of achieving the ethical organization, well developed on both compliance and social responsibility dimensions.

Most critical observers of the market state (e.g., Reich 2007; Frederickson 2005; Denhardt and Denhardt 2003) bemoan the loss of democratic values and citizen confidence in government as a fair and reliable agent of the public interest, if only potentially so. Ethical scandals entwined with acts of incompetence (Macaulay and Lawton 2006; Adams, Balfour, and Reed 2006) deepen the disconnection between citizens and their governments, and between ethical theory and practice. In the era of Enron, Abu Ghraib, Hurricane Katrina, and Blackwater, the revitalization of public service ethics seems essential to avoid the further erosion of democracy and continuing loss of legitimacy for government in society. Citizens are unlikely to answer the call to greater involvement in government and civic life unless it becomes clear that all those in public service are at least attempting to foster a cultural and organizational context within which ethical principles and standards are paramount, and no longer an afterthought at best.

What type of research on public service ethics might begin to address some of the problems discussed here? First, studies focused on understanding the ethical theory/ethical action disconnection within single organizations, whether isolated or as participants in a network, seem vital. Second, we need research on organizations' social responsibility—encompassing fiscal, social (or community), and environmental responsibilities—an urgently needed research trajectory. Third, research on the challenges and opportunities for creating well-developed organizational ethics cultures would be very helpful. Fourth, while public management scholars have appreciated the importance of collaboration in successful networks, a focus in this literature on the ethics of cross-sectoral relationships is badly needed. Finally, and relatedly, we are in need of research that suggests strategies for organizations to succeed in developing healthy and resilient ethical cultures in an environment that is less than supportive of those who would put the public interest first. Regardless of the research agenda ultimately pursued, however, studies addressing this topic are needed, important, and long overdue. The question remains whether there will be enough scholars of public service ethics to address these topics in the coming decades, given how very few ethics scholars are emerging from the field's top doctoral programs.

REFERENCES

Adams, Guy B. 2001. Administrative Ethics and the Chimera of Professionalism: The Historical Context of Public Service Ethics. In *Handbook of Administrative Ethics*, 2nd edition, ed. Terry L. Cooper. New York: Marcel Dekker.

Adams, Guy B., and Danny L. Balfour. 2008. Ethics, Public Values and Market-Based Government. Paper presented at Copenhagen International Public Values Workshop, University of Copenhagen, Copenhagen.

———. 2009. *Unmasking Administrative Evil*, 3rd ed. Armonk, NY: M. E. Sharpe.

Adams, Guy B., Danny L. Balfour, and George E. Reed. 2006. Abu Ghraib, Administrative Evil, and Moral Inversion: The Value of "Putting Cruelty First." *Public Administration Review* 66, no. 5:680–69.

Barrett, William. 1979. *The Illusion of Technique*. Garden City, NY: Doubleday Anchor.

Bauman, Zygmont. 1989. *Modernity and the Holocaust*. Ithaca, NY: Cornell University Press.

Bobbitt, Phillip. 2002. *The Shield of Achilles: War, Peace, and the Course of History*. New York: Alfred A. Knopf.

Callahan, David. 2004. *The Cheating Culture: Why More Americans Are Doing Wrong to Get Ahead*. Orlando: Harvest Books.

Denhardt, Robert B., and Janet V. Denhardt. 2003. *The New Public Service: Serving, Not Steering*. Armonk, NY: M. E. Sharpe.

Ellul, Jacques. 1954. *The Technological Society*. New York: Vintage.

Ethics Resource Center. 2007. *National Government Ethics Survey: An Inside View of Public Sector Ethics*. Arlington, VA: Ethics Resource Center.

Frankena, William. 1973. *Ethics*, 2nd ed. Englewood Cliffs, NJ: Prentice Hall.

Frederickson, H. George. 2005. Public Ethics and the New Managerialism: An Axiomatic Theory." In *Ethics in Public Management*, ed. H. George Frederickson and Richard Ghere. Armonk, NY: M. E. Sharpe.

Friedman, Thomas. 2007. *The World Is Flat: A Brief History of the Twenty-first Century*, 2nd rev. and expanded ed. New York: Farrar, Straus & Giroux.

Harmon, Michael M. 1995. *Responsibility as Paradox: A Critique of Rational Discourse on Government*. Thousand Oaks, CA: Sage.

Hofstede, Geert, and Gert Jan Hofstede. 2005. *Cultures and Organizations: Software of the Mind*. New York: McGraw-Hill.

Macaulay, Michael, and Alan Lawton. *2006*. From Virtue to Competence: Changing the Principles of Public Service. *Public Administration Review* 66, no. 5:702–10.

MacIntyre, Alasdair. 1984. *After Virtue*, 2nd ed. Notre Dame, IN: Notre Dame University Press.

Maesschalck, Jeroen. 2004. The Impact of New Public Management Reforms on Public Servants' Ethics: Towards a Theory. *Public Administration* 82, no. 2:465–89.

McBarnett, Doreen. 2004. Human Rights, Corporate Responsibility and the New Accountability. In *Human Rights and the Moral Responsibilities of Corporate and Public Sector Organisations*, ed. Tom Campbell and Seumas Miller. Dordrecht: Kluwer Academic Publishers.

Milgram, Stanley. 1974. *Obedience to Authority*. New York: Harper & Row.

Moulton, Stephanie, and Barry Bozeman. 2008. Policy Design and the Subprime Mortgage Market: Implications for Managing Publicness. Paper presented at the Copenhagen International Public Values Workshop, University of Copenhagen, Copenhagen.

Poole, Ross. 1991. *Morality and Modernity*. London: Routledge, Chapman and Hall.
Reich, Robert. 2007. *Supercapitalism: The Transformation of Business, Democracy, and Everyday Life.* New York: Alfred A. Knopf.
Ritzer, George. 2004. *The McDonaldization of Society,* rev. New Century edition. Thousand Oaks, CA: Sage.
Rousseau, Denise M. 1995. *Psychological Contracts in Organizations.* Thousand Oaks, CA: Sage.
Schon, Donald. 1983. *The Reflective Practitioner.* New York: Basic Books.
Sennett. Richard. 1998. *The Corrosion of Character: The Personal Consequences of Work in the New Capitalism*. New York: W. W. Norton.
Vanderburg, William H. 1985. *The Growth of Minds and Cultures: A Unified Theory of the Structure of Human Experience.* Toronto: University of Toronto Press.
———. 2005. *Living in the Labyrinth of Technology.* Toronto: University of Toronto Press.

The Status of the Law in Contemporary Public Administration Literature, Education, and Practice

David H. Rosenbloom and Katherine C. Naff

The law has never been central to mainstream public administrative theory and education in the United States. As a field of self-conscious study, public administration was initially defined as a field of management. In the first U.S. textbook on public administration, *Introduction to the Study of Public Administration*, Leonard White famously wrote: "The study of administration should start from the base of management rather than the foundation of law, and is therefore more absorbed in the affairs of the American Management Association than in the decisions of the courts" (White 2004, 56).

There was nothing new in White's echo of Woodrow Wilson's earlier assertion that public administration is "a field of business" (Wilson 2004, 28). In a sense, the law was tangential to public administrative practice before the late 1940s. There was no comprehensive or basic federal administrative law statute until the enactment of the Administrative Procedure Act in 1946. From the 1890s through the mid-1930s, judicial decisions were more likely to prohibit than to direct administrative action (Rosenbloom 2008). From 1937 to the early 1950s, the courts had little direct impact on public administration because they were highly deferential to administrative expertise and they largely acquiesced in the exercise of administrative authority (Pritchett 1948; Shapiro 1968). Beginning in the early 1950s, the judicial role in public administration intensified dramatically (Rosenbloom and O'Leary 1997). The extent to which the courts currently prescribe public administrative values, behavior, and liability needs no documentation or elaboration here (Rosenbloom and O'Leary 1997, chap. 9). It is enough to note that by the 1970s it was reasonable to consider the federal courts as full-fledged "partners" in public administration (Bazelon 1976). Has the status of the law in contemporary U.S. public administrative literature and education caught up with the vast changes to the field's legal framework since its founding? This is the research question directing our analysis.

"CONSTITUTIONS MATTER": THE OBVIOUS IMPORTANCE OF LAW IN PUBLIC ADMINISTRATIVE SCHOLARSHIP AND EDUCATION

During the 2003 Virginia Tech High Table affair, John Rohr and his coauthor Rosenbloom concluded that two words largely sum up their career work, "Constitutions matter." They also joked about whether they would have had careers if the academic field of public administration paid more attention to what is to them the obvious importance of constitutional and administrative law. It now appears that the American Society for Public Administration's (ASPA's) Task Force on Educating for Excellence in the MPA [master of public administration] Degree has affirmed the obvious. Comprising Nicholas Henry, Charles T. Goodsell, Laurence E. Lynn Jr., Camilla Stivers, and Gary L. Wamsley—heavyweights all—the Task Force agrees that, at least in the U.S. context, constitutions do matter:

- The core mission of those offering the MPA degree must be to develop the capacity of graduates to exercise delegated public authority wisely, effectively, *lawfully* [emphasis added].
- The Task Force believes that MPA education should accomplish two goals: First, transmittal of a full awareness of the broad issues of constitutionalism, politics, and democratic theory that are innately embedded in the practice of public administration. . . .
- As to [this] objective, the anchor of American public administration, regardless of level of government, is the United States Constitution, along with the constitutions of the states.
- The curriculum for the MPA degree should be such that it introduces or reinforces students' understanding of their constitutionally delegated authority.
- [Public administrators are duty bound] to ensure that the terms of the public trust are fulfilled and activities within and outside the public agency are consonant with constitutional principles of individual rights, due process of law, equal protection, and the separation of powers. (American Society for Public Administration Task Force 2008, 21)

The importance and urgency of the Task Force's recommendations are highlighted by the assault on the rule of law waged by the George W. Bush administration. As discussed by Rosenbloom (2008) and in much greater detail by James Pfiffner (2008), Bush's presidency ran roughshod over the constitutional separation of powers and guarantee of habeas corpus as well as laws and treaties against torture and domestic surveillance. In Pfiffner's words, "Insofar as President Bush . . . refused to acknowledge the constitutional limits on his executive authority, he undermined two of the fundamental principles upon which the United States was established: the rule of law and the Constitution" (Pfiffner 2008, 245).

Pfiffner does not dwell on the extent to which Bush's actions are concordant with public administration's fixation on executive centeredness. Rosenbloom (2009) takes up this theme, concluding that Bush's theory of a unitary executive branch bears a strong intellectual relationship to the writings of Alexander Hamilton, Luther Gulick, and the proposals of various reform committees, from the 1937 President's Committee on Administrative Management (the Brownlow Committee) to the Hoover Commissions, the Ash Council, and beyond (Arnold 1998). Unitary executive branch theory holds that the president has plenary power to "remove subordinate policy-making officials at will," "to direct the manner in which subordinate officials exercise discretionary executive power," and to "veto or nullify such officials' exercises of discretionary executive power" (Yoo, Calabresi, and Colangelo 2005, 607). It necessarily parrots reformers from Brownlow to Gore in calling for very limited congressional involvement in federal administration (President's Committee on Administrative Management 1937, 1, 3, 22, 49, 50; Brownlow 1949, 116; Gore 1993, 17, 20, 34). It also would necessarily weaken the separation of powers. Reflecting on Watergate, Gulick eventually admitted the error of executive-centered "unity of command": "We all assumed in the 1930s that management, especially public management flowed in a broad, strong stream of value-filled ethical performance. Were we blind or only naive until [President] Nixon came along?" (Shafritz and Russell 2000, 104).

Organizing the modern presidency, as Gulick and his colleagues on the Brownlow Committee tried to do, is no place for naïveté. Rosenbloom (2008, 264) reinforces Pfiffner's conclusions in finding that "the Bush administration's behavior . . . indisputably demonstrates that implementation of a theory of a unitary executive branch poses a clear and present danger to the rule of law." As the ASPA Task Force suggests, the U.S. field of public administration should be rooted in the separation of powers. That means that Hobbes, Locke, and Montesquieu should be in, and Rousseau, Gore, and others who take a benign view of human nature should be out.

THE LAW IN THE LITERATURE OF PUBLIC ADMINISTRATION

There is no easy or universally accepted means of assessing the extent to which the law is covered in the academic literature on public administration. Article and book titles can be misleading. A book on bureaucracy and democracy may or may not provide much attention to constitutions or constitutional and administrative law (Kennedy 2007). Textbooks may incorporate the law into their topical coverage rather than treat it in stand-alone chapters. This being the case, Zeger van der Wal (2008, 55) has done a major service in providing "the results of a literature review and content analysis of the most prominent organizational values in the administrative and business ethics literature, public and private sector codes of conduct, and empirical research on

Table V.1 Coverage of Values in the Public Administration Literature (number of times mentioned)

1. Honesty	434	16. Cooperativeness	191
2. Humaneness	422	17. Responsiveness	184
3. Social justice	402	18. Dedication	183
4. Impartiality	380	19. Effectiveness	181
5. Transparency	379	20. Innovativeness	179
6. Integrity	365	21. Lawfulness	152
7. Obedience	357	22. Loyalty	146
8. Reliability	329	23. Consistency	111
9. Responsibility	327	24. Autonomy	99
10. Expertise	314	25. Suitability	99
11. Accountability	294	26. Representativeness	88
12. Efficiency	276	27. Competitiveness	77
13. Courage	254	28. Profitability	59
14. Prudence	220	29. Collegiality	48
15. Serviceability	215	30. Self-fulfillment	16

values." With respect to the public sector, van der Wal reviewed seven books for coverage of values.[1] He also reviewed *Public Integrity* from 1999 to 2003 and *Public Administration Review* from 1999 to 2002. He identified 544 values that clustered in terms of prominence, as presented in table V.1 (van der Wal 2008, 55).

Given the character of the literature reviewed, one might reasonably expect lawfulness to rank higher that number 21 in table V.1 (van der Wal 2008, 56). If the treatment of the law is not prominent in the literature on administrative ethics and values, it may receive even less attention in such core areas of public administration as budgeting and finance, organization, program and policy evaluation, implementation, and decision making (though perhaps more coverage in human resources management). This of course does not mean that the law finds no prominence in U.S. contemporary public administration literature. There is a trove of scholarship on constitutional and administrative law, and the law is central to the analysis of regulatory policy and administration. In addition, several texts focusing on the law in the context of public administration are available for classroom use.[2] On balance, however, the law seems to be largely a "stand-alone" field within public administration rather than well integrated into the core literature. If that is the case, can we expect the law to receive the treatment that the ASPA Task Force believes is necessary in MPA programs?

THE LAW IN U.S. MPA PROGRAMS

In conjunction with this chapter, Rosenbloom and Laurel McFarland, executive director of the National Association of Schools of Public Affairs and Administration (NASPAA), designed a questionnaire to ascertain the extent to which NASPAA-affiliated MPA programs offer law-oriented courses and JD (juris doctor)–MPA degrees. The questionnaire was e-mailed to the 265 NASPAA-affiliated MPA program contacts (program directors or principal representatives) on July 27, 2008. As of August 12, a total of 86 responses were received.[3] The survey results are available on the internet.[4] Only a few points need highlighting here:

- Roughly 40 percent of the responding programs offer JD-MPA degrees. In most of these programs (80 percent), they account for 5 percent or less of the enrollments.
- In about 60 percent of the programs a student can receive an MPA degree without taking a single law-oriented course.
- Most MPA programs (88 percent) offer at least one course with "law," "legal," or "constitutional" in its name. About 8 percent offer none, and the rest were not sure.
- In order of frequency, law-oriented courses emphasize administrative law (84 percent), constitutional law (45 percent), personnel/human resources management law (36 percent), and environmental law (17 percent). Additional emphases mentioned include housing and community development, local government, collective bargaining, health, elections, nonprofit, and tax law.
- In more than 60 percent of the programs, law-oriented courses are taught by tenured or tenure-line faculty; about 14 percent are taught by in-residence (nontenure/non-tenure-line faculty), and 18 percent by adjunct faculty.
- Where law-oriented courses are optional, the propensity of students to take them is shown in table V.2.
- The main reasons why MPA programs offer law-oriented courses are presented in table V.3.

Why are more programs not requiring students to complete a law-oriented course? The survey results suggest that it may not be a question of availability. The same proportion of programs that do and do not make the requirement offer one such course on a regular basis (55 percent), and the same proportion offer more than one (about 30 percent). Nor is it necessarily a question of

Table V.2 The Propensity of Students to Take Optional Law-Oriented Courses

Percentage Taking Law-Oriented Courses	No. of Programs (%)
Less than 10	21 (38.8)
11–25	26 (40.6)
26–50	6 (9.4)
50+	7 (12.5)

Table V.3 Percentage of Respondents Indicating Main Reasons for Offering Law-Oriented Courses

Reason	Percent
MPA students should have knowledge of the law	77.3
MPA students should have the option of taking law-oriented courses	44.8
There is student demand for law-oriented courses	26.2
Law-oriented courses in the curriculum make it easier to admit students	2.4
MPA programs compete with law schools for students	0

resources. Those programs requiring courses on the law are only slightly more likely to have a tenure-track faculty member available to teach them (63 percent) than those that do not (58 percent). Though it is not surprising that 90 percent of programs requiring a law-oriented course report that the main reason is because "MPA students should have knowledge of the law," even among those programs that do not require such a course, 71 percent agreed that that was a main reason. The same proportion of both indicates that student demand for such courses is a main reason (26 percent). Perhaps differences between programs that do and do not require at least one law-oriented course are related to program structure and enrollments. Requiring any course reduces the number of electives students are likely to take and may require additional sections (and faculty) to keep class sizes within desired bounds. However, in view of the high level of agreement that knowledge of the law is important, one could expect more programs to require at least one law-oriented course.

What, then, does explain the MPA programs that do not require (or in some cases, even offer) a law-oriented course? One reason may be that the focus of the courses listed in their programs is on administrative law, which is only one element of public administration's contemporary legal dimension. The vast majority of respondents (more than 80 percent) did indicate that administrative law is an emphasis in their course. One respondent wrote on the survey that the typical administrative law course "is geared to the federal government process, and the vast majority of MPA students will not work for the federal government." Notably, however, those programs that require a law-oriented course are more likely to also emphasize constitutional law (56 percent, compared with 37 percent) and public personnel law (44 percent, compared with 33 percent). In many programs there remain some faculty who, contrary to the ASPA Task Force, just do not see the need for law-oriented courses. The following comments in response to the survey capture this: "A little bit of legal knowledge is good. If you want more, become a lawyer." Another wrote: "If administrators find themselves with a legal question or issue, there are professional lawyers within the organization, . . . which need to be consulted to ensure legal actions and reduced liability."

If these results are assessed in terms of the recommendations of the ASPA Task Force, it is clear that the law requires greater emphasis in MPA programs. In more than 60 percent of the MPA programs, a student can graduate without taking a single law-oriented course, and where such courses are optional, in the majority of programs, most students do not take them.

IS LEGAL KNOWLEDGE RELEVANT TO PRACTICE?

There is no doubt that the law is relevant to public administrative practice. The law establishes, empowers, structures, and constrains agencies and programs. It mandates procedural, reporting, and transparency requirements. It provides for public participation, representation, and official and agency liability. There is not much agencies can do without reference to legal authority. In the litigious United States, the law is fundamental to a vast array of administrative operations: public-sector human resources management; prison, public school, and public health administration; social welfare; regulation; rulemaking; adjudicating; contracting; street-level and other enforcement; use of resources; and more. Writing in 1980, perhaps Marshall Dimock best summed up what the law means to public administrators: "To the public administrator, law is something very positive and concrete. It is his authority. . . . It does three things: tells him what the legislature expects him to accomplish, fixes limits to his authority, and sets forth the substantive and procedural rights of the individual and group" (Dimock 1980, 31).

The courts, as well as legislatures, often establish public policy and regulate administrative action in these areas, sometimes engaging in a "reinterpretation of statutory law that amounts to substantial alteration of the intent of Congress in enacting the law" (Powers and Rothman 2002, 2). Appreciation of how the courts do so requires at least some grounding in constitutional and administrative law. Public administrators ought to understand their judicial "partners." The administrator should also know "his" or "her" law, but need he and she know much about law generally?

Here the evidence is less certain, just as it is with much research, pedagogy, and andragogy in the field of public administration. Empirical findings from the United States and the Netherlands suggest that general knowledge of the law is important because the law cannot always be applied universally. Administrators recognize that strict adherence to the letter of the law may be counterproductive and contrary to the spirit of the law. A survey by van der Wal (2008, 70, 73, 74) indicates that lawfulness ranks close to the top of values held by Dutch administrators. Yet he found that "as a value in public sector decisionmaking, *lawfulness* ('acting in accordance with existing laws and rules') might seem self-evident and perhaps even trivial given that laws are thought out, formulated, implemented and executed by public sector organizations through the legislative process. On a day-to-day basis, however, many gradations and dimensions seemingly apply to abiding by laws, rules and regulations" (van der Wal 2008, 85–86). Similarly Maynard-Moody and Musheno (2003, 156) observe that in street-level administration, "in many instances, workers cannot respond to the needs of individuals and follow the dictates of law and policy. Workers must continually make judgments about citizen-clients to determine how to apply the rules and procedures and to determine their meaning and value."

Knowledge of the law generally, rather than just of individual statutes, would help to inform judgments about gradations and the exercise of discretion. This is probably particularly true with respect to constitutional law in the United States and its functional equivalents elsewhere. Knowledge of constitutional law is a prerequisite for preventing violations of constitutional rights. As the U.S. Supreme Court reasoned, "where an official could be expected to know that certain conduct would violate statutory or constitutional rights, he should be made to hesitate" (*Harlow v. Fitzgerald* 1982, 819). Without knowledge, there may be no hesitation.

Today, the notion of government is being challenged by one of governance. That is, activities once performed by government at the federal, state, or local level are "diffused" among each other and into the private and nonprofit sectors. Neither can the influence of globalization be overstated (Nye 2002). Among other dimensions, it places new pressures on traditional definitions of sovereignty because multigovernmental coordination is required to address issues, problems, and threats that span geographical boundaries. (The long-standing feud between the state of California and the U.S. Environmental Protection Agency regarding who has the authority to regulate automobile emissions is a case in point; Bensinger and Tankersley 2009.) That is all the more reason for administrators to understand federal and state constitutions. The statutory relationships among national, subnational, and supranational institutions and jurisdictions may become the new foundation for understanding the essence of governance in the age of globalization.

CONCLUSION: FUTURE PROSPECTS

On the basis of the material presented here, one might be tempted to ask whether the glass is half empty or half full with regard to the status of the law in the public administrative literature and education. But there is a prior question: How big is the glass? What are our expectations? In view of the George W. Bush administration's assault on the rule of law and all the "gates" scandals from Watergate on, has the field of public administration placed enough emphasis on the law? From the perspectives of those of us who have been analyzing the law's impact on public administration and teaching it to MPA students for many years, joined now by the ASPA Task Force, the answer is clearly "no." Perhaps this will change, as the ASPA Task Force demands.

First, the Bush administration inadvertently fostered greater recognition of the importance of the rule of law. On Inauguration Day 2009, President

Barack Obama underscored his break with the Bush presidency: "Transparency and the rule of law will be the touchstones of this presidency" (Stolbert 2009). Earlier, in 2006, the American Bar Association condemned Bush's signing statements as "contrary to the rule of law and our constitutional separation of powers" for asserting unchecked presidential authority (American Bar Association 2006). Second, the severe current global economic downturn casts serious doubt on the deregulatory initiatives of the past three decades. Growing interest in re-regulation may well spill over into public administration in the form of greater concern with administrative law provisions for rulemaking and enforcement along with efforts to reduce discretion and employee empowerment to ensure that administrative activities are legally bound. With the 2008 global economic meltdown clearly in hindsight, how appealing is the claim that "our path is clear: we must shift from systems that hold people accountable for process to systems that hold them accountable for results" (Gore 1993, 13)? Finally, the intertwinement of nations and populations with respect to today's globalized threats of climate change, pandemics, potential economic collapse, terrorism, mass destruction, and more requires multinational agreements and supranational order, much of which will be imposed by legal requirements implemented by public administrators.

NOTES

1. These are: T. L. Cooper, ed., *Handbook of Administrative Ethics* (1998); T. L. Cooper, ed., *Handbook of Administrative Ethics* (2001); A. J. Heidenheimer, M. Johnston, and V. T. Levine, eds., *Political Corruption: A Handbook* (1989); A. Lawton, *Ethical Management for the Public Services* (1998); C. Sampford and N. Preston, eds., *Public Sector Ethics: Finding and Implementing Values* (1998); M. Van Wart, *Changing Public Sector Values* (1998); and R. Williams and A. Doig, eds., *Controlling Corruption* (2000).
2. Just a few examples, all published in 2004–5, are Julia Beckett and Heidi Koenig, eds., *Public Administration and Law*; Phillip Cooper, *Cases on Public Law and Public Administration*; Donald Barry and Howard Whitcomb, *The Legal Foundations of Public* Administration, 3rd ed.; and Kenneth Warren, *Administrative Law in the Political System*, 4th ed.
3. The contacts were asked to pass the questionnaire to the faculty member whom they thought might be best able to respond.
4. See www.maxwell.syr.edu/pa/minnowbrook3/PDF percent20Files/Minnowbrook per cent203 percent20Agenda percent209-4.pdf; and www.surveymonkey.com/sr.aspx?sm =BmVxPn77HDNy9099k7yLzusN8lT6MgIWnkv65cYngD8_3d.

REFERENCES

American Bar Association. 2006. *Task Force on Presidential Signing Statements and the Separation of Powers Doctrine: Report.* www.abanet.org/op/signingstatements/aba_final_signing_statements_recommendation-report_7-24-06.pdf.
American Society for Public Administration Task Force on Educating for Excellence in the MPA Degree. 2008. Excellence in PA Report, Part 2, *PA Times* 31 (No. 6, June): 21.
Arnold, Peri. 1998. *Making the Managerial Presidency*, 2nd ed. Lawrence: University Press of Kansas.

Bazelon, David. 1976. The Impact of the Courts on Public Administration. *Indiana Law Journal* 52:101–10.

Bensinger, Ben, and Jim Tankersley. 2009. The President Will Ask the EPA Today to Allow States to Set Their Own, Stricter Rules for Auto Emissions, Sources Say. *Los Angeles Times,* January 26. www.latimes.com/news/nationworld/washingtondc/la-na-emissions26-2009jan26,0,7708082.story.

Brownlow, Louis. 1949. *The President and the Presidency.* Chicago: Public Administration Service.

Dimock, Marshall. 1980. *Law and Dynamic Administration.* New York: Praeger.

Gore, Al. 1993. *Creating a Government That Works Better and Costs Less: The Report of the National Performance Review.* Washington, DC: U.S. Government Printing Office.

Harlow v. Fitzgerald. 1982. 457 U.S. 800.

Kennedy, Sheila. 2007. Book Review: Meier, Kenneth J., & O'Toole, Laurence J., Jr. (2006). *Bureaucracy in a Democratic State: A Governance Perspective.* Baltimore: Johns Hopkins University Press. *American Review of Public Administration* 37, no. 4: 501–4.

Maynard-Moody, Steven, and Michael Musheno. 2003. *Cops, Teachers, Counselors.* Ann Arbor: University of Michigan Press.

Nye, Joseph. 2002. Information Technology and Democratic Governance. In *Governance.com: Democracy in the Information Age,* ed. Elaine C. Kamark and Joseph S. Nye Jr. Washington, DC: Brookings Institution Press.

Pfiffner, James. 2008. *Power Play.* Washington, DC: Brookings Institution Press.

Powers, Stephen P., and Staley Rothman. 2002. *The Least Dangerous Branch?* Westport, CT: Praeger.

President's Committee on Administrative Management. 1937. *Report of the Committee.* Washington, DC: U.S. Government Printing Office.

Pritchett, C. Herman. 1948. *The Roosevelt Court.* New York: Macmillan.

Rosenbloom, David. 2008. President George W. Bush's Theory of a Unitary Executive Branch and the Rule of Law in the United States. *Journal of Political and Parliamentary Law* 1 (August): 237–64.

———. 2009. Reevaluating Executive Centered Public Administration. In *The Oxford Handbook of American Bureaucracy,* ed. Robert Durant. New York: Oxford University Press.

Rosenbloom, David, and Rosemary O'Leary. 1997. *Public Administration and Law.* New York: Marcel Dekker.

Shafritz, Jay, and William Russell. 2000. *Introducing Public Administration,* 2d ed. New York: Longman.

Shapiro, Martin. 1968. *The Supreme Court and Administrative Agencies.* New York: Free Press.

Stolbert, Sheryl. 2009. On First Day, Obama Quickly Sets a New Tone. *New York Times,* January 21. www.nytimes.com/2009/01/22/us/politics/22obama.html?hp.

van der Wal, Zeger. 2008. Value Solidity. Doctoral diss., Vrije University, Amsterdam.

White, Leonard. 2004. Introduction to the Study of Administration. In *Classics of Public Administration,* 5th edition, ed. Jay Shafritz, Albert Hyde, and Sandra Parkes. Belmont, CA: Wadsworth (orig. pub. 1926).

Wilson, Woodrow. 2004. The Study of Administration. In *Classics of Public Administration,* 5th edition, ed. Jay Shafritz, Albert Hyde, and Sandra Parkes. Belmont, CA: Wadsworth (orig. pub. 1887).

Yoo, Christopher, Steven Calabresi, and Anthony Colangelo. 2005. The Unitary Executive in the Modern Era, 1945–2004. *Iowa Law Review* 90:601–731.

Adding Value in a World of Diffuse Power

Reintroducing Public Management and Public Financial Management

Justin Marlowe and Daniel L. Smith

Although public administration is a field of continuous innovation, evolution, and reinvention, at its heart it remains concerned with discovering a better way of doing the public's business. Some of the sharpest differences in public management are grounded in the question of how to accomplish this in a way that sustains public servants' constitutional obligations, preserves or enhances citizens' trust in government, and delivers public goods and services in ways consistent with some definition of equity. It is on these difficult questions about the implications of practice and technique where we find the great diversity of intellectual perspectives that makes the field so vivid. This chapter focuses on the centrality of management technique in contemporary public management. We argue that research in select areas of contemporary public budgeting and financial management has delineated and will continue to illuminate the implications of reform and innovation in management techniques, particularly in our current environment of diffuse, shared power.

Contemporary research on how public resources are generated, allocated, and controlled focuses almost exclusively on technique. This is in large part because the subfield's "clinical detail" (Thompson and Gates 2007), or the technical knowledge needed to understand and observe contemporary practice, changes constantly. Budget processes are reformed and re-reformed; since 1992 there have been at least fifty substantial changes to national governmental accounting and financial reporting rules. Citizen initiatives and other forms of direct democracy have woven a complex and ever-changing tapestry of restrictions on how governments can generate and spend money. Because of these and many other changes, many budgeting and finance scholars are principally concerned with technique, with little time to explore the implications of that technique. Unfortunately, this inattention to implications has, we believe, isolated public budgeting and finance experts from the rest of public management.

Our solution to this problem is to highlight how contemporary research on technique in budgeting and financial management can inform broader issues in public management. The first section of our discussion briefly illustrates how the divergence of public budgeting and financial management from broader concerns in public management is, in proper historical context, a new development. The second section highlights three key areas of technique-focused research on budgeting and financial management that have important implications for broader issues in public management. We attempt to demonstrate the value that each of these three types of work could add to public management, both today and in the future. By reintroducing public management and public financial management, we intend to illuminate opportunities for enriching theory, practice, and training in public administration.

PUBLIC MANAGEMENT AND PUBLIC FINANCIAL MANAGEMENT: FROM ROOTS TO BRANCHES

In terms of both research and practice, innovation and reform in management writ large were symbiotic with those in financial management. As the field of public administration became self-aware, however, more explicit normative concerns displaced attention to managerial technique, and the financial management subfield is home to the most technocratic and ostensibly least normative subject matter. As a result, the relationship between the management and financial management subfields has gone from one of recognized common roots to one characterized by distinct branches, especially since the beginning of the twenty-first century. Yet far from being a natural or even inevitable divide that reflects the changing landscape of public administration, there remains much that the now-insular subfield of public financial management can offer to the broader subfield of public management.

Although the self-aware study of public administration—as a field, if not a discipline—was born in the United States around 1940, its intellectual roots trace back to at least the mid–nineteenth century, to early scholars and practitioners of scientific management. Subscribers to scientific management were focused on discovering the management principles and institutions that best enabled organizations to achieve efficiency in particular contexts. The role of financial management—specifically managerial and financial accounting—in scientific management is clearly illustrated in McCallum's (1856, 42) famous memorandum, in which he argues that management science techniques are crucial to both unit-cost accounting (managerial accounting) and developing an annual financial statement (financial accounting).[1] It is further demonstrated by Poor (1860).

Fast forward about a hundred years, and a private-sector-style management orientation inspired a series of reforms in public budgeting and financial management that had, and continue to have, a direct bearing on public management writ large. First, the performance budget, which focused on output-based efficiency, took center stage. Soon after, the Planning-Programming-Budgeting (PPB) system was introduced (Schick 1966). Schick (1969) highlights PPB's systematic, comprehensive, prospective, and outcome-oriented approach, in which the realities of limited rationality and the need for occasional remediation are embraced. The latest in budget innovations, Performance-Based Budgeting (PBB), reflects the management orientation in which *achieving outcomes*, rather than *controlling inputs*, is the focus. Implementation of PBB at the federal and state levels is widespread, though its impact on governance is ambiguous (Joyce 1993; Willoughby and Melkers 2000; Melkers and Willoughby 2001).

The budgetary reforms of the mid-twentieth century occurred in close conjunction with the broader search for a science of democratic administration. Moreover, the management orientation that inspired them was the antecedent to the field's major movements since 1990—reinventing government, the New Public Management, governance, and management by network. The relationship between the management and financial management subfields, especially the shared performance orientation, remained intact throughout the early 1990s but has essentially disappeared with the dawning of what we might call "contemporary" public management. Under the new paradigm, the dual financial-organizational management orientation—and arguably any attention to resource management—has been replaced in public administration writ large by new and broader concerns that are characterized by complex institutional arrangements and diffuse power. For their part, scholars of the public budgeting and financial management subfield have not explicitly joined in on the revolution; they now occupy a desert island—some would say it is an oasis.

CONTEMPORARY PERSPECTIVES ON PUBLIC MANAGEMENT AND PUBLIC RESOURCES

As mentioned, one way to reconnect these two bodies of inquiry is to highlight some of the contemporary, technique-oriented research on public financial management that has implications for broader conceptual and empirical issues in public management. In this section we highlight three streams of this work.

Interorganizational Networks and Performance

Interorganizational networks are among the most widely explored topics in contemporary public management (Goldsmith and Eggers 2004; Milward and Provan 2000), and yet we have only begun to understand how these networks are structured, how they work, and their implications for accountability, equity, and efficiency in public service delivery. To that end, public network scholars have called for broad-based, comparative, empirical work on the relationship between network structures and network outcomes. But by nature, networks are difficult to study. Their structures are diffuse, dynamic, and sometimes informal, and their goals are often ambiguous or unstated. As a result, much of the empirical work on public network management is on carefully chosen small-*N* samples of comparable networks, usually over comparatively long time periods. That work has produced some important insights, but our understanding of network management is limited to those particular contexts and tasks (Agranoff and McGuire 2001).

Some recent financial management research (Marlowe 2007b; Robbins and Simonsen 2007; also see O'Toole 1996 and Miller 1993) on public "debt management networks" provides new empirical leverage on several aspects of the study of public management networks. Debt management is the process of selling tax-exempt bonds to finance infrastructure and other large public capital projects. At the end of 2008 there were more than 2.3 million of these bonds outstanding from more than 50,000 organizations, including state and local governments, utilities, schools, community development districts, and many others. Those bonds constitute a total outstanding debt burden of more than $2.6 trillion (Federal Reserve Board 2007). Effective debt management is central to the fiscal health of any organization.

Debt management's central objective is to procure the desired capital at the lowest possible cost. Given the information demands of debt issuance, most organizations do not issue debt often enough to justify an in-house debt management staff. Many organizations instead manage this process by assembling "debt management networks" (DMNs) made up of individuals or firms with specialized knowledge. Most DMNs include a group of underwriters—usually investment banks or commercial bankers—that supply the needed capital and advise the issuer on how investors will likely respond to its debt; a bond attorney to assist with the legal affairs; a financial adviser who recommends how the debt should be structured and marketed to potential investors; and others to assist in the numerous tasks required by a typical debt issue. These professionals integrate their expertise and recommendations into a strategy for how and when to sell the bonds. That process is consistent with Agranoff and McGuire's (2003, 4) description of collaborative public management networks as "the process of facilitating and operating in multiorganizational arrangements to solve problems that cannot be solved, or solved easily, by single organizations."

DMNs are an ideal setting in which to address many of the key questions in public network management. They have a clear and widely accepted outcome indicator—the interest rate a jurisdiction pays when it issues bonds—and a widely accepted model of the debt management production function (see O'Toole and Meier 1999).[2] DMN participants are disclosed through state securities and insurance laws, and recent moves by the municipal bond industry have improved debt management's overall transparency, both making

DMNs clearly identifiable and observable. Moreover, though there is enormous variation among public organizations, there are clear similarities in DMNs' structures and compositions. This allows us to better understand how the same DMNs with essentially the same mission perform in different contexts.

Much of the research thus far on DMNs has focused on the relationship between network stability and network outcomes. But taken together, the inconsistent results imply that network stability's effect on performance cannot be understood without proper attention to network structure and context. But as mentioned, this research tends to rely on small-*N* designs that provide only limited controls on network structure and context. Some well-designed studies of DMNs have addressed some of these limitations, and in doing so have produced important insights. Two of those findings are of particular interest for future research on public network management.

The first is that stability's effects on performance are contingent on task complexity (Marlowe 2007a). In particular, DMNs with more complex tasks—defined as networks issuing revenue-backed bonds subject to far more legal and financial constraints than traditional property-tax-backed bonds—are less likely to improve their performance by shuffling network participants. A key question for research, consistent with prior discussions of the key questions in network management, is how task complexity shapes interactions among network members, and whether differences in those interactions account for stability's entire performance dividend.

A second key finding is that DMN instability can be beneficial for routine tasks, and in particular where routine tasks are performed in environments with limited transparency and oversight from network members. Specifically, it finds that borrowers using the same underwriter tend to pay higher interest rates than issuers rotating underwriters or selecting underwriters through competitive, sealed-bid procurement processes (Robbins and Simonsen 2008). A key question is why this happens. As mentioned, some traditions of organization theory suggest that stability stifles innovation and invites complacency among network members (Miller 1993). A separate line of related research takes this research to its natural end; it suggests that stability results in, or is perhaps the result of, collusion or even corruption among DMN members (Butler, Fauver, and Mortal 2009). Future DMN research will help to illuminate these issues.

DMN research is relatively new, but the results thus far are promising. To the extent that public management scholars are concerned with the relationships among network structure and network outcomes, the DMN research agenda is likely to produce important and relevant findings in the future. If we presume that the future of public management will entail networks that are at least as complex as the ones we know today—if not more so—this line of research offers a strong foundation from which to study this complex and all-important governance mechanism.

Are Public Organizations Subject to "Market Discipline"?

The promise of "market discipline" is a key driver of the explosive growth of contracting out, public–private partnerships, outsourcing, and other alternatives to traditional in-house public service production. There is a rich literature on these issues that has to date produced a nuanced set of findings on whether third-party involvement in public services bolsters efficiency, however defined. Third-party involvement in public service provision follows from the assumption that competition among potential service providers, or between public organizations and potential private providers, will incentivize efficiency gains and, where necessary, sanction inefficient service provision by directing attention and resources toward more efficient alternatives. What is less clear is whether these same sorts of sanctions exist even in the absence of formal competition. Put differently, is there a sanction for inefficient public management, even if those inefficiencies are not revealed as the result of formal competition?

The assumptions behind this unique perspective on public-sector market discipline are, in fact, well established in business administration scholarship. This research is based on the "efficient markets hypothesis" (EMH) (Fama 1970), that is, the claim that the market price of an asset—such as a stock, bond, or property—incorporates all information available to investors about that asset. Much of the research in contemporary finance, accounting, marketing, strategy and other fields builds on the EMH by observing how an asset's market price changes in response to new information about its value. For example, accounting scholars often study how companies' stock prices respond to quarterly earnings announcements, stock analysts' predictions, and other news about their financial condition (see MacKinlay 1997). In the wake of the scandals at Enron, Tyco, and other large corporations, there has been a flood of research on whether the quality of corporate governance and internal control have a discernible effect on companies' stock prices and other indicators of business performance (Zhang 2006; Beneish, Billings, and Hodder 2008).[3] Research in this vein has been especially salient in the midst of the controversy about the Sarbanes-Oxley Act of 2002.[4]

At the moment, the evidence on the price impact of financial information on public organizations is mixed. Much of this evidence comes from research on governmental accounting about how changes to the format and content of government financial statements affect the prices investors pay for municipal bonds (for a summary, see Reck and Wilson 2006). Some studies show that bond issuers with evidence of financial problems disclosed in their financial statements, such as high outstanding debt liabilities or cash flow problems, do pay higher interest rates when they borrow money. By contrast, other studies show that those same financial indicators have no long-run impact on bond interest rates. More recent work has examined whether newly required disclosures of governments' long-term financial condition have their own price effects

(Marlowe 2007a; Plummer, Hutchinson, and Patton 2007). This research will continue to develop, and in the process will provide new information about these special aspects of "market discipline." Other research in this vein has explored the claim that management quality matters for municipal bond interest rates in the same way that it matters for corporate credit markets. That literature has reached a loose consensus that, in fact, municipal bond investors reward high-quality public management and sanction ineffective management and constraints on management flexibility (Johnson and Kriz 2005; Wagner 2004; Denison, Yan, and Zhou 2007).[5]

The key finding from the research thus far in this tradition is that, in fact, management matters to municipal bond investors. In general, municipal bond prices and interest rates respond to marginal differences in public organization transparency, financial disclosure quality, performance, and management quality. And by implication, more transparent and better-managed organizations experience lower interest rates and transaction costs in the municipal bond market, both of which lower costs and add value for citizens and taxpayers. Research in this tradition will continue to illuminate when and how public organizations are subject to this peculiar type of "market discipline," and how this discipline does (or ought to) interact with other types of accountability.[6]

Governance and Public-Sector Risk Management

The hollowing out of American public administration implies a new set of challenges and risks. A variety of legal, institutional, and other strategies have emerged to manage those new risks, and how these strategies are developed and implemented is the stuff of the emerging field of public-sector risk management. This new field encompasses everything from traditional liability insurance to sophisticated financial "hedging" strategies like options and derivatives.

What is unclear is how the governance structures and political traditions of public organizations shape risk management strategies. There is evidence, for example, that public organizations tend toward risk aversion; they tend to prepare for "worst case" contingencies, even when there is strong evidence that those contingencies are unlikely. For instance, research on local government "rainy day funds" shows that it is not uncommon for municipalities to keep reserve funds equal to eighteen months to two years of revenue collections (Marlowe 2005; Hendrick 2006; Gianakis and Snow 2007). No contingency except a full-blown disaster could place such substantial demands on local government cash flows. Moreover, a true natural disaster would demand far more than two years of revenue.

We see similar trends in the economic development context. Many jurisdictions are reticent to commit public capital to economic development ventures, except when developers can all but guarantee the safety of that capital. These and many other issues are consistent with Wildavsky's (1988) observation that in some cases extreme risk aversion can actually create new and unforeseen risks. And yet consider that many local governments hold no formal reserves, and there are many documented cases of large public subsidies for economic development where the terms of the subsidy are not even defined in a formal contract. In short, public-sector risk management strategies range from a bias toward the extremely conservative to aggressively risk accepting. It is essential that public management understand how governance structures, political traditions, and management characteristics shape these and other risk management strategies. However, it is difficult to observe in any systematic way how those sorts of "governance" characteristics shape those strategies, and, more important, whether they help to align or distort an organization's ability to identify its optimal risk management strategy.

For these reasons, public management has much to learn from the governance and performance of public employee pension funds. U.S. Census Bureau (2004) statistics indicate that at the end of 2002, there were 2,670 distinct public employee pension systems representing more than 14 million public-sector employees. The total holdings in these funds currently exceed $2 trillion, an enormous sum by any standard. Much of the extant research on public pensions focuses on the risk profiles suggested by their investment strategies. Risk can be measured several ways in this context, but most strategies involve simply observing past price movements of the stocks, bonds, commodities, and other assets the fund holds, and then combining those movements into a series of probability calculations on the fund's future growth or decline. Analyses of that sort consistently show that these funds are extraordinarily risk averse. They are heavily invested in assets that grow at stable but modest rates, and they tend to avoid investments in international stocks and other assets whose values tend to fluctuate, even in predictable ways (Peng 2004).

This is not to suggest that these funds are politically benign or free of controversy. An ongoing issue is whether they should hold investments in politically sensitive regions like Darfur, or whether they should deploy their capital in pursuit of particular political objectives. Pro-union state politicians have suggested, for instance, that pensions divest holdings in companies with questionable labor relations practices, and vice versa. This has been an especially contentious suggestion in the wake of the ongoing problems at the major American automakers. In a March 7, 2008, opinion piece published in the *Wall Street Journal,* Benn Steil captured these dynamics well; he dubbed the California Public Employees Retirement System (or CALPERs) America's principal "sovereign wealth fund."

It is also important to note that public pension fund governance is evolving. Funds known for their risk aversion are slowly adopting more risk-accepting positions. Across the board, public pensions are taking up ever larger positions in international equities and other traditionally volatile investments. In fact, some pensions have specific policies mandating minimum holdings in international markets. Much of this evolution is the result of constant pressure for these funds to produce ever-higher returns on their investments. This is because higher returns lower the contributions that governments must make to these funds. In a world of perpetual fiscal stress, higher returns mean less pressure on near-term budgets.

In short, public pension fund governance is an excellent setting to study the development, implementation, and outcomes of sophisticated public-sector risk management strategies. Risk management is on par with contracting, interorganizational networks, and other contemporary concerns in administrative technique with respect to its sophistication, importance, and centrality to public management's ongoing conceptual development. To the extent that the future of public management research and practice will entail blazing new trails, research on public pension fund management has started the field down one critically important path.

CONCLUSION

This chapter's conclusion is its central thesis: that the management and financial management subfields are in need of reintroduction, and that reconnecting these subfields would be much more than a trivial academic exercise for public administration. Indeed, they have a symbiotic relationship not despite history but because of it, and this fact has not changed with the emergence of contemporary public administration, in which power is diffuse, institutions are loosely arranged, and actors are even more loosely connected. At a minimum, combining research on and the practice of public financial management with those related to public management paints a more complete picture of the system in which practitioners frame and execute public policy. More generally, public financial management theory and practice have substantial potential to inform broader issues in public management. If the future public servant is to effectively traverse the brave new world of contemporary public administration, he or she will require the benefit of research and instruction that are grounded in a more complete and sophisticated understanding of public management and the role of resources and resource management in doing the public's business.

Our approach has been to highlight how contemporary research on technique in budgeting and financial management can inform broader issues in public management. This logic suggests many implications for research, but also—perhaps more important—for training future public servants. First and foremost, matters of managerial technique in the public management and financial management subfields should not be taught or studied in isolation; this argument has been convincingly made before (see Golembiewski 1964). For example, it would be sensible to introduce students to methods of cost allocation as part of a lesson on organizational design, because cost allocation requires a precise and consistent road map of how the support and mission functions of an organization, or network of organizations, are interrelated.

The same logic applies to teaching organizational performance measurement, management, and reporting. There is no reason that standard measures of organizational performance should be taught only in public management seminars while standard measures of financial performance should be taught only in financial management courses. Both sets of measures take into account inputs, activities, outputs, and outcomes, and a public organization's capacity to survive or even thrive is dependent on performing well in both dimensions. Moreover, public financial management has strongly emphasized "plain language" or "popular" financial reports designed to make financial information about public organizations accessible to citizens. Students concerned with how to disseminate performance information have much to learn from the experience thus far with popular financial reporting.

The above examples highlight just two of the many potential intersections between organizational and financial management that might be found in public administration curricula. As a final example, financial management theory and practice also offer a set of conceptual and analytical tools to supplement traditional pedagogical approaches to cost/benefit analysis and risk management, assessment, and communication. Many of the tools developed by finance professionals to manage financial risk—such as value at risk, portfolio theory, and others (Thompson and Gates 1997)—have broad potential applications to other public risk allocation problems. Incorporating lessons on crosscutting "hard skills" such as these into public management coursework is perhaps particularly important for giving future public servants a more sophisticated understanding of public management and the role of resources and resource management in doing the public's business.

NOTES

The authors thank Bill Duncombe and David Van Slyke for helpful comments on earlier drafts.

1. Managerial accounting "relates to generating any financial information that managers can use to improve the future results of the organization" (Finkler 2005, 4); financial accounting, meanwhile, provides retrospective information on an organization's financial position at a specific point in time.
2. That model controls for several factors such as market interest rates at the time of the debt issue, the amount and purpose of the borrowed funds, the likelihood the issuer will repay the debt (i.e., its credit quality), and other factors (Simonsen and Robbins 1996; Johnson and Kriz 2005).
3. Internal control is the system of policies and practices that describe how an organization maintains and protects its key assets.
4. For the implications of internal control on government financial performance, see Marlowe and Matkin (2008).
5. It is important to distinguish bond prices, a direct measure of investor response, from bond ratings, which are formulated by third-party bond raters to benefit investors.
6. Important, but receiving no substantial attention here, is research on the rate at which the value of public services is incorporated (or "capitalized") into property values. The basic implication of this line of research to our argument is that the investor response to public management might also hold for highly "illiquid" assets (i.e., assets that are not bought and sold frequently) like property. For more on capitalization see, among others, Yinger (1982).

REFERENCES

Agranoff, Robert, and Michael McGuire. 2001. Big Questions in Public Management Network Research. *Journal of Public Administration Research and Theory* 11, no. 3:295–326.

———. 2003. *Collaborative Public Management: New Strategies for Local Governments.* Washington, DC: Georgetown University Press.

Beneish, Messod, Mary Brooke Billings, and Leslie D. Hodder. 2008. Internal Control Weaknesses and Information Uncertainty. *Accounting Review* 83, no. 3:665–703.

Butler, Alexander W., Larry Fauver, and Sandra Mortal. 2009. Corruption, Political Connections, and Municipal Finance. *Review of Financial Studies* 22, no. 7:2873–905.

Denison, Dwight, Wenli Yan, and Zhirong (Jerry) Zhao. 2007. Is Management Performance a Factor in Municipal Bond Credit Ratings? The Case of Texas School Districts. *Public Budgeting & Finance* 27, no. 4:86–98.

Fama, Eugene. 1970. Efficient Capital Markets: A Review of Theory and Empirical Work. *Journal of Finance* 25, no. 2:383–417.

Federal Reserve Board. 2007. *Flow of Funds Accounts of the United States.* Washington, DC: Board of Governors of the Federal Reserve System.

Finkler, Steven A. 2005. *Financial Management for Public, Health, and Not-for-Profit Organizations,* 2d ed. Upper Saddle River, NJ: Pearson Education.

Gianakis, Gerasimos, and Douglas Snow. 2007. The Implementation and Utilization of Stabilization Funds by Local Governments in Massachusetts. *Public Budgeting & Finance* 27, no. 1:86–103.

Goldsmith, Stephen, and William D. Eggers. 2004. *Governing by Network: The New Shape of the Public Sector.* Washington, DC: Brookings Institution Press.

Golembiewski, Robert T. 1964. Accountancy as a Function of Organization Theory. *Accounting Review* 39, no. 2:333–41.

Hendrick, Rebecca. 2006. The Role of Slack in Local Government Finances. *Public Budgeting & Finance* 26, no. 1:14–46.

Johnson, Craig L., and Kenneth A. Kriz. 2005. Fiscal Institutions, Credit Ratings, and Borrowing Costs. *Public Budgeting & Finance* 25, no. 1:84–103.

Joyce, Philip G. 1993. The Reiterative Nature of Budget Reform: Is There Anything New in Federal Budgeting? *Public Budgeting and Finance* 13, no. 3:33–45.

MacKinlay, Craig A. 1997. Event Studies in Economics and Finance. *Journal of Economic Literature* 35, no. 1:13–39.

Marlowe, Justin. 2005. Fiscal Slack and Countercyclical Expenditure Stabilization: A First Look at the Local Level. *Public Budgeting & Finance* 25, no. 3:48–72.

———. 2007a. Much Ado about Nothing? The Size and Credit Quality Implications of Municipal and Other Post-Employment Benefit Liabilities. *Public Budgeting & Finance* 27, no. 2:104–31.

———. 2007b. Network Stability and Performance: Does Context Matter? Paper presented at 2007 Public Management Research Association Conference, Tucson.

Marlowe, Justin, and David S. T. Matkin. 2008. Is There a Financial Benefit to Improving Accountability? A Test of the Costs of Financial Control Problems in Local Government. Paper presented at 2008 Meeting of Western Social Science Association, Denver.

McCallum, Daniel C. 1856. Superintendent's Report. In *Classics of Organization Theory,* 5th edition, ed. Jay M. Shafritz and Steven J. Ott. Orlando: Harcourt College Publishers.

Melkers, Julia E., and Katherine G. Willoughby. 2001. Budgeters' Views of State Performance-Budgeting Systems: Distinctions across Branches. *Public Administration Review* 61, no. 1:54–64.

Miller, Gerald J. 1993. Debt Management Networks. *Public Administration Review* 53, no. 1:50–58.

Milward, H. Brinton, and Keith G. Provan. 2000. Governing the Hollow State. *Journal of Public Administration Research and Theory* 10, no. 2:359–79.

O'Toole, Laurence J. 1996. Hollowing the Infrastructure: Revolving Loan Programs and Network Dynamics in the American States. *Journal of Public Administration Research and Theory* 6, no. 2:225–42.

O'Toole, Laurence J., and Kenneth J. Meier. 1999. Modeling the Impact of Public Management: Implications of Structural Context. *Journal of Public Administration Research and Theory* 9, no. 4:505–26.

Peng, Jun. 2004. Public Pension Funds and Operating Budgets: A Tale of Three States. *Public Budgeting & Finance* 24, no. 2:59–73.

Plummer, Elizabeth, Paul D. Hutchinson, and Terry K. Patton. 2007. GASB No. 34's Governmental Financial Reporting Model: Evidence on Its Information Relevance. *Accounting Review* 82, no. 1:205–40.

Poor, Henry V. 1860. *History of the Railroads and Canals of the United States of America: Exhibiting Their Progress, Cost, Revenues, Expenditures & Present Condition*, vol. 1. New York: John H. Schultz & Co.

Reck, Jacqueline, and Earl Wilson. 2006. Information Transparency and Pricing in the Municipal Secondary Bond Market. *Journal of Accounting and Public Policy* 25, no. 1:1–31.

Robbins, Mark D., and Bill Simonsen. 2007. Competition and Selection in Municipal Bond Sales: Evidence from Missouri. *Public Budgeting & Finance* 27, no. 2:88–103.

———. 2008. Persistent Underwriter Use and the Cost of Borrowing. *Municipal Finance Journal* 28, no. 4:1–13.

Schick, Allen. 1966. The Road to PPB: The Stages of Budget Reform. *Public Administration Review* 26, no. 4:243–58.

———. 1969. Systems Politics and Systems Budgeting. *Public Administration Review* 29, no. 2:137–51.

Simonsen, W. and M. D. Robbins. 1996. Does It Make Any Difference Anymore? Competitive Versus Negotiated Municipal Bond Issuance. *Public Administration Review* 56, no. 1:57–64.

Thompson, Fred, and Bruce L. Gates. 2007. Betting on the Future with a Cloudy Crystal Ball? How Financial Theory Can Improve Revenue Forecasting and Budgets in the States. *Public Administration Review* 67, no. 5:825–36.

U.S. Census Bureau. 2004. *Employee-Retirement Systems of State and Local Governments: 2002*, GC02(3)-6, 14.

Wagner, Gary A. 2004. The Bond Market and Fiscal Institutions: Have Budget Stabilization Funds Reduced State Borrowing Costs? *National Tax Journal* 57, no. 4:785–804.

Wildavsky, Aaron B. 1988. *Searching for Safety*. New Brunswick, NJ: Transaction Books.

Willoughby, Katherine G., and Julia E. Melkers. 2000. Implementing PBB: Conflicting Views of Success. *Public Budgeting & Finance* 20, no. 1:105–20.

Yinger, John. 1982. Capitalization and the Theory of Local Public Finance. *Journal of Political Economy* 90, no. 5:917–43.

Zhang, Ivy Xiying. 2006. Economic Consequences of Sarbanes-Oxley. Working Paper, Brookings-AEI Joint Center for Regulatory Studies, Washington, DC.

Teaching Democracy in Public Administration

Trends and Future Prospects

Matt Leighninger

Over the last century, the skills, ideas, and values upheld within the field of public administration (PA) have undergone several major shifts. We seem to be in the midst of another such transition, as PA schools react to new perspectives about the state of democracy and citizenship. Most of these arguments focus on the more participatory aspects of democracy, and emphasize the need for governments to work more directly and interactively with citizens. "Democratic governance" (see box V.1) is one term used to describe this set of ideas.[1] This chapter explores the relationship between PA and democratic governance through interviews with fifteen professors and observers of the discipline.

The fifteen interviewees all have some experience with democratic governance, having taught these principles in the classroom, practiced or researched them in the field, or advocated them in their agencies or associations. They are well-positioned to report on the interplay between democracy, participation, and PA. The picture that emerges from the interviews is that of a field in flux, spurred both by theoretical claims and by the practical needs of administrators, being pushed from a narrow focus on management to a broader conception of governing. The arguments made by the interviewees are by no means entirely new; scholarship in PA has, to varying degrees in its history, always been concerned with citizen participation in the work of government, and a considerable amount of research has been generated on the topic. For example, Nancy Roberts's (2008) edited volume, *The Age of Direct Citizen Participation*, presents a wide variety of arguments in favor of engaging citizens more directly in governance. The contributors to this volume argue that citizen participation can facilitate public learning, build community, improve responsiveness, serve and empower citizens, build trust in government, increase citizen efficacy, promote a shared conception of the common good, and generally reduce citizen discouragement and apathy, among other results.[2]

Box V.1 Defining Terms

The word "engagement" is often used in a general way to describe formal interactions between government and citizens. It has different connotations for different people, but these attitudes are rarely discussed openly. Many public managers think back to poorly planned, poorly structured, legally mandated meetings that were unsuccessful for both officials and citizens. For others, "engagement" has a more positive meaning.

"Democratic governance" is a term used to describe the more successful forms of engagement: ones that involve large, diverse numbers of people, that allow people the opportunity to share experiences and assess a range of policy options, and that lead to action and change at a number of levels.

Finally, the term "citizen" often seems inappropriate, because it is sometimes used in its narrow, legal sense: people who are U.S. citizens. In this chapter, the term is used as a synonym for "residents" or "the public"—people who have a stake in their community.

The people interviewed for this chapter have taken these arguments a step further, describing the ways in which administrators in the field are now driving these changes, and pointing toward new priorities for teaching and research.[3] Eleven of the interviewees are PA professors who address issues of democratic or collaborative governance in their teaching and research. The other four interviewees bring the perspectives of leaders outside the academy who benefit from PA research and are potential employers of PA graduates.

WHY SHOULD PUBLIC ADMINISTRATION EDUCATORS BE RETHINKING THEIR APPROACH TO DEMOCRACY?

First and foremost, the interviewees saw the teaching of democratic skills in PA as "a response to how things are," as John Stephens, one of the interviewees, put it. They either view democratic governance instrumentally, as an important tool for administrators facing new expectations from citizens, or idealistically, as a way to reverse the decline of democracy and public life.

The Instrumental Responses: Adapting to the Needs of Administrators Today

Some of the interviewees, including all the nonacademics, stressed the idea that many administrators have already changed the way they interact with the public, and that the theory and teaching of PA lags behind the practice. "What it takes to run a government has changed," said Bill Barnes of the National League of Cities.

The interviewees named seven reasons for this shift in the citizen–government relationship:

- The erosion of trust in government.
- An increasingly diverse population.
- Recognition that government alone cannot solve public problems.
- The decentralization of many public decisions.
- Less hierarchy within and among organizations.
- Greater capacity of citizens to disrupt policymaking.
- The enjoyment of citizens being involved.[4]

Several interviewees emphasized the last two arguments in particular. On the one hand, citizens today seem more willing and able to insert themselves into the decision-making process, whether or not public administrators planned to give them a role. This is partly due to the continuing development of the Internet, which is "empowering small factions of people with greater levels of information and easier methods of connectivity to others," said Pete Peterson. But when these opportunities are meaningful and well organized, citizens value them intrinsically, not just as levers for affecting issues and decisions, argued John Nalbandian. He sees engagement as a logical response to modernization and homogeneity, a way for citizens to establish and safeguard their identity, and "a way of claiming what is mine, yours, and ours, a way of saying 'we are unique.'"

This rise in citizen engagement work by governments, in turn, creates a new hiring need. There is a rising demand for PA schools to produce graduates who are prepared to work more closely with citizens. "We are looking for graduates with these skills in many different fields," said Leanne Nurse, "and not finding many."[5] It also means a higher demand for training and learning opportunities for midcareer administrators.

The Idealistic Responses: Creating New Arenas for Public Life

Other interviewees justified their teaching and research in this realm not just as a reaction to what is already happening but also as a proactive way of helping democracy function in more participatory, equitable, emotionally fulfilling ways. This view is rooted in the idea that "democracy is an end in itself," as Camilla Stivers said, and that politics can be a fundamentally valuable human activity, not just a way to make decisions and allocate resources.

Rather than starting with the immediate needs of current administrators, this view seems to takes its cues from ideal visions of community as expressed in political theory. The "job of academics is to transfer these ideas into practical usable programs," said Tina Nabatchi. Our intent, argued Angela Eikenberry, should be to "create spaces where the public sphere might exist."

There seemed to be much more agreement than disagreement between the instrumental and idealistic responses to the question. However, the idealists are somewhat concerned that PA should not become too narrowly focused on the needs of managers. "We've lost the public-regarding dimension of PA," said Gary Marshall. Nabatchi worried that "the field of PA is guided to look at deliberative democracy as a potential problem," not as an achievable goal.

But regardless of whether they are motivated by compelling theory or changing practice, the interviewees all seemed to agree that PA is facing a tremendous generational opportunity. "The baby boomers are retiring, and we have to train a whole new generation of public servants," Nabatchi pointed out. "We can't just teach them how to 'manage' the public; we need to help them learn how to involve the public."

WHAT KINDS OF DEMOCRATIC SKILLS DO PUBLIC ADMINISTRATORS NEED?

The interviewees generated a list of skills that are critical for involving the public. These included the ability to

- Work in teams—particularly teams that include citizens and those that include representatives from different governmental jurisdictions.
- Utilize the broad repertoire of newer citizen engagement processes, beyond the standard public hearings and political meetings.
- Facilitate or moderate meetings more effectively, even in the more traditional kinds of formats.
- Engage in conflict resolution, facilitation, negotiation, and collaboration.
- Document, follow up, and evaluate both the impact and the quality of engagement processes.
- Understand when—and on what issues—it makes sense to engage larger numbers of citizens. Understanding when this engagement may not be helpful or appropriate.
- Utilize stakeholder analysis.
- Know how the expanding kinds of information technology and e-government tools influence citizen participation.
- Bring political skills to bear when other powers are opposed to an engagement process.
- Understand policy ethics and how policy decisions affect such issues as social equity, justice, participation, and intergenerational issues.
- Organize for engagement on an issue, in which citizens are asked to take part in discussion and action on a specific public problem or policy decision.
- Create sustainable structures for engagement—regular opportunities for citizens to bring their own issues and priorities to the table.
- Assess community needs, values, opportunities, and challenges—without making sharp distinctions between officials and employees.

IS "COLLABORATIVE GOVERNANCE" BROADENING TO INCLUDE (OR EVOLVING INTO) "DEMOCRATIC GOVERNANCE?"

The interviewees also shed some light on the ways in which different intellectual strands in the PA field weave together and influence one another. Some of the interviewees identified with the term "collaborative governance," the idea that governments, nonprofits, businesses, advocacy organizations, and other groups should work together to make public decisions by consensus whenever possible. Collaborative governance recognizes that governments need the active support of other organizations—often called stakeholders—to control or solve public problems. This field of study began to gain credence in the 1970s, partly because of the work of state and federal agencies in environmental policymaking. Many scholars are now motivated by the belief that "collaborative solutions are generally better, more durable, and more iterative," said Stephens.

Other interviewees identified more strongly with such terms as "deliberative democracy" or "democratic governance." These concepts emphasize:

- Involving hundreds or even thousands of ordinary citizens, not just organizations that claim to represent them.
- Creating arenas where citizens compare experiences, build their knowledge about the issues, and consider a range of policy options.
- Encouraging action by citizens as volunteers, in committees, or by organizations to which they belong, in addition to gathering input for the policymaking process.

Some of the democratic governance adherents thought the differences between the two concepts need to be acknowledged and examined. They pointed out that collaborative governance is all about institutional relationships, and that "citizens are generally excluded as stakeholders in these network relationships," as Nabatchi put it. "A lot of the writing about collaborative governance has to do with how you manage the relationship of organizations in a network—this doesn't have democracy at its heart," argued Stivers.

The two ideas do seem to be in flux, however. As John Bryson said, "The collaborative governance people are receptive to citizenship arguments, and are starting to explore them." Crosby pointed out that collaboration in practice brings up questions of citizenship, representation, and participation. "There is definitely an evolution going on here," said Rosemary O'Leary. Nalbandian saw it as a coherent progression, as the perspective of PA scholars broadens "from [a focus on] institutions to stakeholders to engagement."

Whether scholars are more interested in collaboration between organizations or collaboration that involves ordinary citizens, there does not seem to be a real competition between the two strands of thought. Both collaborative and democratic governance "share some core values," said Stephens. They also share "overlapping skill sets," Nalbandian said. Pat Bonner and

Nurse agreed that all these skills are becoming increasingly necessary and valuable.

To what extent is democratic governance being addressed in the PA curriculum? The distinction between the collaborative governance focus on organizations and the democratic governance focus on citizens may, however, affect how professors view the prevalence of these ideas. The interviewees who come out of the collaborative governance tradition were more likely to feel that significant progress has been made, whereas the ones who identified more with democratic governance saw the glass as—at best—half empty. Crosby and O'Leary reported that collaborative governance concepts have been "mainstreamed" into some of the required courses at their schools. "One of the things that has changed over my career," said Bryson, "is that people have changed their definition of what counts as 'real work.' It used to be that 'talk' didn't count—but our students now understand this kind of dialogue, deliberation, and stakeholder analysis is actually real work."

Interviewees who identified more closely with democratic governance were more frustrated with their lack of progress. "There are a few pockets" of interest and activity, said Eikenberry, "but we're on the margins." Archon Fung, a public policy professor, said that he "doesn't see discussions of participation being very prevalent in any of these fields [PA, public management, or public policy]."

Some interviewees worried that the management orientation of many PA schools may even be turning the tide against a focus on democracy and citizenship. Stivers is concerned that even the titles of PA schools reflect a shift toward more managerial, less democratic interests. "Many PA schools used to have words like 'citizenship' and 'public' in the titles, and they've taken them out." As a field, Eikenberry argued, PA is not encouraging the growth of democratic governance through accreditation or other means.

Perhaps the bleakest picture was painted by Bonner and Nurse, who said they do not even look to PA schools for graduates with the skills needed at the Environmental Protection Agency (EPA). "When someone is a PA graduate, for EPA purposes I'm not sure what we can do with them," said Bonner. "The matrix for preparing people for public service is an outdated Progressive Era model, in which public servants try to solve people's problems for them," said Nurse. "Nothing that I've seen in the degree programs seems to be changing that."

David Kuehn reported that the Federal Highway Administration (FHA) has reacted to this challenge by "increasing the number of midcareer hires, who as a group have more experience with public engagement." Both the FHA and the EPA now run internal training programs that focus on collaborative and democratic governance skills.

WHAT PREPARATION DO PA STUDENTS NEED TO BE COMPETENT IN DEMOCRATIC GOVERNANCE?

Virtually all the interviewees voiced the opinion that, in training students for democratic governance, the overall mindset is as important as the individual skills (listed earlier in this chapter). Three elements of this "democratic mindset" emerged from the interviews:

1. *A new definition of leadership that embraces and explains democratic governance.* "Cross-boundary leadership [that engages stakeholders across the public, private, and nonprofit sectors] now has more legitimacy in PA schools," said Crosby, "but I think now we need more skills in the person who is trying to inspire and mobilize others and the person who is trying to be an engaged follower."
2. *A theoretical and political analysis of how democratic governance fits.* "Administrators need a skills base, and a theory base, but also a politics base," argued Stephens. "Why does this work make sense politically?"
3. *Visions of how democracy can work when the right principles and strategies are applied.* O'Leary thought that students and others have an outdated picture of public participation, one that emphasizes "stale, old-school" methods like public hearings. She said, "We need to educate people about what we mean [about how citizens might be involved in politics]."

Bonner described the necessary mindset more simply: "I just want employees who can approach the public without assuming, right off the bat, that they [citizens] are wrong. I want them to be able to look at a conflict or tension with the public and say, 'It might be our fault, not theirs.' "

All the interviewees seemed to view this line of thinking as part of an ongoing, career-long education. Eikenberry said that "our students will be good public administrators if they're also good citizens, with the skills to participate in public life. If they can think critically and apply some of these ideas, all the more specific skills (like participatory budgeting) they can pick up later." Barnes agreed that "one of the functions of school is to set your brain up so that you can learn more. We need to tease out these underlying issues and help people see what is at stake so that they can wrestle with it a little bit. They will be wrestling with it the rest of their lives."

HOW SHOULD PA SCHOOLS TEACH DEMOCRATIC PRINCIPLES AND STRATEGIES?

The interviewees' responses to this question ranged from opportunities within the PA curriculum to various other kinds of learning opportunities, on and off campus, for students and faculty. Most of the academics mentioned the potential of producing democratic governance "modules" that could be easily incorporated into existing PA courses (as well as courses in other disciplines). "These could take different forms: one third of a course, one quarter, and so on," said Nalbandian. "But each would provide the necessary resources, articles, discussion questions, and assignments."

Several interviewees felt that modules were useful but not sufficient. Marshall envisioned a course specifically on "working with the public." Stivers added, "There is a need for stand-alone courses because there are so many skills to learn." Understanding how to engage citizens productively in budget decisions, for example, may require a different kind of preparation than working with the public on crime prevention, or on racism and race relations.

For both the modules and the stand-alone courses, Bryson thought we need more "examples and cases that show how the big concepts and processes can be accomplished or operationalized using very specific tools. The ideas, processes and procedures, and tools all need to hang together and be illustrated in cases."

Most of the interviewees also emphasized the need for midcareer training opportunities. Fung praised "targeted training modules for professional development." Professional associations like the National League of Cities and the International City/County Management Association already provide democratic governance workshops, and some federal agencies do as well. "For people we hire directly from school, we try to provide them with developmental details in state and local agencies to give them experience working with stakeholders," reported Kuehn of the FHA.

Teaching democratic principles and strategies may not simply be a matter of course content, however. "If we want to teach these concepts," argued Eikenberry, "we professors need to learn them ourselves." She pointed out that professors are generally given very little background in teaching methods, particularly in skills like facilitating class discussion. Democratic governance "challenges the old-school banking style of education," Eikenberry said, and it is hard for the professors who want to break out of that mold to find the resources they need.

Stivers said "engaged learning" ought to be considered the only way to teach civic engagement. "It teaches people that you can learn by doing, and also that ordinary people know something—they know a lot about their lives and they know it in a way that experts don't. This is an important democratic idea: that you have to start from what people already know."

Taking this line of thinking a step further, Stivers, Eikenberry, and others pointed out the irony of teaching democratic skills on campuses that don't necessarily give students a meaningful role in decision making. "[The state of] democracy on campus does have a huge effect on how we teach these ideas," claimed Stivers. However, none of the professors interviewed was optimistic that the traditional mindset of university governance would change quickly. "It makes sense to say 'We need to do this in our own home,' and use more of these ideas on campus," said O'Leary, "But I don't see it actually happening much yet." Stephens agreed, noting, "Universities have a long way to go. After all, they began as medieval institutions and still have many of those characteristics."

WHAT ARE THE MOST PROMISING WAYS TO MOVE FORWARD?

In addition to the suggestions on teaching and learning, the interviewees were vocal about ways to advance the concept of democratic governance within the field. Their ideas could be grouped around three objectives: communicating the dramatic extent of the changes facing administrators today, generating much more comprehensive research that explores what is happening on the ground, and using a variety of supports and incentives, including accreditation, to encourage PA schools in their efforts to teach democratic principles and practices.

Reframing the Discussion around the Dramatic Changes Facing Administrators Today

The nonacademics were particularly adamant about the need for change in PA schools. "This is becoming an urgent situation," said Nurse. "If we don't change, institutionally, the way we interact with the public, we will become irrelevant—governance will happen without us. Citizens won't sit around and wait for us to do this." These comments from Nurse, Bonner, and other practitioners seem to agree fundamentally with both the instrumental and idealistic rationales for democratic governance but were couched in more ardent, imperative language. The analyses presented by the other two rationales could be understood as "how the world is changing *incrementally*" (the instrumental view) or "how the world ought to change *radically*" (the idealistic view). What the practitioners seemed to be suggesting was an analysis that shows how "the world *is* changing *radically*."

As part of this change in outlook, many interviewees thought it was time to shift from abstract claims about deliberative democracy to more practical and immediate kinds of arguments. "I'm very resistant to yet another article that exhorts people on this topic," said Barnes. "We're past that point now. I want either 'here's how you do it' information or research on 'here's what works.'" Bonner agreed that she has a negative reaction to what she calls "deliberative democracy as theology."

Instead of a "normative 'this is the way it should be' message," Nalbandian suggested we move to a "'this is how we understand this' approach. We need to place engagement into an intellectual framework that engages fundamental questions of PA—like issues of accountability and legitimacy."

This approach seemed to suggest a way of combining the idealistic and instrumental viewpoints. "The theory must be embedded into the practice, the 'green book' of how you work with the public," said Barnes. "In that way, it gets built into practitioners' expectations of how the world works." One critical contribution, said Fung, would be to foster "a clear sense and courage about when the ordinary, bureaucratic, nonparticipatory methods for interacting with citizens are not working."

Research That Explores the Lessons, Successes, Failures, and Implications of Democratic Governance Work Now Happening in the Field

The interviewees suggested new directions for PA research that would strengthen this "clear sense and courage." Many of them mentioned the need for more inquiry into the methods, implications, and consequences (both intended and unintended) of involving citizens actively in decision making and problem solving. Too little of the research on civic engagement, Marshall pointed out, has focused on "actual participation," as opposed to voting and volunteerism. The academic journals, agreed Barnes, "ought to take democratic governance more seriously." Of the research that has been done, too much of it focuses narrowly on what happens inside citizen–government dialogues and deliberations, and not enough on the larger organizing and political context that surrounds an effort.

Several of the academics felt that taking the research in this direction means following the traditional PA questions about accountability, inclusiveness, and responsiveness: "These are classic questions we need to answer in a contemporary context," said Nalbandian. How are democratic governance approaches affecting the ways in which needs and goals are articulated in the policymaking process? He cited the involvement of citizens in performance measurement. Stephens asked, "How inclusive are these efforts to engage citizens? Do they privilege certain cultural understandings, or favor scientific arguments over emotion and passion?"

One of the most critical frontiers in the field—and therefore a critical question for research—is the challenge of "embedding" democratic principles and strategies into the day-to-day function of public institutions. Most democratic governance efforts are temporary projects involving large numbers of citizens on particular issues or decisions for a limited time period. It is much more uncommon to find durable citizen structures that have been sustained over time. "This distinction between organizing for temporary engagement and organizing for sustained activity is a central question—an intellectual as well as a practical issue," said Nalbandian. More work needs to be done on the existing examples of permanent structures, looking at how they differ from temporary organizing efforts, and how the two approaches might inform one another.

Aids and Incentives for PA Professors and Schools

The interviewees listed a number of ways to support PA professors and schools as they incorporate democratic principles and strategies into their teaching and research. Nabatchi commended the syllabus exchanges, case simulation competitions, and case teaching workshops that have been developed recently. The groups engaged in these kinds of activities include the Collaborative Democracy Network, the Deliberative Democracy Consortium, the Democracy Imperative, the Program for the Advancement of Research on Conflict and Collaboration at the Maxwell School of Syracuse University, and the Electronic Hallway at the University of Washington.

In addition to all the workshops and training programs offered for midcareer practitioners, Fung emphasized the value of simply "connecting people with others who have done similar things." A number of organizations do this kind of convening work at the national level; others, such as Common Sense California, have taken on similar roles at the state level. One group sometimes left out of all these gatherings, Nabatchi pointed out, is the "growing set of private-sector consulting firms that conduct public engagement projects" for agencies and governments.

Finally, most of the interviewees mentioned the accreditation process as one important vehicle for changing the expectations of what PA schools ought to teach. "The 'core' of what we teach has to expand in response to the complexity of the real-world situations," said Bryson. "PA education needs to train the next generation of public administrators to govern, not just to manage," agreed Nabatchi.

A CHANGING FIELD FOR A CHANGING WORLD

In these interviews with PA professors and observers, we get glimpses of the changing contours of the field. Whether they were pleased or frustrated with the progress of democratic principles in the discipline, the interviewees described pressures and trends both on and off campus that seemed to be forcing the field in new directions.

The interviewees suggested various ways of transforming the teaching of, and research on, democratic governance from a lively side discussion into a mainstream focus of their field. They proposed new and innovative changes to the PA curriculum, such as placing more emphasis on the concepts and skills of leadership, facilitation, conflict resolution, deliberation, recruitment, online technologies, and participatory process design. These new skills may be best learned by doing, for example in case studies, role plays, simulations, internships, and service learning approaches. Others suggested that we should evaluate, and perhaps even accredit, PA programs not only on their traditional skills-based content but also on their process and civic-oriented curricula. Taken together, these proposals suggest a major shift in PA education: Instead of training their students to be managers, PA schools should prepare the next generation of public administrators to play central, convening, facilitative roles in democratic governance.

NOTES

1. The Democratic Governance Panel (a body of thirty mayors and city council members) of the National League of Cities defines democratic governance as "the art of governing in participatory, deliberative, and collaborative ways" (NLC 2004).
2. Another contribution to this discussion is the author's *The Next Form of Democracy* (Leighninger 2006).
3. The full list of interviewees: William Barnes, National League of Cities; Patricia Bonner, Environmental Protection Administration; John Bryson, University of Minnesota; Barbara Crosby, University of Minnesota; Angela Eikenberry, University of Nebraska–Omaha; Archon Fung, Harvard University; David Kuehn, Federal Highway Administration; Gary Marshall, University of Nebraska–Omaha; Tina Nabatchi, Syracuse University; John Nalbandian, University of Kansas; Leanne Smith Nurse, Environmental Protection Agency; Rosemary O'Leary, Syracuse University; Pete Peterson, Pepperdine University; John Stephens, University of North Carolina–Chapel Hill; and Camilla Stivers, Cleveland State University.
4. This chapter focuses on the testimonial of the fifteen interviewees, but scholarly research and public opinion data confirm that changes are afoot in our political culture. Numerous polls have charted citizens' changing attitudes toward authority and the erosion of their trust in government (e.g., see "Trust in Government Remains Low," Gallup Poll, September 18, 2008). Daniel Yankelovich, who inspired many people to rethink their views about citizenship with his 1991 book *Coming to Public Judgment,* now argues that "in recent years, the public's willingness to accept the authority of experts and elites has sharply declined. The public does not want to scrap representative democracy and move wholesale towards radical populism, but there will be no return to the earlier habits of deference to authority and elites" (Yankelovich and Friedman 2011). Some studies, such as the 2008 Civic Health Index published by the National Conference on Citizenship, have confirmed that there is "overwhelming support for laws and policies that would support greater citizen engagement."
5. The skills for which Nurse and Bonner look include meeting design and facilitation, issue framing, and effective recruitment techniques.

REFERENCES

Leighninger, Matt. 2006. *The Next Form of Democracy.* Nashville: Vanderbilt University Press.

NLC (National League of Cities). 2004. The Rise of Democratic Governance: How Local Leaders are Reshaping Politics for the 21st Century. Washington, DC: National League of Cities.

Roberts, Nancy C. 2008. *The Age of Direct Citizen Participation.* Armonk, NY: M. E. Sharpe.

Yankelovich, Daniel, and Will Friedman. 2011. *Toward Wiser Public Judgment.* Nashville: Vanderbilt University Press.

PART VI

Remaining Relevant

> In the final analysis, it would seem that Public Administration cannot survive unless it becomes relevant to current . . . problems, and cannot become relevant until its major academic strengths are brought into contact with practitioners.
>
> —Keith M. Henderson (quoted by Marini 1971, 248)

> There is a need for more theoretically specific formulations designed to relate more effectively to the practitioner.
>
> —Kenneth Jowitt (quoted by Marini 1971, 259)

> The insistence that Public Administration should recover relevance was embedded in arguments quite critical of the contemporary state of the academic literature of Public Administration.
>
> —Frank Marini (1971, 349)

Although the quotations given above are from Minnowbrook I, they just as easily could have been from Minnowbrook III. In both the 2008 new scholars' preconference workshop and the 2008 Lake Placid conference, commentary abounded about the lack of relevance of public administration literature, theory, and curricula. This concern was voiced most strongly by the new scholars—those who had been out of their PhD programs less than eight years. Accordingly, in this part of this book we present the views of four new scholars on the issue of the relevance of public administration.

In "Making Public Administration Scholarship Matter," David M. Van Slyke points out that the work of economists, political scientists, psychologists, sociologists, other social scientists, and management theorists is frequently cited in the public administration literature not only for the contributions those disciplines have made to our thinking about organizations, markets, and governance but also because of the legitimacy that their research and top journals convey. The field of public administration has much to offer these other fields, but it needs to go beyond small ideas, old debates, adherence to methodological orthodoxy, and publishing just for the sake of publishing.

Van Slyke writes that relevant research in public administration is characterized by three outcomes. It is analytically rigorous. It speaks back to, and informs, other social science disciplines and management research, as well as the questions they investigate. And it informs the public—government leaders, policymakers, nongovernmental actors, citizens, and interest groups—and shapes their engagement in the process of governance. The challenges to achieving these outcomes remain, but the opportunities for revision and reform are promising.

In "The Challenge of Remaining Relevant," Kristina Lambright begins by focusing on network management and maintains that public administration scholars need to both update their theories and transfer knowledge in meaningful ways to practitioners. She argues that part of the updating of theories can be accomplished by applying what we know in more traditional management settings that might be applicable to network settings, whereas part of the updating must include developing new theories.

Few practitioners know of the bulk of public administration research, according to Lambright, and if they do know about it, many do not consider it valuable or relevant to what they are doing on a daily basis. For academia to remain relevant, public administration scholars not only need to shift the focus of their research but also need to broaden how this research is shared. Specifically, public administrators must grapple with the challenge of transferring knowledge in accessible and meaningful ways to practitioners. Though Lambright cites research on networks as an example, she explains how her critique is also applicable to the larger body of public administration scholarship. A key impediment to a greater connection between academics and practitioners is the narrow promotion and tenure process, she argues, which focuses on getting articles published in high-prestige academic journals that are not read by practitioners.

In a similar chapter with a different twist, "Has Public Administration 'Repositioned' Itself? Advances and Inertias in Transitioning to the Collaborative Governance Paradigm," Kelly LeRoux argues that practitioners have forged ahead of academics in experimenting with mixed-market service delivery. Theories of governance remain underdeveloped and somewhat untested. And even the implementation of the tools of governance proceeds in an unsure fashion.

Public administration needs to fully reposition itself to deal with the new reality of governance, according to LeRoux. This includes developing a single, coherent definition of governance. It also encompasses changing what we teach in master of public administration programs to include interjurisdictional and interorganizational collaboration, contract management, negotiation, and collaborative problem solving. And it also means adopting a more integrated approach to thinking about governance as market management and a management model that relies on a combination of policy instruments to achieve public purposes. If public administration does not adapt and grow, it risks becoming irrelevant.

In "Public Administration and Management Research: Evidence of Isolation and Unrealized Opportunity," Bradley E. Wright maintains that academic public administration has incorrectly isolated itself from mainstream management literature and practice. The field's treatment of management issues has lost its moorings, he argues, and is no longer firmly grounded in contemporary management theory and research. As a result, the public administration literature not only ignores valuable lessons that can inform practice but is also increasingly ignored by scholars in other fields.

Part of the problem, as Wright sees it, is the field's belief in the uniqueness of public organizations and employees. Though there are certainly differences between the public and private sectors, he suggests focusing on the similarities and utilizing the important findings and theories found in the literature on private management. Moreover, to end the public administration field's isolation, strong works in the field need to be exported into the mainstream management literature.

Finally, Beth Gazley charts the path she sees being taken by the practice and scholarship on collaboration in "Improving Collaboration Research by Emphasizing the Role of the Public Manager." She presents background on this emergent area of study in public administration and outlines what she sees as the principal challenges, asserting that what is needed is a greater interdisciplinary approach to studying collaboration and more emphasis on the roles and characteristics of the individual actors engaged in collaborative activities and settings. She asserts that the variable of time needs to be incorporated into research on collaboration because it is not a one-time event but rather emergent, evolving, and dynamic. To ignore the role of individual actors in collaborative arrangements is to miss an important element of success.

Taken as a whole, these insights from the Minnowbrook new scholars are both sobering and informative, leading to the question of whether the tensions between the academics and practitioners involved in public administration will ever be resolved. We continue this discussion in the last part of this book.

REFERENCES

Henderson, Keith M. 1971. A New Comparative Administration. In *Toward a New Public Administration: The Minnowbrook Perspective,* ed. Frank Marini. Scranton, PA: Chandler.

Jowitt, Kenneth. 1971. Comment: The Relevance of Comparative Public Administration. In *Toward a New Public Administration: The Minnowbrook Perspective,* ed. Frank Marini. Scranton, PA: Chandler.

Marini, Frank, ed. 1971. *Toward a New Public Administration: The Minnowbrook Perspective.* Scranton, PA: Chandler.

Making Public Administration Scholarship Matter

David M. Van Slyke

The occasion to come together as young scholars to critique the field is both a great opportunity and responsibility. The discussions at the Minnowbrook I and II conferences (1968 and 1988) and at the 2008 young scholars' preconference workshop highlight questions about the relevance of public administration scholarship to other fields of scholarly inquiry and to the practice of governance. This chapter reflects my own epistemological concerns about public administration scholarship and a theme echoed throughout the 2008 meetings. That is, too much public affairs research has become emblematic of small ideas, old debates, adherence to a methodological orthodoxy, and continued questioning of whether public administration research informs the real world of governance, public affairs, and scholarship in other disciplines. This chapter describes the contemporary state of the field and some of the obstacles to becoming more relevant, and proposes a vision for what the field could be in the future.

Relevant research in public administration is characterized by three outcomes: (1) It is analytically rigorous; (2) it speaks back to and informs other social science disciplines and management research and the questions they investigate; and (3) it informs the public—government leaders, policymakers, nongovernmental actors, and citizens and interest groups—and shapes their engagement in the process of governance. The challenges to achieving these outcomes remain, but the opportunities for revision and reform are promising.

THE FIELD IN 2008

The field of public administration has been and continues to be plagued by its own intellectual insecurities about its relevance (Frederickson 1999; Marini 1971; Meier 1997). These insecurities include the questions of where the field belongs from a disciplinary perspective within the social sciences, if at all; and the desire to be respected by, and of use to, other social science and management disciplines (Kelman 2005, 2007; Simon 1997; Waldo 1968).

A different but persistent question is whether the field addresses "big" and potentially risky and controversial ideas or pursues more modest, cleverly executed questions, which tend to be viewed as divergent or trivial from the realms of epistemology and practice. Too often, public administration scholars have tended to avoid big and controversial ideas because of the argument that they politicize the field. Perhaps not surprisingly, very few researchers want to work in a politically volatile environment or feel forced to take sides, or worse have their empirical work used to support ideologies that they would not. However, such "big idea" avoidance can also be viewed as a form of academic cowardice. And this avoidance is a way for researchers to hide from the messiness of real policy debates. The field of public administration has been trying for some time to compensate for these insecurities. Past Minnowbrook discussions raised the issue of relevance with respect to the field's positioning or actions with prescriptions to ameliorate that relevance and diminish those insecurities.

Relevance begins with the choice of research questions. A concern expressed among young scholars at the 2008 Minnowbrook workshop was the trade-off between taking on bigger, messier, and more controversial questions that may take more time and potentially have less success becoming published compared with thinking and acting more strategically and employing empirical sophistication on less interesting, smaller questions, with the expectation that there is a greater probability of their work getting published. The decision calculus becomes one of getting published and responding to the structural incentives in place at universities for promotion and tenure in the field versus pursuing more difficult questions that can take longer and may not get published in top scholarly outlets. To be clear, similar problems plague most other academic disciplines, and not all scholars adhere to the discrete end points of that continuum. In public administration circles, the debate continues about what the big ideas are, and what the discipline has contributed by way of thinking—theoretically, analytically, and methodologically—to the pressing problems associated with governance and to the research enterprises of other disciplines engaged in investigating similar problems.

In this respect, public administration has been and continues to be a field of apologists. The work of economists, political scientists, psychologists, sociologists, other social scientists, and management theorists is frequently cited not only for the contributions those disciplines have made to our thinking about organizations, markets, and governance but also because of the legitimacy that *their* research and top journals convey. Sociologists, for example, study public organizations; economists analyze government contracting; and political scientists investigate citizenship and policy design. Yet as a field, public administration should be concerned about the unidirectional flow from the disciplinary social sciences to public administration.

If a study was developed with the question of how public administration scholarship is being used, and all the appropriate design mechanisms and controls were implemented, we would find that our "relevance score" is lower than we desire. Relevance was a big part of the debate at Minnowbrook I and II and continues today, as evidenced by the discussions at Minnowbrook III and in various chapters of the present volume. Yet as Wright notes in a later chapter in this part of the book, articles published in the top U.S. public administration journal, *Public Administration Review*, were only cited 0.02 percent of the time. In the 620 articles published in the top ten management journals in 2007, articles in the *Journal of Public Administration Research and Theory* were not cited at all. The field of public administration must move beyond its apologies for the limitations of its empirical methods and development of theory and toward fuller integration with the social sciences and management disciplines.

Improving the quality of public administration research means significant thinking about the design of graduate and doctoral education (Halperin 1982), and in the departmental cultures of public administration programs regarding what constitutes high-quality research and publication outlets, and incentivizing efforts at cross-disciplinary collaboration. As a number of senior scholars have observed, the field is evolving and improving. However, a commitment by those in the field will be necessary if public administration research is to become more relevant. High-quality research may evolve organically and without specific interventions, because of incremental changes to existing structures, processes, and norms, or because of proactive commitment to change. But relevance begins with the choice of research questions. It is difficult to produce research findings that others may use if you do not start with a question for which someone may be able to use the answer.

The issue of relevance for scholars and the field involves risks, uncertainty, resources, and an outcome time lag that may preclude observable and measurable indicators of productivity and effectiveness. To be sure, there is a continuum of motivations, preferences, incentives, structures, and processes of agreement and standardization that would be needed to gain buy-in and to achieve a robust level of commitment to improving the relevance of public administration scholarship. If public administration research is to have relevance that stands the test of time, then the work of scholars who have changed the discussion and terms of the conversation should be considered. Here one might look at the work of Granovetter on networks, Williamson on transaction costs, Simon on decision making, and Akerlof on the role of information.

If, as scholars of governance (broadly defined), relevance is an important goal and outcome, then the research needs to be stronger, with more emphasis on quality and less on quantity for quantity's sake. Better mechanisms are also needed for diffusing and informing practitioners of research findings and for learning from those engaged in practice. Theory and practice need not be divorced from one another; rather, they can and should complement each other.

OPPORTUNITIES FOR RELEVANCE AND THE FUTURE OF PUBLIC ADMINISTRATION SCHOLARSHIP

As a field of scholarly inquiry, public administration research should be able to answer the questions "For whom?" "Why?" and "So what?" An important part of the public administration scholarly identity is the "publicness" of what we study, of those with whom our research is shared, and how it potentially informs and influences those engaged in the governance process. There are a number of opportunities for public administration scholarship to become more relevant.

One opportunity is to publish in interdisciplinary and intersectoral journals, such as general management and administration outlets. If public administration research is good, it must be capable of speaking back to the disciplines from which it draws its theoretical and analytic foundations. This can help the field and its scholars reach an audience perhaps not familiar with public administration journals and its researchers.

Another opportunity is to reconsider how research is shared and who has access to it. Who are the field's audiences? If public administration considers other fields, such as the natural sciences, the journal *Science* stands out as an important and innovative outlet for several reasons. First, most articles are only five pages long, single spaced. They are written for a general audience, and jargon is generally avoided as much as possible. It is the most widely read publication in the natural sciences and the preferred venue for publishing articles on groundbreaking research in several different fields. The articles are not directed to a single audience, and in addition to new findings, scientific debates and research paradigms are framed in ways that many stakeholders can access and use. Similarly, a different journal and form is one from the social sciences, the *Journal of Economic Perspectives*. It does not follow the same style as *Science*, but the articles are shorter than conventional manuscripts, are less technical, and are intended to reach a broad audience and present ideas, debates, and framing models in a way that is accessible to other individuals besides economists. This does not imply that all scholarship should only seek outlets such as these, but these two publications do reach beyond more narrow disciplinary and subfield audiences.

Reflecting on public administration scholarship and journals, one question for further discussion is whether academic journals are the most effective venue for engagement with practitioners—those involved in the governance process. Though this is not the only, or best, measure of relevance, one can hear stories on NPR or read them in a national newspaper that cite the journal *Science*. Unfortunately, many fewer stories are discussed in these venues that cite a public affairs journal. Public administration is not more difficult to conduct or communicate than research taking place in the natural sciences; but again, faculty, students, and the field have not thought strategically enough about how to communicate scholarly research and translate it into different forms and disseminate it using different media for greater consumption. Writing editorials in national or local papers, preparing a commentary for a trade publication, posting on blogs and other electronic forums, or considering the implications of public administration research and its generalizability to a broader audience are all opportunities for enhancing relevance. Not all public administration research will warrant implementing these recommendations, but some surely will. Beginning a discussion about how to do so could lead to innovations that may result in greater relevance for public administration research.

Pursuing these opportunities requires perseverance. Some scholars have found that publishing research in nonacademic outlets is not valued or materially rewarded, especially for untenured professors. To be sure, there are trade-offs, and for untenured individuals this is between efficiency and productivity and an effectiveness measure that may not be widely agreed upon in the field, or in one's institution or department. The trade-offs can be steep. Such considerations include deciding whether to spend the time rewriting your research in a language and form accessible to a broader set of stakeholder groups or beginning work on another article. Another is the decision about whether to develop a network of policymakers, public managers, and others with whom you can share your work or to begin another article. This proposal would perhaps be more challenging to design and implement in the short term, but it could lead to larger gains in relevance compared with the current modus operandi in the field.

MOVING FORWARD

If the "great minds" of past Minnowbrook participants are considered, a significant issue with which the field continues to struggle is the relevance of public administration scholarship. The argument has been, and continues to be, that public administration scholarship lacks rigor and meaning, scholars in other disciplines do not use our research, and few policymakers use the findings we are producing. For many involved in public administration, the professional academic mission is to make positive changes to the processes and institutions of governance and those that work in and with them. Given that more progress is needed on the relevance of public administration scholarship, a commitment to that change is needed if the field of public administration is to become more relevant.

NOTE

The author thanks Trevor Brown, Jesse Lecy, Matthew Potoski, Michael Rushton, and Jeremy Shiffman for their helpful comments. The usual caveat applies.

REFERENCES

Frederickson, H. George. 1999. The Repositioning of American Public Administration. *PS: Political Science & Politics* 32:701–11.

Halperin, Michael J. 1982. The Relevance of Public Administration Education in the 1980s. *American Review of Public Administration* 16, nos. 2–3:261–64.

Kelman, S. 2005. Public Management Needs Help! *Academy of Management Review* 48:967–69.

———. 2007. Public Management and Organization Studies. In *The Academy of Management Annals,* Volume 1, ed. J. P. Walsh and A. P. Brief. Mahwah, NJ: Lawrence Erlbaum Associates.

Marini, Frank, ed. 1971. *Toward a New Public Administration: The Minnowbrook Perspective.* Scranton, PA: Chandler.

Meier, Kenneth J. 1997. Reforming the Review Process: Right Problem, Wrong Solution. *PS: Political Science & Politics,* September, 561–63.

Simon, Herbert A. 1997. *Administrative Behavior,* 4th ed. New York: Free Press.

Waldo, Dwight. 1968. Scope of the Theory of Public Administration. In *Theory and Practice of Public Administration: Scope, Objectives, and Methods,* ed. James Clyde Charlesworth. Philadelphia: American Academy of Political and Social Science.

The Challenge of Remaining Relevant

Kristina Lambright

One of the key themes at the original Minnowbrook Conference in 1968 was the challenge of remaining relevant (Marini 1971). Although the landscape of public administration has changed considerably since the 1960s, remaining relevant continues to be a challenge facing public administration scholars in the twenty-first century. This chapter reflects on the issue of relevance by exploring two key challenges facing public administration scholars: (1) updating public administration theory and its application to better reflect the emergence of networks and collaborative governance; and (2) transferring knowledge in accessible and meaningful ways to practitioners.

NETWORKS AND COLLABORATIVE GOVERNANCE

During the last hundred years, public administration research has largely focused on vertical relationships in hierarchal bureaucracies and multilayered federalism (Kettl 2000). Although Weber's (1946) bureaucracy has certainly not disappeared, the challenges facing contemporary public administrators are considerably more complicated as a result of the "hollow state" (Milward 1996; Milward and Provan 2000). Complex networks of public, private for-profit, and private nonprofit organizations are responsible for delivering an ever-growing array of public services (Edelenbos and Klijn 2007; Kettl 2000; Milward 1996; Milward and Provan 2000; O'Toole 1997a; Sowa 2008). Drawing on O'Toole (1997a, 445), this chapter defines networks as "structures of interdependence involving multiple organizations."

Networks typically focus on a specific policy or policy area (Agranoff and McGuire 1999), often span different sectors (Agranoff and McGuire 1999), and involve multiple, reciprocal exchanges (Powell 1990). They are particularly well suited for addressing "wicked problems," challenges that must be addressed holistically rather than through fragmented strategies (McGuire 2006; O'Toole and Meier 2004; O'Toole 1997b). Although networks by definition are based on interdependent relationships, they can have hierarchal structures and be rule driven (McGuire 2006). For instance, public contracting relationships are often hierarchal networks (Johnston and Romzek 2008).

Though one advantage of networks is their flexibility, they are also less stable than markets and require complex coordination and accountability mechanisms (Milward 1996; Milward and Provan 2000).

The increasing importance of networks in public administration raises a variety of interesting questions for further research. However, this does not mean that a whole new body of theory unique to networks needs to be developed. As McGuire (2006) highlights, though some of the skills public administrators need to manage collaborative structures are unique to this setting, many of the skills critical in collaborative environments are also essential in the management of more traditional organizations. A rich body of knowledge already exists about management and administration in public organizations. Rather than attempting to reinvent the wheel, public administration research can build on this existing knowledge.

As an example, public administration scholars have focused considerable attention on understanding motivation in the public sector. Most literature in this body of research has focused on examining motivation within traditional bureaucratic structures. Yet understanding motivation in networks is undoubtedly also critical for public managers. If anything, motivation is likely to be more complicated in a network setting compared with a traditional bureaucracy, because public managers do not directly supervise many of the individuals who affect their own performance (O'Toole 1997b). Nongovernmental employees are often responsible for the actual delivery of public services in the hollow state. Yet public managers' ability to individually reward or penalize these nongovernmental employees based on the services they deliver is quite limited. This makes it harder for public managers to motivate the delivery of high-quality public services in network settings.

Public administration scholars can draw on existing motivation theories traditionally applied in bureaucratic settings to answer a range of important questions about networks. Under what conditions would a specific motivation theory traditionally applied in a bureaucratic setting such as expectancy theory (Porter and Lawler 1968; Vroom 1964) also be applicable in a network environment? Under what conditions would the applicability of this same motivation theory be limited in a network environment? To what extent are these conditions consistent across different types of networks? To what extent are conditions of applicability similar across different motivation theories? Scholars could also pursue comparable research agendas in other areas where there are already well-developed theories such as organizational leadership, learning, change, and culture.

TRANSFERRING KNOWLEDGE TO PRACTITIONERS

Although key gaps in our knowledge about networks remain, there has recently been a growing interest among public administration scholars in understanding networks and collaborative governance. Much of the research in this area has important implications for practitioners. However, most practitioners are unaware that this research even exists and certainly do not view it as a valuable resource when confronting network management challenges. For academia to remain relevant, public administration scholars not only need to shift the focus of their research but also need to broaden how this research is shared. Specifically, public administrators must grapple with the challenge of transferring knowledge in accessible and meaningful ways to practitioners. Though research on networks has been cited here as an example, this critique is also applicable to the larger body of public administration scholarship. The discipline as a whole needs to develop more effective ways for transmitting knowledge from public administration scholars to practitioners.

According to Waldo (1968), public administration should strive to be a profession that encompasses theory and practice and focuses on solving the most important problems facing government. Yet, as several contemporary scholars have recognized, there is a gap between current public administration research and practice (Bolton and Stolcis 2003; Box 1992; Streib, Slotkin, and Rivera 2001). In his critique of public administration research, Box (1992) noted that much of the research in our field often fails to link theory to practice and is written in a style that can only be easily understood by other academics. This gap between theory and practice is of particular concern because public administration is an applied field and scholars in our discipline cannot just remain in the "ivory tower." Moreover, with the increasing sophistication of theoretical models and quantitative analysis, this chasm between theory and practice is likely to grow rather than shrink.

A key institution undermining the link between theory and practice is the tenure and promotion process (Bolton and Stolcis 2003). For the most part, research universities heavily weigh publication in traditional scholarly outlets such as peer-reviewed journals and books in this process. As a consequence, this is where scholars focus the vast majority of their research efforts. Yet few practitioners read these publications. Instead, the primary audience for public administration scholars' research efforts is other academics. Scholars can also transmit knowledge to practitioners using the trickle-down approach that occurs in classrooms. Academics are influenced by other academics and subsequently influence their students with these ideas. Think tanks represent another method of knowledge transmission. As an alternative to these more traditional approaches, researchers can engage in collaborative research activities with practitioners. In action research, people in the organization or community being studied are not just treated as passive subjects but are actively involved throughout the research process (Flynn, Ray, and Rider 1994; Mischen and Sinclair 2009; Whyte, Greenwood, and Lazes 1991). Unfortunately, none of the mechanisms detailed here currently transfer knowledge to large numbers of practitioners on a consistent basis.

Finding mechanisms to better connect public administration research with practice is essential. One option is to expand the audience for peer-reviewed journals. To do this, these journals would need to include more articles that use straightforward methodologies, are written in nontechnical language, and address topics that practitioners find relevant and interesting. A possible model for this is the "Theory to Practice" section of *Public Administration Review*.

Another way to better connect public administration research with practice is to encourage more public administration scholars to engage in action research. By participating in action research, scholars will be able to create new networks with practitioners. These networks will not just expand the dissemination of public administration research but will also provide meaningful opportunities for practitioners to become involved in knowledge creation. Though action research can benefit the field in important ways, implementing it on a widespread basis will not be easy because it limits the control that scholars have over the research process. Another challenge is that the type of research projects public and nonprofit administrators are most interested in often will not result in generalizable knowledge. Due to the incentives of the tenure and promotion process, academics tend to only collaborate with practitioners when the partnership is likely to result in research suitable for publication in a mainstream, peer-reviewed journal. However, academic–practitioner research collaborations that do not result in publishable findings still can advance the practice of public administration and should be taken more seriously in the tenure and promotion process. These collaborations can help public and nonprofit agencies solve practical problems and make scholars more aware of the challenges facing contemporary administrators. One strategy to create more incentives for these collaborations is to expand tenure and promotion committees to include practitioners in the review.

By making these recommendations, I am not suggesting that public administration scholars should solely direct their research activities toward practitioners. I am simply arguing that there should be a better balance between theory and practice in public administration scholarship. Though both the options I suggest would require significant institutional changes, the cost of not addressing the current gap between theory and practice is also great.

CONCLUSION

In sum, challenges relating both to the focus of public administration research and the transmission of this research need to be addressed. With respect to the focus of research, public administration theory and its application should be updated to better reflect the emergence of networks and collaborative governance. Equally important, better mechanisms need to be developed to connect public administration research with practice. If these steps are not taken, public administration scholars run the risk of becoming irrelevant to the practice of public administration.

REFERENCES

Agranoff, Robert, and Michael McGuire. 1999. Managing in Network Settings. *Policy Studies Review* 16:18–41.

Bolton, Michael J., and Gregory B. Stolcis. 2003. Ties That Do Not Bind: Musing on the Specious Relevance of Academic Research. *Public Administration Review* 63:626–30.

Box, Richard C. 1992. An Examination of the Debate over Research in Public Administration. *Public Administration Review* 52:62–69.

Edelenbos, Jurian, and Erik-Hans Klijn. 2007. Trust in Complex Decision-Making Networks: A Theoretical and Empirical Exploration. *Administration & Society* 39: 25–50.

Flynn, Beverly Collora, Dixie Wiles Ray, and Melinda S. Rider. 1994. Empowering Communities: Action Research through Healthy Cities. *Health Education Quarterly* 21:395–405.

Johnston, Jocelyn M., and Barbara S. Romzek. 2008. Social Welfare Contracts as Networks: The Impact of Network Stability on Management and Performance. *Administration & Society* 40:115–46.

Kettl, Donald F. 2000. The Transformation of Governance: Globalization, Devolution, and the Role of Government. *Public Administration Review* 60:488–97.

Marini, Frank, ed. 1971. *Toward a New Public Administration: The Minnowbrook Perspective.* Scranton, PA: Chandler.

McGuire, Michael. 2006. Collaborative Public Management: Assessing What We Know and How We Know It. *Public Administration Review* 66:33–42.

Milward, H. Brinton. 1996. Symposium on the Hollow State: Capacity, Control, and Performance in Interorganizational Settings. *Journal of Public Administration Research and Theory* 6:193–95.

Milward, H. Brinton, and Keith G. Provan. 2000. Governing the Hollow State. *Journal of Public Administration Research and Theory* 10:359–79.

Mischen, Pamela A., and Thomas A. P. Sinclair. 2009. Making Implementation More Democratic through Action Implementation Research. *Journal of Public Administration Research and Theory* 19:145–64.

O'Toole, Laurence J., Jr. 1997a. The Implications for Democracy in a Networked Bureaucracy. *Journal of Public Administration Research and Theory* 7:443–59.

———. 1997b. Treating Networks Seriously: Practical and Research-Based Agendas in Public Administration. *Public Administration Review* 57:45–52.

O'Toole, Laurence J., and Kenneth J. Meier. 2004. Desperately Seeking Selznick: Cooptation and the Dark Side of Public Management in Networks. *Public Administration Review* 64:681–93.

Porter, Lyman W., and Edward E. Lawler. 1968. *Managerial Attitudes and Performance.* Homewood, IL: Irwin.

Powell, Walter W. 1990. Neither Market nor Hierarchy: Network Forms of Organization. In *Research in Organizational Behavior,* ed. B. M. Staw and L. L. Cummings. Greenwich, CT: JAI Press.

Sowa, Jessica E. 2008. Implementing Interagency Collaborations: Exploring Variation in Collaborative Ventures in Human Service Organizations. *Administration & Society* 40:298–323.

Streib, Gregory, Bert J. Slotkin, and Mark Rivera. 2001. Public Administration Research from a Practitioner Perspective. *Public Administration Review* 61:515–25.

Waldo, Dwight. 1968. Scope of the Theory of Public Administration. In *Theory and Practice of Public Administration: Scope, Objectives, and Methods,* ed. James Clyde Charlesworth. Philadelphia: American Academy of Political and Social Science.

Weber, Max. 1946. *Max Weber: Essays in Sociology*, trans. Hans. H. Gerth and C. Wright Mills. New York: Oxford University Press.

Whyte, William Foote, David J. Greenwood, and Peter Lazes. 1991. Participatory Action Research: Through Practice to Science in Social Research. In *Participatory Action Research*, ed. William Foote Whyte. Newbury Park, CA: Sage.

Vroom, Victor H. 1964. *Work and Motivation.* New York: John A. Wiley & Sons.

Has Public Administration "Repositioned" Itself?

Advances and Inertias in Transitioning to the Collaborative Governance Paradigm

Kelly LeRoux

On the eve of the millennium at the American Political Science Association's annual meeting, George Frederickson delivered the John Gaus Lecture, "The Repositioning of American Public Administration," in which he foreshadowed the field's continual migration toward theories of governance, cooperation, networking, and institution building. He observed how the increasingly global and transjurisdictional nature of commerce, communication, and environmental dilemmas have complicated public management at all levels. The solutions for managing these problems, he argued, are multijurisdictional and multisectoral modes of collaboration, to include the variety of policy tools encompassed under the umbrella of governance.

Today Frederickson's comments are more salient than ever, yet it appears that the field of public administration has failed to fully "reposition" itself to cope with the problems of a fragmented administrative state. Clearly a "repositioning" has begun, but in many cases the practice of governance, and the implementation of its "tools" (Salamon 2002), proceed in an unsure fashion, while theories of governance remain underdeveloped and somewhat untested. Indeed, a title search of the word "governance" revealed only six *Journal of Public Administration Research and Theory* articles bearing the term since 1999, and only ten published in *Public Administration Review.* Moreover, governance scholarship has been asymmetrically balanced in favor of studying networks and service contracting, to the exclusion of a broader picture that must also include studies of public–private partnerships, intergovernmental agreements, and mixed-market approaches to delivering services. Governance research must not only speak to issues of managing markets in ways that generate the most public value, but it must also speak to the skill sets managers require to achieve cooperative ends. This chapter makes the case for the importance of governance theories to the future of our discipline, outlines the progress we have made toward "repositioning" ourselves to cope with a fragmented and outsourced state, and identifies several items to consider as we look forward.

Perhaps the incompleteness of the repositioning movement can be explained by the inability of the field to render a single, coherent definition of governance. For the purposes of this critique, I define governance and distinguish it from government as follows: Whereas governments are legally constructed institutions that are politically and spatially bounded, *governance* refers to the pursuit of public purposes through government-directed, but not necessarily government-produced, methods. Governance is the process whereby public officials, both elected and administrative, ensure that the needs of citizens are met. It is a process that relies on a varied mix of service delivery arrangements, and it is built on interdependencies between governments, citizens, and public and private (for-profit and nonprofit) organizations. These interdependencies assume many forms, the most common of which are formal and informal networks, contracts for services, intergovernmental agreements, mixed-market approaches, and the use of public incentives to encourage desired behavior in the market. Governance is thus, by definition, collaborative.

NEW REASONS TO "REPOSITION"

Frederickson's rationales for public administration's need to reposition itself are even more compelling today, yet we also face additional, unforeseen challenges. The persistent threat of both human-made and natural disasters has ushered in a new era of mandates for intergovernmental collaboration in the areas of emergency management and disaster planning. Homeland security and other federal mandates of the last ten years have redistributed federal funding to cities in ways that promote certain public objectives like national security while constraining cities' ability to deal with other pressing public problems. Declining discretionary federal resources combined with an economic recession and national housing mortgage crisis have forced state and local governments to become more entrepreneurial, and thus to engage in financial partnerships with the private sector and to maximize alternatives to direct government service delivery.

Public administration must fully reposition itself because America's stronghold in the world economy, technological innovation, and even in military capacity are eroding. Pointing to milestone achievements in U.S. history such as winning the space race and eradicating diseases, Frederickson observed in his Gaus Lecture that every significant accomplishment of the twentieth century could be attributed to American bureaucracy. Arguably, some of the most exciting innovations and discoveries of today are not being made by government but in the private sector. From the production of green energy by the utilities industry to the alleviation of poverty and economic distress by nonprofit social enterprises, some of the most sustainable solutions to contemporary public problems are being found outside government. In some cases, these developments progress without government subsidies. The instruments of governance provide the only vehicles through which government can stake a claim to these innovations; otherwise, these solutions will evolve independent of government and perhaps not in ways that are consistent with the public interest. Thus, the first danger in failing to fully reposition ourselves is that public administration risks diminished relevance as the private sector outpaces government in innovation. The second danger in failing to reposition government to manage the extended state relates to accountability; managers who are not prepared to provide leadership of collaborative governance arrangements are ill equipped to protect the public interest.

ADVANCES AND INERTIAS IN "REPOSITIONING"

Throughout the past decade, those of us working as public administration scholars have made significant progress in repositioning ourselves to deal with some types of governance challenges. The study of managing networks is one area in which this progress is particularly apparent. We have managed to cull important information for practice about the roles and responsibilities of network actors (Klijn and Koppenjan 2000), the power structures within networks that contribute to network effectiveness (Milward and Provan 1998), how to overcome unexpected obstacles facing network participants seeking to mitigate public emergencies (Moynihan 2005), and criteria for assessing network performance (Provan and Milward 2001).

We have also made substantial progress in repositioning the field through what we have learned in the last decade about service contracting. Perhaps most important, we have learned that many of our initial assumptions about service contracting were incorrect. Efficiency is not the sole motivator in the decision to contract out, and sometimes it is not a consideration at all. Other public values, along with political considerations, institutional structures, and market conditions, also drive service delivery choices (Brown, Potoski, and Van Slyke 2006). We are just beginning to learn how public managers use mixed-market forms of service delivery in an effort to balance efficiency gains with other important public values like citizen satisfaction (Warner and Hefetz 2008). Thanks to work by Brown and Potoski (2003), we understand how specific characteristics of public goods and services shape government choices about which sector with which to contract for different types of services.

We are also better equipped today to manage the extended state because of work by Romzek and Johnston (2002) showing us that the ways we structure contract expectations and interact with contract personnel have important consequences for contractor performance. In the new governance era, understanding how to maximize contractor accountability and performance is of paramount importance for both scholars and practitioners. Yet despite the importance scholars accord to accountability and the performance of third-party government actors, fewer than an a dozen master of public administration (MPA) programs in the United States offer students the option of a course in contract management. This points to a major disconnect between what scholarship tells us is important for the field of contemporary public management and how we prepare students for careers in public service.

Frederickson (1999) found that public managers spend approximately 15 percent of their time engaged in interjurisdictional and interorganizational collaborative activity. These types of collaboration require specific skills of managers such as negotiation, conflict management, dispute resolution, facilitation, and process management. Yet most MPA programs have been slow to incorporate exercises for imparting these skills into their curriculum. The fact that most MPA programs do not emphasize the management skills needed for collaborative governance is partially to blame for the lack of progress in repositioning public administration as a field. The discipline would benefit from a more standardized approach to incorporating lessons on collaboration. For example, the National Association of Schools of Public Affairs and Administration might consider making a course in collaborative governance a required part of the MPA core curriculum for the programs it accredits. Such a course might highlight the various tools of governance and focus on developing the skills needed for managing networks and other types of interorganizational and interjurisdictional government partnerships.

Finally, the study of networks and service contracting has somewhat overshadowed the academic attention given to the other forms of cross-sector collaboration that exist within the realm of governance. Experiments with public–private ventures, competitive sourcing and public–private competition, and coproduction are happening everywhere in U.S. local governments. Yet we know little about why governments opt for these forms of collaboration as opposed to direct contracting. Given what we have learned over the last ten years about managers' preferences for mixed-market service delivery, the field may stand to benefit substantially from a greater understanding of the circumstances favoring the use of these alternatives.

TOWARD A FULLY "REPOSITIONED" PUBLIC ADMINISTRATION

Public administration must fully reposition itself for managing an administrative state that is jurisdictionally, functionally, and sectorally fragmented, as public problems continue to transcend these categorical boundaries. This means that we must adopt a more integrated approach to thinking about governance increasingly as market management, and a management model that relies on a combination of policy instruments to achieve public purposes.

Driven by both necessity and creativity, practitioners have forged ahead of academics in the repositioning movement by daily using policy tools that connect them to other sectors and governments to achieve their goals. These policy tools take the shape of networks, service contracts, public–private ventures, the use of public incentives such as tax subsidies, and so on. These tools are employed by practitioners to provide for a variety of public needs that span policy domains ranging from housing and social services to economic development and public safety.

As we look to the future, scholars can move us toward a more fully repositioned public administration through the development and testing of theories that can describe, explain, and predict under what circumstances and contextual conditions managers opt to use various policy tools. We also need theories that can accurately predict the performance outcomes of these tools. Lynn, Heinrich, and Hill's (2002) "logic of governance" offers a model for empirically testing the effects of various factors on performance outcomes, but this framework has been underutilized by scholars studying collaborative service arrangements. Given the need for these models to account for the politics of specific policy arenas and for the institutional contexts that frame managers' choices, it seems unlikely that a single theory of governance will suffice. Governance theories might be differentiated by whether they explain interorganizational, intersectoral, or intergovernmental linkages. For example, urban politics scholars have made great progress in elaborating theories of metropolitan governance that can reliably predict under what conditions intermunicipal cooperation is most likely to occur.

To bring us closer to a more fully repositioned public administration, we also need research that helps us better understand the life cycle of networks, including how they perform over time, why they fail, and why some cease to exist when their mission is fulfilled while others evolve into new structures and take on new problems. As the constellation of actors changes, network outcomes are likely to change. Empirical studies of networks over time can help us better understand the inputs that contribute to their outcomes. Finally, if the field is to fully reposition itself to cope with the realities of a fragmented and outsourced state, MPA programs must do a better job of preparing students for today's public service climate. This includes more coursework in contract management, simulations that equip students with skills for negotiating multiactor arrangements, and a greater emphasis on public managers' role in ensuring that the appropriate balance is achieved between values of efficiency and effectiveness and values of equity and responsiveness.

REFERENCES

Brown, Trevor L., and Matthew Potoski. 2003. Transaction Costs and Institutional Explanations for Government Service Production Decisions. *Journal of Public Administration Research and Theory* 13, no. 4:441–68.

Brown, Trevor, Matthew Potoski, and David Van Slyke. 2006. Managing Public Service Contracts: Aligning Values, Institutions, and Markets. *Public Administration Review* 66, no. 3:323–31.

Frederickson, H. George. 1999. The Repositioning of American Public Administration. *PS: Political Science & Politics* 32:701–11.

Klijn, E. H., and J. Koppenjan. 2000. Public Management and Policy Networks: Foundations of a Network Approach to Governance. *Public Management* 2, no. 2:135–58.

Lynn, Laurence E., Jr., Carolyn Heinrich, and Carolyn Hill. 2002. *Improving Governance: A New Logic for Empirical Research.* Washington, DC: Georgetown University Press.

Milward, H. Brinton, and Keith Provan. 1998. Principles for Controlling Agents: The Political Economy of Network Structure. *Journal of Public Administration Research and Theory* 8, no. 2:203–22.

Moynihan, Donald P. 2005. *Leveraging Collaborative Networks in Infrequent Emergency Situations.* Washington, DC: IBM Center for the Business of Government.

Provan, Keith G., and H. Brinton Milward. 2001. Do Networks Really Work? A Framework for Evaluating Public Sector Organizational Networks. *Public Administration Review* 61, no. 4:414–23.

Romzek, Barbara, and Jocelyn M. Johnston. 2002. Effective Contract Implementation and Management: A Preliminary Model. *Journal of Public Administration Research and Theory* 12, no. 3:423–53.

Salamon, Lester. 2002. *The Tools of Government: A Guide to the New Governance.* New York: Oxford University Press.

Warner, Mildred, and Amir Hefetz. 2008. Managing Markets for Public Service: The Role of Mixed Public–Private Delivery of Public Services. *Public Administration Review* 68, no. 1:155–66.

Public Administration and Management Research

Evidence of Isolation and Unrealized Opportunity

Bradley E. Wright

Public administration is commonly viewed as an inherently interdisciplinary field, defined by the need to address conflicting political, legal, and managerial values and processes (Rosenbloom 1983). As a result, "the development of a more coherent body of public administration theory" may be predicated on recognition of "the utility of each of these three approaches as they apply to various aspects of administration" (Rosenbloom 1983, 219).

There are, however, legitimate concerns that the field may too often ignore the values and lessons of one or more of these areas. In part V of this volume, Rosenbloom and Naff provide very convincing evidence for both the lack of and greater need for emphasis on the law within public administration. Regrettably, this is not the only area in which public administration may be deficient. Kelman (2007) argues that public administration has also slighted the traditional management values of efficiency and effectiveness. Though organizational performance and behavior are topics frequently featured in major public administration journals (Moynihan 2008), this provides little assurance that these issues are given proper attention.

Given that others have highlighted concerns regarding the field's detachment from the law (again, Rosenbloom and Naff, in part V of this volume), this critique focuses on the issues related to public administration's isolation from the mainstream management literature and practice. Rather than a focus on the degree to which public administration has slighted the importance of its management values (Kelman 2007), perhaps a more fundamental issue is that the field's treatment of management has lost its moorings and is no longer firmly grounded in contemporary management theory and research. As a result, the public administration literature not only ignores valuable lessons that can inform practice but is also increasingly ignored by scholars in other fields.

Unfortunately, evidence of this isolation is not hard to find. Even a cursory review of public administration journals can identify articles that focus on management topics without using mainstream management theories or research (e.g., Stoker and Greasley 2008). A more systematic assessment of the extent to which public administration is isolated from the managerial literature also provides compelling evidence. In 2007, for example, only 3.4 percent of all articles cited in the *Public Administration Review* (*PAR*) and the *Journal of Public Administration Research and Theory* (*JPART*) were from the ten most-commonly-cited management journals.[1] In addition, more than two-thirds of these citations (137 of 203) were of management articles more than ten years old. Perhaps even more damning than the infrequency with which public administration research cites published management work is the infrequency with which management journals cite articles published in *PAR* and *JPART.* Of the nearly 70,000 citations included in the 620 articles published by the top ten management journals during 2007, *PAR* was cited only 14 times, while *JPART* was not cited at all. Thus there is considerable evidence that public administration research not only ignores but is also ignored by mainstream management scholars. This isolation not only results in the missing of valuable lessons that could inform public administration theory and practice but also hinders the perceived importance and credibility of the field.

A number of reasons have been previously offered to explain why public administration research has been ignored by the mainstream management literature. Admittedly some of these reasons may suggest the culpability lies outside the field of public administration, such as mainstream management scholars' lack of interest in the legal and political context in which the management issues in public administration journals are framed. Other reasons highlight common serious critiques of the public administration literature, such as the field's reliance on weaker research designs (Kelman 2005; Wright, Manigault, and Black 2004) or even its failure to test and build on applicable contemporary management theories (Van Wart 2003; Wright 2001). Though both are legitimate issues that need to be addressed, the latter is of special concern because it suggests that some of the isolation is intentional and self-imposed. In fact, perhaps the most likely reason for public administration's isolation from the contemporary management literature is the field's belief in the uniqueness of public organizations and employees. Rather than seeing public administration as the intersection of management, political, and legal thought, the legal and political context is often used to justify dismissing or redefining traditional management values and processes so fundamentally that little value is seen in attempting to learn how or even if the lessons of the mainstream management literature can be applied (Allison 1983). Such a view seems to persist even when a scholar is faced with contrary evidence. Several recent reviews suggest that public organizations and employees do not always differ from their private-sector counterparts in the expected ways, and the empirical evidence for some of these differences is surprisingly sparse and inconsistent (Boyne 2002; Rainey and Bozeman 2000; Wright 2001).

Even if differences exist, however, it would not justify ignoring the similarities that have been found in organizing and motivating collective action. Because much of public management research relies on antiquated management theories (Wright 2001), it continues to ignore the considerable evidence that the most prominent mainstream management theories of leadership (Dumdum, Lowe, and Avolio 2002; Lowe, Kroeck, and Sivasubramaniam 1996; Van Wart 2003) and motivation (Latham, Borgogni, and Petitta 2008; Wright 2001, 2004, 2007) are not only applicable in public-sector organizations but also offer valuable lessons to practitioners and scholars alike. Similarities even exist regarding the nature of organizational goals themselves, as the most popular mainstream organizational performance theories (Quinn and Rohrbaugh 1983) and assessment practices (Kaplan and Norton 1992) have not only found public-sector application (i.e., Faerman, Quinn, and Thompson 1987; Walters 2000) but also make an assumption that is consistent with a fundamental model of public administration, that all successful organizations must recognize and address multiple and competing interests.

This does not mean that all mainstream management theories and practices can or even should be implemented in public-sector organizations, merely that public administration scholars need to do more to test if (and how) such theories can be applied when managing in the legal and political contexts of public organizations. For example, given the importance of internal equity and political institutions in determining extrinsic performance rewards, there are valuable lessons to be learned from recent mainstream management research on alternative motivational processes such as task significance (Grant 2007, 2008a, 2008b, 2008c) and transformational leadership (Van Wart 2003). Fortunately, some public administration scholars have begun applying some of these theories in public administration journal publications (e.g., Rainey and Watson 1996; Trottier, Van Wart, and Wang 2008; Wright and Pandey 2010). Another positive sign is that some prominent mainstream management scholars are starting to promote their research to public administration scholars by publishing in public administration journals (Grant 2008c; Latham, Borgogni, and Petitta 2008).

Just as important as the need to import management research into public administration is the need to export our field's research into mainstream management. Public administration has the potential to contribute to the mainstream management literature by investigating the potential effects of structural (i.e., red tape) and contextual (i.e., distributed decision-making authority) constraints on important organizational behavior constructs (i.e., employee role ambiguity and conflict) as well as possible strategies that might help mitigate those effects (Pandey and Wright 2006; Scott and Pandey 2000). Another area in which public administration research could be readily exported into the management literature is in employee intrinsic or prosocial behavior. Here some progress has been made as references to public service motivation research is beginning to appear in top economic (François 2000) and psychology (Grant 2000a, 2008b) journals. Even so, there is still a long way to go, because it is still common to find studies on the role incentives play in public-sector organizations that ignore research on public service motivation and fail to cite any work published in public administration journals (e.g., Burgess and Ratto 2003; Dixit 2002).

Herbert Simon once noted that public administration is often viewed as "an academic backwater" and, as a result, the field and any of its contributions are "nearly invisible to mainstream social scientists" (Simon 1991, 114). If the field of public administration hopes to develop a more coherent body of public administration theory, maximize its usefulness to management practitioners, and gain credibility as a field of social science, then it must work to end its isolation from the mainstream management literature.

NOTE

1. *Journal Citation Reports* was used to identify the ten most-cited journals in management and the frequency with which they cite or are cited by two of the top journals in public administration. In 2007, the ten most-cited management journals were the *Academy of Management Journal, Academy of Management Review, Administrative Science Quarterly, Harvard Business Review, Journal of Management, Management Science, MIS Quarterly, Organizational Behavior and Human Decision Processes, Organization Science,* and *Strategic Management Journal.*

REFERENCES

Allison, G. 1983. Public and Private Management: Are They Fundamentally Alike in All Unimportant Ways? In *Public Management: Public and Private Perspectives*, ed. J. Perry and K. Kraemer. Palo Alto, CA: Mayfield.

Boyne, G. A. 2002. Public and Private Management: What's the Difference? *Journal of Management Studies* 39, no. 1:97–122.

Burgess, S., and M. Ratto. 2003. The Role of Incentives in the Public Sector: Issues and Evidence. *Oxford Review of Economic Policy* 19, no. 2:285–300.

Dixit, A. 2002. Incentives and Organizations in the Public Sector: An Interpretative Review. *Journal of Human Resources* 37, no. 4:696–727.

Dumdum, U. R., K. B. Lowe, and B. J. Avolio. 2002. Meta-Analysis of Transformational and Transactional Leadership Correlates of Effectiveness and Satisfaction: An Update and Extension. In *Transformational and Charismatic Leadership: The Road Ahead*, ed. B. J. Aviolio and F. J. Yammarino. New York: JAI Press.

Faerman, S. R., R. E. Quinn, and M. P. Thompson. 1987. Bridging Management Practice and Theory: New York State's Public Service Training Program. *Public Administration Review* 47, no. 4:310–19.

François, P. 2000. "Public Service Motivation" as an Argument for Government Provision. *Journal of Public Economics* 78:275–99.

Grant, A. M. 2007. Relational Job Design and the Motivation to Make a Prosocial Difference. *Academy of Management Review* 32, no. 2:393–417.

———. 2008a. Designing Jobs to Do Good: Dimensions and Psychological Consequences of Prosocial Job Characteristics. *Journal of Positive Psychology* 3:19–39.

———. 2008b. Does Intrinsic Motivation Fuel the Prosocial Fire? Motivational Synergy in Predicting Persistence, Performance, and Productivity. *Journal of Applied Psychology* 93:48–58.

———. 2008c. Enhancing Work Motivation in Public Service: Connecting Employees to the Prosocial Impact of Their Jobs. *International Public Management Journal* 11, no. 1:48–66.

Kaplan, R. S., and D. P. Norton. 1992. The Balanced Scorecard: Measures That Drive Performance. *Harvard Business Review*, January–February, 71–79.

Kelman, S. 2005. Public Management Needs Help! *Academy of Management Review* 48:967–69.

———. 2007. Public Management and Organization Studies. In *The Academy of Management Annals, Volume 1*, ed. J. P. Walsh and A. P. Brief. Mahwah, NJ: Lawrence Erlbaum Associates.

Latham, G. P., L. Borgogni, and L. Petitta. 2008. Goal Setting and Performance Management in the Public Sector. *International Public Management Journal* 11, no. 4:385–403.

Lowe, K. B., K. G. Kroeck, and N. Sivasubramaniam. 1996. Effectiveness Correlates of Transformational and Transactional Leadership: A Meta-Analytic Review of the MLQ Literature. *Leadership Quarterly* 7, no. 3:385–425.

Moynihan, D. 2008. Public Management in North America. *Public Management Review* 10, no. 4:481–92.

Pandey, S. K. and B. E. Wright. 2006. Connecting the Dots in Public Management: Political Environment, Organizational Goal Ambiguity and Public Manager's Role Ambiguity. *Journal of Public Administration Research and Theory* 16, no. 4:511–32.

Quinn, R. E., and J. Rohrbaugh. 1983. A Spatial Model of Effectiveness Criteria: Towards a Competing-Values Approach to Organizational Analysis. *Management Science* 29:363–77.

Rainey, H. G., and B. Bozeman. 2000. Comparing Public and Private Organizations: Empirical Research and the Power of the A Priori. *Journal of Public Administration Research and Theory* 10, no. 2:447–70.

Rainey, H. G., and S. A. Watson. 1996. Transformational Leadership and Middle Management: Towards a Role for Mere Mortals. *International Journal of Public Administration* 19:763–800.

Rosenbloom, D. H. 1983. Public Administration Theory and the Separation of Powers. *Public Administration Review* 43, no. 3:219–27.

Scott, P. G., and S. K. Pandey. 2000. The Influence of Red Tape on Bureaucratic Behavior: An Experimental Simulation. *Journal of Policy Analysis and Management* 19, no. 4:615–33.

Simon, J. 1991. *Models of My Life*. New York: Basic Books.

Stoker, G., and S. Greasley. 2008. Mayors and Urban Governance: Developing a Facilitative Leadership Style. *Public Administration Review* 68, no. 4:720–28.

Trottier, T., M. Van Wart, and X. Wang. 2008. Examining the Nature and Significance of Leadership in Government Organizations. *Public Administration Review* 68, no. 2:319–33.

Van Wart, M. 2003. Public-Sector Leadership Theory: An Assessment. *Public Administration Review* 63:214–28.

Walters, J. 2000. The Buzz over Balance. *Governing*, May, 56–62.

Wright, B. E. 2001. Public Sector Work Motivation: Review of Current Literature and a Revised Conceptual Model. *Journal of Public Administration Research and Theory* 11, no. 4:559–86.

———. 2004. The Role of Work Context in Work Motivation: A Public Sector Application of Goal and Social Cognitive Theories. *Journal of Public Administration Research and Theory* 14, no. 1:59–78.

———. 2007. Public Service and Motivation: Does Mission Matter? *Public Administration Review* 67, no. 1:54–64.

Wright, B. E., L. J. Manigault, and T. R. Black. 2004. Quantitative Research Measurement in Public Administration: An Assessment of Journal Publications. *Administration and Society* 35, no. 6:747–64.

Wright, B. E., and S. K. Pandey. 2010. Transformational Leadership in the Public Sector: Does Structure Matter? *Journal of Public Administration Research and Theory* 20, no. 1:75–89.

Improving Collaboration Research by Emphasizing the Role of the Public Manager

Beth Gazley

Since the late 1990s, scholars of public affairs and administration have focused increasing attention on the nature of interorganizational and intersectoral collaboration. Collaboration, or "co-labor," manifests itself through strategic alliances, partnerships, joint ventures, teamwork, and other forms of coproduction, with some level of interdependence and shared responsibility among the actors. Public-sector collaboration research seeks to understand these activities in the particular context of public service provision (O'Leary et al. 2008). Social science scholars have derived their conceptual frameworks of collaboration from a number of disciplines. Business studies contribute an understanding of the dynamics in strategic alliances. Neoclassical economics, sociology, and anthropology help to explain how individuals and groups are motivated to engage in mutual action and reciprocal behavior. Policy sciences identify the challenges of effective collective action.

In the decade leading up to 2008, the year of Syracuse University's Minnowbrook III Conference, the public administration field exploded with research on collaboration in its many forms: interorganizational, internetwork, and intersectoral, and within communities, work units, and social groups. Dozens of panels at academic meetings, multiple journal issues, and hundreds of articles and chapters have been dedicated to collaboration research. Several volumes on "collaborative public management" were produced in 2009, with an equal effort in the nonprofit literature.

The study of collaboration is a vibrant and exciting research area because it is highly contextual, depends on many circumstances, offers many applications, and enjoys much policy and philanthropic attention. The field of collaborative theory—describing its antecedents, characteristics, actors, and outcomes—has strengthened, growing increasingly integrative across fields and theoretical perspectives. Many of these research efforts are aimed at helping public managers and policymakers understand the most useful or important elements of partnerships in the public-sector context. And many of them are moving collaboration research beyond its original normative tone, to understand both its risks and rewards. But some challenges remain.

The complexity of collaborative activity presents paradoxes to many observers—especially, perhaps, in the public-sector context (Connelly, Zhang, and Faerman 2008). The term "collaboration" is frequently misused in practice and misapplied in research. Even those practitioners who actively engage in collaborative activity are not always sure what it looks or feels like (Gajda 2004). Normative and practical tensions abound. For example, public-sector collaboration depends on some amount of institutional flexibility and discretion, but also on stable and publicly accountable systems. Further, the same legislation that gives an agency its fiscal independence may also expect that agency to collaborate across institutional boundaries and thus increase dependence in other ways. Finally, the emphasis on collaboration as an end in itself—somewhat like the early days of public-sector privatization activity—can deemphasize a practical understanding of the circumstances where collaborative activities would not be worth the effort.

There are at least two epistemological limitations at present in the collaboration research in public administration: its disciplinary scope; and its analytic scope, particularly with respect to the underemphasis on the individual actor. In my view, these are more perceptual than empirical limitations. But they do pose research challenges.

THE LIMITED DISCIPLINARY AND ANALYTIC SCOPE OF PUBLIC-SECTOR COLLABORATION RESEARCH

Practitioners easily learn that collaboration requires more than statutory authority and that success depends on more than passive compliance. Scholars learn this lesson with rather limited observational and theoretical tools. Until we study collaborative activity with at least the same level of sophistication as it manifests itself in practice, we severely limit the utility of our research for practitioners. At present, to understand collaboration theory in the public administration context is like being handed a Bowie Knife when a Swiss Army Knife with fifteen tools is needed to do the job. Our tool to provide useful analysis is improving, but it is not yet up to the task.

This metaphorical tool I describe is complex because it understands any form of policy implementation, including collaborative activity, as something that occurs in multiple dimensions, at multiple levels of governance, and within multiple contexts—sectoral, institutional, individual, financial, political, and so on. To illustrate my argument more specifically, it is useful to note two limitations on the current approach to collaboration research.

First, although I mentioned above that these challenges are mostly perceptual, incorporating the element of time into collaboration research is a serious empirical challenge. Many scholars point out that interorganizational collaboration is a process, "a journey, not a destination" (Gajda 2004, 68; see also

Gray 1989). The emphasis in the social sciences on cross-sectional data has made it particularly difficult to understand the performance of organizational systems that depend on evolving relationships. Network studies—also often erroneously viewed as static systems—are in a similar situation. In past discussions on how to improve the situation (including a conference held by Syracuse University in 2006 on collaborative management), scholars have observed the need to share more data, to increase the sources of research funding, and to improve the general commitment to long-term data collection efforts.

Second, we face an even more challenging paradox. Collaboration is viewed largely as an institutional phenomenon in public-sector research, even though individual actors make it happen. A personal anecdote can illustrate my point. My preacademic career included a managerial position in a public–private partnership that supported a successful infant health program. This program, which was located in a very poor New England city, only gained momentum after a public official with great credibility and moral authority got representatives from every health agency together in the same room. Executives from the region's public and private hospitals—individuals who should have known one another much sooner—met across the table, brought together by a common objective. They stayed in the partnership because of resources and results, but it was committed individuals who got them there and who have always represented some of the glue that keeps the program running.

In our research I believe that we have the most difficulty understanding the role of the individual in collaborative activity. Some of us are uncomfortable with administrative discretion. Others find their research frameworks and data sets insufficient to address slippery notions like "trust." Nonetheless, although Herbert Simon and Dwight Waldo may have disagreed about the core values that should drive the study and practice of public administration, they held one crucial point in common: It is individuals who are ultimately responsible for its success. This perspective is still present today—Bailey and Koney (2000, 29) argue that "although strategic alliance research focuses on organizations, the implementation . . . has as much to do with individual relationships." Despite the persistence of this argument, however, scholars still struggle with its application.

Current scholarship shows that public managers rely on a combination of personal traits and institutional, environmental, and experiential factors when they implement policies across sectoral and organizational boundaries. For example, though a public manager may be compelled to collaborate through legislative mandate, the quality of that partnership depends on much more. The manager's level of bureaucratic discretion, institutional capacities, the nature of the joint effort, and past experiences and relationships will all also contribute, as will culture, institutional norms, and institutional incentives and constraints. One limit on these qualities of collaboration is that the personal traits we now include are mainly experiential—for example, training or a prior collaborative experience. We should also work to understand how collaborative skills are built on personality traits and attributes such as sex, political ideology, and motivations in line with burgeoning research on "public service motivation."

A field largely absent from much public administration research is that of human behavior, including sociology, social psychology, and cognitive theories. These disciplines have generated some of the most useful research on individual philanthropic activity and civic engagement in the nonprofit sector, so they are likely to be equally useful in the public sector in understanding collective behavior. Vigoda-Gadot (2003) suggests that a broader disciplinary scope could explain the "philosophy of collaboration" in terms of three constructs: the creation of common views, common social norms, and common managerial strategies. In another example of a multidimensional approach, Kumar, Kant, and Amburgey (2007) use a study of Indian forest managers to frame managerial attitudes as a function of socialization factors, personality traits, organizational culture and other job-related factors, and external environmental events such as political pressure.

To understand the individual's role in collaborative activity, there is also a potential connection between research on leadership and research on collaborative behavior—note, for example, the rise of new terms to describe managerial behavior in collaborative environments, such as Morse's (2008) and Connelly's (2007) conceptual but untested discussions of "collaborative leadership" (there are older uses of the term, but rarely in the public management context). Leadership research suffers from the same complexity, limitations, and paradoxes as collaboration research, but it could have much to say about the qualities that managers bring to collective action. Collaborative leaders take certain roles ("sponsors" and "champions"; "formal" and "informal" leaders), rely on certain qualities (reputational leadership), have certain attributes (mutuality, openness), require certain training (negotiation and dispute resolution), and work to balance their hierarchical and collaborative roles (Bryson and Crosby 2008; Morse 2008). The broader research on leadership in the public sector can be applied to nonhierarchical, collaborative situations in particular. Such efforts, combining knowledge from leadership studies with that of collaboration, might help us discover, for example, whether (and which) leadership traits are antecedents to effective collaborative action.

From a geographic point of view, scholars who conduct research at the local levels of government may be most likely to understand the possibilities here, because the spirit of collaboration is in large part rooted in community experiences, including the experiences of local government managers. These individuals are especially accustomed to working side by side with their commercial and nonprofit counterparts (as contractors, consultants, and volunteers), and to have experience serving together on boards. In these local partnerships, public managers could most readily recognize that "the critical element depend[s] more on having the right kind of people involved . . . than relying on traditional . . . institutional arrangements" (Abramson, Breul, and Kamensky 2006, 24).

WHERE DO WE GO FROM HERE?

Although I write mainly about research challenges, these also suggest an expanded view of how we teach students about collaborative public management. To teach public administration with the broader disciplinary scope suggested here, academic curricula will need to become more inclusive, and academic departments will need to become either more diverse internally or more willing to allow students to seek courses elsewhere. This would present a problem for many campuses where administrative units' fiscal health depends on keeping student credit hours in-house. But some academic institutions have figured out how to offer enough curricular diversity in-house, and we should see more in the future and actively study their experience. Academic administrators might also consider taking a more deliberate and focused approach to teaching collaborative skills in public affairs programs.

In academic programs, and in research as well, the notion of "collaborative capacity" requires much greater attention—the resources and processes that support effective collaborative activity (Gazley 2008). To accomplish this, we need to link our teaching of collaborative practices to functions that support other elements of management capacity, such as fund-raising or human resources management. For example, Waugh (2008) identifies this link when he observes that high personnel turnover in an agency can require a constant rebuilding of the relationships on which collaborative activity depends, and can severely limit collaborative performance.

Further, our curriculum often treats collaborative management as a subsector or function of other popular topics such as network management, rather than as a distinct form of management. Much of the current research on collaboration has been produced through the study of networked public service provision, and network scholars have been active participants in building public-sector collaboration theory. They have helped to explain the forms of exchange, the value of coordination, and the development of mutual objectives in highly collaborative networks. Nonetheless, it is important to keep in mind that not all network activity is collaborative, and not all collaborative activity is networked. Collaboration management must be treated as an activity distinct from network management (McGuire 2006).

CONCLUSION

If we are to understand the nature of public administration in the new arena of highly networked and collaborative settings, public administration's conceptual and research tools must also continue to match the complexity of the activities we study and teach about. Dwight Waldo, who presided over the

Minnowbrook I Conference, understood public administration as a broad, cross-disciplinary field. The paradox, of course, is that our academic field already struggles with defining its boundaries because it draws on so many other disciplines (political science, economics, law, sociology, psychology, management, finance). We should worry less about the boundaries and focus on bringing in—and bringing up to speed—more scholars from nontraditional public administration fields who might be interested in contributing. We lose nothing by maintaining Waldo's perspective and expanding our notion of the disciplines we should engage.

If the Minnowbrook watchword forty years ago was "relevance," my choice today would be "realism." And to me, a realistic public administration is a humanistic discipline, where the public manager is the central actor. Although the tools may have changed, this argument is no more than a return to the roots of a large portion of public management research and theory, where administrative leadership, bureaucratic discretion, and the "human and social side of public organizations" have long been topics of interest (Vigoda-Gadot 2003, 9).

These considerations seem to have particular salience and urgency in this post-9/11 decade. In the emergency management context, for example, Waugh (2008, 160) writes that "developing trust and respect are the first tasks of the professional emergency manager . . . in an environment where interpersonal skill is more important than technical expertise and informal relationships outweigh formal authority." The extent to which we can deepen our understanding of these effective qualities and learn how to capture them at more widespread levels of governance will remain one of the most intriguing questions of this generation of scholarship.

REFERENCES

Abramson, Mark A., Jonathan D. Breul, and John M. Kamensky. 2006. *Six Trends Transforming Government.* Washington, DC: IBM Center for the Business of Government.

Bailey, Darlyne, and Kelly M. Koney. 2000. *Strategic Alliances among Health and Human Services Organizations: From Affiliations to Consolidations.* Thousand Oaks, CA: Sage.

Bryson, John M., and Barbara C. Crosby. 2008. Failing into Cross-Sector Collaboration Successfully. In *Big Ideas in Collaborative Public Management*, ed. Lisa Blomgren Bingham and Rosemary O'Leary. Armonk, NY: M. E. Sharpe.

Connelly, David R. 2007. Leadership in the Collaborative Interorganizational Domain. *International Journal of Public Administration* 30:1231–62.

Connelly, David R., Jing Zhang, and Sue Faerman. 2008. The Paradoxical Nature of Collaboration. In *Big Ideas in Collaborative Public Management*, ed. Lisa Blomgren Bingham and Rosemary O'Leary. Armonk, NY: M. E. Sharpe.

Gajda, Rebecca. 2004. Utilizing Collaboration Theory to Evaluate Strategic Alliances *American Journal of Evaluation* 25, no. 1:65–77.

Gazley, Beth. 2008. Intersectoral Collaboration and the Motivation to Collaborate: Toward an Integrated Theory. In *Big Ideas in Collaborative Public Management*, ed. Lisa Blomgren Bingham and Rosemary O'Leary. Armonk, NY: M. E. Sharpe.

Gray, Barbara. 1989. *Collaborating: Finding Common Ground for Multiparty Problems*, 1st ed. San Francisco: Jossey-Bass.

Kumar, Sushil, Sashi Kant, and Terry L. Amburgey. 2007. Public Agencies and Collaborative Management Approaches: Examining Resistance among Administrative Professionals. *Administration and Society* 39, no. 5:569–610.

McGuire, Michael. 2006. Collaborative Public Management: Assessing What We Know and How We Know It. *Public Administration Review* 66, no. 6 (Supplement): 33–43.

Morse, Ricardo S. 2008. Developing Public Leaders in an Age of Collaboration. In *Innovations in Public Leadership Development.* Armonk, NY: M. E. Sharpe.

O'Leary, Rosemary, Beth Gazley, Michael McGuire, and Lisa Blomgren Bingham. 2008. Public Managers in Collaboration. In *The Collaborative Public Manager: New Ideas for the Twenty-first Century*, ed. Rosemary O'Leary and Lisa Blomgren Bingham. Washington, DC: Georgetown University Press.

Vigoda-Gadot, Eran. 2003. *Managing Collaboration in Public Administration: The Promise of Alliance among Governance, Citizens and Businesses.* Westport, CT: Praeger.

Waugh, William. 2008. Mechanisms for Collaboration in Emergency Management: ICS, NIMS, and the Problem with Command and Control. In *The Collaborative Public Manager: New Ideas for the Twenty-first Century*, ed. Rosemary O'Leary and Lisa Blomgren Bingham. Washington, DC: Georgetown University Press.

Conclusion

Challenges and Opportunities, Crosscutting Themes, and Thoughts on the Future of Public Administration

David M. Van Slyke, Rosemary O'Leary, and Soonhee Kim

All academic disciplines have had enduring theoretical, empirical, methodological, and conceptual debates. Since the debate between Waldo and Simon, there has been continued unrest in the academic field of public administration. Such field definition and debate by Waldo, Simon, and others is a trend line that has continued over the course of the Minnowbrook meetings. Though scholars may no longer "genuflect" as a sign of reverence to either Waldo or Simon, the camps and general axioms by which scholars define themselves have retained a more lasting currency.

The discussions and debates at the Minnowbrook III gatherings reflect, in part, this history. A large poster of Waldo was on display at the 2008 meetings because of his vision in inaugurating the first Minnowbrook Conference. However, a healthy tension remained among groups of some scholars, who might be defined more as managerialists, and others, who see the field of public administration more through a lens of political philosophy. The two sets of lenses are not mutually exclusive, of course, but rather build on and inform each other. The value of these distinct perspectives is that they illustrate that public administration is not a united field; it is still evolving, maturing, and manifesting itself in different ways, with different subfields, drawing on varying tools of inquiry.

Although the Waldo–Simon debate formally may be over, the larger question of what the field of public administration stands for continues to percolate in an unsettled state—one that is at an intersection. The field of public administration is growing more open to many points of view. Questioning and discussion about the role and influence of the field continues. As George Frederickson commented in his final plenary remarks at Minnowbrook III, this general theme has constructively given rise to a field that continues to develop in its scope, rigor, and relevance. The desire to differentiate scholars, subfields, and topics in dichotomous ways has had some beneficial outcomes, but at Minnowbrook III the field showed signs of capitalizing on the synergies of cross-field collaborations and moving beyond its either/or notions of where one resides intellectually.

A number of books have been written about the current state of the field; many others have been written about specific topics covered in this book. Edited volumes often bring together different voices and build from a foundation of expert legitimacy. The perspectives are often heavy either on commentary or empiricism; a strong combination is uncommon. What makes this book different—and we argue relevant—to those who work in and study public administration is that it is *both* historical and forward looking, with contributions from some of the field's established, senior leaders *and* from a number of new scholars who are or will become leaders in the discipline. Therefore, the perspectives use history as one set of evaluation criteria, are based on experience, present new thinking, and also set forth questions and propositions about where the field could be—and in many cases should be—headed in the near term. These perspectives help frame the future of a field that has achieved a great deal but still has a significant distance to travel. In this chapter we present the major challenges and opportunities, as well as crosscutting themes that emerged at Minnowbrook III, reflecting a growing openness to new ideas, coupled with enduring issues that span the decades.

GLOBALISM

The most prevalent and important issue addressed at Minnowbrook III was the impact of globalization on the field. This is the most important change since Minnowbrook II, and certainly since Minnowbrook I. Public administration as a field of academic study has gone through several stages since its inception; globalization has posed unprecedented challenges, and it is not an exaggeration to say that globalization has caused a revolution in public administration in terms of increased studies in comparative public management, more public policy research that crosses international boundaries, and the increased role of international organizations in governance.

Several speakers at Minnowbrook III lamented the fact that the public administration perspectives taught to PhD students in their typical "intellectual history" courses are *U.S.* public administration only, or, as Yilin Hou put it in his closing plenary remarks, "public administration with American characteristics." Hou pointed out that remnants of government operations can be traced back to ancient civilizations in Asia, including examinations for public servants in the Sui Dynasty (AD 581–618) in China.

Advocating for a global public administration, Hou commented, "There are no doubt many universal features in government practice. But can we arrive at a global perspective from here? To build a more generic theory or theories, we need to broaden our views and work on new assumptions that do not take country-specific phenomena as a given."

Minnowbrook III participants also analyzed new dimensions of connectedness, interdependency, knowledge sharing in governance, and collaborative public management among government agencies and across international boundaries in the twenty-first century. Several authors of the chapters in part II of this book provide concrete examples concerning how comparative public administration research and practice have responded, and continue to respond, to globalization's challenges. Some propose the integration of a global perspective in public administration scholarship similar to Hou's idea. Bowornwathana analyzes a growing number of international organizations and regional networks of public administration that influence more comparative studies on good governance, government effectiveness, the New Public Management, government reforms, and transparency in developed and developing countries. Hou, as well as Poocharoen, also underscore the demand for scholarship that emphasizes comparative public administration with a global perspective for the twenty-first century.

The insights and analyses presented by these academics call for scholars in public administration to engage in critical dialogue on issues concerning the development of rigorous research methods for comparative studies with a global perspective. This of course is nothing new. What *is* new is how far reaching the global perspective has become in the field. It is difficult to find a public administration scholar anywhere in the world today who does not have some sort of comparative experience or perspective. The Minnowbrook III scholars hasten us to better understand the values of democratic governance, transparency, accountability, and effectiveness at the local, national, and international levels. Also cited as important is more research on the effects of international development programs and government reforms on government and governance in developing countries.

To paraphrase Hou's closing plenary remarks, the current generation of public administration scholars is fortunate to be witnessing another wave of social experiments: the reforms in transitioning and developing countries. Thus, one step we can all take is to pay much more attention to public administration in other countries in general and to transitioning countries in particular. Training in comparative studies and sensitivity to global issues is critical to effective governance in an increasingly interconnected and interdependent international environment. Also essential is solid training in traditional and current theories. Despite inadequacies, traditional theories from the diverse social sciences, management, law, and organizations are not necessarily wrong, but they do require some revisiting. In some cases, theories need "upgrades" with new, wider, and more accurate insights. Innovation will not come out of a vacuum; familiarity with previous research is an essential starting point. Incorporating a global perspective will allow for the expansion of current theories, and the testing of new assumptions and hypotheses in different cultural and political contexts.

TWENTY-FIRST-CENTURY COLLABORATIVE GOVERNANCE

If globalization was the most talked about challenge and opportunity at Minnowbrook III, then collaborative governance came in a close second. This theme has been interwoven in a variety of chapters in this book, including those dealing with deliberative democracy, public participation, teaching and relevance. In part III, Kim argues persuasively that there is an increased need for theories and models to understand collaborative leadership in local governance in global communities. The discussions and debates at Minnowbrook III broadened this perspective to the state/provincial, regional, and federal levels, both domestically and internationally. McGuire, Brudney, and Gazley explain that modern emergency management is a good example of today's challenges in collaboration. They note that emergency management includes a more diverse set of actors than ever before, stronger professional norms and training, and greater attention to network governance and performance management. It also has built-in tensions between command-and-control approaches and collaborative engagement. Emerson and Murchie present a relatively new issue—global climate change—that was not yet on the radar screen at Minnowbrook I and Minnowbrook II. The challenges of climate change present opportunities for public administration to develop new collaborative approaches, primarily in the areas of mitigation and adaptation. One lesson from Minnowbrook III is that collaborative approaches to public administration are here to stay.

Several discussions and debates at Minnowbrook III centered on the fact that governance in many countries is changing from hierarchical and stovepiped orientations with government as the dominant actor to more networked forms of governance. In the latter form, government is an important institutional actor, but not the only or most important one. Governance forms and functions are evolving and manifest themselves and their connectedness to others through networks, contracts, and a range of information technology innovations. At the same time, scholars of public administration are examining new and complex questions about authority, responsibility, the rule of law, and citizen engagement. These are representative of current inquiry. What these new forms of governance suggest is that collaboration is the required norm, and that power is becoming diffused through a number of institutional mechanisms and policy instruments. As a result, "new" managerial tools—such as facilitation, negotiation, collaborative problem solving, and dispute resolution—are taking on heightened prominence. Accordingly, a different type of professional training and education will be needed to prepare public administrators to work with a range of institutional and individual actors and across governance domains and sectoral boundaries. Emerging from these governance changes is a field of public administration practice that is becoming more professionalized than in the past in terms of systems, processes, and tools.

Professionalization, however, does not connote increased democratization. Rather, governance is taking shape across political forms, philosophies, cultures, and citizenship. Some of those forms seek more active citizen engagement and participation, while others are evolving toward that state in only the most incremental of steps. This is one indication that while governance has become more global, diverse, and represented by complex governing arrangements and values, it also has departed from the long dominant norms embedded in Western notions of democratic governance. These changes will require more research and engagement between scholars and with practitioners. They may very well be topics on the agenda at the Minnowbrook IV Conference in 2028.

THE ROLE OF INFORMATION TECHNOLOGY

Coming in a close third as the most debated and discussed challenge and opportunity at Minnowbrook III was the future role of information technology (IT) in the public sector. This topic spilled over into the topics of the management of organizations, collaborative governance, citizen participation, and globalization. In part III of this book, Pardo, Gil-Garcia, and Luna-Reyes synthesize the changing role and functions of IT in public organizations and governance. They provide insights into the applications and implementation of IT in a networked and IT-enabled public administration. They propose an emphasis on designing IT applications for enhancing interorganizational information integration, sharing knowledge in collaborative governance, solving transnational problems, and utilizing analytical tools to deal with complex and uncertain problems. In addition, they address the demand of competency development of public servants for collaborative governance and the cross-boundary information sharing that is necessary for governmental transformation to respond to challenging issues in the twenty-first century.

Another challenge concerning the role of IT in governance involves the expanded scope and complexity of web-based social networks in which government employees and citizens communicate. On the basis of on an analysis of various web applications called social networking media tools, which emerged in private settings outside any business or government context, Mergel argues in part IV for the potential positive influence of the active utilization of these tools on increased transparency, accountability, participation, and collaboration opportunities.

These chapters are indicative of the conversations at Minnowbrook III about the impact of IT on public administration, which is often linked to the increasing importance of globalization. Several questions are representative of the cross-cutting themes that emerged. What is the impact on public administration of advanced IT in an increasingly globalized environment? This question brings up many subissues, including regulatory policy in a global economy, national security, and transnational cybersecurity concerns. What are the effects of the challenges of globalization and advanced IT on government reforms and innovation efforts in both developing and developed countries? Here the hot topics include increased knowledge transfer among local government leaders at the national and international levels, and expanded regional networks for solving global issues across countries. How should civil service systems assist public managers in developing a global perspective? The issues discussed included competency development regarding global leadership, IT leadership for enhancing government effectiveness, and democratic governance in different political and institutional contexts. How do comparative public administration studies and development management studies in diverse regions contribute to establishing institutional and managerial capacity in individual countries? How do they enhance knowledge sharing and collaborative abilities for resolving complex regional and global issues? Compelling subissues that arose included comparative studies of the effects of international nongovernmental organizations' computer training programs for youth on employment in Africa and South Asia, and comparative studies on the utilization of online citizen participation programs and their impact on public trust in governments.

DELIBERATIVE DEMOCRACY AND PUBLIC PARTICIPATION

Another prevalent issue at all the Minnowbrook conferences encompasses the tensions among deliberative democracy, public participation, and the organizational mechanisms and managerial actions taken to incentivize public engagement in policy discussions and implementation. This continues to be an issue without clear parameters or reconciliation. The three perspectives offered by leading experts in the field in part IV are reflective of the discussions and debates that brought together more practitioners than any other issue. Nabatchi focuses on historical tensions and offered a persuasive argument for why more democratic engagement is needed. She also argues that public managers are important to facilitating this dialogue. Mergel proposes more research on the impact of social networks on relationships among citizens and public-sector employees. Thomas offers a framework for considering when and how to involve the public and presents a set of decision heuristics that should aid those public managers to whom Nabatchi refers. Leighninger, in part V, offers a practitioner perspective shaped as a result of his own boundary-spanning activities between practice and scholarship. He not only synthesizes the results of his research on this issue but also suggests changes that need to be incorporated in the curricula of public administration programs so that public involvement is viewed as important and valuable by those implementing public programs.

These chapters build on one another and present an integrated perspective on bringing about more effective involvement between public administrators and the public. The most important lesson is as Thomas suggests: Involving the public need not be a static and discrete choice between involvement and no involvement. Rather, the choice is one of *when* and *how best* to involve the public. The recommendations that Nabatchi and Leighninger offer are important building blocks for finding equilibrium between the Waldo and Simon perspectives on political philosophy and management decision making. Mergel shares some intriguing perspectives on twenty-first-century tools on how to get there. The Minnowbrook perspective that public engagement is critical to governing a healthy democratic state is alive and well.

THE ORGANIZATION OF THE FUTURE

The debates and discussions at Minnowbrook III concerning organizations of the future, reflected in these chapters, tended to be more in the Waldo camp than the Simon camp. Participants, for the most part, tended to address issues concerning preserving democracy, for example, rather than how to create a more efficient bureaucracy. In part I, Piotrowski maintains that public-sector employees need clear signals that nonmission-based values, such as due process, equity, integrity, and transparency, are essential parts of their jobs. Guy, Newman, and Mastracci focus on the emotional part of public-sector work and argue that this component needs to be addressed in theory and in practice. Isett calls for a retreat from faddish pseudomanagement solutions that sound good but are often promoted without systematic analysis. She advocates a greater emphasis on evidence-based organization solutions. Moynihan calls for a reframing of performance management from a narrow technique to a tool to further democratic governance. Bearfield calls for an examination of the images of race that are prevalent in the field and new, robust analyses that catalyze our understanding of the role that race and ethnic background play in public administration. Gooden maintains that social equity research needs to go one step further and be used for concrete, positive, action-oriented change. Jones and Givens argue persuasively that the issue of homeland security is many times more important in 2008 than it was in 1988 and in 1968, and that it presents opportunities for public administration to develop new organizations, new academic programs, and new areas of research.

What is clear is that public organizations of the future will look different than today in their size, scale, personnel, network complexity, and direct connectedness to programs and citizens. More institutional actors and stakeholders from across both governments and the private sector will be involved in policy design, program development, and the financing, arranging, and delivery of services. Information technology will enhance the scale and scope of available data and information for decision making. However, only leadership's commitment to structural changes to existing organizations will create a more effective set of conditions for the use of information in shaping decisions and in policymaking. Continued political changes to existing and new systems of governance will vary from scaling back to expanding the reach of public organizations. What is necessary is for leaders in public organizations to think and act more strategically and flexibly. For this to happen, organizational structures will need to become more malleable so they follow and complement strategy, rather than adhere to the current strategy of having to succeed by overcoming static organizations rigidly fastened to their old structures.

Nowhere will these changes be more important than in the development, modification, and implementation of management tools for public purposes with the intent of strengthening governance capacity and democratic values. But caution must be exercised: The historical, cultural, political, and economic values of many nations are deeply embedded in their governance systems. Such intertwined values shape a nation's decisions in its policies and the development of its public administration systems. Careless and casual conversations often speak of globalization and democratic governance as though these are two sides of the same coin. To do so, however, is to mistake the significant differences that characterize the implications of globalization for the governance of nation-states. The future public organization's evolution needs to be informed by more comparative studies of public administration with a focus on generalizability. This may necessarily preclude large-scale studies of Western and non-Western nations, but it may include more bounded regional studies that are informed by administrative and policy learning from more developed countries' successes and failures.

The only way to achieve such learning in a more efficient manner than currently exists, however, is to move toward more institutionalized systems and multilateral networks for knowledge transfer and organizational learning, both within and across countries. These are ambitious goals, and we do not offer such direct statements unaware of the antecedent changes that must take place in organizations and in governance systems as they exist today. Knowledge sharing and diffusion are more than positive buzzwords; they represent intentionally moving forward and beginning the long process of trust building and collaboration that starts with smaller efforts at cooperation and then coordination. These issues are sure to resurrect themselves at Minnowbrook IV in 2028.

TEACHING THE NEXT GENERATION OF LEADERS

A range of recommendations for strengthening public administration curricula, teaching, research, and practice were presented at Minnowbrook III. In her closing plenary remarks, Susan Gooden, for example, talked about the continued need to lure students and professors of color to public administration. Paul Light, in his closing plenary remarks, talked about the field's students "getting chopped up" in the real world of practice, and the need to do a better job educating them. The contributions in part V range from Leighninger's prospective agenda on teaching democracy to Marlowe and Smith's argument that public management and public financial management have much to learn from one another in maximizing synergies in order to catalyze research and practice. These are reflective of the diversity of ideas about teaching that were debated at Minnowbrook III. Robinson presents the case that the field of public administration needs to communicate more effectively and brand the value of a master of public administration degree. He asserts that value is in "the eye of the beholder," and his findings suggest that potential employers may find greater value in more specialized graduate training—such as in social work, educational administration, or emergency management—than in a more generalist program like those offered in graduate schools of public affairs.

Adams and Balfour assert that public administration programs have moved away from exposure, discussion, and training in ethics. Their argument is that the ethical issues public administrators must address in today's environment are not questions with dichotomous and normative responses. Rather, these issues entail decisions that need to be made in policy and implementation environments marked by complexity and network governance. They involve a range of ethical considerations that street-level workers—both governmental and nongovernmental—are going to have to interpret and about which they will have to exercise discretion. Such interpretation and discretion may lead to decisions and ethical issues that are not easily resolved. Similarly, Rosenbloom and Naff make the case that a limitation of current public affairs curricula is their deficiency in administrative and constitutional law. Their argument is more firmly focused on a federal perspective, but it can certainly be extended to state and local government domains, as well as international arenas.

Perhaps most surprising is that in 2008 the areas of ethics and law are considered to be in a state of crisis with respect to the emphasis placed on them in today's public affairs programs. In the past, these topics were firmly grounded in the curricula. Critics, such as Curtis Ventriss in his Minnowbrook III closing plenary remarks, argue that the pendulum may have swung too far from generalist training in law and ethics to more policy-, economics-, and management-oriented courses that have analytical and technocratic dimensions. The argument for a balance between the Waldo and Simon perspectives as they are operationalized in graduate public affairs degree programs is indeed a challenge the field will need to continue to consider and address in concrete ways.

REMAINING RELEVANT

The most constant theme across the Minnowbrook conferences—from 1968 to 1988 to 2008—was the challenge of remaining relevant. As Beryl Radin phrased it in her Minnowbrook III closing plenary remarks:

> Why is it so difficult for our community to have an impact on the world of practice? This is true for management reform efforts both inside the United States and globally. This is found in World Bank efforts as well as those from the United States Agency for International Development. Here in the U.S. we look at the National Performance Review, PART, and the creation of the Department of Homeland Security and realize that influences on these efforts have rarely come from those in the public administration community, especially the academic part of that community. They are more likely to come from the private sector and reflect a different set of values than those traditionally associated with the public side of administration or management.

Among Minnowbrook III's new scholars, the desire to fully connect scholarship with practice was voiced early and often at the preconference workshop, as well as at the Lake Placid gathering. It is no accident, then, that the five chapters in part VI concerning the challenge of remaining relevant were all written by new scholars. Van Slyke calls for relevant research in public administration that is characterized by three outcomes: It is analytically rigorous. It speaks back to, and informs, other social science disciplines and management research, as well as the questions they investigate. And it informs the public—government leaders, policymakers, nongovernmental actors, citizens and interest groups—and shapes their engagement in the process of governance. LeRoux argues that public administration needs to reposition itself to deal effectively with the realities of governance and cross-jurisdictional management, and Gazley proposes an agenda to make this happen. Lambright echoes this sentiment, adding not only that new venues for knowledge sharing and transfer are needed but also that the promotion and tenure system needs to change to bring together the worlds of scholarship and public affairs. Wright argues that public administration has isolated itself as an academic discipline to its detriment.

David Rosenbloom, in his closing plenary remarks, listed five proactive steps the field of public administration might take to make it a stronger, more robust field. His suggestions, which are here paraphrased in part, are directly applicable to the relevance issue.

First, we need to aggregate knowledge, in the sense of making it cumulative. We are diffusing valuable knowledge at a high rate. In a sense, however, the more we diffuse, the less we know, because our research is not aggregated or accumulated into substantial bodies of knowledge. There are three reasons for this: (1) The field either lacks or does not use a common framework. (2) Public administration pays inadequate attention to its own intellectual history. (3) We lack sufficient time to read broadly. We are under such pressure to create new knowledge that publication has become "supply side": Authors produce books and articles that are read by few people beyond those willing to devote time to them, because they need them for their specific research and writing. Again we are producing more knowledge but running the risk of knowing relatively less. Although it is impossible in today's publish-or-perish world, it would be wonderful if we could all simultaneously have a one-year moratorium on publishing in order to read broadly.

Second, we need to maintain public administration's methodological and epistemological pluralism. Public administration's quirkiness with regard to ways of knowing contributes to its creativeness and richness. Any effort to impose a single or hegemonic methodology or epistemology will narrow and weaken the field.

Third, we need to maintain public administration's value diversity. The field's major values run the gamut from technical efficiency to social equity and beyond. Prescribing a single set of values—whether utilitarian, instrumental, egalitarian, libertarian, or contractarian—will make the field increasingly irrelevant to today's complex policy problems.

Fourth, we need to continue to promote boundary spanning. Minnowbrook I emphasized the need for boundary spanning. Today, we should expand our boundaries by paying greater attention to comparative administration and developments in related fields, such as economics, sociology, business administration, and political science.

Clearly, the issue of relevance will continue to be on the public administration radar screen for years to come.

THE SINGLE CERTAINTY

The discussants and contributors profiled in this book present cogent perspectives on the challenges that lie ahead for the field of public administration. Several questions invariably arise from those perspectives. Susan Gooden summed up the challenges of public administration in 2008 in her closing plenary comments:

> The current public administration superhighway is filled with lots of great vehicles. The vehicles I reference here metaphorically represent the various scholars who are very busily driving along. Some may be traveling faster or slower than others, but these vehicles are all moving forward. They share some important commonalities in terms of an engine (solid academic preparation and credentials), [and] a sturdy steering wheel (research agenda). . . . Despite their commonalities, each vehicle possesses a unique vehicle identification number all of its own. So although they may have similar makes and models, . . . they are each unique in important ways. The problem though, is that these vehicles, far too often, travel only in their own lane. . . . So, the challenge becomes for us to travel into other lanes . . . to improve our overall contribution to the field. This may

> involve such radical actions as equity riding in the backseat of a leadership vehicle; accountability riding in the backseat of an equity vehicle, and so forth, in order to make a greater contribution to our understanding of the complex nature of the governance and administration problems we are trying to solve.

Several participants at the 2008 Minnowbrook III Conference focused on the bifurcation of the academic and practitioner worlds of public administration and asked why some scholars and practitioners continue to posit questions with expected outcomes that are dichotomous. When the question is raised about whether public administration is an academic field that developed from the world of practice or a field where practice grew out of the academic field, we might ask why these are thought to be mutually exclusive. If one important goal for the field is to be more relevant, several avenues have been identified in the chapters of this volume that set markers for future consideration. As raised at Minnowbrook III, is the value of public administration as a boundary-spanning discipline? If the answer is yes, with all the expected permutations, then it may be the case that the field needs to become more effective at moving fluidly between scholarship and practice.

It may well be that the value of public administration is its interdependence with the broader research fields in the social sciences, law, and management. We can strive for a much closer integration with those engaged in the art and practice of public administration at all levels of government and with those who serve as participants in networked governance and service delivery. This interdependence and a closer integration may be the means to the desired end of becoming more relevant in the value we create. Yet, as Todd LaPorte remarked in his closing plenary comments, this will become increasingly difficult; public issues and problems are arising and changing at an accelerated pace. Global climate change and homeland security are two examples addressed in this book. Scholars' capacity just to describe what is happening, much less analyze it, is being challenged. Connected to this, public problems are becoming more complex, and the stakes are higher if a public or quasi-public organization fails. LaPorte asked, "How good can public organizations be, given the hands they are dealt?"

The chapters presented in this book represent the range of topics debated and discussed at Minnowbrook III. Their breadth and depth illustrate areas of concern and continued tension, such as those between the bureaucratic and democratic ethoses that are cornerstones in the foundation of public administration, as well as the need to bridge the gap between public administration practitioners and researchers. The concerns expressed at previous Minnowbrook gatherings—such as the relevance of public administration research, its utility for practitioners, and its impact in shaping social science scholarship in other fields—remain issues yet to be addressed in a manner that the participants at Minnowbrook III considered to be satisfactory.

Progress continues to be made in both the intellectual diversity of topics and the empirical sophistication with which studies are being designed, data gathered, and findings analyzed. The quality of public administration research is improving, and its use and dissemination are on the rise. More publication outlets exist for high-quality research and commentary than ever before, and policymakers increasingly cite research as informing their decision making. Practitioners are developing more innovative ways to implement public programs. Yet many more opportunities remain for collaboration among scholars, and between scholars and practitioners. Further investigation is needed into a range of challenges where practice currently outpaces scholarship, such as the role of networks, the globalization of governance, and the new system processes and tools that are currently being implemented in a variety of countries.

The myriad scholars and practitioners who gathered at Blue Mountain Lake and Lake Placid in 2008 represented disparate and diverse points of view, but they demonstrated a single certainty: The field of public administration will continue to be challenged to be more creative and relevant in its scholarship and in its practice for many years to come.

Contributors

Guy B. Adams is a professor of public affairs at the Harry S. Truman School of Public Affairs of the University of Missouri–Columbia.

Danny L. Balfour is a professor of public administration at the School of Public and Nonprofit Administration of Grand Valley State University in Grand Rapids, Michigan.

Domonic Bearfield is an assistant professor of public administration at the Bush School of Government and Public Service of Texas A&M University.

Bidhya Bowornwathana is an associate professor in the Department of Public Administration of the Faculty of Political Science at Chulalongkorn University in Bangkok.

Jeffrey L. Brudney holds the Albert A. Levin Chair of Urban Studies and Public Service at the Maxine Goodman Levin College of Urban Affairs of Cleveland State University.

Kirk Emerson recently stepped down as director of the U.S. Institute for Environmental Conflict Resolution of the Morris K. Udall Foundation, which she had served since its inception in 1998.

H. George Frederickson is the Edwin O. Stene Distinguished Professor of Public Administration at the University of Kansas.

Beth Gazley is an assistant professor of public and environmental affairs at Indiana University–Bloomington.

J. Ramon Gil-Garcia is an assistant professor in the Department of Public Administration and the director of the Data Center for Applied Research in Social Sciences at the Centro de Investigación y Docencia Económicas in Mexico City.

Austin Givens is a PhD candidate at Virginia Commonwealth University.

Susan T. Gooden is an associate professor and director of graduate programs at the L. Douglas Wilder School of Government and Public Affairs of Virginia Commonwealth University.

Mary E. Guy is a professor and director of the master of public administration program at the School of Public Affairs of the University of Colorado–Denver.

Yilin Hou is an associate professor of public administration and policy at the University of Georgia.

Kimberley R. Isett is an assistant professor at the School of Public Health of Columbia University.

Dale Jones is an associate professor of public administration and director of the National Homeland Security Project at the L. Douglas Wilder School of Government and Public Affairs of Virginia Commonwealth University.

Soonhee Kim is an associate professor of public administration at the Maxwell School of Syracuse University.

Kristina Lambright is an assistant professor of public administration at the College of Community and Public Affairs of Binghamton University.

W. Henry Lambright is a professor of public administration and political science at the Maxwell School of Syracuse University.

Matt Leighninger is the executive director of the Deliberative Democracy Consortium.

Kelly LeRoux is an assistant professor in the Department of Public Administration at the University of Illinois–Chicago.

Luis F. Luna-Reyes is a professor of business at the Universidad de las Américas in Mexico.

Justin Marlowe is an assistant professor at the Evans School of the University of Washington–Seattle.

Sharon H. Mastracci is an associate professor in the Department of Public Administration at the University of Illinois–Chicago.

Michael McGuire is an associate professor at the School of Public and Environmental Affairs of Indiana University–Bloomington.

Ines Mergel is an assistant professor of public administration at the Maxwell School of Syracuse University.

Donald P. Moynihan is an associate professor at the Robert M. La Follette School of Public Affairs of the University of Wisconsin–Madison.

Peter Murchie works for the U.S. Environmental Protection Agency's Regional Climate and Clean Energy Team in Seattle.

Tina Nabatchi is an assistant professor of public administration at the Maxwell School of Syracuse University.

Katherine C. Naff is an associate professor of public administration at San Francisco State University.

Meredith A. Newman is professor and chair of the Department of Public Administration at Florida International University.

Rosemary O'Leary is Distinguished Professor of Public Administration and holds the Howard G. and S. Louise Phanstiel Chair in Strategic Management and Leadership at the Maxwell School of Syracuse University.

Theresa A. Pardo is deputy director of the Center for Technology in Government at the State University of New York at Albany, where she is also an associate research professor in public administration and policy and an affiliate faculty member in informatics.

Suzanne J. Piotrowski is an assistant professor of public affairs and administration at Rutgers University–Newark.

Ora-Orn Poocharoen is an assistant professor at the Lee Kuan Yew School of Public Policy in Singapore.

Scott E. Robinson is an associate professor at the George Bush School of Government and Public Service of Texas A&M University.

David H. Rosenbloom is Distinguished Professor of Public Administration at American University in Washington and Chaired Professor at the City University of Hong Kong.

Daniel L. Smith is an assistant professor of public administration at New York University.

John Clayton Thomas is professor of public management and policy at the Andrew Young School of Policy Studies of Georgia State University.

David M. Van Slyke is associate professor of public administration at the Maxwell School of Syracuse University.

Bradley E. Wright is associate professor of political science at the University of North Carolina–Charlotte.

INDEX

Page numbers followed by f indicate figures, those followed by t indicate tables, and those followed by b indicate boxes.

CPSIA information can be obtained at www.ICGtesting.com
Printed in the USA
BVOW02s0403040315

390275BV00001B/9/P